PROJECTS
IN WOOD

Mitchell Beazley

PROJECTS IN WOOD

David Field

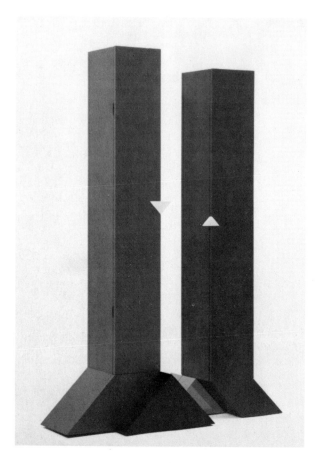

Edited and designed by Mitchell Beazley International
Ltd., Artists House, Manette St., London WIV 5LB

Project Manager/Art Editor	*Kelly Flynn*
Managing editor	*Frank Wallis*
Editor	*Mary-Sherman Willis*
Associate Art Editor	*Mike Brown*
Associate Editor	*Alan Wakeford*
Contributing authors	*Alan Smith*
	Peter St. Hill
	David Savage
	Tim Imrie
	Maggie Ellis
Technical advisers	*Peter Collenette*
	Paul Connell
Production controller	*Philip Collyer*

ISBN 0 85533 576 9

Typeset by MS Filmsetting Limited, Frome, Somerset
Reproduction by Chelmer Litho Reproductions, Maldon, Essex
Printed and bound by Koninklijke Smeets Offset b.v., Weert,
Netherlands

FOREWORD

The furniture with which we surround ourselves has a profound influence on us. At the most basic level it simply may not work—a chair is too low; too high; a bed sags; a drawer sticks. At a different level it may not relate to our taste in things. It works but is not conceived in a style to which we respond— we are indifferent to its appearance. Mass-produced furniture attempts to combine practical needs and fashionable styles at a convenient price while the custom-made piece hopes to satisfy the needs of individual expression.

All furniture forms a part of the man-made environment and in doing so directly reflects or influences our standards, values and aspirations. In this sense furniture can achieve the status of a work of art. However, unlike fine artists whose concern is in communicating the truth of their own vision, furniture designers must take on responsibilities to other people. These are not just contractual responsibilities, but ones which come from an understanding that their work, together with all designed objects, directly determines the quality of the world in which we live – and for that reason the work must be good. The designers chosen to appear in this book take up that challenge in various, highly personal ways.

If there is an emphasis on design, it is because design is the key: a set of ground rules that gives meaning to an idea. Making is the method of translating that idea into reality and in that sense is a means to an end, not the end in itself. However, it must be added that skilled makers can bring to furniture qualities never imagined at the drawing board and it is often these qualities that bring furniture into the realms of art.

From the interviews with the designers, which begin on page 48, different approaches to work emerge. Some are interested in mass production, looking for ways of working in the furniture industry to bring better design to a wider range of consumers, while others are so intensely interested in wood as a material and in the process of turning it into objects of beauty, that they truly represent an extension of a tradition going back 5,000 years. The interviews, as well as offering impressions of what kind of people they are, serve another important purpose: they contain clues to that most elusive of all things, the wellsprings of inspiration. In furniture making, as in all art, one can teach the principles of good practice, but flair, talent and genius are inherent.

In the first sections of the book I have attempted to clarify an approach to design and while I realize that this alone cannot teach someone to design, it may reduce the confusion often experienced when confronted with the world of designers. Most of them are not the high-flying, fast-living, outrageously-clothed contenders so favoured by the glossy magazines, but people who recognized the complexity and seriousness of designing. They are aware of the social implications of what they do and base it on sound research. These pages may seem a little theoretical, but we cannot discuss design—and its translation into practice— without first defining what we mean by it. If better work is to be done it is essential that all designers, however experienced, constantly question the value of their work. For newcomers it is likewise essential that they are not sent down the wrong path. Do not look for easy answers—there are none—but then nothing worthwhile ever comes easily.

Projects in Wood is a furniture book which brings together the theoretical and the practical—design and making. It should not be surprising, for they are extensions of one another, as is illustrated by the contents. A woodworker with a reasonable degree of competence can make anything in the book. But armed with a greater understanding of the design process it is hoped that he or she will use the projects as examples from which to develop his or her own ideas.

The collaboration between the publishers and the designers has been an attempt to provide a foundation from which you can build the confidence to design your own furniture. If it encourages you to explore the intellectual pleasure of design and offers you the practical knowledge to translate it, it will have achieved its aim.

David Field

CONTENTS

PROJECTS IN PRACTICE

THE WORKSHOP

MATERIALS

INTRODUCTION

Projects in Wood is a book about making furniture in the small workshop. Its author, David Field, is a lecturer in the furniture department of the Royal College of Art and one of Britain's best-known designers and makers. He has set out to do far more than simply to provide a catalogue of projects that the home woodworker can make: by discussing in detail the principles behind good design, and by illustrating those principles with examples of his own work, and the work of some of the most original British furniture makers, he has produced a book that encourages the reader to create his or her own designs, to suit particular needs or tastes, and which provides all the information needed to do that.

The first section of *Projects in Wood* is devoted to the elements of design. Well-designed furniture has to be functional as well as beautiful—a chair may appear slim, elegant and finely made, but if it collapses under the weight of a normal human being it is useless. Furniture has also to be fitted into rooms, and the most beautiful dining table ever made is similarly useless if it is too big for the space it has to occupy. Subjects that may at first glance seem formidable—anthropometrics, physics and aesthetics—are part and parcel of good design. In fact, they simply mean that furniture must be designed so that people can use it, so that it will withstand hard use, and so that it pleases the eye. Finally, David Field discusses some seeming imponderables—style, taste and fashion—and the problems that arise in designing specific pieces of furniture.

The colour section, which begins on page 46, shows the end results of putting the principles into practice. It illustrates some two dozen finished pieces of furniture, ranging from dining tables to mirrors. Interleaved with the illustrations are interviews with the designers in which they talk in practical terms about the design principles set out by David Field and their own philosophies of furniture making.

The 80 pages following the colour section take the pieces of furniture illustrated in it and, through exploded working drawings, show how they were constructed. The drawings and accompanying text contain enough information to enable the home craftsman to build each piece, but beyond that, additional working drawings and text show how each design can be varied to provide more than 100 possible projects. This section knits together all the sections of *Projects in Wood*, showing how design principles are applied, how a designer's individual style—described earlier in the interviews—is expressed in his work, and drawing upon the techniques described in the final two sections. It contains a wealth of ideas which can be applied across the whole range of furniture making.

The book's final two sections deal with the practicalities of the workshop and the materials used in furniture making. Jigs, tools that increase the scope of woodworking machinery, are discussed and explained, and the materials section goes beyond wood to look at the ways glass, metal and plastics can be used in the making of modern furniture. The section also covers veneering and finishing, and fixtures and fittings such as hinges, knockdown joints, and catches and stays.

This chapter should provide you with the tools for designing any piece of furniture in wood that you desire, and ensure that the result looks and functions as you intended. It will not tell you *what* to design, but it should show you *how*. However, if you do not feel up to the challenge of invention, you will find no shortage of projects to follow step-by-step in the following chapters. But we hope you will refer back to this chapter to explore the stylistic or structural options open to you, to mark your project with a personal stamp.

The discussion starts, necessarily, with the theoretical aspects of design. The section illustrates the balancing act that a professional designer performs to satisfy the need for utility on the one hand, and beauty on the other. By learning how to "look at" the shapes of objects the way designers do, you should be able to make your own designs with confidence.

After the theoretical, comes the practical—the nuts and bolts of integrating furniture with the shape and the needs of human beings. Furniture craftsmen often do this intuitively, drawing from their own experience and common sense. Industry has made a science of it, called ergonomics, to measure how best to fit machinery to human beings so that both work more efficiently. We draw a bit from both so that you can make truly fitted furniture. A section treating furniture as structures translates the physics of mechanics into the language of the furniture designer.

Having arrived at a general shape and structure, the style of a piece of furniture will begin to emerge. The following section breaks down the elements of style, taste and fashion, helping you distinguish among these often confusing notions and arrive at a personal statement with your furniture.

Finally, some specific problems you might encounter in designing particular items of furniture are laid out in the form of a checklist. You will then be prepared to transform your ideas and jottings into working sketches and a mock-up list—the final step before the benchwork begins.

The meaning of design

The ability to design is within all of us and we practice it daily, mostly subconsciously, when sorting and ordering our lives. The choice and combination of clothes to wear, the arrangement of food on a plate, the way we comb our hair or apply make-up are all examples of design thinking. Design is concerned with judgement and discrimination in decision-making, whether this is applied to personal dress or to the complex social and psychological implications in the work of professional designers—those who earn their living by it.

Designers are concerned with, and mainly responsible for, the man-made environment. It is their work which conditions the objects and images that surround us and affect the way we live. From this we can see how design is an important and complex human activity, with far-reaching social responsibilities. It is important because we cannot easily escape its effects, especially in towns and cities. And it is complex because it draws upon the worlds of both art and science.

If designers fail to exercise judgement and sensitivity in their work, we all suffer, physically and psychologically. Everyone has experienced badly-designed products which break or cause injury, and we can all recall the oppressive effects that some buildings or city areas evoke, which have been erected seemingly without heed to aesthetics. In this sense, designers can forestall some of the more unpalatable aspects of industrialized societies, for well-designed objects do more for us than simply perform their intended tasks.

The designer, therefore, is in a field that involves concern and response to social conditions exercising his or her skill as a problem-solver. Of course, not all categories of design demand a high social consciousness, but the answers to the seemingly simple questions of why?; what for?; how?; with what? are never easy to answer, even in the most elementary projects.

A design vocabulary

It is precisely because design is such a complex subject that we must be sure of the terms we are using when we analyze the content of a design. As I have said, design is an activity that combines art and science, and it is often discussed in terms of its esthetic or visual content, or in terms of its functional content. These two components—the visual and the functional—are hardly satisfactory for describing the full range of facets involved in designing, because the exact meaning of the terms are seldom fully understood. But the terms can serve as a general starting point.

Even in a simple analysis, we are dealing with very abstract notions because many of the effects of design can only be sensed or felt and are impossible to measure. It helps to define things clearly to avoid confusion, but categorizations must be done with care, because it is the object as a whole that we are considering, and all the design elements that make it up are subtly interconnected and interdependent. Some objects, for example, function primarily as visual things—thrones, for example. And, on the other hand, the visual form of most objects is determined, at least in part, by its function.

The meanings of function

The function of an object can vary enormously from person to person. The function of a chair to the person buying it, for example, may be that it should support him comfortably and safely when he sits on it. But its function to the retailer is to produce profit and promote the image of the store. To the manufacturer, its function is to generate a return for his shareholders and keep his employees in work. To the designer, it is often a function geared to earning a reputation, publicity and design awards; and to a furniture maker in a small workshop, the real function of that chair could well be to develop his or her craft skills and bring work satisfaction. The chair will even be expected to function by satisfying some abstract emotions—to evoke status or security or promote a feeling of informality, or simply to fit into a particular style. Thus, the function of an object varies with a person's relationship to it. When the term is used correctly, it refers to the purpose to which something is put.

Function is a curious word and its incorrect use has led to all manner of misconceptions, epitomized by such maxims as "form follows function." Because function can vary considerably, form, which is supposed to follow it, presumably also can vary. But we will see that function in fact limits form by restricting the choices a designer can make about an object's appearance.

Visual elements of design

The other word most commonly used when discussing an object in design terms is "visual." This too is misleading, because it refers to the terms "see," "perceive" and "look at." Even though we can see from the moment we are born, we have to learn to recognize and interpret the images over a long period of time. This recognition is known as "perception." Once we have recognized the object, our perception of it is largely concerned with meaning, rather than with content. We tend to ignore information beyond what we need simply to recognize an object.

The meaning of the things we perceive is all-important. For example, when a car is about to run someone down, he does not need to know what make of car it is or whether it has chrome fenders—only that it is a car and that he should get out of the way quickly. He recognizes instantly the collective signs that indicate "car" and he takes the appropriate action. If he had to analyze all the components before he could act, there would be few people left to read this book.

But if meaning takes precedence over content in perception, it is the visible content of objects—the individual features of an object that we see and their interrelationship—which gives the overall meaning we perceive. It is precisely this assembly of features which is the concern of designers. They have to look at objects attentively, and to analyze the individual forms in far greater depth than is necessary for the average individual, in order to understand how they interact and produce desirable effects. Traditionally, this has been taught through the process of drawing, which requires a person to concentrate his eye on the individual aspects of the subject—something which does not happen naturally when we simply perceive things. Designers, therefore, learn to look at objects in order to be able to design.

By manipulating the size, shape and relationship of various components, designers can create an object which, for most people, looks right. Whether it appeals to them or not is a matter of taste; it does not change the facts of the design. For the designer or design critic, the concern is for understanding why it looks right; for the man in the street, it is sufficient that it does.

Taste aside, what is visually exciting to those who naturally look at an object can be visually distressing to the ordinary person. There is an analogy in contemporary classical music. A person who has listened to it a great deal, studied music and is aware of the difficulties of composing, may greatly enjoy a musical performance. Another person without such a background might find the same performance laborious and difficult to listen to. Both can share a taste for classical music, but one has developed his knowledge of it and hears it differently from the other.

So it is with looking at things. People who have practiced, who have studied the appearance of objects in depth, will interpret what they see differently from those who have not. Therefore when we use the term "visual," we must realize that what we look for as designers, and consequently is important to us, may be entirely different from the criteria of the uninitiated. They are likely to respond to antique furniture in general, for example, because it is old. A practiced eye, however, will be much more selective and perhaps respond to only a few pieces at most. The popularity of bad reproduction furniture relies on the fact that most people only need to perceive the overall effect of antiquity or of traditional feeling in a piece before buying it. As long as this requirement is satisfied, they will happily remain visually indifferent.

For most people, it is important that an object has a feeling of rightness that falls within a particular area of taste. Those new to design can take courage from this because, provided they are not too ambitious, they can achieve this quality quite early in their attempts. It is a question of being able to familiarize themselves with the variables of a design, and then to assemble them into a recognizable pattern or style. (We discuss this process at greater length on pages 32 to 37.) But even after they feel they have mastered a style, they must not stop looking at things, for only by doing so will they progress to better work.

The requirements of design

To the two very general ingredients of function and appearance, we must add the aspects of ease and economy. To understand all aspects of design, however, we should regroup all these elements into three basic requirements, which can be summarized as: (a) the conditions demanded from the object while it is in use—its usefulness; (b) the requirement that the design is conceived in terms of economy and ease of use—its efficiency; and (c) the provision of an acceptable appearance—its degree of beauty.

Anyone who designs something tries to satisfy these three requirements. The difficulty is to do so without compromising one requirement for another—a predicament that designers repeatedly confront and rarely resolve to their total satisfaction.

Usefulness

The first requirement of usefulness specifies that for an object to work, all the components must be related geometrically to one another so it does its intended job. This is a simple enough statement, but drawers stick and doors fall off their hinges because the designer has failed to ensure that they will work properly.

As long as the design works properly, then an object can be any shape the designer wants it to be. In practice, he is asked to provide drawings for an object in a particular category, for example, a chest of drawers. And because most objects have traditional precedents, limitations are imposed on the final design.

DESIGN / Applying the principles

It is surprising how pervasive are the forms of the first reliable inventions on future generations of objects; designers constantly refer back to them even when there is no longer any physical need. To illustrate: most new solid-state cash registers slavishly resemble the old mechanical models, even though the silicon chips that run the new machines are so small that the designer could make the register any shape he wanted. The new machines mimic the old shape, which originally was determined by the size and action of the mechanisms it had to house.

The second requirement of usefulness is that all the components be strong enough to handle the forces that come from repeated use and abuse. With some objects, it is necessary to calculate these with extreme accuracy (objects such as precision machinery, automobiles, buildings, bridges and so on). With furniture, this is not so and many successful pieces have been produced through beefing up a succession of broken prototypes until they no longer break. (Toby Winteringham followed this method successfully to arrive at his chair at the top of page 60.) It is advisable however to have some knowledge of the strength of materials and the behaviour of components within a structure, if only to reduce development time and frustration (see pages 24–31).

Through calculation, the minimum cross-section necessary can be determined for any material. The designer should not choose sections below this, but he or she is *not* prevented from choosing bigger cross-sections. These days there appears to be some moral benefit derived from using the least amount of material possible—minimalism—but this is only a style, and is often more expensive to achieve than by using more material: labour is usually the major cost factor in manufacturing, not the material. Not only does the designer have the choice of using bigger sections than those actually required, but these can also be any shape as long as they still remain strong enough. It is interesting to realize just how many revered objects are fabricated from large, generous cross-sections—far larger than are necessary for them to work. Many famous buildings are notable in this respect. In fact, some designers feel that thicker structural members will actually inspire confidence in an object, and so they purposely over-build.

A third aspect of usefulness concerns accessibility. Of course, no object exists in isolation and would have no meaning if it did. Every object relates to other objects, and indeed, to man. If it is to work satisfactorily, this must be taken into account: the design must provide accessibility, which is a general term referring to how easy it is to use. Hand tools, for example, need to provide access for the hand and be easy to hold. The better tools take careful account of the way the hand moves, its shape, and its strength and sensitivity, so that they can be used as long as necessary without injury or fatigue.

Furniture provides a good example of another kind of access. Not only must the furniture be anthropometrically adequate (see pages 16–23) but because it is used within a definite space (inside a house or outside in a garden) it must not limit the working of that space. Furniture which is made to be moved or to be fitted into restricted spaces such as alcoves or corners, and which relates in scale to the architecture, has been designed with access in mind. This thinking provides us will all sorts of convenient facilities for eating, sleeping, sitting down and storing things which do not impede our movements from room to room. We retain access to the house. It may be stating the obvious, but there are too many examples in day-to-day living where this does not happen.

Access of a third kind is usually associated with complex objects such as machines. This is access for maintenance, including cleaning and repair. Those who have attempted to repair or replace components in a car will probably have scraped knuckles to prove the importance of this requirement.

The need for access also applies to furniture. A storage cabinet using touch latches (see pages 216–217), for example, to hold doors shut should not have a grooved and glued back, but one that is screwed on. This is because if the latches jam for any reason (something they are prone to do) there is access to the stored contents by unscrewing the back, without having to break open the door.

To satisfy all three requirements of usefulness can become a designer's nightmare. Consequently, the design process inevitably involves degrees of compromise because the components have to work properly as a whole, be strong enough and *still* provide access. But because the object would not function at all if the first two requirements were not satisfied, usually access is compromised in favour of expedience.

Ease and economy

When we speak of the economy of a design, the term goes deeper than simply tallying the retail cost of an object. It is to *not* choose a difficult and cumbersome means to an end when an easier, more efficient method is possible. This is the goal of human ingenuity—a kind of natural selection for objects, where the most effective survive to influence future generations. It is the purpose of most man-made objects to reduce the trouble, discomfort and risk in our lives, save us time and most importantly, effort.

Very few objects are absolutely essential to basic survival. As long as we have only heat and shelter, our existence is not threatened, but its *quality* would be. The objects we design therefore are valued for their convenience and their efficiency, and their evolution centres on further reducing the physical burdens in our lives. They ease our existence, and when we pay money for well-designed objects we are looking for greater ease. How much greater depends not just on the cost of materials and labour, but also on the particular sense of value we get from owning the object, and how much we benefit from the tasks it performs for us. The term "high added value" is a marketing term that describes what all manufacturers try to accomplish in a product. It is a quality so essential or desirable that people are willing to pay prices for the products greatly exceeding the cost of manufacture.

No designer can be entirely free from the limitations imposed by the price of things he or she designs. But cost constraints are a matter of choice, whereas the constraints of usefulness cannot be sidestepped—the object must work. Designers are pressured to produce high added value in the broadest terms, but we should realize that we do not have to make everything as cheaply as possible. It is important to emphasize this because designers often feel they are powerless to do much about it. The value of an object can mean its degree of usefulness in social or moral terms, rather than merely its financial worth. If all aspects of value are reduced to cost, it could become a short step to the conclusion that the same is true of people.

The erosion of a sense of value, more and more replaced by "cost effectiveness" in product designs, is traceable to the corruption of the term "economy." Manufacturers display a mindless preoccupation with feasibility, doing technically feasible things just because they are possible, and then pursue projects regardless of cost or consequence, as they did, for example, with the Concorde. Supersonic commercial jets are certainly feasible, but hardly practical in a business sense.

It is not surprising to find many designers, their sensibilities ignored, themselves becoming manufacturers to try to regain a sense of value. The growth of small furniture workshops—not a significant threat to industrial production except by challenging the standards of the products—is a move that could form the basis of the next generation of industries, as long as the small workshop is not construed as a means of opting out. Designers are *not* privileged to opt out of their culture, but they are privileged by virtue of their skills and understanding to do something about the quality of life in their culture. The importance of their role as cultural activists becomes clearer when we discuss the third requirement for good design—appearance.

Appearance
It was mentioned earlier that the man-made environment, which for most of us forms our world, is essentially the combined effect of the work of designers. Thousands of objects combine to create this environment and the manner in which we perceive them, either singly or collectively, conditions the quality of our lives. Therefore it is important that this "artificial" designed environment be emotionally supportive. Is it to this end that designers concern themselves with the appearance of things.

We have dwelt with the natural tendency of designers to try to make objects that are useful and efficient and have discussed the value of doing so. However, when they try to give these objects an acceptable appearance, they find a conflict. In furniture, for example, we create enormous problems for ourselves by requiring surfaces that are fine-sanded and highly polished, perfectly straight rails, precise curves or flush-fitting joints. All these details could be omitted and the piece would still work perfectly well. And yet we purposely set out to contradict the premise that the design must be efficient. So why do we make life difficult for ourselves with unnecessary complications?

The answer is, of course, that these visual elements are not unnecessary, but of critical importance. Designers and manufacturers commit enormous amounts of effort and time to arrive at an appropriate appearance in an object. And people demand it in the things they buy. So it is right to conclude that for an object to simply work well is not enough.

All objects, to varying degrees, have a role in satisfying our spiritual needs in addition to our physical ones, and they achieve this largely through appearance. A furnished room can represent an extension of an individual personality, and can tell a story about the occupant. In the objects and images he chooses and the way he uses and displays them, there are references to aspirations and fears, levels of self-respect or self-confidence, individual standards and values. The same is true of large "designed" environments—towns and cities reflect the values of the culture that builds them.

When appearance reflects our established values, the designer becomes involved in the realms of art. It is for this reason that there has existed the tradition of teaching design and art side by side—they are inseparable. This implies that the designer's real responsibility is not to the client or those who pay for the work, but to his fellow human beings. The fact that a designer can choose the appearance of things does not necessarily make him an artist, however. His involvement with art calls on him to understand that the appearance of things can profoundly affect the quality of our lives and those of future generations, and he therefore must make responsible and informed choices. The designer who works as an artist is the one who makes people believe that the phrases "standard of living" and "quality of life" *can* mean the same thing.

It would be easy to think by now that appearance is more important than whether or not an object works properly. But a sense of value can be communicated through all the senses—the rich smell of leather or the feel of silken fabrics conjure up vivid memories and associations. However, the value of an object that works efficiently and reliably cannot be underestimated, even though we have accustomed ourselves to a world full of cut-rate objects that disappoint us when we use them. How refreshing is it then to use a well-engineered machine—a thoroughbred car or a high-quality kitchen appliance—or to operate well-made furniture with drawers and doors that fit. The experience lingers and is discussed, often with incredulity. A person even develops an affection for these dependable objects—a favourite rocking chair or a jacket. They become an asset to own, and not a burden.

But when efficiency is compromised for appearance, our experience of the object is diluted. Our high expectations are quickly overshadowed by disappointment and annoyance, especially if we paid a high price for the object.

We are after the best of both worlds, and every good designer must skilfully manipulate the rational, in solving his design problems, and the irrational, by infusing the visible environment with art.

DESIGN / Planning for people

How a piece of furniture fits the human frame, adapts to the way human beings will use it and conforms to the physical characteristics of the human body can make the difference between a good design and one that is utterly useless. Therefore, serious designers use anthropometrics, a science that studies the comparative dimensions of the human body, to arrive at the initial scale and dimensions of a piece of furniture.

Anthropometrics has standardized certain body measurements so that a designer starting from scratch can get an idea of the parameters that are imposed by the human frame on his design. From this he gets a notion of the physical proportions of the "average person" his furniture is meant to fit, and can estimate the limits of the visual and physical reach of a person.

It must be stressed that these are very general figures, calculated to accommodate the average-sized person, much the way clothing sizes aim to fit an average range of physical proportions. These figures cannot be guaranteed to satisfy persons at the extreme ends of the size scale. Therefore, a designer should always refine the data given here by adding personal observations and then, if necessary, amend the preliminary sketches to better fit a particular case. To make furniture for children, for example, the crucial measurements given in the following pages should be adapted to fit the child's size, allowing room for growth, of course. And the designer should make careful note of how people use furniture in daily life, and record their practical needs that are or are not met by the furniture they use.

Typical furniture heights from the floor	
250 cm/98 in	Ceilings
188–198 cm/74–78 in	Windows and door tops
104 cm/41 in	Counters for eating and drinking
96.5 cm/38 in	Work benches
91.5 cm/36 in	Kitchen work surfaces
83.8 cm/33 in	Food preparation surfaces
73.8 cm/29 in	Eating surfaces
71 cm/28 in	Most tables
68.6 cm/27 in	Desks and general work surfaces
66 cm/26 in	Typing tables
52.5–73.8 cm/21–29 in	Chair arms
40.6–50.8 cm/16–20 in	High occasional tables
35–48 cm/14–19 in	Chairs, benches and stools
30.5 cm/12 in	Low occasional tables

A chart of heights
The chart above gives the accepted heights of most furniture. The height of a ceiling will affect the height of a bunk bed. The height of a door will limit the height of an assembled storage cabinet that has to pass through the door into a room. Work benches, kitchen worktops and food preparation surfaces tend to be roughly the same height; other tables are lower.

Anthropometric proportions
The measurements below indicate the average dimensions of men and women. These figures in turn determine the dimensions of furniture. For example, a person's reach to the side limits the width of a door. The stretch to the front limits the depth of a shelf. The length of a person's thigh determines the depth of a chair seat, while the distance from floor to knee controls the height of the seat.

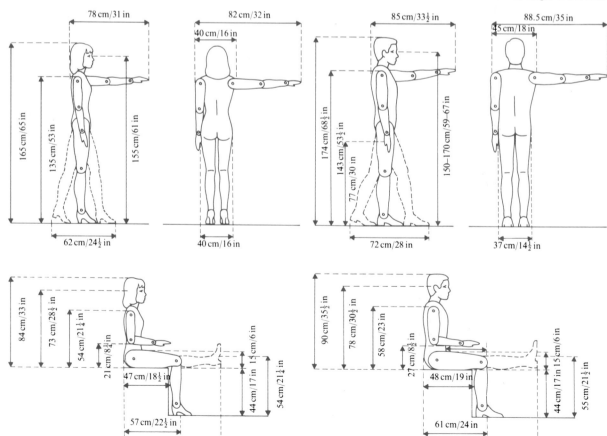

16

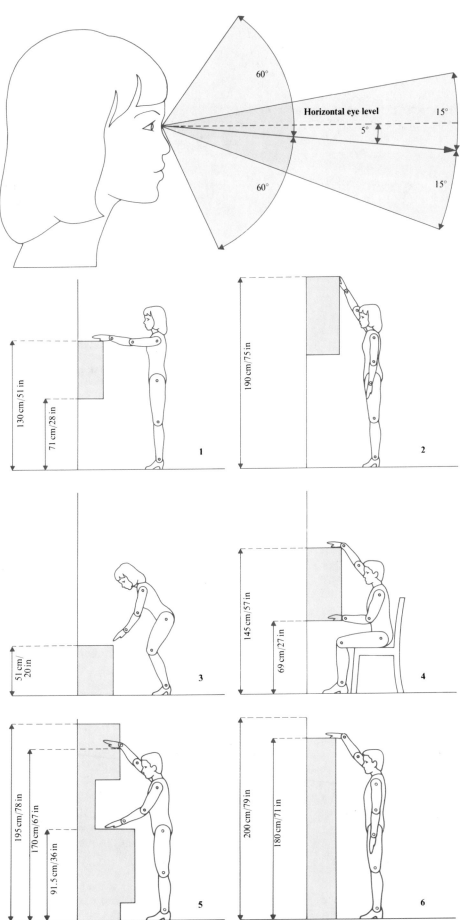

Ranges of vision

A person's range of vision will determine the best place to put high storage to display objects. Normal eye level for men is 150 to 170 cm/59 to 67 in. For women it is 140 to 168 cm/55 to 66 in. The natural line of sight is 5° below horizontal, and most objects are in focus in a cone 15° around the line of sight. Without moving his head, the person has a range of vision in a 60° cone around his line of sight.

The central storage range

1. Store frequently-used or heavy objects requiring two hands to hold in the central storage range, at a height easy for the average person to reach and manoeuvre the item. This zone is between 70 cm/28 in and 130 cm/51 in from the floor.
2. Less essential items not as frequently put away and retrieved should be stored above ...
3. ... or below the central storage range.

Vertical reach

4. A person's vertical reach while sitting is approximately 145 cm/57 in from the floor. Storage above a work surface such as a desk should not exceed that height, though in practice the person's reach may be even less, as he stretches over the protruding desk to grasp the object.
5. Vertical reach over a surface from a standing position is similarly restricted. Comfortable reach is at 170 cm/67 in, while a full stretch can extend to 195 cm/77 in.
6. Vertical reach without a protruding work surface is considerably greater: 180 cm/71 in to reach an object comfortably, and 200 cm/79 in at a full stretch.

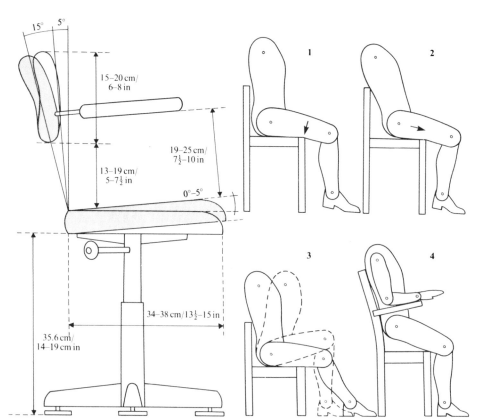

Some dimensions that çan be altered in an adjustable chair include the height and tilt of the backrest and the seat, and the height of the armrest, making it adaptable to a wide range of body sizes.

1. If a chair seat is too high, the front of the seat puts uncomfortable pressure under the thighs, just behind the knees. The blood supply to the legs, which flows in the arteries at the back of the legs, will be cut off.

2. Because the feet do not rest firmly on the ground, a person sitting in a high seat will slide forward, especially if the seat is horizontal and slippery.

3. If the seat is too low, a person becomes cramped in the chair, or stretches his legs out in front. Even a spry person has difficulty getting out of the chair from this position.

4. An armrest that is placed too high from the seat tends to lever the sitter out of the chair, which exerts uncomfortable pressure on the shoulders.

Human beings sit down in order to relax certain parts of the body and to relieve the strain of standing. As a person sits down on a seat, the body's weight is taken off the legs and feet and is transferred to the buttocks and the back of the thighs. To further relax, a person leans against the backrest and is supported at two principal points that help the spine maintain its natural curvature: at the pelvis and at the upper torso, or thorax. A chair must therefore be designed to fit these points of support, and yet must not restrict a person from shifting position, which he does periodically while seated to reduce fatigue.

The seat

The seat height is one of the most important dimensions of a chair. If the seat is too high, it causes uncomfortable pressure under the thighs and eventually cuts off the blood supply to the legs. If the seat is too low, the sitter must assume a crouched position, losing the benefits of a shaped seat. In general, however, a low seat is a better design than a high one, because a tall person can sit on a low seat more comfortably than a short person can sit on a tall seat. The ideal height allows the sitter to have both feet flat on the floor, leaving a small gap under the thighs, just behind the knees. That is a soft, sensitive area which should not come under pressure.

The seat height is so crucial to comfort that it is the primary adjustment to be made on an adjustable office chair, which is specifically designed for long-term sitting for a broad range of body types. The added expense of making these specialized chairs has become cost effective for the companies who buy them, although in design terms the range of styles is limited. It is interesting to note the increased use of adjustable office chairs in the home as well as the office.

The width of a seat must accommodate the spread of the buttocks on a relatively small area around the centre of the pelvis. Additional space is needed to allow for shifts of position and for thick clothing.

The seat depth is calculated by estimating the length of the thigh. As a general rule, designers make hard upright seats shallower than soft padded seats, especially if they are in low or reclining chairs. But in any circumstance, the seat must not be too deep, or the back will not come into contact properly along the backrest.

The surface composition of the seat varies according to how the seat will be used. It can be solid, smooth or shaped, covered with fabric or caning, or layered with padding. A person generally will be more comfortable on a soft seat than on a hard one, but if the surface is too soft the body weight is distributed over a broad sensitive area of the pelvis and thighs, which is not ideal for sitting. Instead, the best area is a small central spot under the centre of the pelvis, where there is a good supply of blood. For sitting over long periods, the padding on a seat should depress only about $1.2\,cm/\frac{1}{2}\,in$ to give support without inducing fatigue.

Carved and sculpted seats in solid wood give the impression of being more comfortable than flat seats, but unless the seat was designed to suit a particular size, the advantages are minimal. However, texturing the surface of the seat increases friction and allows a

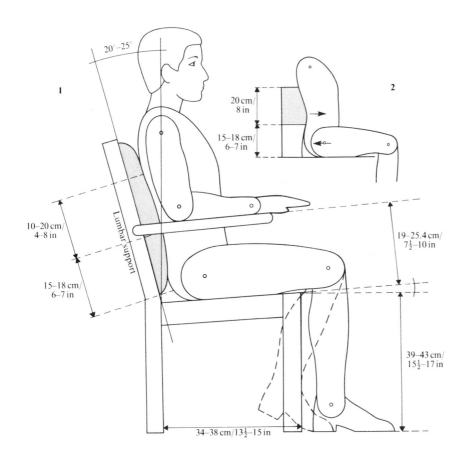

20°–25°

20 cm/
8 in

15–18 cm/
6–7 in

1

2

10–20 cm/
4–8 in

Lumbar support

15–18 cm/
6–7 in

19–25.4 cm/
7½–10 in

39–43 cm/
15½–17 in

34–38 cm/13½–15 in

An armchair of fixed dimensions
1. These are the general dimensions for an upright armchair with armrests. The armrests should have at least 48.3 cm/19 in between them, and should be about 10 cm/4 in wide across the arm to be comfortable to lean or sit on. A rounded, convex backrest should have a radius of 2 to 3 times the depth of the seat. So if the seat is 38 cm/15 in deep, the radius of the back should be 76–114 cm/30–45 in.
2. The backrest supports the middle or lumbar region of the back, and allows room for the buttocks and the area just below the lumbar region. This support should allow for elbow room, so that the sitter can arch his back to relieve strain. Therefore, the backrest should be between 30.5–35.6 cm/12–14 in wide to allow the elbows to move backwards.

person to keep his seat more easily and with less effort than if the seat were smooth. This is accomplished by covering the seat with a layer of coarse fabric, straw caning or by somehow roughening the smooth surface. The front edge of the seat should be rounded to prevent injury to the vulnerable areas behind the knees when getting in and out of the chair.

There should be a space *under* the seat for two reasons. First, if he can place his feet under the seat, a person can project his body's centre of gravity forward more easily to rise smoothly out of the chair. The same is true in reverse, when the sitter lowers his body gently into the seat. Secondly, the sitter can take the strain off the middle back, or lumbar region, while he is sitting by putting his feet back under the seat and arching his back. This position reduces fatigue on the back and allows the chair to be used for longer periods—an important consideration for office workers.

The backrest
Backrest cause the most problems to designers concerned with fitting chairs to people. The profile of the backrest must give support at the right points to avoid backache and the angle of the backrest must be suited to the way the chair will be used either for relaxation or for work. It should be shaped to accommodate the curve of the spine, with the emphasis on giving support to the lumbar region (the small of the back and the area of the body potentially under most strain when someone is sitting).

The tilt of a backrest helps to position the body comfortably and to prevent the sitter from gradually

sliding forward. A sloping, roughly textured seat base used with a tilted back will further help to prevent this tendency to slide, but is often a disadvantage on chairs used for working, such as office chairs. For this reason the seats of working chairs are usually horizontal or very slightly tilted.

As well as providing support for the small of the back, a designer must also ensure that there is sufficient space for the buttocks and, in a chair that reclines, support for the shoulders also. With steep angles (130° gives a position which is highly relaxing) a head restraint should be considered because conversation, reading or watching television becomes difficult at that angle without it. A pillow or cushion at the back of the head satisfies this requirement.

Armrests
Armrests perform several functions. They can provide side support to a seated worker, allowing him to shift his position and lean on the armrest. Or they can be used for leverage, to pivot someone in and out of the chair by pushing on the armrest. Visually, they add an element of containment and security to the design, seeming to hold the sitter inside the chair. And in the case of the carver chair usually positioned at the head of the table, they assign status.

The two critical dimensions of the armrest are the spacing between the armrests themselves, and the distance between the seat and the top of the armrest. Additionally, the armrest should be strong and wide enough to bear the weight of someone sitting or perched on it.

The dimensions of a table are determined by the kinds of tasks performed on it and the number of persons who require access to it. Even though there are accepted figures for the sizes of a table according to its use (see page 16), allowances must be made for the equipment and machinery that might be placed on top of it. Such is the thinking, for example, behind the Peter St. Hill split-level desk (pages 94–95) with one side at a lower level than the other to accommodate a typewriter or a computer terminal with a video screen.

Dining tables

Something as simple as eating can require quite different table dimensions depending on where the eater lives. In China, for example, where people scoop their food from bowls with chopsticks and bite into their meat to cut it, the preferred table height is closer to the mouth, at roughly 92 cm/36 in, or the height of a western kitchen counter. Westerners, who use knives and forks, need to be able to push downward to manipulate their utensils. A more comfortable height for them is 71 cm/28 in.

Whatever the culture, eating is a social ritual in which the eaters share food and conversation, and the shape of the dining table can facilitate this ritual or impede it. A round table allows everyone to see each other easily if it is less than 153 cm/60 in in diameter. An oblong table, however, creates a seating hierarchy with a "head" and "foot" of the table.

In general, each place setting should be allotted 62 cm/24 in, with the allowance increased to 92 cm/36 in at the corners of a rectangular table.

Extendable tables can be designed in many shapes and the mechanisms to expand and contract them can be bought ready-made to install. There are two factors influencing the design of the table. The first is the placement of the table legs and the second is the extending mechanism, which must be designed so that the table can easily be converted by one person from one form to another.

Worktables

Unlike dining tables, the design of a worktable, whether it is a desk or a kitchen counter, becomes a very personal thing. Worktables must suit an individual to use for long periods under conditions that require concentration and energy and in which unnecessary fatigue must be avoided.

Therefore, the designer must be sensitive to the personal requirements of the user, his or her size and that of the machinery being used. He should ask how the user of the table works: does he require a large uncluttered expanse of surface; a surface that can be adapted to several functions; numerous cubby-holes and drawers? Storage receptacles should be well integrated into the table so that they are easily accessible as the worker stands or sits in front of his work. This is an area where the experiences of the designer are a valuable resource. A sketchbook is useful to record the dimensions and the characteristics of work surfaces.

A circular dining table
A typical circular dining table of approximately 153 cm/60 in diameter seats 8 persons comfortably, allowing roughly 62 cm/24 in for each setting. At this diameter, a seated diner has difficulty reaching an object at the centre of the table. A good solution to this problem is to build a revolving turntable into the centre of the table to pass dishes of food among the diners. A table larger than this one would make conversation across the table difficult.

Note the placement of the table legs; set in 25 cm/10 in from the edge of the tabletop, they do not obstruct the diner from pulling his chair comfortably under the table.

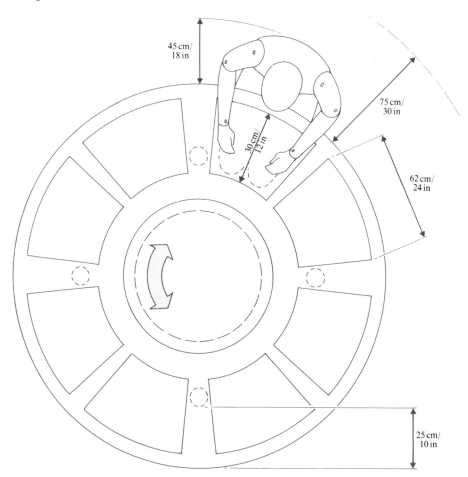

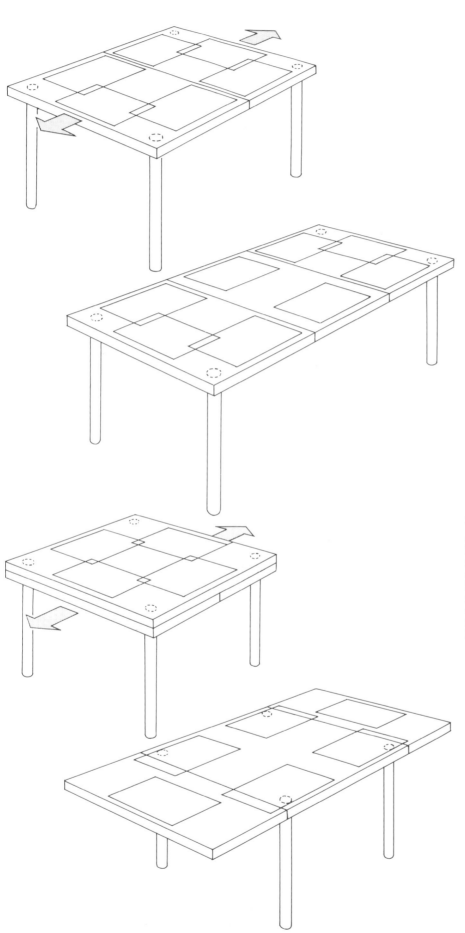

A well designed extending table
Closed, this table seats 6
persons generously. It is
extended, using a slide-and-
drop leaf mechanism, to
accommodate 8 diners with no
loss of comfort because the
table legs, which are fixed at
each corner, are still well out
of the way of the seated diners.
The mechanism even leaves
enough room under the table
to allow the diners to cross
their legs without knocking the
table frame.

A badly designed table
Unlike the table above, this
small square four-seater uses a
hidden-leaf mechanism to
expand into two extra place
settings. The four place settings
in the middle of the expanded
table are now situated directly
over the table legs, blocking
the seated diner from pulling
his chair under the table.

Beds

The size and shape of a bed is usually determined by one primary factor: the mattress. Few designers bother to make their own mattresses because commercially-manufactured mattresses are generally of good quality and come in standard sizes to match standard-sized bed linen. The best mattresses support the spine, but are not so heavy that they are difficult to lift.

However, the designer can control the springiness of the bed and its height from the floor. For soft mattress support there can be a sprung under-frame or wooden slats or, for a harder sleeping surface, a solid plywood platform. Any mattress support should allow the mattress to breathe or it will become musty. Solid wood platforms should be perforated with air holes.

A bed positioned above the floor keeps the sleeper out of draughts, is easier to make and allows for built-in storage underneath. If the bed is too low, it is awkward and uncomfortable to sit on its edge; too high, and it is difficult to climb onto.

Bunk beds are usually designed to accommodate children and should be built with safety in mind. They should be detachable for use as single beds as the children grow. The ladder treads should be close together and rounded on the front edge

Storage

The human frame puts the emphasis on *access* in the design of storage because it is the dimensions and anatomy of the human body that determine how easily a person can lift and manipulate objects. Ideally, storing something should not cause strain from moving things at awkward angles, difficulty in manoeuvring the object, or danger from having to stand on an unsteady surface to reach the stored object. Therefore, a person's size—whether a child or an adult—affects the general dimensions of the storage unit.

There are several other related factors such as the area needed around the unit to open it. There is the visibility of the items being stored, which could necessitate glazing the doors, installing lighting or making shallower shelves. And finally, there is the frequency with which the objects are used, and the size, weight and value of the objects.

This very general discussion of storage covers some of the physical requirements that human beings place on storage furniture, whether it is a jewelry box or a kitchen cabinet. The human body also determines the size and shape of things to be stored. The most notable example is clothing, stored folded in drawers, shelves and boxes, or hanging from a rack or from hooks.

The dimensions of beds

1. These are some general dimensions for a bunk bed, suitable for two growing children. The safety rail and the ladder are detachable and the bed can be dismantled into two single beds.

2. The minimum space between two beds should be increased if there is to be storage under the beds. The beds should be easy to move for room cleaning or bed making, but should not move accidentally. Fit the base with wheels with built in stops to do that.

3. A bed frame should be designed with a space under its edge at least 15 cm/6 in deep so that the bed-maker has room for his feet under the bed while lifting the mattress. This facility helps to avoid back strain.

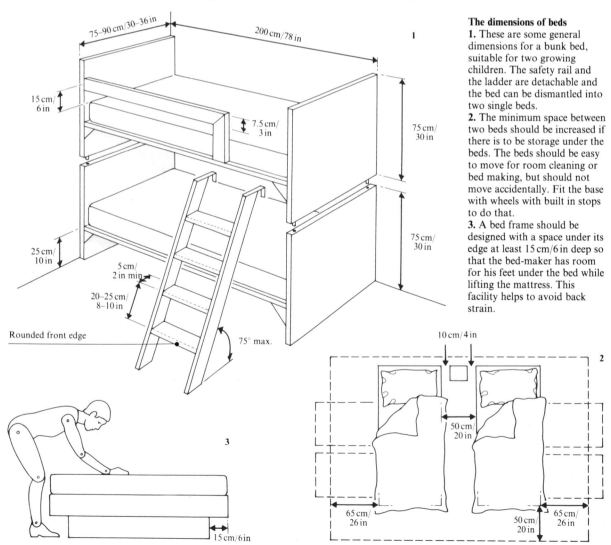

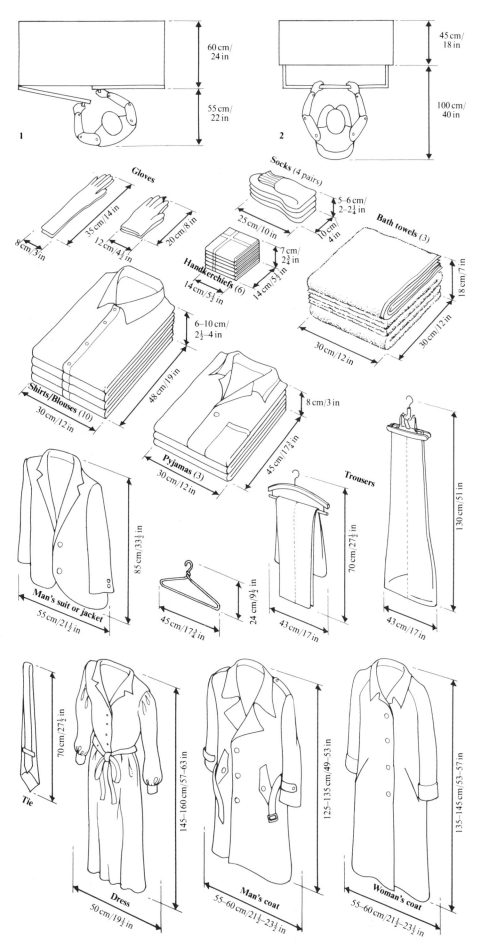

Clearance for doors and drawers

1. A design must allow enough space to open drawers, doors, flaps and lids to gain access to stored items. The door or flap should remain open until closed, and not have to be held in position while the user searches for the item.

2. The weight of stored objects is important to consider as well as the size: a heavy full drawer taxes the strength of the user, and can cause injury if it falls out of the carcass. Drawer glides and stops, and reducing the size of the drawer all help to overcome the problem.

Storing clothing

By generalizing the size and shape of clothing, how it is folded and how often it is used, it is possible to predict the dimensions of clothes storage units such as wardrobes, bureaus and closets. Additionally, sub-units of storage such as drawers, shelves and hanging racks can be strategically positioned.

Small items such as gloves, socks, underwear and handkerchiefs, which are used frequently, are stored in small drawers at least 25 cm/10 in deep in the central storage range (a zone between 70–130 cm/28–51 in from the floor).

Medium-sized items such as folded pyjamas and shirts—also often used—need wider receptacles: a drawer or shelf at least 30 cm/12 in wide and positioned in the same central storage range as socks. Less frequently used items of the same size, such as sweaters and bath towels, can be stored in the same-sized receptacles, but outside of the central storage range, in low drawers or high shelves.

Certain large items, such as coats, suits and long dresses, can only be stored hanging. The position of a clothes rail allows for space 45 cm/18 in deep and 25 cm/10 in high around the rail, plus a maximum of 160 cm/63 in under the rail for long dresses.

The designer could use these figures to estimate how much clothing an individual owns and then tailor a storage unit to fit a specific need. Or, by averaging the volumes needed to store a range of items, and by taking into account how often the items are used, the result would be a general-purpose unit.

23

Furniture in everyday use has to withstand being pushed, pulled, tipped, dropped, sat on and loaded with heavy items such as books or bodies. In short, it has to be able to cope with a number of forces, which, if unaccounted for in the design, result in furniture that does not perform properly, or even breaks down completely when it is used. So it is essential that structural weakness be designed out of an object at the earliest stages and that the designer familiarizes himself with the properties of stability and rigidity so that his design stays together, works safely and does the job he intends it to do.

Fortunately, a structure does not have to be nondescript or ugly in order to work. In fact, many designers believe that an object designed from a good structural standpoint automatically becomes beautiful. In reality, good structural practice merely determines the minimum size and the position of the components of the piece. And any piece of furniture that ignores structure in favour of aesthetics will soon lose its appeal when it breaks, wobbles, tips over or crushes fingers.

Stability

A rigid structure can be unstable, and *vice versa*, but a successful design must be both stable and rigid. When not in use, all objects are stable. An object rests on the ground in a particular position and it stays there: it is in equilibrium. If, when it is moved, it remains or returns to this "upright" position, it has what is termed a stable equilibrium. All furniture should aim for this. It is achieved when the centre of gravity of the structure and the load fall vertically within the area of the base.

This load is not always stationary. It can move, as, for instance, when someone sits on a chair and leans back. The shifting load changes the position of the centre of gravity; shifted far enough and the centre of gravity will move to fall outside the area of the base. At that moment, the chair loses its stable equilibrium and topples over.

In general, any object, including furniture, is more stable if its centre of gravity is low to the ground. The object would have to be tilted much farther for its center of gravity to move outside the area of its base. Calculating exactly where to find the centre of gravity of an object is a complicated task, but it is safe to say that the wider and heavier the base, the lower the

centre of gravity will be and the more stable the object.

Just as a load may not always be static, it may also not always be constant. A structure must be able to support the shifted weight of an open drawer or door without toppling over or splitting at the joints.

Finally, the designer must consider the weight of the structure itself, which is essentially a static load produced by gravity. A top-heavy, unstable structure places extreme strains on the joints, and in extremes it can break down under its own weight.

The forces needed to overcome friction—when moving furniture across the floor or opening and closing doors and drawers, for example—can also strain a structure. These forces are usually transmitted to the weakest part of the structure (usually to the joints). It is thus important to consider at the design stage whether furniture should move easily or resist movement. If it is to move, castors, glides and even small wheels solve the problem by reducing friction. On the other hand, a bench intended to stay put can be made to do so by placing a rubber cap or a wide serrated foot at the base of each leg.

Predicting forces

Many people new to furniture design never fully understand the size or the direction of the forces acting on a structure when it is in normal use, or how certain structures transmit and withstand these forces. "Normal" use of course includes some amount of unpredictable and abnormal abuse, because people will often stand on a chair or sit on a table. This is exactly the kind of treatment that cracks the joints and fractures the rails in ordinary furniture. A good designer will allow for the more obvious abuses, but how much strengthening is really necessary?

Most furniture makers get around the problem by copying a standard pattern and assuming it has been tested. These craftsmen do not have to understand why a certain chair rail is needed or where it should be placed to be most effective. They may never even make a calculation, and yet the results are satisfactory, largely because most existing pieces of furniture are overstructured and, by containing more bracing than they need, incorporate a large safety factor. Yet if the forces acting on a chair are fully understood, it is astonishing how thin the bracing needs to be. A fine example is the Toby Winteringham chair on page 60.

Rigid and unstable
1. This table is rigidly built, but force applied to the edge of the top easily tips it.

Stable and not rigid
2. This table is stable, but its top is too flexible and will not provide a rigid surface.

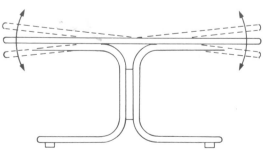

Stable equilibrium

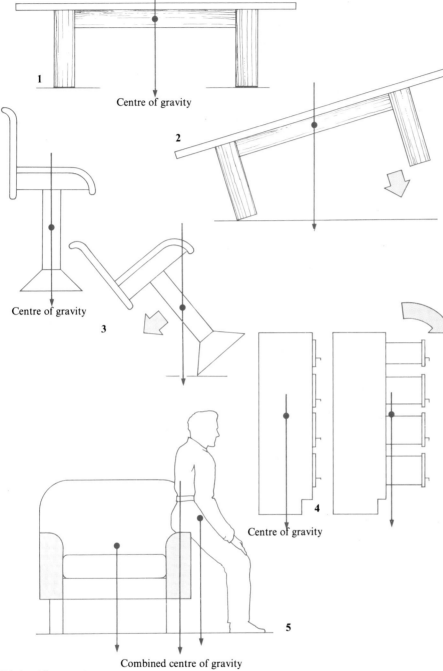

1

Centre of gravity

Centre of gravity

3

Combined centre of gravity

Centre of gravity

2

4

Stable equilibrium

1. At rest, the center of gravity of this table falls within the area between its points of support, where its legs touch the ground. It is in equilibrium.

2. When the table is tipped up, the centre of gravity still acts within the area of its points of support, and the table will return to an upright position when it is released. It is in stable equilibrium.

3. The bar stool at rest is in equilibrium. But when it is tipped back, its centre of gravity shifts outside the area of its base, and it will lose its stable equilibrium and fall backwards.

4. A tall filing cabinet with all its drawers open often will have its centre of gravity shifted to outside the area of its base, and topple forward.

5. The effect of someone sitting on the arm of a chair shifts the chair's centre of gravity to outside its points of support, and the chair will tip over.

Frictional forces

6. The force needed to overcome the frictional forces between the chair legs and a pile carpet is greater than the force needed to push the chair across a polished floor.

7. Castors or glides reduce the frictional forces on an office chair.

8. A combination of great weight and thick legs increases the frictional force on a workbench, and helps keep it stabilized in use.

Frictional forces

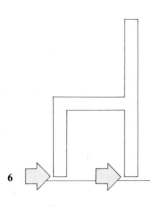

6

7

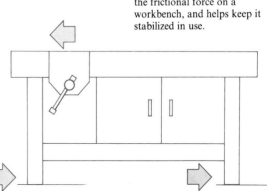

8

Copying an existing design can be risky, even if the designer has planned the structure to be safe to the user *should* it break down. Windsor chairs, and most cane furniture can still be used with stretcher rails broken and joints loose because they were designed with enough supporting joints to compensate for the broken members and to keep the piece intact—up to a point.

To calculate the myriad forces within a piece of furniture is a complex operation, but you need a general understanding of how they work. Gravity is a force that can distribute itself though a structure and result in radically different local forces. The weight of a hinged door, for example, acts to pull it from its frame and the top hinge has to resist this; most of the support is provided by the bottom hinge. A door in equilibrium that swings freely without sagging or tearing its hinges out can be achieved by setting both hinges into the frame. This spreads the load acting on them, effectively increasing their strength.

The design of a cantilever chair needs to take a different kind of force into account—the force exerted when a beam moves on a pivot or fulcrum. The placing of a fulcrum is crucial: position it correctly and a man can use a crowbar to lift a rock many times his own weight. The same force can be destructive (for example, to pry open a locked box) and it is this negative application of which the designer needs to be aware.

The cantilever chair is essentially a beam supported at one end and acting on a fulcrum. It must be able to withstand much greater force than a conventional chair with a leg at each corner simply because the force applied to acts like a lever on a chair frame . A person sitting down heavily on such a seat can apply a force roughly twice his or her own weight. That force is transmitted to the floor principally through the fulcrum and the chair's legs. The effect is like trying to force open a steel box with a thin wooden crowbar: if the seat timber is not strong enough, the seat will snap off at the fulcrum—the steel pin that holds it to the legs. Similarly, if the pin at the fulcrum is weak, it will break

The designer must, if possible, reduce leverage by shortening the seat to reduce the leverage, or by adding bracing.

Similar forces will be applied to the flap of a desk if someone leans on it heavily. Even if the flap does not break away immediately, it is certain to work loose quickly. The remedy is to build strong stays or sliding battens called lopers on which the flap can rest. These take the strain off the hinges by moving the fulcrum on which the force is acting—the hinged edge of the flap—nearer to where the load is being applied. In simple terms, less leverage is applied to the hinge.

A stay that restricts the swing of a door is useful in a badly designed cabinet, where the door can open out all the way and collide with the narrow face of an open drawer. The drawer will act as a fulcrum against the

---

A triangle of forces

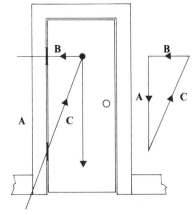

The effects of pivot points

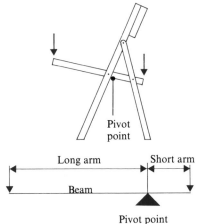

A triangle of forces
The forces acting on the hinges of a door form a triangle of forces. Side A of the triangle is the weight of the door pulling down through the centre of gravity. Side B is the upward resistance to the door's weight, provided by the lower hinge, which supports most of the door's weight. Side C is the inward resistance provided by the top hinge to keep the door upright. And so the force of gravity produces quite different directions of force on the top and bottom hinges.

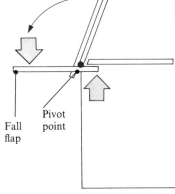

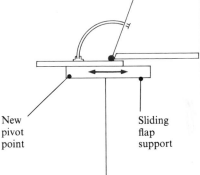

The effects of pivot points
In principle, the two arms of a beam on either side of a pivot point balance when the product of the weight applied to the beam on the short arm, multiplied by the length of the short arm equals the same product on the long arm.

If the beam is highly stressed, for example, the seat of a cantilever chair or the fall flap of a desk, move the pivot point closer to the end bearing the weight—the front of the seat or the flap—by shifting the position of the supports (which function as pivot points) closer to the front.

face of the door, and even a small velocity swing can create a force great enough to tear the hinges off the carcass *and* damage the surface of the door.

Stresses

The effects of force on furniture are felt most strongly on the joints, where the wood itself is at its thinnest cross-section, and where the forces are the most concentrated. For a designer to calculate a force is only the beginning. He must then be able to predict the stress—the effect of the force on a specific area of material. The actual amount of force is less important than where it is being concentrated. As we have seen, even a small force, if it is concentrated on a small area, can create enough stress on the material to break it.

All materials vary in their ability to absorb stress, and so the choice of material—wood, metal or plastic—together with its thickness or cross-section in the design, must relate to the structure and the loads it must tolerate. For example, chair frames made of oak or beech are far stronger than those of the same design made of mahogany.

In practice, materials are either plastic or elastic under stress. Plastic materials deform when they are under stress, and they stay deformed even after the stress is removed. Elastic materials, as the name implies, return to their original shape once the stress has been removed, provided they have not been overstressed. In furniture, the stresses of normal use must fall within an "elastic limit", which means that the design can exploit the elasticity of a particular material, but must not exceed it. For example, a chair made of tubular steel is a great deal more resilient, or elastic, under an applied load than a chair of the same design made from wood. It has the ability to bend under stress and then to return to its normal shape when the stress is removed. In furniture, it is critical that structures absorb stress without any permanent changes of shape.

To a certain extent the ability to absorb stress in a structure can be increased by providing a greater cross-sectional area in the members and at the joints, or by cross-bracing.

A related type of deformation of material under stress is known as creep, which is a gradual, though permanent, change of shape. It is evident in shelving made of planking that is too thin. When the shelves are loaded with books, they eventually bow under the weight, and remain bowed even after the books have been removed. That is creep. It can be remedied by supporting them from below using a beam.

While materials under a load may not visibly deform, they all experience some form of internal change. These changes are a result of three different forms of stress: compression stress, tensile or pulling stress and shear or tearing stress. They are illustrated below and on the following pages.

A stay to prevent a collision
The point of collision between a drawer and a door becomes a fulcrum, exerting leverage to pull off hinges and damage the door. Stays prevent collision.

Stresses on wood
1. The same force exerts less stress on a large cross-sectional area than on a small one because the stress is spread over the larger area.
2. Under compression, the molecules of wood are being pressed together; in tension they are pulled apart.
3. Under shear stress the molecules to slide against each other.

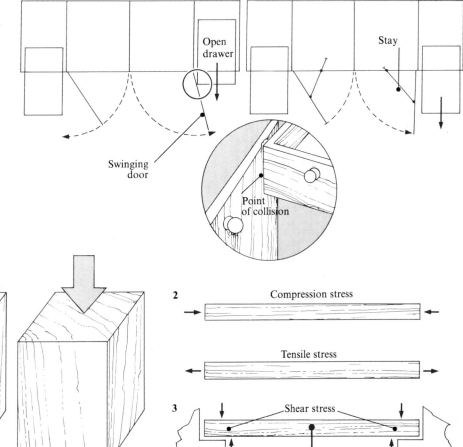

Shear stress occurs when the molecules of a material are being forced in different directions, as when the two blades of scissors slice through paper, and it is present in a beam spanning two supports when pressure is exerted in its middle.

It is shear stress that causes the problems in corner joints, where the inherent weakness of wood along the grain combines with the presence of a fulcrum at the base of the joint to create immense stresses. A designer can partially overcome the problem by gluing the joint as well as screwing or doweling it, because most modern adhesives resist shearing better than wood does. In fact, a glued corner is likely to break along the layer of fibres next to the glue line, rather than in the glue line itself. Another solution is to increase the area of the contact surfaces of the joint by making a more complex combe joint instead of a simple mortise and tenon. This way, the stress on the corner is dissipated and spread over a larger area.

The poor shear strength of wood along the grain is the reason why hinges are relatively easy to tear off if they are simply screwed down and not set in. Where the stress is especially high, on bureaus and table flaps for example, one solution is to use a dovetailed counterflap hinge, which has been inset into both the flap and the carcass. The inset hinge reduces the shear stress in the wood by distributing the stress over the area of the hinge plate, rather than concentrating it on the point where the screws penetrate the wood.

Corner joints are also vulnerable to the alternating shear stresses that come from twisting and bending the joints, and from the continual expansion and contraction of wood through the seasons. This is all the more reason to reinforce the corners of large thin-walled boxes and frames.

Stresses in bending

A beam spanning two supports illustrates how materials such as wood react to being bent, experiencing the combined effects of tension, compression and shear stress. The bottom edge of the beam elongates under tension, while the top edge compresses. At the points of support the load causes shear stress, as the force of the load is counteracted by the resisting forces at the supports.

But timber beams rarely fail at the points of support, where the shear stress exists, because the resistance to shear stress across the grain is good. Instead, the beam usually cracks in the middle of the span, where the greatest tensile and compression stresses are. Timber, as a material, is weakened by natural faults and cracks in the grain, which change its uniform resistance to stress. The faults become the weak points in the beam, and it is there that failure will occur.

How well a beam resists bending depends on a combination of two factors: its width and which way up it is used. Just as a steel rule flexes more easily if it is bent on its face than on its edge, a wooden beam will be able to better support a load and resist bending if the load is placed on the beam's edge. Surprisingly thin boards, used on edge, make excellent supports for heavy shelving units if they are deep enough.

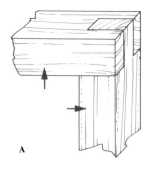

Shear stresses on a corner joint
With outward forces acting on either side of a corner joint (A), the bottom edge of the joint acts as a fulcrum and the fibres next to the glue line fail under shear (B).

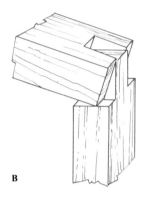

Even with the surface area of the joint well glued, the weak shear strength of wood along the grain will cause the joint to break in the fibres along the glue line.

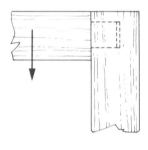

Shearing a mortise and tenon
A mortise and tenon joint, typically found in chair frames, is greatly weakened once the tenon no longer fits snugly in the mortise channel because of shrinking resulting from changes in the atmosphere.

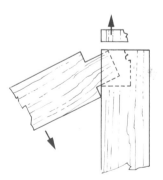

A force applied downward on the frame translates—using the bottom of the mortise as a fulcrum—into leverage against the top of the mortise. Combined with the poor shear strength of wood across the grain, the leverage breaks out the top of the joint.

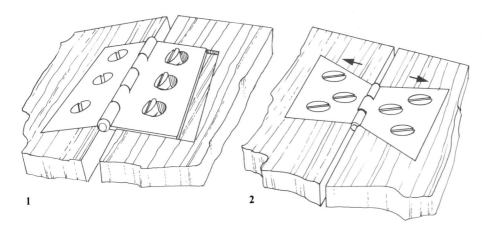

1   **2**

Dovetailed hinges
1. Conventional butt hinges can more easily be pulled out of the wood because it is only the hinge screws that resist the pulling force.
2. Dovetailed hinges overcome this difficulty by exploiting the good shear strength of wood *across* the grain. The flared shape resists the pulling force across so that less of the stress is borne by the screws.

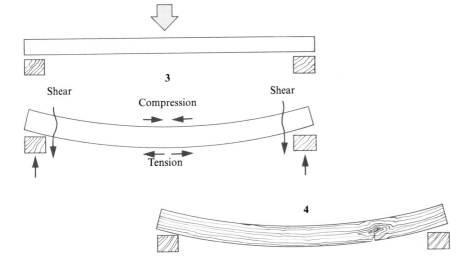

3

Shear   Shear

Compression

Tension

4

Bending a beam
3. On a beam spanning two supports with a load applied in the middle, three stresses occur simultaneously: the top is under *compression* while the bottom is under *tension*. At each support point is *shear* stress, where there are combined forces downward from the load and upward from the resisting supports.
4. The beam will break when the wood fails under stress: when the combined compression and tension crack the wood. Knots in the wood weaken it, and the break will occur at the weak spot.

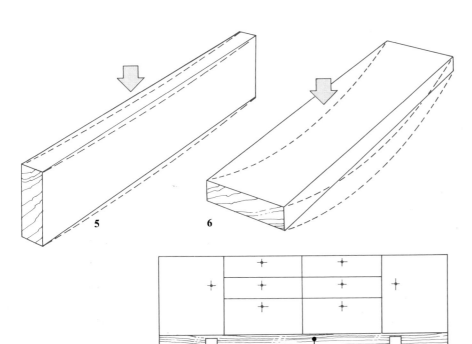

5   **6**

7   Beam

Flexing a beam
5. A beam bends to the extent that its top edge can be compressed and its bottom edge stretched. The thicker the wood, the more material there is to compress and to stretch, and the harder it is to bend the beam. In short, the beam has a high bending resistance.
6. Turning the beam on its face effectively puts a thinner beam under load. It has a weaker bending resistance and therefore flexes more easily than the same beam on edge.
7. Beams used on edge resist bending well enough to be able to support heavy storage units.

Strengthening box frameworks

One of the most difficult shapes to make correctly in cabinetmaking, and yet one of the most useful, is a box. Practically all forms of storage are made of boxes called carcasses by cabinetmakers.

A four-sided box—one with no front or back—reacts in two ways under force. If a single force is exerted on a side, the box simply leans sideways so that the opposite sides of the box retain their parallel relationship. Designers call this racking or parallelograming. But if two forces act from different directions on the sides, the box twists, losing the parallel relationship of its sides. Racking and twisting exert immense shear stresses on the corner joints.

Modern carcasses of slab construction are made of manufactured board fastened with knock-down fittings (see pages 214–215), which have far less shear strength than do the formerly-used dovetails. Therefore, the carcasses of slab construction must be designed with extra bracing, and there are two ways of doing that, both of which exploit the bending resistance of beams used on edge.

The first restricts twist by making one of the five sides of the carcass absolutely flat, by screwing the back of the box to the wall, or the base to the floor, for example. A movable carcass can be reinforced with a torsion box—a six-sided box that acts as a base and is especially resistant to twisting.

The second way resists racking by making any two adjacent edges absolutely straight and at right angles, usually by bracing the edges with beams. Variants of these methods of bracing boxes include the T-frame, and the cross-brace, both illustrated below, and the technique of slotting in the back of the box, rather than simply butt-joining it.

Frames

The bracing assemblies described above are known as frames and they permit thin-walled constructions of surprising strength. Frames are used extensively in cabinetmaking, not only to strengthen storage carcasses but also to stiffen thin tabletops, chair seats and beds. Frames themselves constitute furniture—to support and brace the fragile pane of glass in a mirror.

Whatever the application, frames must be generally rigid: they must resist a change of shape under load

Racking and twisting

1. Racking occurs when a force is applied in one direction, tilting the box so that its opposite sides are still parallel.
2. Normally, however, more than one force acts on a box. The box then twists, or racks in two directions. The sides of the box lose their parallel relationship.

Increasing rigidity

3. A free-standing four-sided box becomes more rigid if one of its sides is kept completely stiff to resist twisting. A six-sided torsion box built into the base is a good solution.
4. The box also will become rigid if two adjacent edges are kept straight and at right angles to prevent racking.

Often a designer will use a combination of a stiffened base and a pair of reinforcing stiff uprights (pilasters) to increase rigidity. A T-frame prevents racking by holding two sides stiff and at right angles to each other. Cross-bracing resists racking by keeping each corner at 90°. Many designers use steel rods at the back of a carcass for the bracing.

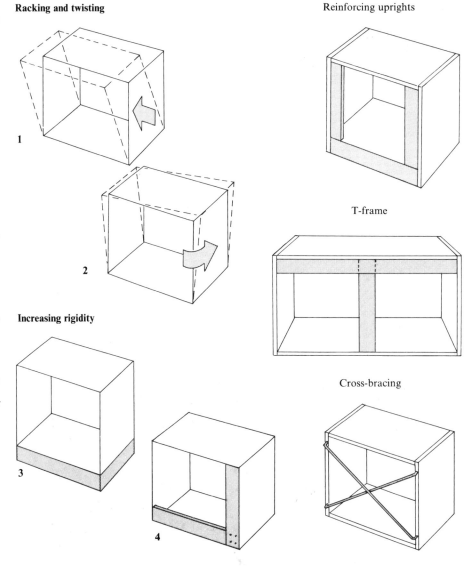

Racking and twisting

1

2

Increasing rigidity

3

4

Reinforcing uprights

T-frame

Cross-bracing

either by racking or twisting. There are three principal forms of frame, although there are many derivations of these types. The first is the continuous frame cut from a solid piece of wood. The second is the stiff-jointed frame, joined only at the corners. The last is a braced frame, where the strength of the corner joints is less important than the presence of diagonal cross-bracing.

As we have seen, the joints are ordinarily the weakest point in wooden furniture because of the leverage exerted on the joint. These problems can be circumvented by manipulating any of the five variables that affect the strength of the frame.

Variables

● The cross-sectional area of the rails of the frame: Thick rails are stronger than thin ones and resist bending better. There is less stress on the joints if the rails are stiff because the rail is absorbing the stress and not transmitting it to the joints.
● The depth of the joint: Deep joints composed of thick, long tenons and mortises are stronger because thicker cross-sections resist shear stress better. Additionally, a deep joint provides a larger surface area for glue contact, which itself increases the shear strength. Deep joints are a natural consequence of having thicker rails.
● Which face of the rail beams the mortise or tenon is cut into: If the joint is cut into the edge of the rail, rather than into the face, not only will the beam resist bending better and thus transmit less stress to the joints, but the joint itself also will resist shearing better.
● Whether the structure is braced: Bracing, especially cross-bracing, relieves shear stress at the joints by stopping the frame from racking.
● Whether the rail beam end is fixed or free: If the frame is open-sided (a U-frame, for instance), two parallel rails will be free at one end and unbraced. From the discussion of leverage, we have seen how great the forces are on a beam supported only at one end. These are, incidentally, the same forces at work on the joint of an unbraced table leg or chair leg.

A designer has a good deal of freedom, therefore, to decide whether to use thick rails and deep joints or to replace them with small, light rails and bracing. The two structures may be equally strong, but will give dramatically different visual messages.

Slotting-in panels for rigidity

Frames

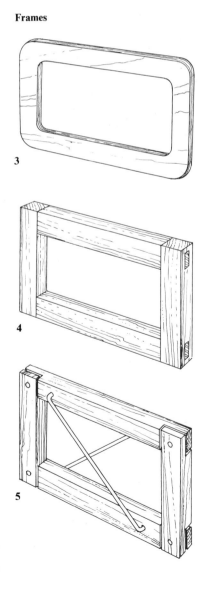

1

2

3

4

5

Slotting-in panels for rigidity
1. Fitting on a fifth panel—the back of the carcass, for example—adds to the rigidity of the structure, preventing racking by keeping the corners at 90°. The panel is usually slotted, or rebated, into the sides of the carcass to increase the glue surface of the joint.
2. Shelves, also rebated into the sides of the box, prevent the box from twisting by keeping two facing sides parallel. Shelving, basically beams used on edge, is an effective type of bracing for boxes; the more shelving used, the more rigid the box.

Frames
Frames are bracing assemblies used to increase the rigidity of panels in furniture. There are three basic forms:
3. The continuous frame, cut from a single piece of wood. This type of frame is wasteful of materials, but quite strong if it is cut from plywood. The layers of wood with grain running perpendicular to each other provide a uniform strength to the material.
4. The stiff-jointed frame, with its corners usually joined with a through-mortise and tenon or with a mitre joint. This is the most widely used frame, easy and economical to build.
5. The light-jointed frame with cross-bracing. The structural weakness of the joints in this frame is compensated for in the cross-bracing. This is the strongest of the three.

We can all recognize a design style. In furniture, you may or may not know what are "art nouveau" or "art deco" pieces, for example, but if you see enough of them, you can distinguish the pieces from each other and perceive that they fall into separate categories.

To designers, *style* is that set of visible characteristics or symbols that identify a piece of furniture with others having similar signs or characteristics, allowing you to categorize furniture designs. The signs for art deco, for example, include bold outlines, geometric decorations and the use of new materials such as plastic. Art nouveau, on the other hand, is recognizable for its sinuous lines and plant-like shapes.

Many people confuse style, taste and fashion. For instance, you may say that a piece of furniture has gone out of style. But it is in fact impossible for any designed object to go out of style because either an object belongs to a particular style or it does not; nothing can alter that. Style is a fact. Every piece of furniture belongs to some style or other because style was built in as part of the process of design and cannot be omitted.

Furniture may certainly go in and out of fashion, however. You may remember how quickly we abandoned the spindly look of the 1950s, for example, for the geometric and pop-art furniture of the 1960s, and then the stark, sculptural look of the 1970s, which gave way to the playful, brightly colored furniture of the Italian new wave in the 1980s. Often, fashion comes full circle; every century has had its revivalist periods.

It is because we become so quickly familiar with our surroundings that fashions emerge. *Fashion* is the style that is most currently in vogue, and the pursuit of fashion seems to reflect the strong need in people to stand out in a crowd. The most significant aspect of a fashionable style is that it is new. As one style ages, new ones are created; it does not matter whether the design has merit or has value (see pages 12–13), so long as it is different. Fashion seems to most benefit those in the fashion industry—the magazines and other trendsetters who have a vested interest in having us continue to consume more furniture. It is a source of frustration to many designers, who see themselves cast in the role of "stylists"— designers of built-in visual obsolescence.

Whether or not you can identify a particular style, you might often describe a piece of furniture as having style, or being stylish. But in fact you are simply saying that you have a particular affinity to the style of the piece, and that you prefer its style to others. This only means you have a *taste* for the furniture.

People have taste; objects cannot be tasteful. But the taste for a particular style of furniture can be either a collective or an individual choice. And so the term "tasteful" can mean a restrained, subtle style which is the least likely to offend a large number of people. It means being widely acceptable, neutral and anonymous. It is not surprising that blandness is the chief characteristic of furniture that tries to be all things to all people—the kind of furniture often found in public places like hotels and offices.

Recognizing styles, exercising taste and being fashion conscious has nothing to do with your ability to make judgements about what is good, or "of value" or beautiful in a design. The hype and excitement of creating a new fashion may result in a striking object (often at the expense of efficiency) which may be hailed as a design breakthrough. But it is only after time, when the style has become familiar and is superseded by the next fashion, that you can really judge, at which point many pieces of furniture will be found wanting and will disappear forever. But the designs that are the result of true imagination never bore us, even though they may have gone out of fashion.

If beautiful, well-designed furniture of various styles have anything in common, it is in the way that they continue to absorb us over the years. This is the test of a good design. Consider, for example, how "modern" Charles Eames's up-holstered lounge chair and ottoman look today, although they were designed in 1949.

The fact that styles exist can also serve as useful starting points for designers, and can help to focus the mind if the design options appear to be too wide. For example, suppose you were trying to design a desk, and, having worked out the appropriate dimensions, the overall storage capacity and the area of the top, you suddenly became stuck on the actual form of the desk. What to choose, when almost any form is possible? By choosing a style, you will find your much needed guidelines. In fact your taste is constantly at work selecting out certain elements of the style you favour to become part of your design. Your taste for a particular style may be the first and the final arbiter in your designs, and you will have to struggle to try out ideas in a style for which you have no taste.

The limitations of a style actually provide a framework within which a designer progresses. Your goal is to develop and modify aspects of a style, adjusting the details as your sensitivity dictates, to give individuality to the work so that the style can evolve. This is called the style of evolution.

It is easiest to explain the style of evolution by describing what it is *not*, and that is the style of fashion. The style of fashion is the style that develops in response to a fashion. Chinese Chippendale is an example, when a fashion for Oriental furniture in the 18th century spawned a hybrid style—British furniture with curious Chinese details appended. The Victorian era is replete with styles of fashion; odds-and-ends from cultures as ancient and far-flung as the Egyptian and the Greek were tacked on to follow the British fashions of those times, with little regard to the integrity of the furniture itself. Those pieces have been widely discarded.

The style of evolution, however, is constantly developing on preceding designs, constructively, using familiar shapes and materials. The Scottish Arts and Crafts master, Charles Rennie Mackintosh (page 37) did not try to redefine the chair when he made his famous sculptural high-backed chair, and yet this work had a major effect on the course of chair design. It is not always originality that creates the magic of a good design, but instead, how the individual parts of the chair are related—the idiosyncratic personal elements of a design. Without it, a design is dull and toneless.

The style of evolution
These three sideboards represent the style of evolution over the past 100 years. Each builds on the piece that precedes it, and at the same time breaks new ground. Thus the designs evolve and endure.

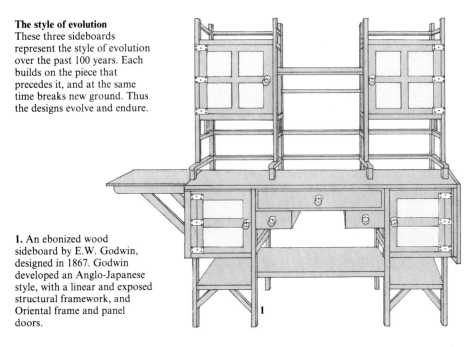

1. An ebonized wood sideboard by E.W. Godwin, designed in 1867. Godwin developed an Anglo-Japanese style, with a linear and exposed structural framework, and Oriental frame and panel doors.

2. A sideboard of painted wood by Gerrit Rietveld in 1919. The exposed framework of the previous piece is emphasized, but the frame and panel doors have become slabs held in precise relationship by the vertical and horizontal frame pieces. The piece is reminiscent of the Dutch de Stijl painter, Piet Mondrian. The gallery—the super-structure of shelves and cabinets in the Godwin piece—is reduced to a single shelf.

3. A credenza by Roberto Licenziato Monti for Ambiance International in 1982. In this piece, the framing disappears and the slabs become more prominent. The style comes from the interplay of the panels of different colours and sizes. The gallery is now a simple rail along the back—a stylistic reference to the preceding pieces.

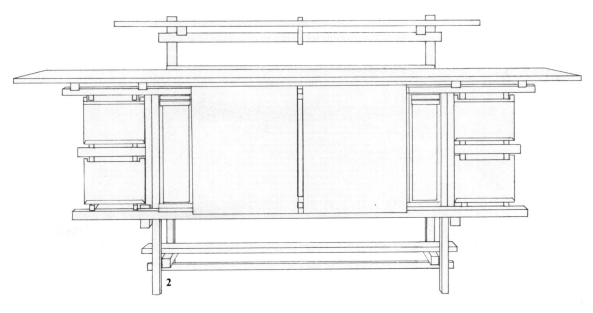

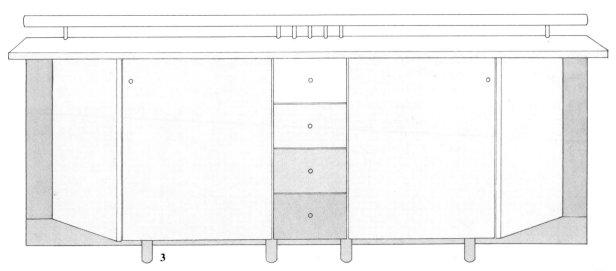

The styles of the furniture in this book are not definitive and it is unlikely that the reader will like them all equally. They are simply a range of stylistic approaches that have been adopted by practising designers and makers working with wood. They are all contemporary styles, some influenced by fashion, and others more by tradition. They demonstrate that timber has an enormous range of applications and as a material is as "modern" as titanium or composite plastic (and probably is more flexible), and they show how diverse our tastes can be.

No one style is more important than any of the others. You may say that some styles are more fashionable than others, but that is largely irrelevant to their importance. You will obviously have your preferences, responding more to some of the pieces than others,

quite naturally. When you do, look closely at them and try to understand why. Is it the serene confidence of a Ron Carter chair or the response to the material in the work of Alan Peters or John Makepeace which attracts you? Make your choice, confront the piece and dissect its qualities. In doing so, you will begin to understand how to respond to a design challenge and the reasons behind a choice of style for yourself. It is only by analyzing the work of others that you will begin to inject a sense of purpose into your own work.

As you will discover, this is a difficult thing to do. To start the process, I have listed the qualities of some of the stylistic groups appearing in the book. This is always a dangerous task because my conclusions may not agree with the designers' own thoughts about their work. But these are not comprehensive lists—only an

Style of fashion
The "Carlton" bookcase, nearly 2 m/6 ft high and wide, was designed in 1981 by Ettore Sottsass for the Memphis Group of furniture designers in Milan. It has been painted in bold primary colours, suggestive of Rietveld slab construction (see page 33), which enjoyed a European resurgence in the

1980s. The piece was clearly not conceived with utility in mind; a book placed on it would only interfere with the design. Instead, it serves to decorate a space and exude a feeling of fashion and fun— perhaps with tongue in cheek. But its shortcomings as a design limit its longevity.

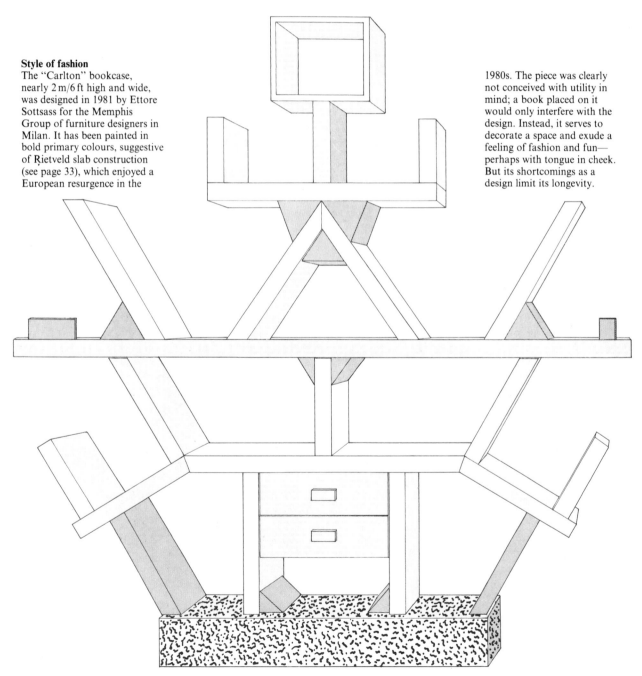

appetizer. If they provoke disagreement, then the process has begun to work. I have given the styles a name in the hope of communicating their essential ingredients.

The style of conscious restraint
The first is epitomized in the work of Ron Carter (page 52). This style is characterized by these elements:
● The furniture is identified by its *simple* detailing (chamfers and rebates) which is used sparingly.
● The material is used confidently. There is no fear of large cross-sections, but these are handled with subtlety and they never appear massive or bulky.
● There is a minimum number of components, and these are used to maximum effect.
● There is absolute control of the thicknesses and overhangs, and the proportions are founded on anthropometric requirements (see pages 16–23) and structural good sense.
● There is a preponderance of traditional methods of construction.

The style of engineered simplicity
The work of David Colwell (page 61) is one of the few examples of this style. The furniture designed by Michael Thonet in the 19th century, composed of simple bentwood shapes, is another. It is far from "simple" to achieve, but has become the hallmark of Colwell's approach to furniture. These are the characteristics to look for:
● The designs exploit the full potential of the inherent properties of the material (in this case, ashwood) which influences the final form of the piece.
● Low technology processes such as steaming and turning are used to achieve the maximum structural benefits *and* economic advantages from the wood.
● There is nothing superfluous. Each component of the structure contributes to the structural efficiency of the piece and ultimately to its form.
● Any detailing of the components reinforces the part they play in the overall structure.

The style of response to the material
This is often the style adopted by designers working in the countryside close to their materials. They are therefore better placed to choose the quality and diversity of timber, and have the space to store it and season it well. John Makepeace (page 56) and Alan Peters (pages 134–135) are among the very best manipulators of this style. From their work you will recognize the following:
● Solid timber often is used throughout.
● The grain and figure of the wood are exploited for their decorative qualities.
● The structure often is determined by the need to allow the timber to move.
● The final form is determined on the bench, often as a spontaneous process to exploit the unique qualities of a particular board or tree.
● The mark of the tool often is left on the wood surface for texture or the surface is deliberately tooled.
● The joints are exposed and used decoratively or they are strongly stated, often in contrasting woods.
● There is a generous cross-section of material, and the structural members tend to be heavy or massive.
● Natural-looking finishes predominate, particularly oils or waxes.

The style of abstract form
Today this style is often the most difficult to distinguish from the style of fashion. It can be seen clearly and is seriously defined in the work of Floris van den Broecke (pages 53 and 57).

Among the recognizable characteristics at present are:
● The use of precisely controlled simple geometric shapes.
● A bold combination of materials and/or colours.
● The form is pre-determined before the piece is made and is influenced by the making process only in terms of the quality of workmanship.
● The material is often chosen dispassionately, either for its overall structural strength, or for its colour or texture, and it is used solely to achieve the form. The form is not determined by the inherent visual qualities of the material, as it would be in the style of response to the material.
● The effect of the piece will be controversial. It is generally the intention of designers working in this style to evoke a response to the work. In many cases the formal structure of the work will question existing furniture archetypes.

These four styles, which I have arbitrarily chosen and named, are all what I term styles of evolution (see page 33). Although the designers who use these styles will continually change and develop the appearance of their furniture, the styles themselves will be eclipsed only when they cease to have any philosophical relevance, as did, for example, the super-ornamented furniture of the late Victorian period, which was deemed too bourgeois in the early 20th century. However, the styles of fashion, such as the ultra modern Hi-tech, Post Modern, Eclectic and Hardedge styles will be superseded as soon as a new look appears on the horizon.

Do not imagine that you can consciously produce work without style, because you may unconsciously refer to a style. For example, you might limit the variables by using simple machined sections in timber or standard extruded metal parts, and paring down everything to its minimum requirement. But even that is a style. You only have to look at the work of the Bauhaus or the Shaker movement, the minimalists or so-called functionalists—the evidence of style is readily recognizable. Or as soon as you apply that formula to another piece of furniture, a style will emerge— designing a matching table and chair, for example.

It is ironic to note that those "functional objects" of the Bauhaus period, where the style was ostensibly dictated by the function and thus they were supposedly designed *without* style, give us such a strong feeling for the 30s. We can see quite clearly now that they were deluding themselves.

By definition, decoration is regarded as an addition or an afterthought to serve as adornment, or more specifically, to elaborate and ornament; to add richness, gaudiness, gilt, ostentation, enhancement and embellishment. In reality it has even wider implications than that.

Decoration is present in all designers' work, but what are they doing when they decorate something? One purpose might be to "invest the object with order" another definition which gives us a clue. Decoration in this sense unifies the visible elements of an object and satisfies a basic human craving for order. In decorating objects—that is, giving order to the objects that are used and seen by people—we are injecting an order into the way we live our lives. The decoration of Aztec temples or Gothic cathedrals are prime examples of how humans have used visual symbolism to support the very fabric of their civilizations. Realistic symbols were used as "reminders" on everyday objects as well as on religious artefacts as a stamp of the person who made the objects, and perhaps as a way of infusing the object with the spirit of the symbol.

Abstract adornment provides balance, harmony or symmetry, and emphasizes an object's shape, the grace of a curve or the regularity of a line. Abstract *patterns* such as geometric repeats are common because they so effectively achieve visual harmony. Although there is some direct symbolism in certain patterns, especially those using realistic images such as leaves or acorns, the power of a pattern is really in its repetitiveness and if used properly, it is very powerful indeed. The extreme sense of order and discipline evoked by Islamic decoration is testimony to this.

This ability of decoration to instill order to a whole is as important today as it was in primitive times. The decorative styles of prominent buildings—"centres of culture" such as churches or theatres—are directly determined by the need to symbolize these values. They capture the spirit of an age.

Decoration of furniture

Historically, the decoration of furniture often had a more prosaic purpose. It resulted from the need to give a tolerance in manufacture. Before the introduction of powered machinery or abrasive papers, flat surfaces and accurate fitting were extremely difficult to achieve. Decoration served to disguise this fact by covering surfaces and panels with texture. Light is broken up and scattered by a textured surface rather than being reflected uniformly and so any imperfections are not easily noticed.

The choice of decoration that craftsmen used to disguise their work slowly evolved as their technique developed. Planed mouldings, linenfold panels, punched backgrounds, "egg and dart" tracery, "ball and claw" feet are all decorative motifs developed from a strict and economic procedure with hand tools. The craftsman worked in a carefully planned sequence to gain the maximum effect from the minimum number of cuts. Even so, there were bound to be inaccuracies. If you look closely at the cabriole legs of some Chippendale chairs you will discover a considerable difference in their shapes and dimensions. Normally this escapes notice because the surface decoration and the shape of the legs distracts us from comparing them. If the legs were straight and unadorned, we would notice immediately if one was larger or slightly curved more than the other.

Further evidence of the early craftsmen's reliance on decoration to mask limited techniques can be found by comparing the sophisticated work of town workshops supported by wealthy patrons with the country craft equivalents of the same period. The country workshops, whose clients were of more limited means, produced pieces that followed the basic shape of the style but omitted the customary decoration for which their clients could not pay. In these pieces any inaccuracies are exposed for all to see. But the furniture from these workshops does not suffer in its simplicity.

The uses of decoration
This couch, built between 1815 and 1820 in Philadelphia or Baltimore, is based on one by Thomas Sheraton, but the decoration refers directly to the American Revolution: the Greek lines symbolize classical Greek democracy; the eagles stand for the recently won American independence.

Surface decorations unify the piece. The incised lines along the base and the scrolls at the end of each foot accentuate the profile of the couch. The patterned upholstery fabric visually ties the head and foot cushion to the main body of the couch.

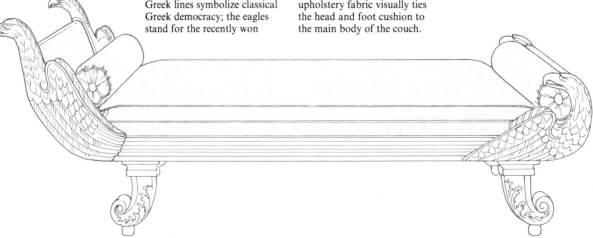

Just the opposite, because those pieces tell an honest story of the values and background in their manufacture.

When techniques improved in the 19th century, and flat unadorned surfaces became more easily possible with machines, decoration was still an important stylistic ingredient because it was still needed for its symbolic value. It represented tradition, enabling Victorian furniture designers, for example, to evoke the spirit of heroic ages, principally Greek and Roman, in the "revival" pieces of the time.

Decoration is still used that way today, to symbolize traditional and therefore known and unthreatening values. Known quantities, the familiar images, are the ones most people feel happy with. People demonstrate this by buying enormous amounts of reproduced antique furniture.

During an economic boom period a cultural confidence emerges and people will buy modern furniture (and abstract paintings). In recession, however, uncertainty and insecurity pervade their lives and they opt for the known styles of former times (or realist painting). Mass-marketed furniture, while not attempting to mimic antiques, draws upon a traditional esthetic and is successful as a result. Many designers resent this because they do not understand the reasons for it. It is simply that much modern furniture is often too threatening or demanding in its symbolism. It rejects traditional values, including decorating, rather than *extending* them.

Even today, we can see decoration being used as a method of conjuring up known and endearing objects to people. However, if we can begin to see its value in a wider context, as the very act of sorting and ordering all the elements of a piece of furniture—of unifying the piece and affording it an individual character which is not alienating to people—then the use of decoration can be seen to be of as much value to designers now as it has been in the past.

Decorative effects

1. This chair by Charle Rennie Mackintosh, built in 1903, is an elegant elaboration on the standard ladderback. The repetitiveness of the slats becomes a decorative element. Stretching from the floor, the towering chairback is then topped with a grid.

2. Georges Jacob, working around 1770, infused a chair of the period with Chinese motifs by simulating the texture and colour, and even the construction, of traditional bamboo furniture—as was the fashion in France of that period.

3. Robert Venturi's laminated office chair, made for Knoll International in 1984, is recognizably modern in construction, but the decorative reference to Queen Anne style harks back to the early 18th century

4. A typical Queen Anne chair from New York, made of walnut around 1750, is beautifully crafted and so solidly built it does not need reinforcing rails. Any lack of symmetry is disguised by the curved cabriole legs with a shell on each knee, the ball-and-claw feet and the carving on the cresting.

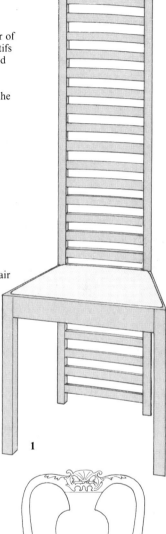

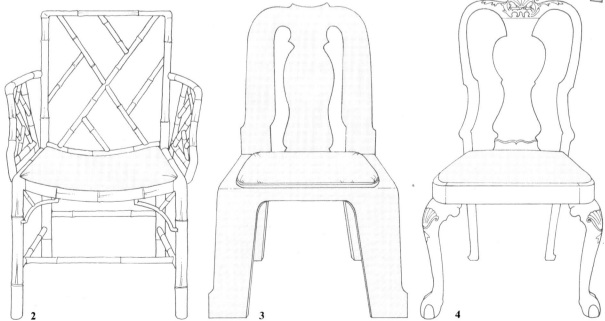

Professional furniture makers differ from serious amateurs in two ways: they usually have to satisfy a client as well as themselves, and they get paid for what they do. The way in which they work is the result of long experience and the amateur can benefit from that experience. He is paid nothing, and his client is himself, but—money aside—the aim is identical.

Every specific piece of furniture—whether requested by a client or made to satisfy a personal need—is initially a problem. The key to successful making is to define the problem and to find a solution. The most efficient way of doing that is to follow three successive stages: the brief, the drawings and the working model or prototype.

The brief

The brief is a formal statement of what is required of the piece to be made. It is put together by asking questions—what is this piece of furniture for, where is it to be placed, what wood should it be made of, what colour should it be, and so on. Each answer is a step towards a solution. Not only does the brief start you off on the right foot, it lets you know when to stop: it is easy to overdesign an object because the goal was not clearly seen at the beginning. If the brief is clear from the start, even though it may alter slightly as work proceeds, the completed object will fulfill the original need.

Asking the right questions sounds simpler than it is. You are looking for three things. You need to know how the piece will be used, approximately what it will cost to make, and what style it should be—style includes both materials and finish. Unless the questions are put carefully, the conclusion may be wrong. For example, you may think that what you need is a desk, when in fact what you need is a place to store papers, something like a filing cabinet. A friend may ask you to make a double bed, but omit to tell you that the room it is intended for is big enough to take only a single bed. A deep, over-stuffed sofa may not merge happily into a room furnished in painted rattan.

Another factor likely to complicate matters is best termed "emotional". It is a particular problem for professional designers seeking to satisfy a client. If questioning reveals that the piece is intended to be a status symbol (often true of handmade furniture) it may need embellishing with a colourful inlay, a high-gloss finish or a dramatic veneer. If, on the other hand, it is supposed to exude a hardworking, highly practical quality then the timber could be rugged and the cross-sections especially heavy.

These subtle, sometimes irrational influences on design thinking should be analyzed as thoroughly as possible before you embark on your project. If you are designing for yourself, they may be subconscious. If you are designing for someone else, they may be counter-productive and prevent you from understanding exactly what is wanted.

In fact, it is the subjective nature of design that often makes it difficult for professional designers to extract a proper brief from their clients. Without close questioning—particularly of people who know what they want but have difficulty communicating—the designer may assume a freedom that was never granted. One way of coping with this problem—and equally effective when you are designing for yourself—is to phrase questions negatively. Ask not "What do you like?" but "Is there anything you positively cannot stand?" People usually have an easier time describing their dislikes than their likes. At least you will be able to reduce the available options, even if you do not know precisely which are acceptable in a positive sense.

If you should ever be involved in designing and making a piece of furniture for a fee, remember that it takes a lot of courage for someone to commission a piece of furniture. Buying from a furniture store has few unknowns or risks. A person can see what he is paying for and is familiar with the procedure. If he is commissioning a piece, however, he is buying a designer's expertise in interpreting his needs, as well as paying for a piece of furniture. Unless he has worked with the designer before, this can be a nerve-wracking process. But if he sees the act of commissioning as involving him in solving his own problems—with you acting as a catalyst—then it can be exciting.

Developing the idea with sketches

Once you have the information which outlines the nature of the design problem (from the brief) you can begin to develop ideas likely to solve it. The best approach is to start by outlining a number of possible directions and then to select the most promising one. For most designers, the method of working these ideas through is by *drawing*. There are several reasons why drawing is so important.

The ability to think visually is probably the single most important skill for a designer and like other skills can be learned and developed. The better you are at manipulating images in your imagination, the better you will become at creating new ones. To take full advantage of this ability, drawing becomes necessary.

There are two types of drawing. The first communicates with others (working drawing and presentation drawing) and the second communicates with yourself. It is this second type of drawing which is important in developing visual thinking. When you are designing you are using this type of drawing as a thinking aid. "Thinking sketches" allow you to record, store, manipulate and communicate those pictures you generate in your imagination. The idea is developed by bouncing it from the imagination to the paper and back to the imagination again. The more you draw, the better you will become at translating those imagined images and these in turn, being on paper, will inspire further images—and so the idea develops.

Do not worry about technique or drawing skill at this stage—sketches can be crude but still highly informative and, after all, they are only being done for your purposes. Choose a sketchbook which is a size you feel comfortable with. Some persons feel intimidated by large blank sheets of paper and so they use pocket-sized note books, which can be carried to record things of interest. In this way you build up a storehouse of inspirational material for the future.

Thus drawing has three distinct uses. First you can use it as a tool to enable you to "look at" objects (pages 12–13). If you draw existing objects you will learn about the way they are constructed, their proportions and the relationship of one component to another. Second, you can use it as a tool for externalizing the images in your imagination, as an aid to visual thinking in the development of an idea. Third, it is used as a device for communication. Different types of drawing can impart information about your intentions to your client, or to a craftsman who will make up the piece, quite clearly and unambiguously.

And so the activity of developing an idea, somewhat simplified, happens something like this: you will have listed the objective limiting factors when you wrote the brief and you will have opened up the subjective opportunities by sketching out several possible ideas. Now comes the point where many people believe the design process begins—the meshing of the objective and subjective parts of design. The goal is to provide a solution which both satisfies the brief and allows you to make your statement as designer and maker. The better designer you are, the less compromise will be necessary on either side. There *will* be a degree of compromise, however, and it is a balancing act. If you compromise on opportunities in order to stick rigidly to the brief, you may end up with a dull and predictable object (better in this case to see if it is possible to adjust the terms of the brief). Conversely, if you compromise the brief by giving way to your imagination, you can easily end up with an object which does not work in its intended location. (Better in this case to temper your enthusiasm and save that idea for a later date.)

Refining and preparing for making

A furniture manufacturer will often commit resources to build a succession of prototypes of a furniture design to refine the idea, once it has gone as far as possible on paper. This is logical, as he cannot risk the return of 10,000 faulty chairs because it would bankrupt him. So very thorough testing is required before his products are released on the market place. But for the small-scale designer/maker, the time and expense of making a series of prototypes, when probably only six chairs are required, does not make sense.

Instead, furniture makers rely on experience, and for this reason much design adjustment goes on during the process of making. Further refinement often goes on over several commissions of a similar nature. Some apprehension in making a design up for the first time can be removed by producing full-size mock-ups. These are different from prototypes in that they are made from cheap materials, often workshop scraps (cardboard or chipboard) and can be constructed in different ways, glued or nailed up quickly, to give you different types of information. You may require confirmation that your piece is anthropometrically correct, and so you produce a mock-up that you can sit in and test—but it does not have to resemble your idea visually.

Similarly, to test the visible proportions, you can make a full-size cardboard mock-up that does not need

any structural strength. Place the mock-ups in an area similar to the final intended location and then make your decisions. It is a common mistake to make things too large because the judgement on size is made in a workshop with a high ceiling. When the same object is placed in a domestic room, the piece seems to grow in size. Similarly, in a workshop we subconsciously equate "bench" height with "table" height without realizing that benches can be as much as a foot higher. Size is relative, and it is important to be sensitive to it. It is during the mock-up stage that you can begin to see the difference that very small dimensional changes can make.

It is during this stage of refinement that you should be looking ahead and *organizing* the construction stage. Remember that any materials, special cutters and particular finishes can take weeks to be delivered. So the moment you know what you will require, order the materials. Do not forget the smaller things at this point. You could be irritatingly delayed, and the project be forced to grind to a halt, for lack of screws, sandpaper or glue. If you have stocks of timber available, select sufficient amounts for the job—make a detailed cutting list—and begin the conditioning process by bringing the boards into the workshop. Cut any thick boards at this stage to give time for them to settle down.

Make lists of your requirements by mentally going through each construction stage, checking as you go that you have all the necessary materials and equipment and considering the available alternatives should there be difficulties. Try to be ahead of your requirements at every stage.

Once you have decided the final format of your design you will need to make a working drawing—one which correlates all the information necessary to make the piece. One-fifth scale drawings with full-size details are normally sufficient for most pieces, although chairs and any shaped work should be drawn full-size unless they are very simple.

It should be possible to draw full-size rods—which are plans, elevations or cross-sections drawn onto a board and used in the workshop to check the dimensions of components—from the information supplied from these working drawings. If you are presenting an idea to a client, do not commit yourself to highly detailed working drawings until you are certain that the idea has been fully accepted. You will save time and effort if you wait. Working drawings are for your information anyway, and it is doubtful that they will be of interest to most clients.

Finally, if you are making furniture for clients, be very careful about letting them see a half-completed product. They will often request this out of interest and sheer curiosity but a piece of furniture covered in scraper marks and closeted in clamps does not in any way resemble the finished article. Many people, having seen their piece in this state, begin to worry about the eventual outcome. It is often far better to be firm, to encourage them to be patient and to capitalize on the heightened sense of excitement when the piece is finally delivered.

It should be clear by now that designing furniture is a complex business, further complicated by the subjective element in the decisions you face whenever you make something. You will be tackling the requirements of good design to make a piece that works well and efficiently, and look acceptable. You will have had to clarify your thoughts about style and to have arrived at a style that satisfies your taste. And still you may have doubts.

This checklist may help smooth out the process and help you organize your thoughts. It brings together the variables of design that have been touched upon in this chapter, including anthropometric and constructional restrictions. And it is laced with the author's own guidelines, extracted over 20 years of experience and often learned the hard way.

Eventually, you may also develop your own design checklist, garnered from your own experiences. We hope that this one will serve as a useful starting point.

Furniture in general

When you are designing furniture in general, whatever it is, you must consider:

Weight

Furniture often has to be carried, moved about and transported. If it is excessively heavy, it can cause personal injury. The risk of damage from dropping or not being able to control the piece as it is being manoeuvred is greater than the risk of damaging surrounding objects. Door frames and walls are generally more durable than furniture, and damage to them is easier to repair.

Size

Large sizes of furniture should be avoided because furniture must fit through minimum door widths and be capable of being moved up or down stairways. Try to design the piece so that it can be disassembled into components and bolted together once in the room. This will help in the handling of the finished piece. Furniture makers should also know the size and capacity of their car or van, although this is not to suggest that it is a design prerequisite, but only that it is useful to keep in mind; the furniture will have to be transported somehow.

Size should be in proportion to the scale of the architecture—especially be conscious of standard ceiling heights. Student designers often design furniture too large; if in doubt, mock up the proposal and test it in a domestic environment.

Tolerances

Rooms are never built with walls that are square, flat or plumb. If building-in furniture, allow for this by using:

● Adjustment devices such as feet that can be raised or lowered.
● Scribing strips—pieces of timber or board which can be shaped to the wall *on site*, and then connected to the furniture.

● Design techniques to avoid problems on the site. If for example it is possible to design wardrobes that do not have to go right up to the ceiling, then adopt that format.

● Design objects that are set into spaces or protrude from them. Never attempt to make them flush because sooner rather than later you will confront a sloping wall.

Study the way household carpenters cope with building inaccuracies. Much can be learned of use to the furniture maker by doing so. A range of techniques is used by designers of industrial furniture which allows greater tolerances in construction. Sometimes known as "designers gaps", they reduce the need for extremely accurate fitting. Because designers understand that most of us look at objects only superficially, they "design in" spaces between components deliberately or make use of mouldings, rebated edges and the shadows they create. They design pieces with overhanging tops or inset rails and rarely make surfaces flush. These are tactics to allow a greater degree of acceptable inaccuracy and consequently a greater speed of production. "Designer gaps" are not a substitute for good workmanship—far from it—but they can be of limited use to furniture makers starting out. The point of "problem avoidance" is to design within the scope of your making ability or the limitations of your workshop and equipment.

Room characteristics

These are the considerations for custom-built pieces. First, an awareness of the room characteristics is essential. Before you even begin to design, be aware of the following list of dimensions and measurements in the room:

● Ceiling heights.
● Door widths and heights.
● Positions, sizes and height of power outlets from the floor.
● Height and thickness of baseboards.
● Window sizes and the heights of sills.
● Depth of carpet—furniture can rock on thick carpet.
● Uneven or sloping floors—especially critical with tall furniture.
● Source of lighting—natural or artificial.
● Colours, tones and textures within the room.
● Characteristics of the other furniture in the room.
● Traffic patterns through the room, established by the position of doors and windows, and those artificially created by the position of furniture such as a table which has to be walked around.
● Ranges of temperature and humidity in the space where the furniture is to go.

Seating

When you design objects to sit on, you must:

● Relate sizes, angles and seat shapes to good anthropometric practice (see pages 16–23). Remember that the body is not flat.

●Design for stability (see pages 24–25). Chairs can tip very easily in normal use.

●Use glides or wheels when appropriate so that chairs slide backwards easily when moved and do not tip backwards.

●Take care to avoid a "top heavy" structure. A chair should be balanced at around seat level so that it can be lifted without the tendency to turn turtle.

●Remember that people will always tend to lean the chair backwards on the chair legs.

●If you use three legs only, ensure that the single leg is positioned at the front and *not* the back, or the chair will be unstable.

Design for strength

●Chairs are abused. Imagine the worst abuses and design for them.

●Relate the structure to the material with which you will build.

●If stretcher rails are included in the design, remember that people will use them as "ladders". Try a ladder configuration of rails, or if this becomes impossible, then make the rails strong enough to take the weight.

●Remember that uneven floors can cause a chair structure to become overstressed.

Design for safety

●Avoid dangerous "scissor actions" in folding furniture. A spacer between crossing and moving components helps considerably to avoid pinched fingers. Keep the gap about one finger's thickness wide.

●Armrests on chairs used with tables should clear under the table by at least a finger's thickness to prevent the crushing of hands as the chair is pulled under the table.

●Avoid sharp corners or protrusions—remember that sharp corners and knobs are at the eye level of children.

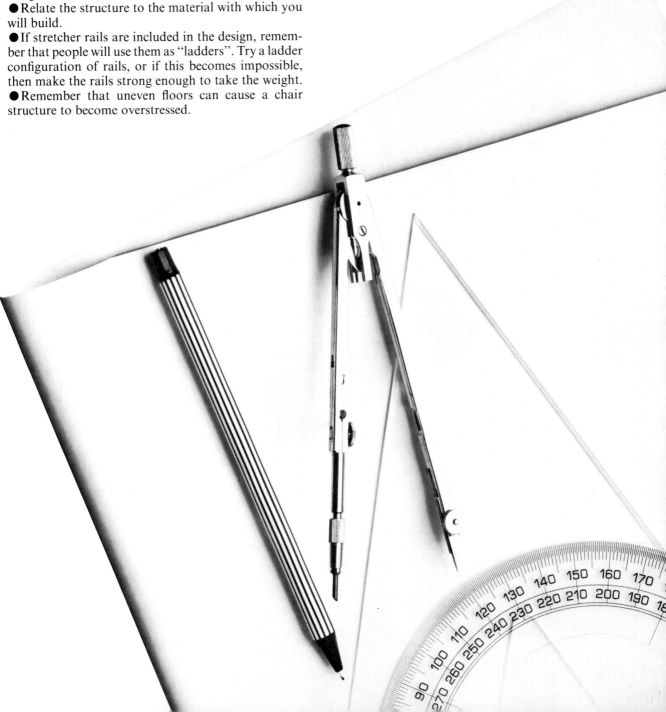

● Do not design chairs with open back areas. Children can fall backwards through these as the author did as a young boy sitting on a Thonet bentwood café chair.

● Consider the appropriateness of linkable or stackable chairs. These clever designs can solve several furniture problems.

● Decide whether your approach should be to create a chair which has a sense of space or of volume.

A spatial chair frame such as Toby Winteringham's on page 60 allows the eye to see through and beyond the chair frame—it occupies less visible space.

A chair with volume obscures the space behind it. Size for size it appears to occupy more space.

Both approaches have their uses, but they must be appropriate to the space.

Points on using upholstery (in seating)

● Avoid shiny fabrics—people will slide out of the seat.

● Use closely-woven fabrics which will not catch on clothing or sag and wrinkle in use. Ultraviolet light causes upholstery foams to decompose—this is one reason for the use of heavy muslin undercovers and tightly woven top coverings on mass-produced upholstered furniture. These are submitted to "rub tests" to determine their durability and wearability. They also have to comply with regulations on fireproofing—become conversant with these if your designs involve a lot of upholstery work. As a limited guide, leather or pure wool coverings satisfy most requirements. There are spray fabric finishes to fireproof others, however.

● Consider the stain resistance of the fabric: spray-on finishing liquids can protect vulnerable light-coloured fabrics, but make any cleaning less successful. Fabrics can be upholstered in a way which makes their removal for cleaning easy or they can be "dry shampooed" in place. Consider those options.

● Design upholstered components so that replacement of fabric is easy and does not involve the dismantling of the chair frame. Recovering could take place three or four times in the useful life of a chair.

● Ventilate cushions so that upholstery does not burst at the seams when sat upon.

Storage

Design for access (see pages 16–17).

● All containers should relate to the contents to be stored in them. Consider the sizes and weights of the contents to determine whether they should be stored high up or low down, in drawer compartments, trays or cupboard spaces. Analyze your options for storage and choose the most appropriate.

● "Visual" access is important. Narrow shelving at high levels and deeper shelving at lower levels helps. Avoid making storage too deep so that objects get lost at the back of the shelf.

● Use removable backs so that if locks or catches jam, access to the contents is still possible without destroying the carcass.

● Shelving should be adjustable where possible because storage requirements change.

● Access for cleaning should be provided. This often means having removable shelving and "designing out" any areas difficult for access or tedious to clean.

Design for stability

● Storage pieces can be large and consequently heavy, especially when full, so make sure that they cannot tip onto the user when opened.

● Never underestimate the weight of contents such as books, records or clothes. Build beams under shelving to stiffen them and add support points for clothes rails to prevent them from bending.

Structural considerations

● Large furniture structures can become distorted on uneven floors, resulting in doors and drawers that jam. Fit adjustable feet to avoid this.

● To get stiffness without enormous weight, consider structural principles on pages 30–31.

● Carcass sides can bulge outwards if the structure is very tall. Fitted central shelving can prevent this by bracing the carcass side.

● Use sufficient knock-down fittings and hinges, and follow the manufacturer's recommendations.

● Consider transport and access to houses. Do not make individual pieces too large or too heavy to move into the spaces they must inhabit.

● Lay-on doors and drawers give greater tolerances than those flush with the carcass front, and they offer the opportunity of using adjustable hinges to align the doors more easily.

● If solid timber is used for storage furniture, consider suitable supported structures such as a frame-and-panel for doors, for example, and design to allow the wood on these wide surfaces to move.

Design for safety

● Always fit drawer stops to prevent heavy drawers from sliding all the way out.

● Avoid sharp corners.

● Remember handles are often placed at a child's eye level. Screw-on handles are better because, as protruding handles tend to be knocked off, these can be removed for transport and manoeuvring.

● Use stays where possible to prevent crushed fingers between doors and door frames.

● Always specify polished edges on glass and never use anything less than $6\,mm/\frac{1}{4}$ in for horizontal surfaces. Vertical glazed doors can be $3\,mm/\frac{1}{8}$ in if they are framed.

● Lift-up lids can be heavy and if dropped can easily crush fingers, so use clamping stays on articles like linen chests. See page 217.

It is often considered that storage is required only for us to file our belongings and place them out of sight. There are, as a result, many examples which although they satisfy these two requirements ignore the special requirements demanded by individual items. Wardrobes for example, should protect clothing from light, dust and insects as well. Make sure that you satisfy the *full* range of individual storage requirements in your designs.

Surfaces: Tables

Determine the size, shape and height of the table top by carefully analyzing the use it is to be put to—list these requirements. See pages 20–21.

●Recognize the range of uses some tables have to accommodate, such as food preparation *and* eating.
●Consider your options in materials and finishes from the point of view of use first, and appearance next.
●Position the supports so that they do not interfere with people either sitting at, standing by or walking past the table.
●Keep bracing and any stretcher rails well out of the way of the legs and knees of the user—including when the legs are crossed.
●Remember that tables can occupy large areas of space. Consider versatile extendable or expandable tables. Take care that they are not cumbersome to convert (one person alone should be able to extend or to close them) and that they work as well in one position as in another.
●Occasional tables are often designed too low. A seated person will often have to bend double to use one; someone passing may crack his shins against it.

Structural considerations

The stability and often the rigidity of a table is determined by the type and position of supports. Table legs can provide a stable format but limit the position of people using the table. Central pedestals can overcome this problem but often only with a decrease in stability. Pedestal tables invariably twist or tip or both. Understand these inherent characteristics and adopt a design format which makes the least compromise for the given circumstances.

If tables are to be pulled across the floor, the support structure can undergo considerable stress. Although it is rare for table legs to break, the joints between legs and rails (or tops) are extremely vulnerable, and fail all too often. Castors or gliders can be used on table legs.

If using solid timber for table tops, become familiar with the techniques used for dealing with cross-grain movement. These include clamps, shrinkage plates, buttons and slot screwing (see page 202). Remember that for large table tops, movement in the order of $10\,\text{mm}/\frac{1}{3}\,\text{in}$ is not unknown. Warping—that is, twisting, bowing or cupping—of boards should also be anticipated, and appropriate bracing applied to preserve the flatness of the top.

Consider the advantages of demountable understructures (removable legs or separate pedestals) on tables. This will make transport and installation easier, and reduce wear and tear on the joints.

Design for safety

●Avoid pointed corners or sharp edge profiles. They are easily damaged and damage people.
●If glass tops are used, place them in frames and use toughened glass of sufficient thickness for surface area. (Incidentally, remember that people's legs can be viewed through a clear glass-topped dining table—a sometimes disconcerting effect).

●If tables extend, ensure that the mechanism does not trap fingers. Ensure that the conversion from one size to another can be accomplished by *one* person without difficulty or danger, preferably in as few operations as possible.

Beds

Stability is rarely a problem with beds because they have a large surface area and are placed low to the ground. Rigidity, however, is less easy to achieve with some design formats. Do not underestimate the stresses on bedframes; they have to withstand more than the weight of a sleeping person. Horizontal racking is a common fault (see pages 30–31).

Depending on the nature of the mattress support base, sagging can be a problem. A slatted or board-based double bed will invariably require central support. Commercially manufactured spring platform bases give uniform support to the heavier sprung mattresses and do not require this support. But these are heavy and bulky to move.

Provide for mattress ventilation by perforating a platform bed with holes, or by designing the bed with slats.

Storage under the bed

Because beds occupy such large areas, consider using the area beneath the bed for storage.

Analyze the storage requirements of bedside units. Consider capacity, access and heights and do not forget the requirements of breakfast in bed.

Lighting

People read in bed. Decide whether lighting should be integral or separate from the bed structure.

Knock-down requirements

Beds need to be transported and installed. Mattresses are soft and can be bent around corners, but bed frames cannot. It is therefore advisable to design a bed in smaller component parts to be assembled on site. Manufacturers solve the problem by splitting a double bedframe lengthways or using two single bed bases linked together under a double mattress to make larger beds.

Comfort

Of all furniture, beds probably have the most stringent comfort requirements. We spend one third of our lives in bed and no other furniture has to accommodate us for such long stretches of time. Learn about mattresses from the manufacturers. Mattresses vary widely in hardness among the manufacturers and some require special treatment—turning at intervals—to get the best results from them. See page 22.

Bedheads

Most bedheads are designed for decorative purposes and do not work as supports for people sitting up in bed. Analyze the anthropometric requirements and angle bedheads accordingly. Create a close fit between mattress and bedhead to block drafts.

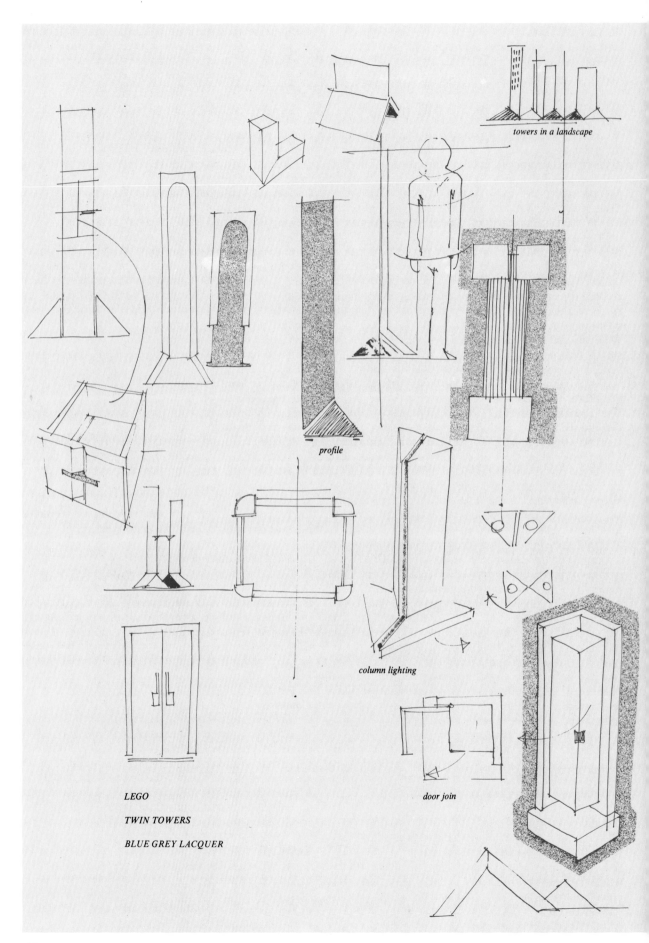

towers in a landscape

profile

column lighting

LEGO

TWIN TOWERS

BLUE GREY LACQUER

door join

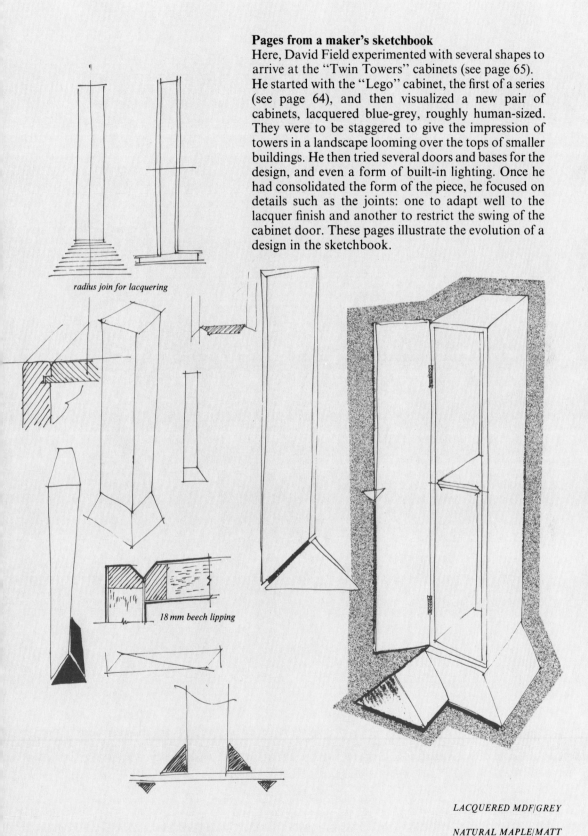

Pages from a maker's sketchbook
Here, David Field experimented with several shapes to
arrive at the "Twin Towers" cabinets (see page 65).
He started with the "Lego" cabinet, the first of a series
(see page 64), and then visualized a new pair of
cabinets, lacquered blue-grey, roughly human-sized.
They were to be staggered to give the impression of
towers in a landscape looming over the tops of smaller
buildings. He then tried several doors and bases for the
design, and even a form of built-in lighting. Once he
had consolidated the form of the piece, he focused on
details such as the joints: one to adapt well to the
lacquer finish and another to restrict the swing of the
cabinet door. These pages illustrate the evolution of a
design in the sketchbook.

radius join for lacquering

18 mm beech lipping

LACQUERED MDF/GREY

NATURAL MAPLE/MATT

PROJECTS IN CONCEPT

Wood certainly must be the most accommodating of materials for turning design ideas into reality. Metal joints may be less bulky, and plastic may be more malleable, but each of the 17 designers featured in this chapter has chosen wood to translate his or her furniture from sketches to full-blown objects. And each has his or her own reasons for doing so.

These designers and makers are all well established as working in a contemporary British idiom. Although they represent profound differences in style and working methods, their furniture is generally characterized by restrained, clean lines and a minimum of ornament. There are few "pyrotechnics in wood," as Ron Carter would say (page 74).

But, being British, they draw liberally from the past, both in the high degree of workmanship they expect from themselves, and in the refined and urbane quality of their designs. Some, like David Savage (page 66) and Alan Peters (page 70), rely on a traditional British crafts workshop system to implement their work. Many—David Field (pages 48–50), Tim Wells (page 59), John Makepeace (page 79) and Alan Peters—were apprentices themselves as young boys. But other designers are more directly the products of the love affair that Britain and the rest of Europe had with industry during the late 1960s and early 1970s—perhaps best typified by Scandinavian furniture. Ron Carter directs his design energy to the production-line, and only actually *makes* prototypes. Many young designers—Paul Connell (page 67) and Toby Winteringham (page 62) and Jonathan Baulkwill (page 54)—aspire to this way of working in the future.

Whatever their origins, designers today are better educated than ever before, often with a strong dose of the fine arts and of art history. For that reason, a hint of the Bauhaus and the work of Gerrit Rietfeld (page 35) can be detected in the work of Paul Connell, Petra Gomann and Anthony Thompson (page 78); of Arts and Craft tradition in Alan Peters's and John Makepeace's work. And throughout can be felt influences as varied as the cool, natural look of the Scandinavian School and its great master, Alvar Aalto, to the colorful fireworks of the Italian New Wave.

Every one of these designers is a professional earning a living. You may not wish to become as involved as they are in designing and making furniture, but their approaches to their work may illustrate the constraints and motivations behind all good furniture design.

David Field

David Field, the author, approaches the design of furniture with the passionate commitment of a vocation. His academic and work experience have given a sophistication to his work and a wordliness to his thinking. He is persuaded that the profession of designer entails specific moral and social responsibilities, which require designers to be participating members of society (see pages 12 to 15). To that end he has been teaching furniture design since 1973, and he is a dedicated teacher.

Field began his design work as a mechanical engineer, working from the age of 16 as an apprentice for the electronics firm, Marconi Limited in 1963. "I dropped naturally into an apprenticeship," he says, "because I'd shown a particular bent for technical subjects and mathematics, and I had an ability to draw. So it seemed a logical path to go."

In 1969 he entered the Central School of Art in London to study industrial design. "It happened that they had recently amalgamated the furniture and industrial design departments. And as time went by, I found I was far more interested in furniture than in designing kettles and refrigerators."

In 1969, he was accepted at the Royal College of Art, in the furniture school, because, "I knew that David Pye was there, and that he was an aesthete and a discerning academic—the stuff good professors are made of." Pye, a cabinetmaker and designer who Field describes as "*the* authority on design theory and practice in Britain today, a person with a no-nonsense approach to dispelling myths about design" was to be a powerful influence on Field's thinking. The other was Ron Carter (see page 74).

Field says, "I arrived at the RCA, and was firmly put down in the first week. I can remember saying that I wanted to produce 'non-status' furniture, only to be rebuffed by the comment 'Impossible!'. I was stunned by the fact that anybody could be so emphatic in matters of art and design. But the explanation from Pye was clear: 'If you project your furniture as being non-status, you are immediately affording it status.'

"From that moment," Field says, "I could see that design was not an act of divine inspiration held together by esoteric jargon, and that some aspects of the subject could be taught." He adds, "I have taught ever since, through every conceivable medium," and "through the work—furniture for industry, individuals, public bodies and private collections."

Field's design philosophy is partly derived from Pye and Carter, he says. Pye emphasized the notion of workmanship, as distinct from "craftsmanship" which "has the connotations of corncob dolls and large hairy things hanging on the wall." The best work is a synthesis of the highest levels of design thinking and workmanship. "There are qualities that a skilled maker can bring to bear, that enhance the object he is making so that it falls firmly into the realm of Art, with a capital A," he explains. "These are qualities that can't be planned on a designer's drawing board."

Field says that Carter showed him that "craftsmanship is an attitude of mind, a response to all materials. It means that you make well because the idea demands it—the idea simply won't come off if the object isn't made well—and not just because you have a preoccupation with perfection."

continued on p. 50

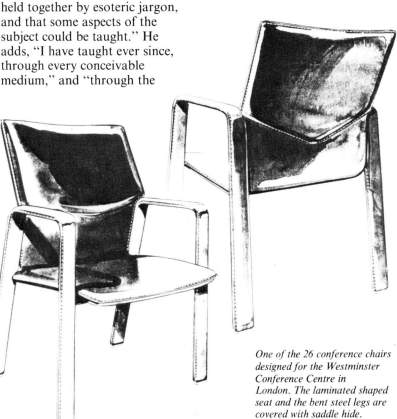

One of the 26 conference chairs designed for the Westminster Conference Centre in London. The laminated shaped seat and the bent steel legs are covered with saddle hide.

David Field's highly practical dining table seats 8
when opened, 4 when closed. Its top converts in
one operation to half its original size by means of an
ingeniously simple pivoting mechanism that consists
only of a dowel fitted into a pivot hole under the table
top. The maple table legs are overlapping frames
which visually reiterate the folding planes of the top.
See pages 82-83.

PROFILE

David Field

There can be the highly regulated craftsmanship of the cabinetmaker, with flawless joints and finish. Or there can be free craftsmanship, rougher and less refined, such as might be used by a boatbuilder. Both types of craftsmanship are valid under the appropriate circumstances, Field says, and it is a measure of the designer's sensitivity to the circumstances that he chooses the craftsmanship correctly, just as it is a measure of his sensitivity to the user of the object he is making. "It's a choice, to use a highly polished finish. It is simply a technical option and in the end a matter of style."

Field says he has been fortunate in his teachers. "Their support was of value because of their work and the way they presented an argument. For example, David Pye could judge the merit of things he didn't personally like." Field recalls that in 1976 Pye chose a grey cabinet of Field's, similar to the ones on pages 64 and 65, for a British Crafts Council exhibition, saying, "Not at all my cup of tea, but it has merit." The exhibit consisted of examples of exceptional design and craftsmanship, he says, and the cabinet was included with a whole range of objects, including a Norris plane and a British riding saddle.

It seems appropriate, then, that Field should find teaching so rewarding. From 1976 to 1979 he taught at the London College of Furniture, and since then has been a tutor at the Royal College of Art. He says, "I think of it as people of more experience and people of less experience getting together and tackling problems. And to be able to discuss what I'm doing is an enormous advantage. If you're going to develop in your work, dialogue is essential. I don't have to consciously seek it because teaching is a two-way street and I get a lot from my students."

He paraphrased the architect Norman Potter, who wrote that teaching art and design is to "advance the fruits of your experience with positive uncertainty," driven simply by the "positive belief that better work is always possible."

But Field says he is often vulnerable as a teacher and consequently takes it very seriously. "Teachers expose themselves to criticism. Very few designers can take that. These kids are incredibly bright and you can't fob them off with palliatives. You must be active, not passive."

In his work, Field is amassing a collection of impressive clients, and his pieces have been shown in galleries and museums every year since 1976. In 1978 he lived in Hong Kong, as a consultant for the Hong Kong Trade Association to advise them how

> **" Craftsmanship is an attitude of mind. It means you make well because the idea demands it—the idea simply won't come off if the object isn't made well—and not just because you have a preoccupation with perfection. "**

to restructure their furniture industry for trade with the West. He says that their industry was composed of small workshops, equipped with adaptable woodworking machinery and handmade jigs. "They did the most amazing things with a radial arm saw and a mortiser," he says. "They made double-locking, 3-way mitred mortise and tenon joints that were rather like a Chinese puzzle, using no hand tools."

He finished his stay there by making a series of designs based on Ming dynasty furniture. Because of the small cross-sections that were needed, the pieces were more stable in the high humidity, and were better suited for being produced in workshops with restricted space and no capacity for flow-line productions. And the style appealed to Western taste.

Today he has a flourishing workshop in Chiswick, a London suburb. He finds he needs to stay a step ahead of his clients, who tend to request designs based on what he has already done. "I did metal inlay, and then lacquered things. Now I'm finding myself working in solid timber much more, and doing an enormous number of boardroom tables."

His ideas for designs come from other sources than furniture. The metal inlay came from looking at steel straps on packing cases; the lacquered finish was inspired by the way British fishing boats are painted. Architecture has always influenced him. "It's so prominent and visible, you can't really miss it. Usually it's the way the building is detailed that interests me."

"I keep a sketchbook," he says, "which is a storehouse of information, a visual notebook with addresses, drawings, references to parts and materials. I take it on holidays rather than a camera because it makes me sit and look, rather than snap and not look."

In the future, he would like to reduce the amount of furniture made at his workshop, and only make prototypes for manufacture. "I would like to form an association with a new generation of graduates who are superb makers. I'm a reluctant maker in many ways," he says.

He says, as many designers do, that he is never satisfied with his work. "I realized the other day that I'd made perhaps 400 or 500 designs in my career so far. And out of those, I only thought two or three were any good. But later I thought, Mies van der Rohe or Charles Eames probably only started getting it right in their mid-50s. So there's hope."

Hugh Scriven

Hugh Scriven describes himself as a "designer first and a craftsman second. As far as using wood and the techniques of woodworking go, it is a means to an end," he says. "I'm doing it in order to produce objects and to realize ideas; the craftsmanship in between is pleasant but it is not why I am doing it."

For Scriven, the design has always been the motivating force behind his work and he often produces a series of pieces in which he pushes the design idea as far as he can before moving on to a new project. The rectangular table illustrated on pages 88–89 is number three in a series of four in which the fourth was actually round but which still used the same design for the supporting legs. Even so, he is careful not to push an idea beyond functionalism. "I'd feel uncomfortable designing something that couldn't be used at all."

His work in general is characterized by strongly sculptural form and by use of colour, and in fact, at the end of his first year at Kingston College of Art, in Surrey, he was of two minds whether to do sculpture or furniture design.

The course at Kingston focused on design work with very little emphasis on craftsmanship. It was not until he began at the Royal College of Art in 1970 that Scriven began to learn about that side of furniture making. He realized then that in order to develop his own ideas, he would have to be able to make his own pieces. "I didn't want to work for a large firm where the marketing director was dictating the designs. I thought I would have more freedom to produce more ideas if I was making things for myself," he explains.

After leaving the RCA in 1973, he went to work for Rob Corbett in Norfolk, where he undertook repair work and joinery as well as commissioned work to Corbett's designs. He was doing very little of his own design work, and after three years he felt it was time to move on. Ashley Cartwright (see page 71), whom Scriven had known from the RCA, had just found himself a workshop at Brackley and was looking for someone to share it.

Brackley is only a few miles from the site of the Prescote Gallery, now closed. In the late 1970s the gallery director Anne Hartree had a profound effect on Scriven's career, and on the careers of several young British furniture makers. She encouraged Scriven in his speculative work, which he exhibited and sold at Prescote, and she helped him to find commissions.

Although he confesses to "not liking to work for people I don't like," Scriven's approach to commissioned work is professional. "I regard solving the client's functional problems as a prime necessity but I hope they'll want my style at the same time," he says. "I try to design a piece that'll do the job they want it to do, but I hope to surprise them too. I see that as part of my job as designer—to go further than they've imagined.

"After I've visited the client's house I start sketching. I start with scribbles, developing the idea, and then it might go to model form if it's a very three-dimensional piece. With some of my designs, it's very difficult to get a sense of what is going on with the understructure without constructing a model. Or I develop ideas through drawings alone. There are no real rules."

This desire for freedom in ideas extends into his choice of materials: "Wood is an easily manipulated material which I happen to have acquired a certain amount of skill in using. To me the design is what's important and wood is a versatile material for ideas, but I also like using leather and plastics."

His latest commission, and his largest to date, is for the library furniture at Templeton College, Oxford University, involving study tables, a large table for reading newspapers and magazines, the librarian's desk, and storage units. The work will

> "*Craftsmanship is pleasant, but it is not why I am doing it at all.*"

be coloured in red, blue and grey and incorporates stained plywood, Formica- and leather-covered surfaces and Plexiglass lighting units. This is an important commission that marks something of a departure for Scriven because, until now, he has done little work on whole interiors. Although Tim Wells (see page 59) is helping him on this project, as a rule he would rather avoid the organizational difficulties with large scale productions.

Once this commission is completed, Scriven plans to teach at The Wendell Castle school near Rochester, New York. He has taught in the past and this combination of teaching and designing is something he feels may develop further because he dislikes being stuck in the workshop five days a week. "I like having access to people and other ideas. I'm not aiming in any particular direction but I wouldn't be surprised if I took on a larger teaching role and could still develop my own work."

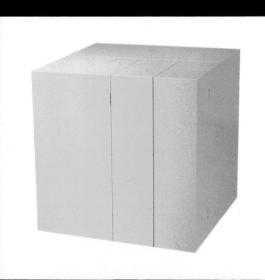

top: **Floris van den Broecke's** cube desk seems more like a clever puzzle than the highly versatile work station that it is. It can be left closed up and function as a sculpture – the effect heightened by the jonquil-yellow lacquer finish. Or it can be gradually opened out to reveal scores of cubby holes and storage spaces, and pull-out desk surfaces. See pages 92-93.

opposite, top: **Ron Carter's** Witney 2 dining table is made of ebonized mahogany and seats 6 or 8 persons comfortably. At 145 cm/57 in in diameter, this table is large for a round table, but its size is not too unwieldy for the average-sized dining space (see pages 22-23). As massive as it is – its top is 32 mm/1¼ in thick and its six legs are cut from beams 75|mm sq/3 in sq – the effect is lightened with the subtle bevel along the lip of the top and the severe stopped chamfer along the legs. See pages 84-85.

opposite, bottom: **Jonathan Baulkwill's** writing desk's apparent simplicity belies the involved design thinking that allows for the movement of the wood from which it is made. Baulkwill has chosen a light maple, with its grain aligned to run across the desk and down, rather than along, the sides. This way, the wood will expand and contract at the same rate across the grain in the top and sides. The secret to the assembly is a range of hidden dovetails that knits the sides of the carcass together. See pages 90 to 91.

Jonathan Baulkwill

Despite his young age—he is only 21 years old— Jonathan Baulkwill has always firmly directed himself in making furniture. He has plotted his schooling and subsequent work with a level head to become a well-rounded designer and maker.

His first experience with wood came at boarding school, where he had free access to experiment in a workshop. At 16 he chose Shrewsbury Technical College near Wales over several other schools "because it suited me the best and had a good atmosphere for making my own things. I didn't think an apprenticeship was right then. I needed more of a balanced training in cabinet-making and design." He made the desk on page 52 and the revolving bookcase on page 72 there.

At 18 he moved on to the Ravensbourne College of Art, south of London in Bromley. "I knew that when I left Shrewsbury, if I wanted to set up shop and make furniture, the only way I could get more recognition was by improving the design aspect," he says. At Ravensbourne, he made the gentleman's dresser on page 68.

The college had another advantage over a wood workshop, in that it allowed him to experiment with other materials. He used the school's vacuum former to shape the plastic trays in the gentleman's dresser. He also experimented with steel under-structures.

Currently he is working for Martin Grierson in his London workshop, "to get a sense of commercial procedures, as well as to improve my making skills." He declares himself to be "quite interested in designing for industry," and if he could find a temporary position in a good Italian firm he says that he would eagerly accept.

He sees his immediate future as a matter of developing his methods of design, and he has been trying to develop a personal working program which allows a quick response to clients' requests. "I want to become more practiced at producing a design." This methodical approach to getting a design off the drawing board is typical of the realistic attitude of some young designers, who consider it critical to making a profitable piece of furniture.

Baulkwill describes his method of working through the design process as a detailed and logical step-by-step process. He makes a careful analysis of the brief, which includes the definite costs and a list of constraints imposed by the interior into which the furniture will be put. Then he works up a sketch proposal, selecting and developing the more promising ideas largely by intuition, he says. His drawings are small, sketched in perspective, sometimes concentrating on a particular promising detail. At this stage he begins to consider his materials. A full-sized mock-up model follows, at which point he can make the changes in the thickness of the material or the degree of shaping which can only be accomplished confidently after seeing the proposal in the round.

Baulkwill's personal taste tends toward the smooth, clean lines of Scandinavian furniture, represented especially by Alvar Alto. But he cites a long list of diverse influences besides. The modernists Gerrit Reitveld (see page 35) and Marcel Breuer are evident in his early work. He also admires the work of Alan Peters (see page 70) for its simplicity and that of Hugh Scriven (see page 51) for his use of colour.

His preoccupation with wood is central to his design approach. He speaks with passion about the intricate and subtle qualities of grain and the effects of light on it. Much of his work attempts to exploit these qualities, especially in light timbers where careful finishing can enhance the figure without it becoming too dominant. The process of working with timber is the central impetus for his involvement with furniture. Other materials are used to set off the timber itself.

> *"It is important to me that people like my designs. They must be user-friendly."*

He believes that his work is in a transition stage. His designs now include stained woods to create highlights. But the colour must be used "with imagination and restraint," he says. He mentions the highly colourful furniture of the Italian firm Memphis (see page 37). "I think that one purpose of the Memphis designs is to cause a strong reaction in people and stirring people up. I do like to get a reaction from people, but it is important to me is that they like my designs. They must be user-friendly.'

Baulkwill's future plans will keep him moving, "otherwise I could get into a rut." He has applied to study in the Furniture Department of the Royal College of Art, but he may find work with another designer instead. His eventual goal is to set up business on his own. "I still need a non-commercial atmosphere," he says. It is certain his next stage will be as much a conscious decision as those of the past. "Up until now I've always had very set decisions. There hasn't been much doubt," he says.

Peter St. Hill

Peter St. Hill graduated from university in Australia in 1980, having studied English and specialized in journalism. A job at a Melbourne newspaper made him realize that he was less suited to recording events than to making them happen for himself. With this realization he decided to change careers, and he took a job as a carpenter/joiner renovating Victorian terrace houses in Sydney. "It was not a difficult decision. I knew that I was good with my hands and enjoyed making things and it was a job where I could be directly responsible for my own standards," he says.

It was during this period that he discovered a book by James Krenov (a Swedish cabinetmaker who works and teaches in the United States) entitled *The Fine Art of Cabinetmaking*. "The book was the first influence pushing me towards furniture making and I can remember feeling that every paragraph contained pearls of wisdom," he says. "I know differently now. The approach to the subject was far from realistic—a sort of romantic ideal, but at the time it touched my imagination. At any rate, it seemed a positive progression from general carpentry."

Having discovered the world of furniture craft and wanting to be part of it, he applied to the John Makepeace School for Craftsmen in Wood at Parnham House, Dorset. There he was able to enhance his furniture making skills under the tutorship of Robert Ingham and Alan Peters (page 70) and he met several design lecturers involved with the course. He says of that period: "In retrospect, Parnham was everything I had expected and more, and I am grateful for the experience. It was a unique education. I was, however, prepared to leave the course at one stage and came away from the place utterly confused."

It is only after 18 months of practical experience with a professional workshop that the value of his time at Parnham has become apparent to him. "Furniture making had become a definite commitment when I was in Australia," he explains. "I decided to do it in depth, but all I knew at that stage was that I enjoyed working with my hands. I knew that cabinetmaking seemed more challenging than joinery, and logically a good course would complete the transition. However it takes much longer and it is only with time that a personal direction and a meaning emerges from the work. Parnham exposed the potential. It confirmed to me that I could make well. My recent practical experience has provided a direction and confidence and now it is up to me to take things further," he says.

It is with furniture, the objects themselves, rather than timber, that his interest lies. He believes that craftsmanship applies to all materials and that timber, although highly suitable for

> *"It is about time that people started thinking about what constitutes good design, and only then about making it well."*

furniture making, is only one of a number of materials to choose from "Having a preoccupation with the material or the making process can lead to disappointment. Unless a piece of furniture is carefully thought out first and not rushed into, all that skill and choice material can be wasted," he says. Therefore, a methodical approach easing him into a project is an important part of his designing process.

"Most projects begin with in-depth research, but not in the conventional way," he says. "I do a lot of reading, take long walks to help concentrate my mind, and then I sit at the drawing board and begin drawing. I do work speculatively most of the time and have never analyzed the actual process point by point. Too much self analysis can confuse the issue—if the work emerges and you feel good about it then leave it at that—at least until the ideas stop flowing."

His standards in design are high, and although he believes that furniture should be made as well as possible, the end result is more important to him than the act of making. This is illustrated by his comments about the current state of furniture craft.

"I like very little of current American craft furniture—most of it is far too self-indulgent in technique," he says. He disapproves of the flamboyant shapes and improbable-looking constructions of American-made pieces. On the other hand, "In Britain, although making standards are high, makers are either firmly entrenched in tradition, or deny it totally and stab uneasily at the frontiers of Art. It is about time that people started thinking about what constitutes good design and only then about making it well—both sides of the Atlantic," and then added for the benefit of his Australian colleagues "and both sides of the Pacific."

Back in Australia now, he is setting up a furniture development workshop and intends to follow that with a factory, which will exploit an emerging design awareness there he says. Then he plans to start a series of retail outlets.

John Makepeace's cherrywood dressing table is a
stunning example of this designer's integrated
approach in his designs. The eye is first caught by the
flared legs, which anchor the piece to the ground and
at the same time sweep upward to the exposed
mortise in the table top – itself as massive as a
butcherblock. The legs literally bite into the top,
flaring slightly to mirror the flare of the feet. The
three drawers are all cut from the same plank of
wood; the grain figure flows from one drawer to the
other, punctuated by the round knobs.
See pages 100-101.

top: **David Field's** split yew table is made of solid and veneered yew, with small block feet of ebony. The split in the top allows the base to peek through and visually unifies the piece. See pages 102-103.

bottom: **Floris van den Broecke's** square-cylinder-triangle table is part of a series that explores those three geometric shapes. The contrasting colors isolate each component. See pages 108-109.

Floris van den Broecke

Floris van den Broecke came to work in the furniture field by an unusual route. The son of an illustrator, he studied fine art, principally painting, at the Arnhem Academy of Fine Art in Holland, from 1961–66. Toward the end of that period he began to worry about the isolated and limiting nature of painting. From that point he became interested in design. He felt that "if art is about the ends in life, then design is about the means" and applied to the Royal College of Art in London to study furniture design. He found that the analytical approach of painting, together with the craft element, were transferable to furniture. He did not have to start from scratch in order to produce useful objects. "I can remember the excitement over the concept of transferable disciplines—the idea that objects could be both art and useful. From then on it became a case of 'Fasten your Rietveld'."

Not illogically, because Gerrit Rietveld, also Dutch (see page 33), had worked from a similar premise during the early part of the century. Pierre Paulin, the designer for the company Artifort, also had a great influence on him and as a direct result, van den Broecke experimented with upholstered furniture.

It was then that Ron Lenthall, an RCA technician and cabinetmaker who was a legend among the students, drew his attention to the potential of timber. Lenthall would make the furniture according to student design drawings. Although he did not exercise a design influence, his understanding of the limits that timber could be worked, together with his inherent sensitivity to designs, taught van den Broecke the value of skilled workmanship in art.

Van den Broecke regularly works with timber but, unlike many designers in the book, his work is not material-based, in the sense that timber is not its starting point. He says, "response to a material, as I see it, is a response to its appropriateness and is a learned process. Through experiment one builds up an experience of knowing how right a material is for a particular application."

This is expectable from a designer who is consciously seeking to make artistic statements in his work. He accepts that furniture can be art by accident but his approach is not to make a distinction. "There is no point in making furniture which is *not* demanding—there is plenty of that around already."

To this end he sees his workshop as a place to experiment with speculative pieces. He is not running a business, although he does take on occasional commissions if he feels that they offer him the opportunity to further develop a formal aesthetic premise. In these circumstances, he requires the

> **" There is no point in making furniture which is** not **demanding— there is plenty of that around already. "**

freedom to design as he pleases on the assumption that clients would not have sought him if they had not wanted his style of work.

His approach is painterly. His ground rules are the spatial and pictorial relationships that painters manipulate because he believes that the disciplines of fine art will yield the best results in design work. If the approach to work is disciplined and constrained, he says, "design begins where chance ends." The sources of inspiration are broad, he says. "Anything may trigger an idea, the way a person sits, seeing a particular material or structure or pursuing a certain set of esthetic or functional values. I have recently become interested in the way in which people change their lives and I would like to postulate some answers with furniture."

He translates concept into furniture this way: "At first you just sit down and talk—with a client or friends—and then sit down again and draw until you can see an idea that approximates a solution. It's very simple at this stage. The next stage is quite disciplined—at least for me it is, for I like to get the piece drawn up as near as possible to the finished article. There is a lot of editing and measuring going on at this point and a scale model may be necessary or a full-size mock-up.

"Much depends on the time available and this is why discipline is necessary. It goes without saying that nothing is ever an immaculate conception. I must build one judgement onto the next. It is different with making, but only slightly. I prefer designing but would not be satisfied without making something every now and then. Of course, some maintain that you can't be a good designer if you don't make things, but this is only true to a certain extent."

He often refers to the advantages of being an outsider coming into furniture design from an unconventional route, and he has made full use of them. He has a host of successful one-man and group exhibitions to his name, consultancies with architects, and a teaching role at the Royal College of Art.

Tim Wells

Tim Wells says, "About the only thing I ever did at school was woodwork and technical drawing." Clearly, he was destined for a career as a designer and craftsman. He left school in 1974, aged 16, and immediately started work for John Makepeace (see page 79) whose furniture he had seen at a small exhibition in his village hall. Makepeace's workshop was then at Farnborough in Warwickshire, about 20 miles from Brackley, where Wells grew up and where he now has his own workshop with Ashley Cartwright and Hugh Scriven (see pages 71 and 51).

After a five-year apprenticeship with Makepeace, he went to work as a craftsman in Makepeace's cabinetmaking workshop, which had by now moved to its present location in Parnham in Dorset. Working for Makepeace, he learned about running a shop, he says, but he ultimately wanted to carry out his own designs. And so with the help of the Prescote Gallery in Banbury, in 1980 he set up on his own.

At first, the influence of Makepeace dominated his work, with its emphasis on traditional handcrafts and the inspiration it draws from the organic qualities of wood. But because Wells has been financing his own work by making furniture for other designers, including Cartwright and Scriven, their influence also

surfaces in his work. Nearly all of the designers he respects are contemporaries noted for their adventuresome use of new materials. "I am not very interested in what happened in the past, and I know very little about that," he says. "What I do appreciate and try to use are traditional methods and techniques, although with new materials and manufactured boards. There are new ways of jointing which I am now using."

One of these modern designers for whom he makes furniture is Fred Baier, a favorite of Wells because of his flamboyant use of sculptural shapes and bold colors. Baier's style is in direct contrast to Wells's own. "I like simple structures and I always design myself out of any

---

> " To set up a really sharp hand-plane and take off a whisper of a shaving that is perfect – that's great. "

---

complicated ones, mainly to keep the costs down," he says.

Nevertheless, he feels that at the moment he is in transition in his development because he has kept himself open to new influences and ideas, although he describes himself as still deeply involved with wood. "Wood is fantastic," he says. "No piece of wood is the same and I've no reason to change the materials I work with now because I totally enjoy what I do. To set up a really sharp hand-plane and take off a whisper of a shaving that is perfect—that's great." In his business, Wells does "a bit of everything," both undertaking commissions and doing speculative pieces. He makes one-of-a-kind items as well as small production batches. The speculative work he has exhibited, has in turn brought him clients for commissioned pieces.

In his relationship with a

client, he sees himself as problem solver: "The client presents the problem and you design the solution. When I get back to the workshop after seeing a client, I think about the function they're after and start to work out ideas. I don't do a lot of drawings—I'm not very good on that side—but I do think about the project a lot, in the bath or whatever, whenever there's spare time."

Because he works in hardwood, with a special preference for homegrown English timber, his jobs have to be carefully planned and costed out. The wood may have to be prepared a month or more in advance and there must always be enough timber in store not just for the current job, but for the one after that as well. These were not things his apprenticeship had fully prepared him for. "It's frightening costing jobs at first because you can lose a lot of money easily" he says.

It is a mistake he has not made too often, because he has already outgrown his workshop—a corrugated iron hut across the yard from the main workshop. The hut has been turned into a cabinet shop, while Wells shares the machine-shop with Scriven and Cartwright, which is useful because he makes extensive use of power tools. "All the donkeywork is done by machine," he says. "I don't agree with doing everything by hand. If they [machines] are used correctly, there's nothing wrong with it; nine times out of ten a machine does a better job than doing it by hand. The only joint I won't cut by machine is a dovetail—I don't think a machine-cut dovetail is good, perhaps visually more than structurally."

Wells is about to leave for the United States to work as a craftsman for Wendell Castle ("One of my all-time heroes") in New York. His long term plans are less precise: "All I know is that I enjoy the sort of work I do and as long as there is someone to sponsor it or pay for it, I shall carry on doing it."

opposite, top: **Toby Winteringham's** carver chair, made of beech, has been pared down to the bare structural essentials. Its spare proportions conjure up Shaker furniture. The seat is perforated with holes, lightening the design even further. See pages 118-119.

opposite, bottom: **Ron Carter's** Scarthin Nick conference chair has an Oriental quality, with its deep, inviting seat framed by low sweeping arms. The curved top back rail, which protrudes slightly at either end of the back frame, accentuates the sweep, like the peaked eaves of a pagoda roof. The padded and upholstered seat and back, however, firmly identify this design as Western. See pages 120-121.

left: **David Colwell's** C-3 chair has been designed for production in a small workshop, using steam-bending equipment. The wood is young ash, prized for its flexibility and strength. The seat, slightly dished, is made of maple. See pages 116-117.

right: **Adrian Reed's** deceptively simple "Suzy stool" is made of beech and can be constructed in two heights, for sitting at a table or at a bar. Folded, it is roughly 65 mm/2½ in deep; the hole in the seat allows it to be stowed away, suspended on a wall. See pages 122-123.

Toby Winteringham

Toby Winteringham embodies the paradoxical nature of many young furniture makers. First, there is the romantic who uses traditional woodworking techniques and works purely for the love of his craft. Next, there is the realist, aware of the need to run an efficient business.

As a result, Winteringham says, "I make things that look like contemporary design and are uncluttered—very square, dead plain and simple." But he adds, "I appreciate handcraft technique that has taken centuries to develop."

Winteringham first developed an interest in carpentry from watching his architect father working around the home. At sixteen, he went to the Solihull College of Art, south of Birmingham. His real interest was in graphic design, and he became a skilled technical artist. He noticed that many "people doing graphic design often wind up doing furniture. Most people have to chose between three-dimensional and graphic design." He then made the transition himself to furniture design, which he found combined creativity with utility.

After two years at Solihull, Winteringham went on to Kingston College of Art in Surrey to take a course in three-dimensional design in wood, metal and plastic. There he had the time to experiment in designing for materials other than wood—notably textiles. He also got a grounding in the history of design and says he benefited from the projects set by visiting lecturers such as Jane Dillon (furniture) and Betty Barnden (textiles) who were practicing British designers.

At the time, he says, he could see himself as a furniture designer, but he was put off by the thought of working for a large design firm. Because he was developing and improving his woodcrafts skill—for the first time he was actually making furniture—he says that gradually "it dawned on me that I could do furniture design freelance."

After Kingston, in 1975, Winteringham studied furniture design at the Royal College of Art in London. He was left to his own devices and at the time he was strongly influenced by an exhibition of Shaker furniture he had seen at the Victoria and Albert Museum in London. His work reflects the functional nature and minimal decoration of this kind of furniture, as seen in the chair on page 60 (top). His current work is more decorative.

After the three-year programme at the RCA, he decided to set out by himself as a designer/maker. With the aid of a grant from the British Crafts Council and a small inheritance he bought his

> "*Sometimes the gut reaction is the best.*"

premises in the town of King's Lynn in Norfolk. In retrospect, he feels he would have preferred to set up a workshop with someone else, not only from the financial and business points of view, but to provide a stimulating working environment where ideas could be discussed—something like college.

After four years at King's Lynn, he has come to terms with running a business. "I've learned to delegate jobs that can better be done by others, like bookkeeping." But he feels it is a struggle not to give more of himself to his work than is sensible in business terms. Most of his work is custom-made commissioned pieces, although he will produce the occasional speculative piece, such as the mirror on page 72 (top), for an exhibition, to sell later.

He regards his early work as essentially two-dimensional pieces that could be designed easily on paper. "If I was stuck for an idea and trying to find the answer to a problem, I would make it incredibly complicated. Totally absurd. I would include all the possible applications and then refine it down, eliminating all the things I did not need. You can waste time," he admits, "but occasionally it's an important part of the process." To be safe, he keeps all his drawings. "You never know. It could always come in handy later on."

The mirror on page 72 illustrates this process. Winteringham says this mirror is the last of a long series of experiments with a design. "This mirror was the throw-away design. I did it without thinking. Sometimes the gut-reaction is the best," he says.

Lately, he says, he had needed to see the piece first as a model before finally making it. He uses models to test the relationships of shapes and the strength of the structure. For example, he tested the chair on page 60 by sitting and leaning back on it, and then pivoting on the legs. Then he dropped it on a front leg from a height of three feet. Although his pieces are professionally tested, he finds the trial-and-error method useful.

Winteringham feels he must keep making to design with confidence, but if his business is to grow at its present rate, he will not have the time to do the necessary handwork. He therefore envisions his role changing to one of designer-prototype maker and thus resolves and conflict between the creative and business sides of his work.

Adrian Reed

"I don't think that I have ever cut a dovetail" may seem a surprising remark to come from someone in a book about designing and making furniture. Yet Adrian Reed provides a distinct contrast to other craftsmen. Still in his twenties and studying furniture design at the Royal College of Art in London, he retains a youthful commitment to design ideals, uncompromised by having had to operate in a commercial environment.

Just how much he can resist the pressures to compromise, only time will show. He is confident that in the end good design will prevail over economic pressures. His optimism is reflected in the thesis he is now writing for the RCA: a study of the way industrial design has evolved not so much through market forces but through the development of techniques used to produce furniture.

Reed was brought up in Leicester where his father owned a hardware store and timber yard. Therefore from an early age he became interested in making things in wood and other materials. At school when set a project he was quickly able to work out how it should be put together, and he was one of the first students to complete a new course in design and craft technology.

From school he went to Loughborough College of Art and Design in Leicestershire, to do a year-long course in art foundation before moving to Manchester Polytechnic to study for a degree in three-dimensional design in wood, metals and ceramics. From there he went straight to the RCA.

Reed acknowledges that perhaps because of his limited experience and his immaturity as a designer, most of his work evolves through physically trying out ideas using pieces of wood, metal, padding and upholstery. He might start off with some scribbles, but "these are all but incomprehensible to anyone but myself." He finds it difficult to design only on the drawing board and his work is mainly by trial and error. He realizes that

---

"*I don't think I have ever cut a dovetail.***"**

---

he needs to develop skills in visualizing objects to better create designs that work on the drawing board. At present he completes his standard drawings *after* he is satisfied with what he has produced. He does this more for the purpose of keeping a record and as guidelines for the craftsmen who replicate his design. And he has been using models to work out his ideas in three dimensions.

David Colwell (see page 75) has had the major influence on his work and particularly on the development of the folding stool (see page 61), he says. Reed especially admires Colwell's designing and making skills, and he is impressed by such things as the way Colwell's workshop is laid out, because it reflects Colwell's attitude towards his work—that everything should be interlinked.

The folding stool, for example, resulted from a set of personally defined parameters—the angle of the seat had to be adjustable for comfort; the height had to be suitable for a drawing board; it had to be transportable; and it had to be easy to store. Obviously, some form of fold-up seating was required, but it took a number of prototypes to refine his ideas and the operating mechanism. Initially, there was a square hinged seat set on a cross-legged frame. But because the seat was hinged only on one edge, it required two hands to open it out. Slowly the idea began to emerge of a circular seat hinged on opposite sides and fixed to an X-shaped frame. Now when the seat is lifted, the planks forming the legs fold into each other and the seat flaps down so that the stool can be stored flat. Reed even invented a special hinge for the folding mechanism that is less obtrusive than a conventional butt hinge.

Just how successful the stool is can be seen in the great commercial interest it has generated. Reed is a bit worried by this early success because he feels pressured to come up with the "right" design and in a short space of time. "Success can be restrictive, it makes you play towards caution ... it reduces one's confidence to make mistakes," he says.

His direction for the future tends towards design—"making is a means of fulfilling a design"—and he does not feel the need to make a piece of furniture himself. He does not think he has the potential to become a top craftsman. "It's good to make mistakes, but sometimes I make too many," he says.

Reed is determined to keep his options open within designing. "What is more beneficial to me is the acquisition of know-how, of what can be done with different materials," he says. He currently is developing an office chair in which the angle of the seat and back can be adjusted to suit the user by manipulating only one lever. This has taken him into metalworking and design engineering. Ultimately, he feels that he will move into commercial design after he finishes at the RCA.

top: **David Field's** plan chest was designed for the Shipley Art Gallery to keep their collection of prints. The wedge-shaped base stabilizes the top-heavy structure, while still leaving enough foot room to stand in front of the chest. See pages 126-127.

above: **David Field's** Lego cabinets look more like sculptures . Field designed these laquered boxes based on drawings of fishing boats with brightly painted hulls. The resulting block shapes remind him of Lego building blocks. See pages 128-129.

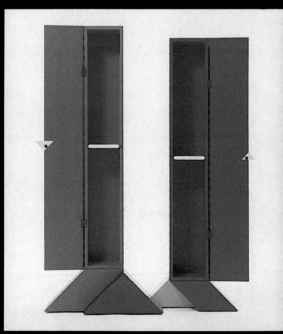

above: **David Field's** Twin Towers are mismatched; one is slightly smaller and painted a lighter shade of gray. The effect is of towers in a landscape. The cabinets, with their totem shapes are domestic altarpieces, says Field. See pages 128-129.

top: **David Field's** 5° cabinet is made of solid maple, limed white. Designed to double as liquor cabinet and display cabinet, this piece has an oddly distorted quality because practically every vertical line is slightly canted at 5°. See pages 130-131.

David Savage

David Savage's approach to furniture is people-oriented and at the same time rooted in tradition. This is visible not only in the classic lines of his designs, but also in the way he has structured his workshop to allow him to spend more time designing.

Of his work, he says quite simply, "I make furniture for people's homes, and not for the art gallery market. I try to make pieces for people to live with, that are human in scale and concept. I do things that people are comfortable with and enjoy using and get recurring pleasure handling and touching, rather than a piece that makes people go zowie!, and then loses impact over the long term."

That long term value in a design came a concern for Savage when he was in college, studying fine arts at Oxford University and at the Royal Academy of Arts in London. At both schools he received "a heavy infusion of fine arts," spending hours looking at the classical and Renaissance art in the Ashmolean Museum at Oxford, and roaming the art galleries near the Royal Academy in the West End of London, soaking up what he describes as a "wide experience of art."

His interest in furniture began after college, when he was working as a freelance commercial designer. He started making furniture for his house and that rekindled a boyhood love of making things—of turning his designs into physical objects. To get the skills he needed to make his pieces, he found the old furniture-making district in London's East End and went knocking on doors. "I would stay and talk as long as they would talk to me," he said. Several old craftsmen were especially helpful and encouraging. Savage is a self-taught craftsman, who learned by "dragging knowledge out of people," he says.

In 1972 he started his design studio in the loft of his London house. He gradually began to make pieces on commission, at first subsidizing them by his other design work. He moved his workshop to Devon last year, having had enough of living in London.

His country workshop resembles the old crafts workshops that used to flourish in England, in which the master craftsman had a young apprentice and several paying students. The only difference is that Savage's shop is fully equipped with modern machinery. Savage has a full-time apprentice to whom he pays a nominal fee, and two full-time students who pay him a yearly tuition. "This is a good way of generating some cash flow," he says, and in addition it gives him some free time to work on special projects.

"Clients tend to like to go for things you've already done," he says. "I don't mind doing a cabinet I've done before, but it tends to be a stifling approach. My ideas get clogged up."

Instead, he prefers to solve specific design problems for clients, taking their homes and even their personalities into consideration. Usually, clients approach him with a rough idea of what they want and how much they are willing to spend on it. Savage explores the possibilities with them and sometimes finds that he has to break down their preconceptions, so that in the end they have redefined what they want. Savage then visits the clients' home to get a sense of the overall style, the colours, shapes and textures there.

This interaction with clients is evident in the commission he received to build the cabinet on page 69. A young couple living in London had a few precious objects they wished to display. Because they were also contemplating starting a family, some form of glass-fronted cabinet was needed. He saw that the cabinet would be hung between two Georgian windows and decided that a slim, elegant design would be the most suitable. The cabinet had to be distinctive, and yet not dominate its contents. The resulting piece is made of pearwood, a light, evenly-grained wood which Savage much admires.

> *"I make furniture for people's homes"*

Once this conceptual stage has been teased out with sketches and perhaps a scale model, he produces some fairly precise workshop drawings. At this point he decides on the method of construction and is able to calculate the time it will take to cut up all the joints and assemble the piece. He even draws up a cutting list so that he can order exactly the lengths of wood he needs and then produce an accurate estimated price for the piece.

In his mind he can now visualize the piece as a whole, but he remains flexible to any modifications that may have to be made in the mock-up. Because he has been consulting closely with his clients all along, it is rare that the final piece will have to be modified in anything but detail.

As to the future, Savage feels that "I'm still learning from wood and I'll stick with it while I'm still getting ideas from it. It's a challenge to design and create in a material that's always changing itself and each piece is different, rare and wonderful."

Paul Connell

Paul Connell began working in wood in a furniture factory at the age of 16, soon after leaving school in 1972. He says that he spent his days clipping drawers together and only lasted two weeks on the assembly line. But by then he had decided he wanted to do "something in furniture," he says.

After a stint at a furniture restoration shop he began working with a friend in a small workshop producing furniture for a London interior design firm. Equipped only with a radial arm saw, a router, a skillsaw and a portable drill, the shop churned out as many as 40 low tables a day. For a while he found the high-production line approach in a small business stimulating—a kind of a thrill, he says—but soon he wanted to think about designing.

In 1977 he applied and was accepted to the John Makepeace School of Craftsmen in Wood at Parnham House in Dorset, during the second year of the school's existence. He says he was accepted, despite his lack of formal education, because "they were looking for someone who would use the experience," and who was interested in the business aspects of woodcraft, as well as being willing to improve his skills in furniture making and designing.

Parnham offered a marked contrast to his previous experience of restoration and production line work. "I had been working to a lower standard. Restoration was more haphazard, patching things together rather than getting it right the first time. Parnham improved my standards of making," he says.

At the end of the two-year programme, he returned to London and immediately went into business, picking up a brisk trade. "Having to work for myself, I got so much more done. The pressure of earning a living and keeping a shop going gets you off your backside. I enjoyed the work. It was something to get your teeth into."

He was especially successful doing one-of-a-kind commissions, although he tried his hand at designing lines of furniture and marketing them at furniture stores. Of the designs, he says, "We realized it had to be very simple, for simple living. It was slightly Oriental in its simplicity," with some splashes of colour, such as red-stained ash handleknobs. "It was a style we thought would be timely."

Connell has continued to design, so much so that he no longer makes furniture himself, but instead subcontracts his work. "Making has become too much of a routine," he says. "The natural thing was to take

> " Making has become too much of a routine "

design further," to design larger things with more variables to consider. This conclusion has led him to enroll in architecture school, and he is currently a first-year student at Kingston Polytechnical School in London. For him, "furniture is the wrong scale in which to put more design thinking. There are fewer variables in furniture. A building has plumbing pipes, heating ducts, electrical conduits—all sorts of inspiring bits" to assemble into a working system, he says.

He is used to thinking about three-dimensional objects abstractly, and he says his designs are usually triggered by making drawings, which he considers a kind of shorthand. "The process of drawing is a search for something, and I'm not quite sure what it is until I get it. I start doodling and see what comes of it." A single piece of furniture often "sparks off a whole concept of a room," he says, generating a complete line of designs, from a sofa bed to a video trolley.

Because of his studies, Connell is "keeping the business ticking over until I make a definite decision about architecture" and how far he can pursue the career of an architect. But he says he can already detect the effect that the discipline is having on his design thinking, helping him to analyze a structure in ways that are new to him.

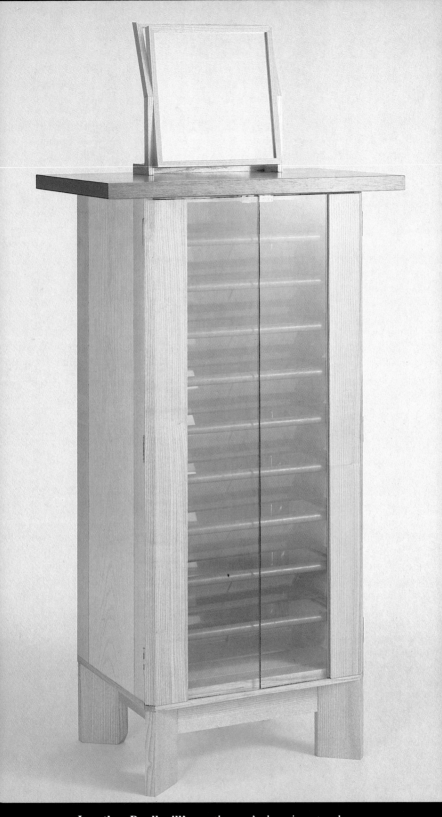

Jonathan Baulkwill's gentleman's dressing stand
uses brightly stained woods to contrast with the blond
maple he works with usually. The corner pieces and
top outline and contain the carcass, while the
matching drawer handle rails seem to float behind
the swinging glass doors. See pages 136-137.

David Savage's pearwood cabinet was designed with a Georgian interior in mind, which accounts for its elegant proportions and restrained detailing – only a bead along the door frame and a flare of the molding along the corners at the top and the bottom of the carcass. See pages 132-133.

Alan Peters

Alan Peters is a descendant of the British Arts and Crafts School of furniture and one of its most articulate apologists, having recently published a book on the subject. In 1948, at the age of 16, he became an apprentice to Edward Barnsley, one of the master craftsmen of the Cotswold Arts and Crafts movement, whose simple designs in solid wood had for decades represented the antithesis to ornamented Victorian furniture of late 19th century Britain.

But Peters, who lives in rural Devon and describes himself as "still a country boy," is anything but naive in terms of design. After a five-year apprenticeship with Barnsley and another two years of training, he came to London to enroll in the Central School of Art, one of the few art schools in Britain that had a separate crafts-oriented department of furniture. But the school was in a transition that reflected a new atmosphere in the 1960s, towards industrial design and automated systems of production, and away from hand-built furniture. Peters began to explore new materials and, until 1975, used metal extensively.

Then, in 1975, Peters received a British Crafts Council grant to travel to Japan to study furniture decoration. "I'd always had a feeling for the East. I'd been influenced by the Chinese Ming furniture I'd seen at the Victoria and Albert Museum in London,"

he says. The trip was a revelation. Peters could see first-hand the inspiration behind the British Arts and Crafts tradition. He says he was most inspired by the architecture and joinery. "I liked the modular approach of construction and the lovely sweep of the roofs." Later, during a trip in 1980 to Korea, "I really warmed towards the Korean work. Korean furniture is more elegant, simpler in form, centuries ahead of its time," he says. The chrome and steel furniture coming out of Milan today reminds him of those graceful, spare shapes.

Peters explored the architecture in Korea as well. He noticed the round beams in the buildings. "I liked the shape of

> **" I like the honesty of the crafts approach. They say 'we've got it right, now that's enough'. "**

the intersections of round timbers. The Koreans use cypress, which grows straight and cuts like cheese. It was only natural that they would use the timbers round," he says. He later used this shape in his own work.

Peters returned from the Orient with a new sense of direction. "I was intrigued by folkcraft. I like the honesty of the crafts approach. They say 'we've got it right, now that's enough.'"

As a result, "I rebelled against the clinical look of industrial design and came back to my first love—wood. I started moving into solid construction and making special joints. And so I'd returned to my roots."

Peters had "become hooked on wood" during his childhood, when he had had a brisk business making and selling model Spitfire airplanes fashioned from tree branches. He credits his grandfather, an inventor, for giving him an ability to solve

constructional problems. His father, a metal worker and amateur painter "who saw beauty in the most unusual things", indirectly encouraged him to see wood as a source of inspiration for furniture.

As a material, wood has rewarded him by adapting to his design needs. For example he is working on two projects at the same time. One is the furnishings for a 12th century stone chapel that will be simple and plainly made. Another is a corporate reception desk, which will be modern—slick and smooth. With wood, he can accomplish both, although he says "I prefer the 12th century church."

"There is a difference between having real design quality, and being over-fussy". He refers again to the Korean esthetic. "Take the finish for example. The Koreans didn't fuss with that. It doesn't have to do with tools. It's a way of thinking."

His plans for a piece of furniture originate practically in the log. He buys mostly unsawn local woods; only 30 percent of his timber is exotic, he says. He then has the logs milled at a friend's timber yard, where he can supervise. "One can make decisions while the log is cut. I can ask for specific sizes and grain direction. It takes time at the beginning, but I never have to chase around for the right wood later on."

The majority of his work is one-of-a-kind commissioned pieces. "I enjoy working with people. We bounce ideas off each other. And I quite like having things to knock against, like space or budget restrictions. I think it's a healthy thing.

Peters employs three craftsmen in his shop—the youngest, a 16-year-old apprentice. He makes periodic forays into London, and returned to the Orient once again in 1981. His future plans include more trips to the East and perhaps the writing of another book. "I've achieved everything I've wanted to do. The only thing I have left to do is to improve my work," he says.

Ashley Cartwright

Ashley Cartwright is one of the few designer/craftsmen involved in making garden furniture. He is in fact the only one on the British Crafts Council's index listed as working in that area, although about half of his work is also in cabinetmaking.

Educated at Kingston College of Art and at the Royal College of Art in furniture design, he went to work for John Makepeace (see page 79), then based at Farnborough Barn in Oxfordshire, in 1973. Although he had experimented with a number of materials while at Kingston before homing in on wood while at the RCA, it was the time he spent designing and making for Makepeace that consolidated his concern for craftsmanship. "I learned an immense amount about making while I was there," he says, "And I suddenly realized how much I hadn't done at the RCA and I regretted not making more of the opportunities of learning from the craftsmen working there."

Ever since his college days he had wanted a workshop where he could design and make his own work, so when Makepeace relocated his business and set up his school in Parnham, Dorset, in 1976, Cartwright decided that the time was right to look for a place on his own. The converted stables at Brackley, which he shares with Hugh Scriven (see page 51), whom he knew at the RCA, and Tim Wells (see page 59), proved an ideal find: the

59), proved an ideal find; the right location and big enough to accommodate all their machinery and benches.

Besides exhibitions at nearby Prescote Gallery, other sources of clients have been through word of mouth, through write-ups and commissioned pieces in magazines and through the Crafts Council's Index. As a result, most of his work is commissioned, which he prefers because he enjoys tackling the specific problems involved. He says, "The thing that I really get most interest and excitement out of is dealing with finding a workable and visual solution to a design problem. What's important to me is the sense of something having a presence, something that works physically and visually."

Although there are relationships between the ideas behind his garden furniture and his cabinet work, the pieces themselves reflect very different working methods. "There is a much more earthy, dynamic and faster approach to making garden furniture," he says. "It's a more direct way of working in which the bandsaw really comes into its own for cutting and creating shapes."

The timber is often left rough-hewn and the pieces built into simple, apparently effortless shapes, designed to specific requirements. One such piece is

> " Then I draw, draw, draw, making marks on pages, pages and pages until something connects to the idea or the brief I've laid out for myself. "

the seating illustrated on pages 156–157. This was designed for the maze in the gardens of Grey Court, a large country house on the river Thames. The design here was influenced by the setting itself. "The design is four straight

planks joined in a chevron fashion and, where the planks connect, the joint is a confusion, so there is a small maze within the seating itself."

Cartwright has exploited elm for his garden furniture because it resists rotting (it was used to make drainpipes years ago), and is still available despite the decimation of trees in Britain by Dutch elm disease. For cabinet-making he prefers the lighter-coloured maple and ash.

When working on commissions, Cartwright believes it is vital to visit the site and to draw the clients into the creative process. He then waits for a couple of weeks for ideas to germinate before starting on the actual designs. "Then I draw, draw, draw," he says, "making marks on pages and pages and pages until something starts to connect to the idea or the brief I've laid out for myself." He then goes on to make a full perspective drawing to show to the client, but although he does make models, "they are usually fairly quick and seldom take longer than half an hour."

Cartwright has just completed his largest cabinet-work commission to date, a thirty-two seat conference table for St. Hilda's College at Oxford University, an important and well-publicized job for which he used Tim Wells's help in the construction. He does not feel precious about having other people work on his designs, though he is eager to remain in control during the making, when decisions often are made.

Although he has no precise long term plans, he is happy to continue the present mixture of designing and making. He also teaches part-time at Rycotewood School and at John Makepeace's school at Parnham. Teaching he feels is important for a variety of reasons: "I don't think of teaching as just a tail-end tag that can be disregarded. It is important for the discussions, the contracts, the sense of regeneration and the change of getting out of the workshop."

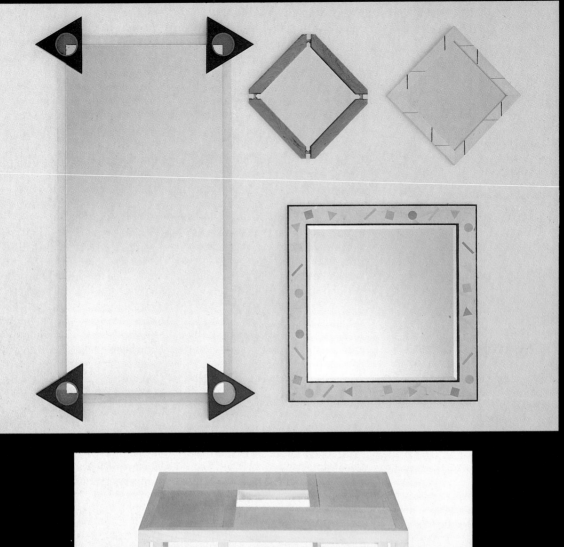

opposite, top (clockwise): **Paul Connell's** mirror features four triangular clips with glassed-in disks. See pages 142-143; **Anthony Thompson's** mirror has a gap left between miters in the frame. See page 145; **Petra Gomann's** mirror frame is shot through with inlaid colored woods. See page 144; **Toby Winteringham's** mirror frame is dotted with floating geometric shapes. See page 146.

above: **Ron Carter's** hat and coat stand is made with the utmost simplicity, with just a hint of a hook at the ends of each arm. See page 147.

opposite, bottom: **Jonathan Baulkwill's** revolving bookcase is for the armchair reader to keep his books at his elbow. The cube is lightened by the internal spokework and by the square holes that pierce the top and middle. See pages 140-141.

Ronald Carter

When Ronald Carter says, "I'm more for the simple life, myself," he is not describing himself as a country craftsman working in bucolic solitude. Carter is one of the most prolific designers of furniture in England, and has won scores of awards and honors. He has divided his career between consulting in the furniture industry and being a part-time tutor of furniture at the Royal College of Art, where he taught many of this book's contributors, including the author.

What he is describing instead is the apparent simplicity of his designs and his wish to avoid "pyrotechnics in timber." His first concern is with design. To him, "making skills are a means to an end. I can make these things as well as the next man, but I never make a thing for the thing's sake." And so he spends his week in his second floor office in Covent Garden, where he has been working since 1974, and only sees his workshop on the weekends, when he visits his country house in Oxfordshire.

Carter says that as a boy he wanted to be an architect, but for lack of £30 annual tuition he was sent to study the jewelry trade at a junior school of art with an intense fine arts curriculum. His professors urged him to become a painter, but he did not think he was good enough. He still paints when he has the time, however.

At college in the early 1950s, he studied interior design, but when he entered the Royal College of Art in London to follow up his studies, there was no interior design course, and so he moved on to furniture design. Among his teachers was David Pye, one of the finest wood craftsmen in Britain, who has "an infectious enthusiams for quality of design. It was an absolute revelation," Carter says. "In those days, the furniture industry in Britain was in a terrible state. The Danes were flying high. The students believed that it was a simple task to go in, sort it out and revolutionize it." Carter has been oriented to industry ever since.

Afterwards he went to New York City as a staff designer for Corning Glass Works, chosen from the RCA as a talented young designer who could apply form and detail. After a year he came back to teach at the Birmingham College of Art, and he worked as a freelance designer in Birmingham and in London. Finally he came to London in 1956 to begin tutoring at the Royal College of Art. By 1960 he was in business and was one of the first designers of mass-produced fitted storage furniture.

In 1974 he was appointed a Royal Designer for Industry by the Royal Society of Arts, which puts him in the company of 100 designers who have been so

---

> *" I never make a thing for the thing's sake. "*

---

honored, including Alvar Aalto and Charles Eames. He has made furniture for a long list of organizations including the British Broadcasting Corporation, Holy Trinity Church in London and St John's College in Cambridge. He has also made domestic furniture for clients such as the art collector Lord Rayne.

Since 1980, Carter has been in partnership with Peter Miles, and their company produced Carter's designs in this book. The company, located in Derbyshire makes high quality furniture for the retail and contract markets and for commission.

His methods of designing are loosely structured. "I've never been a great mathematician," he says. "I prefer to make it and try it out." Often, the capability of the factory that will produce the furniture affects his designs. In first designing the line for Peter Miles, he was uncertain of how his new factory would be equipped and what skills would be available to make his furniture. So he kept his new designs as simple as possible. Now that the factory is to be fitted with a lathe, he wants to make turned versions of some of his old designs.

Carter says he is never satisfied with his designs and is continually revising them. The revisions sometimes produce successful designs that seem to violate all the rules. The Liverpool bench on page 77 breaks all the anthropometric rules, he says, because its back is vertical and its seat uncushioned. And yet people like to sit on it because it looks inviting. In reference to chairs, he paraphrases the American architect, Philip Johnson: "If you like a thing well enough, you'll find a way of sitting on it."

In the future, Carter says he would like to re-establish himself in the mass furniture market, in what is known as flat-pack or knock-down furniture. "There is a need for someone to make more of a contribution in that area. There's no reason why it can't be very good indeed." Similarly, he would like to design lines of furniture for companies interested in upgrading their existing products.

He is encouraged to see "some young enthusiasts among the furniture makers who are becoming involved in the industry. This is where the changes are going to come from." Of himself, he expects "more of the same, only better."

David Colwell

"As far as craftsmanship goes," says David Colwell, "there are some things that I am fairly good at, but I am certainly not a craftsman first and foremost, by any means. I've always been interested in manufacture more than in craftsmanship."

Although he now concentrates most of his energies on small-scale batch production of wooden chairs, Colwell's career has been far removed from that of the traditional craftsman.

He trained in furniture design at Kingston College of Art in Surrey and at the Royal College of Art in London, but at both places he worked almost exclusively in plastic and steel, not wood. After graduating from the RCA in 1969, he built up a highly successful design practice in London designing commercial interiors and winning contracts from some of the giants in British industry. He also designed film sets and worked on special effects for advertising and for feature films.

His firm, Trannon, came about through what Colwell describes as a complete set of coincidences. In 1978, he rented a house in Wales to do some work on chair design. He liked the neighbourhood and bought an old schoolhouse in the heart of rural Wales, which he has converted into his home and his workshop and from which he and his two

assistants now turn out a range of six different items: four chairs and two tables.

Trannon embodies Colwell's search for a new and more appropriate system of production to what he sees as the wasteful technologies of the mass-market furniture industry. "In terms of the whole conservation issue," he says, "the low-energy requirement of working in timber, as opposed to working in plastic or metal, is important to me. The system that I favour is one where you use low energy and high labour content in order to make something which is going to last for longer, which means you're going to get more value out of it."

His preference for young, unseasoned ash also reflects his concern for appropriateness. It is strong, impact-resistant, comparatively cheap and ideal for steam-bending. It also grows quickly. "I make sure not to use very much material in the chairs I design," he emphasizes. "And the fact that ash is a fast-grown tree is important from an ecological point of view. It can be grown commercially in a way that most timbers can't be."

Nevertheless Colwell believes that to develop alternative means of production, he must build on his experience in industry, and not turn his back on it. To do so would, in any case, be out of character for a designer who includes among his influences automobile-designer Alec Issigonis, the creator of the Austin Mini. Colwell regards the Mini as a prime example of a design that uses a technology appropriate to the product. "The brilliance of the Mini was in its design, which combined sophisticated engineering with compact size at a reasonable price," he says. "The design was making-oriented, determined by the processes of pressed metal, rather than styling. And it was done by an engineer, not a designer. What I try to do is similar. I try to let the object be itself."

Another example from

industry that he is fond of citing is the bicycle. "A bicycle is very, very close to what you want from furniture," he says. "Minute variations on a standard object in the hand-built end of the market, which is the sharp end of design development, produce a very high-performance object. I like to think that my own furniture is similar."

All the elements of his furniture are cut and shaped by machines, but are then assembled and finished by hand. He says: "The machining we do is not particularly interesting. What is interesting is the steam bending, which few people do to our scale. We bend unseasoned, freshly

> **"** *A bicycle is very, very close to what you want from furniture.* **"**

harvested wood and so the process is more agricultural. There is a flow of materials."

He generally works in batches of up to fifty pieces at a time, half of which are kept in stock and half supplied to order. Although he sells some of his work through shops, much of it is still supplied to customers direct from Trannon.

His knowledge of the economics of production has persuaded him to limit the range of his designs in order to get the maximum cost effectiveness out of his investment.

"I'm interested in economics of scale, making the scale more harmonious with the manufacturing process," he says, adding that he has modelled some of his processes and philosophy on those of Michael Thonet, the 19th century pioneer of mass-produced steam-bent furniture.

Of the future, he says: "I think that teaching will play a slightly more important role. It seems to me that if one discovers anything at all from doing something like this, it is a pity not to pass some of it on if you believe in it."

David Field's bed, designed for London advertising
executive Bob Maclaren, satisfies his request that
the mattress seem to float off the ground. The
headboard is slightly angled to serve as a backing for
the pillows. Two built-in sidetables are set at the right
height for the Tizio bedside reading light. See pages
148-149.

Petra Gomann/Anthony Thompson

The careers and styles of Petra Gomann and Anthony Thompson make a study in similarities and differences.

Both went to the London College of Furniture at about the same time, Gomann completing her course in 1981, Thompson his in 1982, and both are determined to make their living solely through their craft. To that end, both had their own workshops even while at college, and since leaving three years ago they have shared the same workshop in south London, just across the Thames from the old heart of the British furniture industry in London's East End.

They have even both been influenced by the same school of simplicity and austerity in furniture design, a tradition that begins at the turn of the century with Josef Hoffmann and Eileen

> **" The moment I realize there is no challenge in something, I drop it. "**
> Petra Gomann

Grey and continues on through the De Stijl movement and the Bauhaus to the contemporary classics of modern Italian and Scandinavian design. They share too a horror of what Gomann calls the "klinker klunk" detailing of eclecticism, although

Thompson, playing the devil's advocate, admits to being tempted to produce "an unbelievably expensive, totally overcrafted chest of drawers."

However, while their similarities have helped to support them, their differences of character and background have still allowed each to develop as a designer/craftsman in his and her own right. They never set up together as a formal partnership and although they continue to work together occasionally on large-scale projects such as custom-made kitchens, they have always felt it important for each to build up their own network of clients and to work on their own projects, for both have strong attitudes towards their work.

Thompson studied engineering at Cambridge University before going to the LCF and this early training is reflected in his design thinking: "A piece of furniture is a very functional item. The structure isn't there solely to hold it together; it has a relationship to the form. When I design a piece, I try to make the structure part of the way it looks."

For her part, Gomann's attitudes to design are characterized by an almost ruthless pursuit of simplicity and an obsessive quest for perfection. When she arrived in England from Germany in 1971, she initially took up a series of secretarial jobs that left her

creatively frustrated. "The moment I realize there is no challenge in something," she says, "I drop it." The LCF finally provided her with the challenge she needed. As the only woman in her course, she had to overcome the sexism of the machine-shop. With no background in woodworking, "I had immense difficulties. Wood is so unpredictable, and if I made a little splinter in the wood, I'd spend an hour sanding it out."

So far they have worked almost exclusively in wood, partly through choice but partly too through necessity. As Thompson says, "I would like to do more metalwork, but we're

> **" When I design a piece, I try to make the structure part of the way it looks. "**
> Anthony Thompson

not set up for that, and there's the problem of small quantities which would be uneconomical. You have to design for what you are capable of making."

Their designs for the mirrors on page 72 (top) typify both their similarities and differences. Although the two are very much alike, Gomann's can be seen as an exercise in precision veneering, while Thompson's displays an engineer's interest in construction: "The joints that hold the mirror frame together developed from just sitting in the pub scribbling on beer mats and thinking about ways of putting things together, thinking about the possible ways of using one small piece of wood to join two larger pieces."

One thing they agree on is the future. Being relatively fresh out of college, they both want to work on the quality of their clients, to become better known. Above all, they are determined that they will design only what they make and make only what they design.

John Makepeace

In contrast to many of the designer/makers in this book who feel that they have a kinship with the furniture industry's production-line processes, John Makepeace is an example and a proponent of the designer-entrepreneur in wood furniture. He believes in the value of learning making skills as a part of the design training. To that purpose he started the John Makepeace School for Craftsmen in Wood in 1976.

Makepeace's life is quite different than the one he had anticipated: to enter the Church by way of Oxford University. He had always been interested in cabinetmaking, and at the age of 18, he abandoned his studies and looked for an apprenticeship in furniture making. That was in 1957, when "people were giving up such work rather than going on. But for me it was almost as much a vocation as going into the Church, and I knew I would have to make sacrifices."

Eventually he found a chance to train with cabinetmaker Keith Cooper, paying a fee of £2 a week. At the same time he took a course in woodworking, and two years later he went to Birmingham to teach. In the holidays and on weekends he produced his own furniture in a garage workshop in Warwickshire. In 1963 he bought a group of broken-down farm buildings which he converted into a house, a workshop and a gallery to show his work. During the following decade he established a thriving business, employing several craftsmen and exhibiting his work all over the world. Some of his standard products were picked up by large furniture retailers. And all along he had students working with him.

The idea of forming a school for wood craftsmen was "a lovely challenge at the back of my mind," he says. By 1976 he saw that, "no art school was going to produce a woodworker with the sensitivity that wood needs." He decided to buy Parnham House, a Tudor mansion in Dorset in which to develop his business and set up his school.

Makepeace accepts ten students a year for his two-year course. The first year is devoted to learning the nuts and bolts of

> *"The best designers are imaginative people who are highly sensitive to other people."*

woodworking, business practice and design theory. The second year develops their business philosophy. Students study marketing and accounting and they are responsible for buying their own materials and for finding clients for their projects who will pay for their work. Makepeace looks for individuals who are well-rounded and "could be successful in a variety of careers. We don't choose students just because they have a commitment to working in wood," he says. "The craftsman needs to develop a number of talents—handling people, organization, communication. The best designers are imaginative people who are highly sensitive to other people's needs." As a measure of the success of his approach, 90 percent of his students are now self-employed.

Makepeace has a separate workshop with seven craftsmen employed to produce his own work, which consists mostly of one-of-a-kind pieces commissioned by organizations and collectors. Although he has made pieces in other materials besides wood, his commitment to wood borders on devotion. "Wood calls for total concentration. It requires a spontaneous response by the maker. To determine its final form on a drawing board is unnecessarily arbitrary."

Unsurprisingly, his work is often influenced by the way a tree grows, and is characterized by flowing lines and flared, trunk-like legs. These sculptural shapes often call for daring constructions, involving the bending of difficult woods such as ebony and rosewood, using dozens of laminations. He buys complete trees and mills them into boards to keep a continuity of materials in his pieces. "I like to make individual pieces or a group of furniture from the wood of one tree," he says. He works in some 20 varieties of timber, air dried in the seasoning shed for three years outdoors, and seasons them a second time indoors.

Recently, Makepeace has been channelling his energies in a new direction, to develop a use for "small roundwood"—young trees under 20 cm/8 in in diameter which are thinned from the forest to allow the best trees to grow to maturity. Thus far they have been used mainly for firewood. He believes that this wood has useful characteristics of strength and flexibility which should be more widely exploited by the construction and furniture industries. To research the potential, he is setting up a School for Woodland Industries at the 330 acres of woodland purchased by the Trust a few miles from Parnham.

top: **Ashley Cartwright's** maze seating was designed for a garden that is itself a maze. The bench zigzags along the ground, the separate sections linked together visually by the lovely puzzle joint at each bend *(right)*. See pages 156-157.
bottom: **Ashley Cartwrights's** garden table is made of solid oak. The four broad legs sweep upward to support the top, the way a tree trunk flares up into its branches. See pages 158-159.

PROJECTS IN PRACTICE

At this stage, you should be ready to turn theory into practice; this chapter gives general instructions for making the 27 projects illustrated in colour in the preceding chapter, along with dozens of variations on those designs.

Undoubtedly, you will wish to tailor these designs to suit specific needs. You may like a design for a dining table, for example, but in fact need a coffee table or a side table. You may like the shape of a particular design, but not its finish or the colour of the wood that was used. Or you may like the general structure of a piece of furniture, but find that the prescribed dovetails are too tedious to make, or that a certain cut is beyond the capability of your machinery.

In all of these circumstances, you have the capability to alter the design to suit you. With the information in the preceding and the following chapters, you can take any of the designs presented in the following pages and

alter them to fit your needs. You can change overall heights, for example, modify the finish and even tamper with the structure. The only requirement is that you inform yourself about what is possible and what is not, and that you know what the consequences of your changes will be. Otherwise, the designs are in your hands.

You will notice that the dimensions in this chapter are given in millimetres, followed by the rough equivalent in inches. Designers tend to work in millimetres because their work is often highly precise. We have included the Imperial measurements for those who visualize sizes best in inches. But we assume that whatever system of measurement you habitually use, no measurement is final until it is checked against the work in progress. We have included for your use a conversion table from metric to Imperial units on the last page of the book, page 224.

David Field's folding table is elegant enough for a dining room and hard-working enough to use as a kitchen work surface. The whole table is made of ash; the top is plywood veneered with ash on one side and laminated on the other with Formica. It is an easy table to make. The bottom consists simply of two interlocking frames which support the hinged top. The top is held in place by a metal pin around which the top pivots. There is a simple formula for properly locating the pin so that the top will be exactly centred over the frame whether the top is opened or closed.

Anatomy of the table
The table legs and support frame are made of solid maple 18 mm thick and 75 mm wide. Four planks 685 mm long will be needed for the tall legs, and four planks 610 mm long, and 93 mm wide, for the short legs.

These are butt-jointed with biscuit joints.

The framework is mortise and tenoned into the legs, with a middle plank 25 mm thick and 100 mm wide that braces the framework and houses a pivoting pin. It is mortised and tenoned into the long rails of the frame, roughly one third of the way. Two pieces 1448 mm long, and two 800 mm long will be needed for the frame. The middle plank is also 800 mm long.

The tabletop is made of 18 mm plywood in two sections, each 750 × 1220 mm. They are held together with 3 brass dovetail hinges, inset to the laminated surface of the table. The undersurface is counter-veneered (see pages 194–195) to prevent the laminate from separating.

A brass pin 10 mm in diameter and 20 mm long is set into the middle plank and fitted into a corresponding hole in the laminated side of the

top. A strip of baise runs along the supporting edge of the frame to allow the top to pivot smoothly.

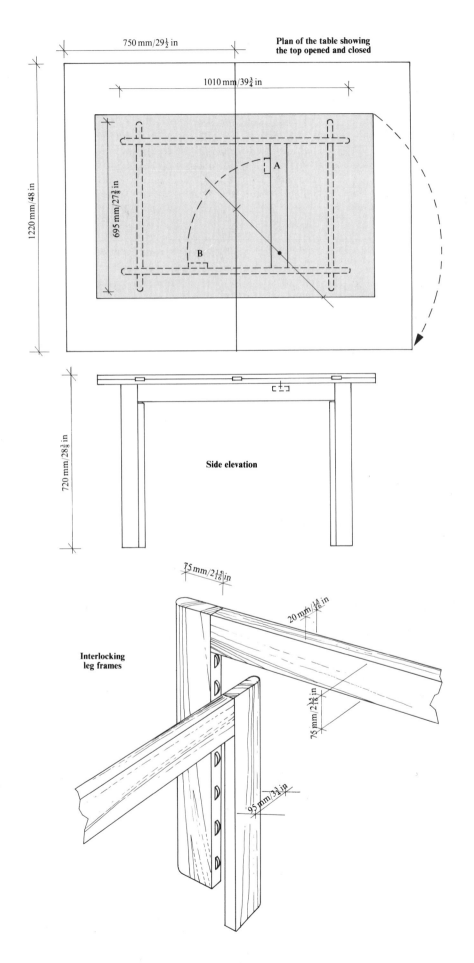

Plan of the table showing the top opened and closed

750 mm/29½ in

1010 mm/39¾ in

1220 mm/48 in

695 mm/27⅜ in

A

B

Side elevation

720 mm/28⅜ in

Interlocking leg frames

75 mm/2¹⁵⁄₁₆ in

20 mm/¹⁴⁄₁₆ in

75 mm/2¹⁵⁄₁₆ in

95 mm/3¾ in

How to make the table

First make up the legs and underframe, mortise and tenoning the corner joints. Round off and smooth the outside corners of the frames.

Make the top by cutting out the sections of the top in plywood, laminating one side in Formica and the other side in ash veneer. The edges should be lipped with ash. Hinge the two sections together with 3 dovetail hinges.

To calculate the exact position of the centre plank, the pivot pin and the pinhole, place a rod of the opened table top on the floor and centre a rod of the top closed and of the table frame over it, as shown here.

Draw the two diagonals of the large rectangle (the open top) to find the centre. Draw a line along the centre line to the edge of the small rectangle (the folded top) and another line at 45° to the same edge. The midpoint along the second line is the pivot point of the top.

Having calculated this, you can assemble the frame. Simultaneously biscuit join the frames, placing the shorter frames *within* the larger ones and mortise and tenoning the centre rail in position so that the pivot point centres on the width of the plank. Glue and C-clamp the sections and let them set. Then finish with two coats of lacquer.

Drill a hole at the pivot point to take the pivot pin and glue the metal pin in place. Then cover the pin, and the two support rails, with baise stripping to protect the table top from scratches and allow the top to pivot smoothly. Finally, set the top in position by drilling a hole in the laminated surface for the pin. Screw two 50 mm stop blocks under the table at **A** and **B** to restrict the arc of the pivoting top.

Ron Carter's circular table is a sociable table because it allows everyone sitting at it to see and talk easily to each other. This elegant example, made in solid mahogany, has a refined and rather dignified air which makes it suitable as a small boardroom table, or as a dining table. The success of the design comes from a subtle blend of structural and decorative features which are further enhanced by the striking use of a dark stain to finish the piece. Note how the use of a hexagonal frame and six legs set well back from the edges reflects the circular nature of the table, at the same time as maximizing the leg room—four legs would not have provided such a satisfactory combination. The slight chamfer cut on the edge of the top and the bold stopped chamfers running most of the way up from the floor on the outside of each leg are confident details which add further interest and soften the overall lines of the piece.

Anatomy of the table
The top is planked up from 32 mm thick mahogany boards and cut to a diameter of 1450 mm. The rails are made up of 80 × 32 mm mahogany and the legs are 75 mm square. The top is held to the base by twelve turnbuttons.

How to make the table
Plank up the mahogany boards slightly oversize and then, with the top surface face down, cut to the final diameter. To do this accurately, use a jig made of thin plywood about 250 mm longer than the radius and approximately 150 mm wide.

Attach the router base plate to one end either by screwing up through the plywood (countersinking the screw) or by using double-sided tape. Then measure the radius cf the table from the router cutter and pin the other end to the top. The router can then be

pivoted on the pin as it cuts.

To form the angle on the table's outer edge either buy the appropriate angled cutter or use a straight cutter with the router still attached to the plywood to remove most of the wood and then clean up the angle with a spokeshave.

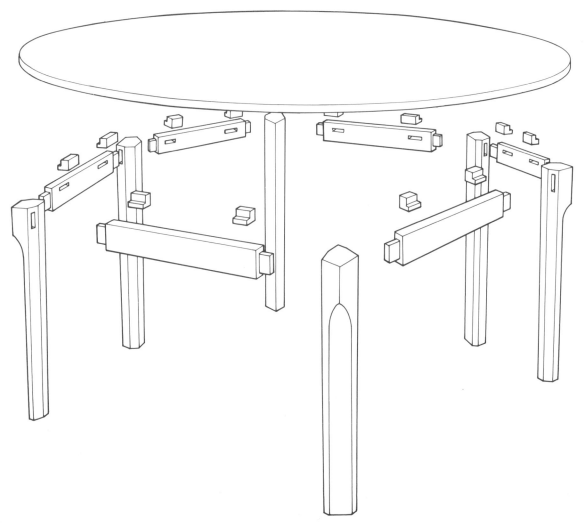

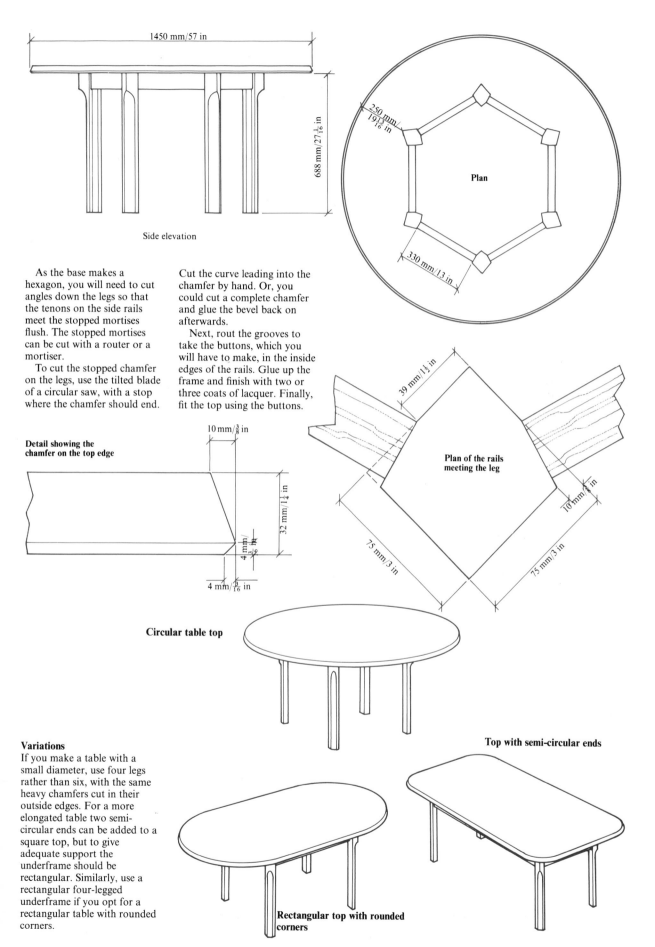

1450 mm/57 in

688 mm/27 $\frac{1}{16}$ in

Side elevation

250 mm/ 19$\frac{3}{16}$ in

330 mm/13 in

Plan

As the base makes a hexagon, you will need to cut angles down the legs so that the tenons on the side rails meet the stopped mortises flush. The stopped mortises can be cut with a router or a mortiser.

To cut the stopped chamfer on the legs, use the tilted blade of a circular saw, with a stop where the chamfer should end.

Cut the curve leading into the chamfer by hand. Or, you could cut a complete chamfer and glue the bevel back on afterwards.

Next, rout the grooves to take the buttons, which you will have to make, in the inside edges of the rails. Glue up the frame and finish with two or three coats of lacquer. Finally, fit the top using the buttons.

Detail showing the chamfer on the top edge

10 mm/$\frac{3}{8}$ in

32 mm/1$\frac{1}{4}$ in

4 mm/ $\frac{3}{16}$ in

4 mm/$\frac{3}{16}$ in

39 mm/1$\frac{1}{2}$ in

Plan of the rails meeting the leg

10 mm/$\frac{3}{8}$ in

75 mm/3 in

75 mm/3 in

Circular table top

Variations

If you make a table with a small diameter, use four legs rather than six, with the same heavy chamfers cut in their outside edges. For a more elongated table two semi-circular ends can be added to a square top, but to give adequate support the underframe should be rectangular. Similarly, use a rectangular four-legged underframe if you opt for a rectangular table with rounded corners.

Top with semi-circular ends

Rectangular top with rounded corners

85

DINING TABLES / Ron Carter

A drop leaf table has a number of advantages over other types of dining table. Its surface area can be quickly and easily increased simply by raising one or both leaves which are then supported on gate legs that pivot outwards from the frame. The leaves fold down to store unobtrusively against the sides of the centre section, making the table highly practical where everyday space is limited.

Ron Carter's table has beautifully clean lines and has the advantage of being simple to make. Here 32 mm thick solid ash has been used with two semi-circular ends that flap down on brass hinges.

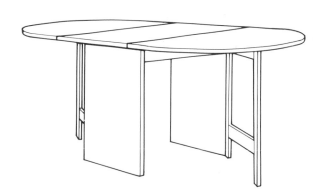

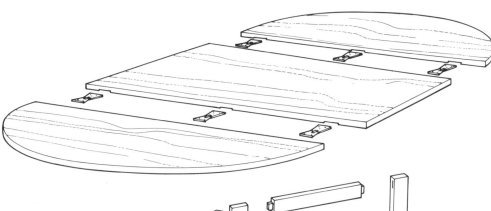

Anatomy of the table

The top consists of three parts: a rectangular centre section 1308 × 510 mm and two semi-circular leaves each with a radius of 654 mm. These are each connected to the top with three dovetailed flap hinges. The frame is made of two planked up boards with two crossrails running between them at the top.

Turnbutton fixings are used to join the centre section of the table to the base structure to allow the top to expand and contract across its width. The gate legs, consisting of very simple frames, which pivot on butt hinges hung on diagonally opposite sides of the base structure.

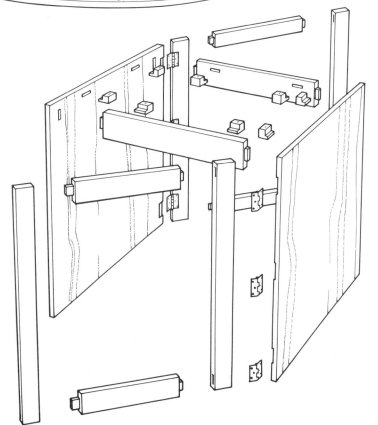

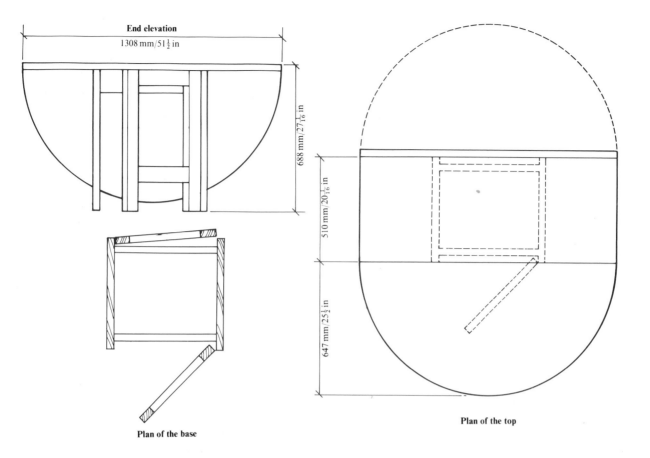

End elevation
1308 mm/51½ in

688 mm/27 1/16 in

Plan of the base

510 mm/20 1/16 in

647 mm/25½ in

Plan of the top

How to make the table
Plank up the three sections forming the top of the table and use a router to cut a radius around the two end pieces, forming a semi-circle. Also use the router to cut a chamfer along the outside edges, if preferred. Lay the sections out in position face down and hold them together with sash clamps. Mark the position of the hinges, then set them into the underside and fasten them in place.

Having planked up the side, cut the mortise and tenon joints to hold the crossrails and then rout the grooves for the turnbuttons.

Make up the two frames for the gate legs, again using mortises and tenons. Hinge these to the diagonally opposite inside edges of the base legs so that they shut to form a neat box. Next assemble and glue up the base structure, giving it two or three coats of lacquer. Finally fit the top section and leaves over the base section and join them together with the turnbuttons. The gate legs will need to open about 45° to provide adequate support for the leaves, so screw small blocks of ash to the undersides of the leaves when the legs are pivoted out to this angle. These will act as stops.

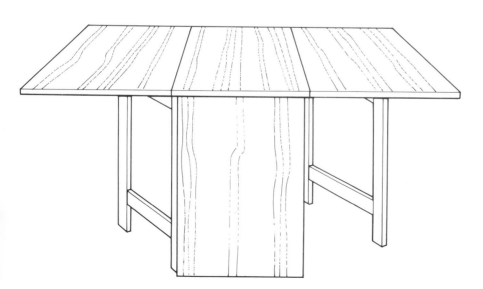

Variation
The proportions of the top can be altered to any size so long as the base corresponds to the folding positions. This variation, however, is based on the same dimensions as the table described above except that the semi-circular folding ends have been replaced by rectangular ends.

DINING TABLES / Hugh Scriven

It is the unique unconventional wider structure of **Hugh Scriven**'s dining table which sets it apart from the ordinary. At first glance it seems that the designer has set out deliberately to shock by creating a table that almost appears to defy gravity. Yet it is because of the outward splayed legs, which do not directly bear the weight of the table, that the table is remarkably practical, providing good leg and foot room for the persons sitting around the table.

Made from cherry, the table is relatively easy to construct using mortise and tenon joints. And the heavy chamfers on the legs give rise to interesting details particularly where they meet the central upright and the three chamfers all meet at one point. The chamfers on this table illustrate how such detailing can make a structure based on straight-edged timbers take on a flowing, almost curvilinear apperance.

Because of the forces put on some of the mortise and tenon joints, it is necessary to dowel the tenons fairly close to the shoulder, as well as to glue them securely.

How to make the table
Glue the top together, if possible book matching the planks down the centre; and use stopped plywood tongues in the joints.

Next cut the frame pieces to size and then cut all the

mortises and tenons. The angled mortises are cut using a block sawn to the correct angle, with the piece to be mortised clamped on top of it on the mortiser. At mitres A and B in the central diagram 4 cut in a 9 mm plywood tongue.

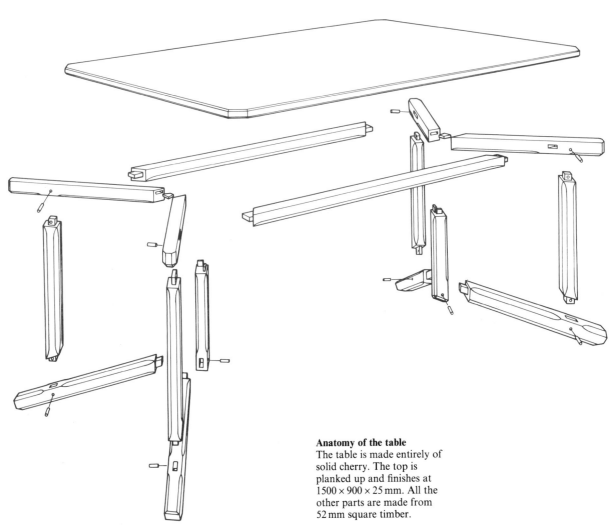

Anatomy of the table
The table is made entirely of solid cherry. The top is planked up and finishes at 1500 × 900 × 25 mm. All the other parts are made from 52 mm square timber.

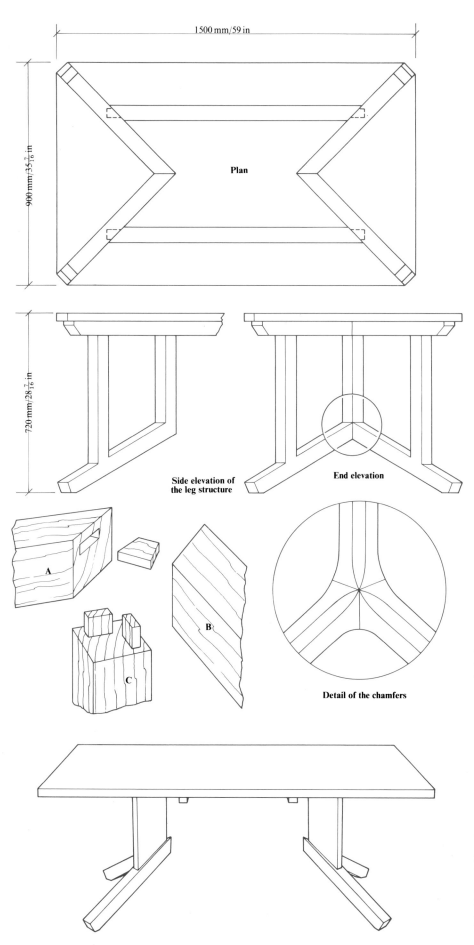

Plan

1500 mm/59 in

900 mm/35 7/16 in

720 mm/28 7/16 in

**Side elevation of
the leg structure**

End elevation

A

B

C

Detail of the chamfers

The short upright (C) has two tenons at the top; one goes into A, the other into B.

Next cut all the chamfers down the edges, being careful to stop them before they reach the ends. Glue up the two end frames starting with sections A and B and when these are dry glue them to the three uprights and two legs. Where there are angled pieces to glue up use clamping blocks. When the frames have been assembled, glue them to the two long rails. Remember to peg all the tenons near the shoulders with oak dowels.

Finally, clean up the frame and apply two coats of lacquer before fixing it to the top with expansion plates screwed to the side rails and to the top.

Variation

This alternative foregoes the use of chamfers along the frame section and instead leaves the edges clear and sharp. The effect is to give the piece a more angular look that some people may prefer.

There are few pieces making up the uprights. These are mitred together in pairs and through-tenoned into the top with wedges banged in to hold them secure. It is the same technique used by Floris van den Broecke on his occasional table (see pages 110–111) and makes a decorative feature of the joints on the table surface. Remember to arrange the planking of the top section so that the tenons are not driven through a join between two boards.

DESKS / Jonathan Baulkwill

Apart from the clean, elegant lines of **Jonathan Baulkwill**'s attractive writing desk, it is noteworthy for the ingenious way it is constructed and how its structure is able to cope with movements in the solid maple from which it is made.

Essentially, it is a craftsman's piece requiring a high degree of skill and accuracy to assemble. Dovetailing features strongly in its making.

Because the design calls for the grain of the maple to run across the top of the desk and *down*, rather than *along* the sides, which is usual practice, the top and sides expand and contract in the same direction. However, this arrangement causes problems when it comes to joining the sides to the legs, but this is neatly overcome by the inclusion of loose tongues, which are dovetailed into the sides along their lengths, and into rails. The rails are mortised into the legs, and thus support the top.

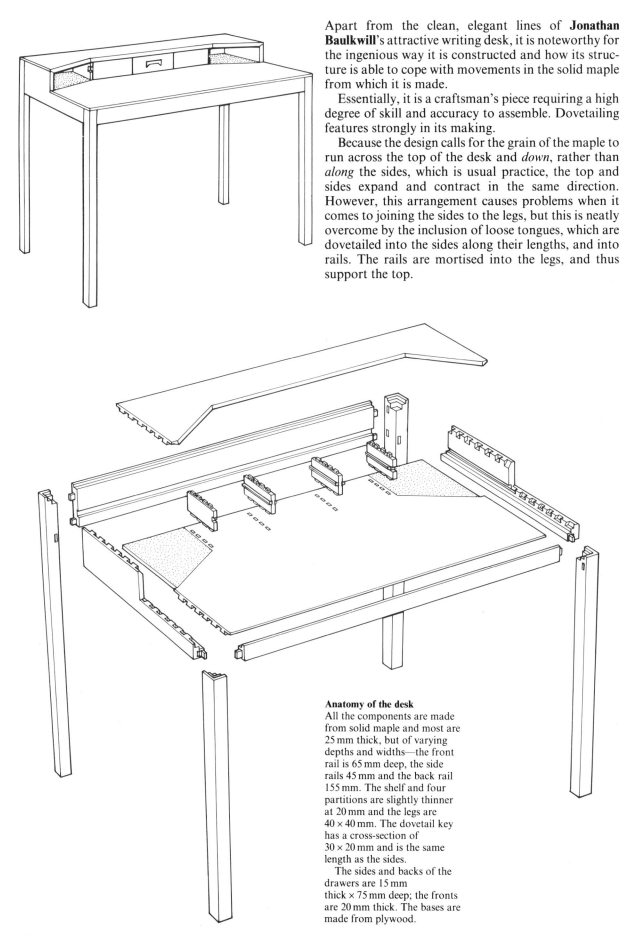

Anatomy of the desk
All the components are made from solid maple and most are 25 mm thick, but of varying depths and widths—the front rail is 65 mm deep, the side rails 45 mm and the back rail 155 mm. The shelf and four partitions are slightly thinner at 20 mm and the legs are 40 × 40 mm. The dovetail key has a cross-section of 30 × 20 mm and is the same length as the sides.

The sides and backs of the drawers are 15 mm thick × 75 mm deep; the fronts are 20 mm thick. The bases are made from plywood.

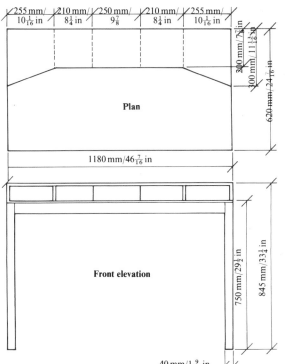

255 mm/ 10 1/16 in | 210 mm/ 8 1/4 in | 250 mm/ 9 7/8 in | 210 mm/ 8 1/4 in | 255 mm/ 10 1/16 in

300 mm/ 11 13/16 in
300 mm/ 11 13/16 in
620 mm/ 24 7/16 in

Plan

1180 mm/46 7/8 in

Front elevation

750 mm/29 1/2 in

845 mm/33 1/4 in

40 mm/1 9/16 in

Finally cut the mortise and tenons for fitting the dividers in the shelf unit.

Now the gluing up can begin. First glue the top to the sides, making sure that the side rail can still move. Then glue the legs to the back, front and side rails, remembering only to glue the front tenons of the side rails. Put the dividers of the shelf unit in dry and line the base of the outside pockets with leather. Now glue the shelf and dividers to the top and sides.

Make up the drawers using lap dovetails at the front and dovetails at the back. Set the plywood bottom in a routed groove. The drawers slide on runners which are screwed into a 5 mm deep groove on either side of the dividers.

The desk can be finished off with two coats of lacquer.

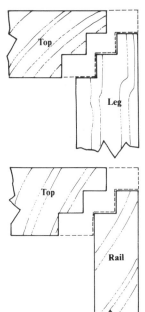

Top

Leg

Top

Rail

How to make the desk

Plank up the tops of the desk and shelf, leaving enough extra length at each end to trim off the sides. Then start by connecting the back, front and side rails to the legs.

Rout a dovetail groove along the bottom inside face of the sides and then make similar grooves in the separate rails, which should be tenoned each end to slot into the mortises cut in the legs. The rails and sides form a channel into which the loose tongue can be slotted. Profile the tongue with a router to match the profile of the channel (see the detail far right).

When you come to assemble the piece, only glue the front tenon and leave the back tenon and tongue dry to allow the top and sides to move along the side rails. Next cut secret lap dovetails on the sides, desk top and shelf, and cut housings along the sides at the back where the top meets them. Also cut a corresponding housing in the back to take the top. Then cut rebates along the top edges of the back and front rail and along the bottom front edge of the desk top and the bottom back edge of the shelf. The sections then come together in a double rebate and the top of the legs will have to be rebated to accommodate this (see diagrams far right). The back and front rails are mortised and tenoned into the legs.

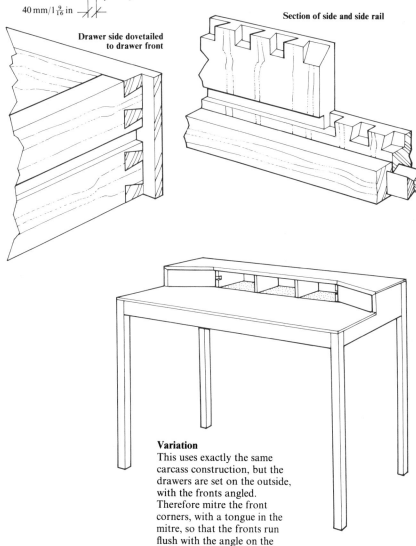

Drawer side dovetailed to drawer front

Section of side and side rail

Variation

This uses exactly the same carcass construction, but the drawers are set on the outside, with the fronts angled. Therefore mitre the front corners, with a tongue in the mitre, so that the fronts run flush with the angle on the ends of the shelf.

DESKS / Floris van den Broecke

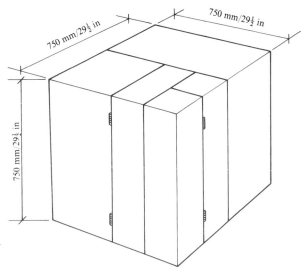

750 mm/29½ in
750 mm/29½ in
750 mm/29½ in

Floris Van den Broecke's ingenious cube desk looks as complicated as a Chinese puzzle or a Rubik's cube, and it might seem too daunting to attempt. But its principle could not be simpler: take a cube, divide it in half, divide that half, then divide it a third time and then a fourth. The result is five parts hinged together that pack up neatly, or unfurl to take any shape you need. It even can be made to open out from the right or from the left.

Each segment of the cube is loaded with storage spaces; the smallest pair, filled with shelves, can be opened out without disturbing the rest of the desk. There are two pull-out work surfaces.

Anatomy of the desk
The desk is a 750 mm cube, made of 18 mm thick medium density fibreboard (MDF). It is subdivided four times, and 1.5 mm is left as a gap between each of the five subdivisions. All vertical dimensions are the same; the top panels must be laid on and the side panels set in. The carcass is biscuit-jointed together.

Inside the subdivisions of the cube are drawers, adjustable shelves supported by magic wires (see page 215), two leather-covered work surfaces that pull out on filing cabinet drawer runners, a tilt-out bin and some pigeon holes. The drawers are side-hung and made of 18 mm thick mahogany joined with dovetails with a false front that can be finished before assembly and screwed on. The large shelves are covered with protective textured black vinyl. The shelves and sliding trays are made of 18 mm MDF. The pigeon holes are made of 9 mm MDF.

There are 12 twin wheel castors, 65 mm in diameter, placed under the sections of the cube so that they can be rolled around smoothly. Each segment is hinged to its neighbour using three, 50 mm solid drawn brass butt hinges at each join—a total of 15 hinges. Extra-long hinge screws will be needed to hold in the MDF. The cabinet is held closed with five magnetic catches.

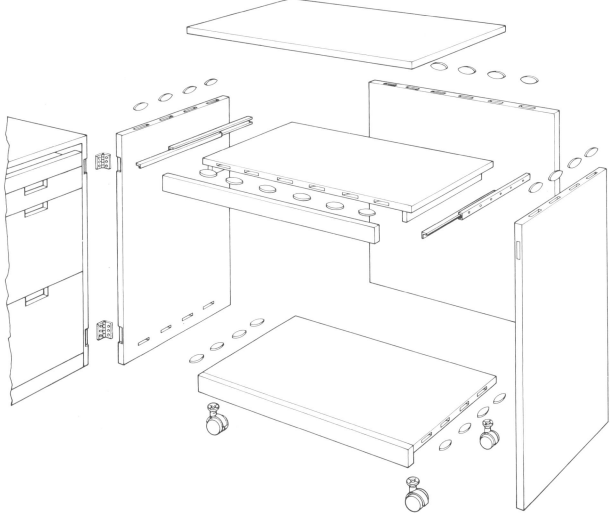

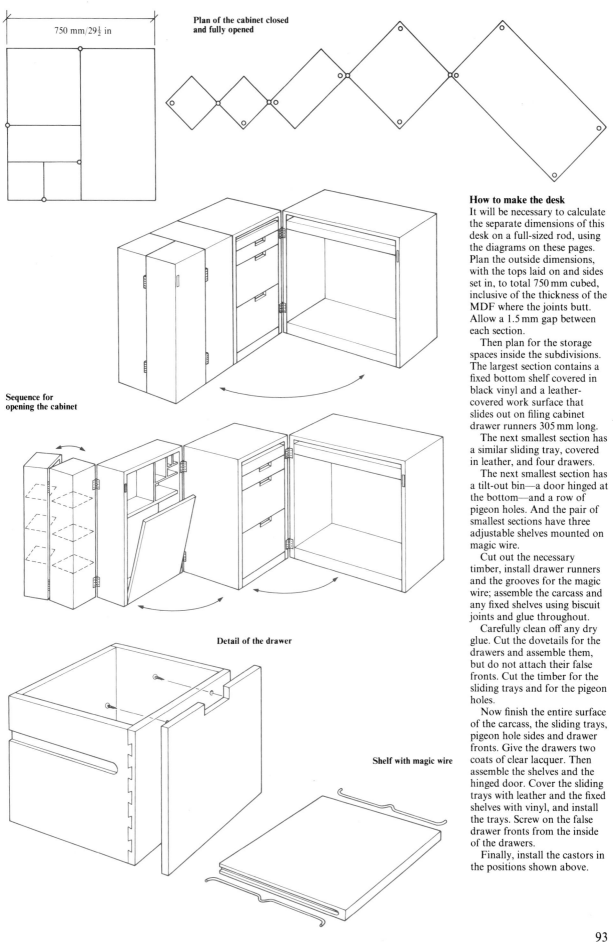

750 mm/29½ in

Plan of the cabinet closed and fully opened

Sequence for opening the cabinet

Detail of the drawer

Shelf with magic wire

How to make the desk

It will be necessary to calculate the separate dimensions of this desk on a full-sized rod, using the diagrams on these pages. Plan the outside dimensions, with the tops laid on and sides set in, to total 750 mm cubed, inclusive of the thickness of the MDF where the joints butt. Allow a 1.5 mm gap between each section.

Then plan for the storage spaces inside the subdivisions. The largest section contains a fixed bottom shelf covered in black vinyl and a leather-covered work surface that slides out on filing cabinet drawer runners 305 mm long.

The next smallest section has a similar sliding tray, covered in leather, and four drawers.

The next smallest section has a tilt-out bin—a door hinged at the bottom—and a row of pigeon holes. And the pair of smallest sections have three adjustable shelves mounted on magic wire.

Cut out the necessary timber, install drawer runners and the grooves for the magic wire; assemble the carcass and any fixed shelves using biscuit joints and glue throughout.

Carefully clean off any dry glue. Cut the dovetails for the drawers and assemble them, but do not attach their false fronts. Cut the timber for the sliding trays and for the pigeon holes.

Now finish the entire surface of the carcass, the sliding trays, pigeon hole sides and drawer fronts. Give the drawers two coats of clear lacquer. Then assemble the shelves and the hinged door. Cover the sliding trays with leather and the fixed shelves with vinyl, and install the trays. Screw on the false drawer fronts from the inside of the drawers.

Finally, install the castors in the positions shown above.

DESKS / Peter St. Hill

Here is a desk which confidently breaks with tradition by having a split-level top, made of medium density fibreboard (MDF) with a maple veneer, rather than an uninterrupted work surface. Space permitting, it can be worked at from either side; the lower level is at the right height for using a typewriter or word-processor, while the higher level is best for writing. See pages 20–21 for more on table heights.

The desk makes a particular feature of the exposed structure, which resembles two tables half-lapped over each other. And there is an interesting use of joints. If preferred, the front rail running underneath the higher leaf can be made inconspicuous by stopping it a quarter of the distance from each end. Apart from giving the higher leaf the appearance of floating it also improves access to the back of the lower work surface.

A three-drawer unit is suspended from the lower leaf while the cabinet on the opposite side is freestanding on castors. This means that where space is restricted the desk can stand against a wall and the cabinet simply can be wheeled round to the lower side.

St. Hill has painted the storage units pale pink and sky blue to harmonize with the pale maple.

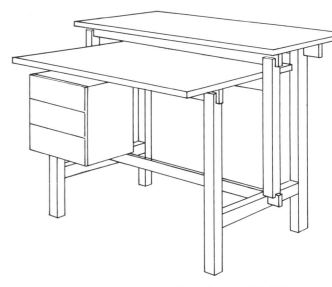

Anatomy of the desk
The desk tops can be made from 18 mm thick fibreboard or chipboard edged with solid maple lippings and covered with maple veneer. The higher leaf is 900 × 500 mm, the lower one 1090 × 600 mm. The six legs and two side rails are made from 45 × 45 mm solid maple, while the crossrail into the side rail at the bottom, the forward crossrail underneath the lower top and the two crossrails underneath the higher top are all made from 45 × 18 mm maple. The back crossrail underneath the lower top is 45 × 23 mm.

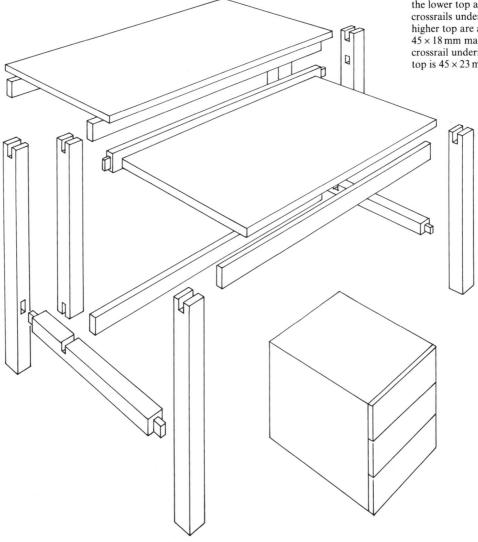

Front elevation

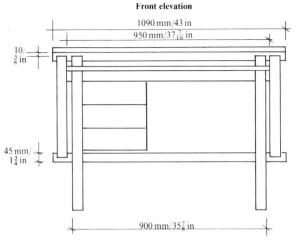

1090 mm/43 in

950 mm/37 7/16 in

10/ 3/8 in

45 mm/ 1 3/4 in

900 mm/35 7/8 in

Side elevation

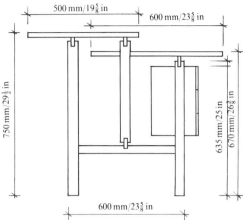

500 mm/19 5/8 in

600 mm/23 5/8 in

750 mm/29 1/2 in

635 mm/25 in

670 mm/26 3/8 in

600 mm/23 5/8 in

How to make the desk

Glue maple lippings to the edges of the fibreboard tops, taking them through the corners rather than mitring them. Then cover with maple veneer and finish with two coats of lacquer. Next cut the halvings and mortise and tenons in the lengths of solid sycamore to make up the base frame. Glue up, and prefinish if you prefer to do this at this stage.

Cut the slabs of MDF to form the carcasses of the storage units and fix in the drawer runners by gluing them into 5 mm deep grooves cut with a router. Then biscuit joint the sections together.

The drawers are made using housing and mortice and tenon joints, but before gluing them up, spray the fronts at the same time you finish the carcasses and door of the cabinet.

Screw through from the inside of the drawer carcass to hold the unit in place against one of the legs of the frame and the front rail.

Finally screw castors onto the inset base of the cabinet. These will virtually be concealed by the sides, back and door of the carcass.

Exploded drawer cabinet

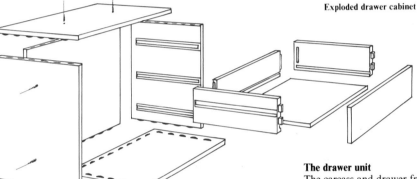

The drawer unit

The carcass and drawer fronts are made of 18 mm thick fibreboard, while solid maple 15 mm thick is used for the sides and back and 20 × 5 mm for the drawer runners. The drawer bottoms are made of 6 mm thick birch plywood.

Exploded freestanding cabinet

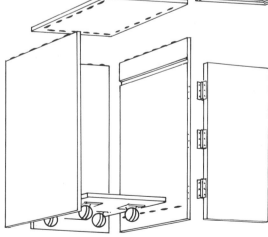

Jointing detail for the base section

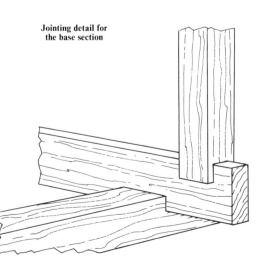

The cabinet

The carcass, drawer front and door are made from 18 mm thick fibreboard, while solid maple is used for the 15 mm thick sides and backs and the 20 × 15 mm drawer runners. The bottom is 6 mm thick birch plywood. Three 30 mm long brass hinges are needed.

95

DESKS / Ron Carter

There is a hint of the Victorian schoolroom and the teacher's desk in **Ron Carter**'s simple design—practical because it is so versatile. Made from a mixture of veneered and solid mahogany, stained very dark, the desk contains three useful drawers, the centre one lockable, set inconspicuously in the front rail, and two drawer boxes. As these are not fixed, they can easily be removed or repositioned, so there is some flexibility in how the work surface is arranged. The upstanding surround prevents papers and pens from falling off and contains the work surface, making it an ideal desk for personal correspondence, and either domestic chores such as book keeping.

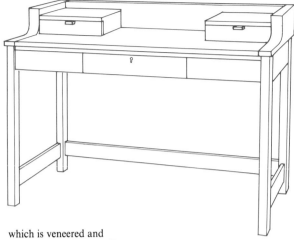

Anatomy of the desk
The desk is made of a veneered plywood top 20 mm thick and lipped on the front edge; the lipping is mortise and teroned to the front legs. There are two side surrounds, cut to a curved profile and joined to a back upstand—all of solid timber 55 mm thick and 150 mm wide.

The frame is of solid timber 100 mm thick, with one long back rail and two short side rails. The rails are mortise and tenoned into legs 45 mm square and 698 mm tall. Three bracing rails 70 mm wide are mortise and tenoned near the base of the legs at the sides and the back. The carcass base is cut from 18 mm plywood,

which is veneered and rebated to the frame rails.

The drawers are dovetailed, with handles dovetailed into the fronts of the box drawers. Underhanging lips at the bottoms of each flush-faced desk drawer act as handles. The central desk drawer is fitted with a small drawer lock.

How to make the desk
Cut the top out of the 20 mm thick plywood and glue a 10 mm wide lipping onto the front edge. Then apply the mahogany veneer. Next cut the profile on the side surrounds before joining them to the back

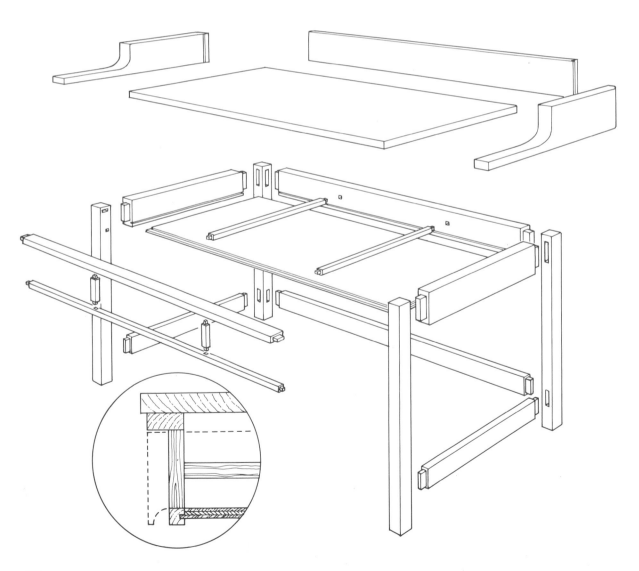

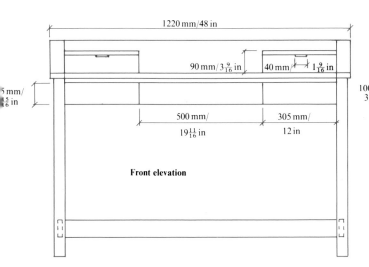

Front elevation

1220 mm/48 in

90 mm/3 9/16 in   40 mm/1 9/16 in

5 mm/ 5/16 in

500 mm/ 19 11/16 in   305 mm/ 12 in

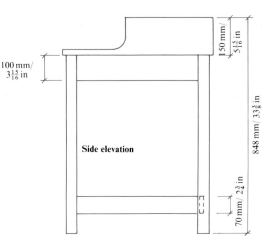

Side elevation

150 mm/ 5 15/16 in

100 mm/ 3 15/16 in

848 mm/ 33 3/8 in

70 mm/ 2 3/4 in

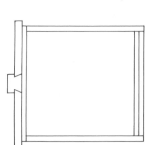

Box drawers

upstand. Glue the surround to the work top using loose tongues to give the connection greater strength. Now round off the back corners.

When making up the base frame, first cut all the mortises and tennons in all the rails, legs and uprights. Cut out the

railsand bottom panel, and they also have to drop down 15 mm from the bottom edge so that a curve cut in the inside edge can act as a handle to open them.

The drawer boxes for the work top are made out of solid mahogany and mitred

Drawer box

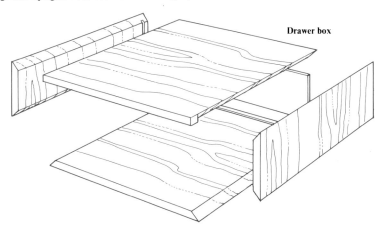

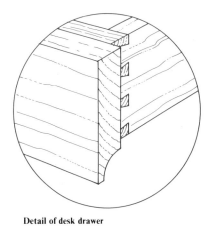

Detail of desk drawer

carcass base from 18 mm plywood veneered with mahogany, and route a rebate along the four edges. Next rout a groove in the relevant rails to take the base, so that its top finishes flush with the top edge of the lower front rail. Prefinish any parts that will later become inaccessible. Glue up the two end frames first, then the rest of the structure, including the veneered plywood panel.

Attach the base to the top by screwing up through the side and back rails, which will mean counter-boring the screws.

Make up the drawers to go underneath the top using dovetails for the back corners and lap dovetails at the front. The plywood drawer bottoms are grooved into place. The drawer fronts have to overlap the uprights separating the top

together, with loose tongues in the mitres. The top section overhangs by 15 mm so there is no need to mitre this part of the edge. The drawers themselves are made in exactly the same manner as the drawers described above but instead of using lapped dovetails at the front, use ordinary dovetail jointing and glue on a false 15 mm thick front afterwards so that it will cover the carcass sides and bottom edges and sit flush with the top when the drawer is in. Dovetail a handle to the false front before gluing it on.

Variations
The desk can be built without the work top drawer units, but retaining the three underneath. And if an uninterrupted work surface is required, it is better to do away with the surrounding upstand.

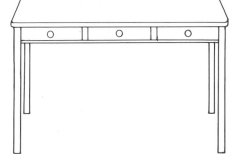

DESKS / Paul Connell

Paul Connell's desk was designed specifically as a moveable typing desk. For this reason it has been set on lockable castors, and the dowels built into each end of the work surface, while preventing things from falling off, also provide a comfortable grip to manoeuvre it by.

It is a busy piece of furniture with many exposed structural components purposely exaggerated by being stained blue to contrast with the very white finish of the maple. This has been achieved by first bleaching the maple and then spraying it with a lacquer containing a white pigment. An air of lightness is maintained by suspending the drawer units containing the drawers from the work top and frame, which gives them the appearance of floating.

Anatomy of the desk
The top, planked up from boards, and the drawers and drawer cabinets are made from solid maple, with the exception of the drawer bottoms and backs which are 6 mm thick plywood. Solid maple is also used for the leg frames. The drawer runners, however, are made from chipboard, with maple lippings and grey

Formica glued to both faces. Four lockable castors are screwed into the bottom of the feet. Black round-headed screws are also needed as these will be left exposed for a decorative effect.

How the desk is made
First, plank up the top and put it to one side. Then turn the

side dowels on a lathe and rout a 15 mm deep groove the thickness of the top down their length. Cut mortises and tenons to join the leg frames and then use a circular saw and a chisel to cut the stopped chamfers with bevelled ends on the lower sections of the legs. Cut the angles on the pieces tenoned to the top of the legs, and then chamfer the lower outside edges of the crossrails

so that the end grain is not exposed.

Next, drill all the fixing holes, remembering that the holes through the top rails into the underside of the work top should be slotted. Also drill 20 mm diameter × 10 mm deep holes in each leg for the dowels to support the side drawer cabinets. Now glue up the frames.

Bleach and finish the top (see pages 206–207), and then lip and glue Formica on the central drawer runners,

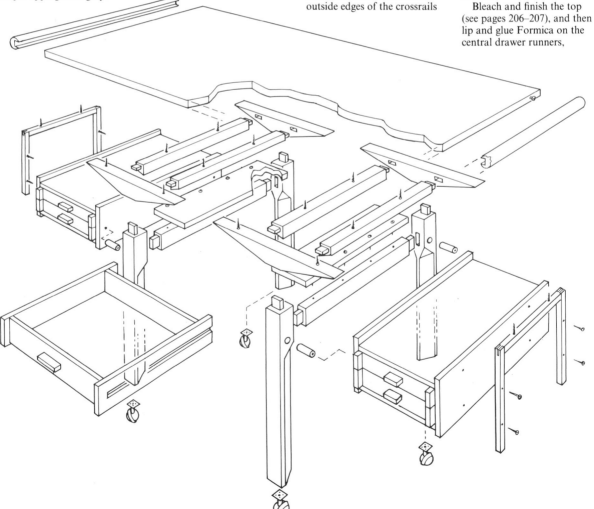

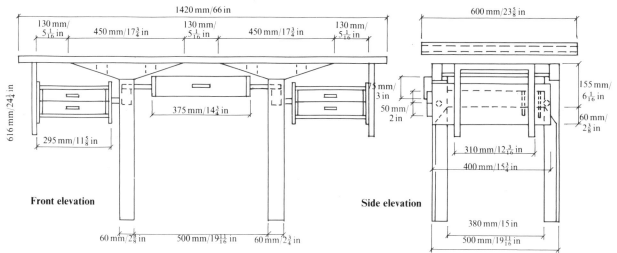

Front elevation

1420 mm/66 in

130 mm/ $5\frac{1}{16}$ in   450 mm/$17\frac{3}{4}$ in   130 mm/ $5\frac{1}{16}$ in   450 mm/$17\frac{3}{4}$ in   130 mm/ $5\frac{1}{16}$ in

616 mm/$24\frac{1}{4}$ in

375 mm/$14\frac{3}{4}$ in

295 mm/$11\frac{5}{8}$ in

60 mm/$2\frac{3}{8}$ in   500 mm/$19\frac{11}{16}$ in   60 mm/$2\frac{3}{4}$ in

Side elevation

600 mm/$23\frac{5}{8}$ in

75 mm/ 3 in

50 mm/ 2 in

155 mm/ $6\frac{1}{16}$ in

60 mm/ $2\frac{3}{8}$ in

310 mm/$12\frac{3}{16}$ in

400 mm/$15\frac{3}{4}$ in

380 mm/15 in

500 mm/$19\frac{11}{16}$ in

staining the lippings blue. Screw the runners onto the lower crossrails so they are flush with the outside edges.

To fix the dowels in place on the work top set keyhole plates in the grooves so they can lock over screws driven into the edges of the top.

Make the central drawer and four side drawers from 15 mm thick maple, with 6 mm plywood bottoms stained blue. The drawer handles are also maple, stained blue, and are attached using black round-headed screws, which are slightly counter-sunk and left exposed.

With the top placed upside down, locate the two leg frames around the central drawer and screw them to the top.

Finally, make up the two side drawer cabinets and the blue stained suspension frames, drilled with slotted holes for attaching them to the top.

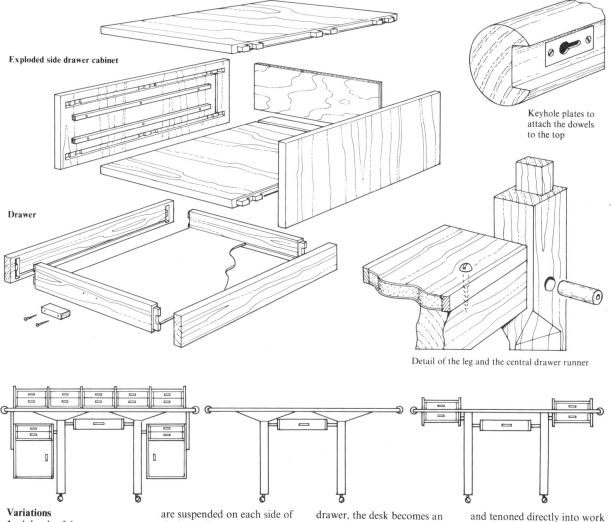

Exploded side drawer cabinet

Drawer

Keyhole plates to attach the dowels to the top

Detail of the leg and the central drawer runner

Variations

1. A bank of drawers rests on the work top and two cabinets are suspended on each side of the leg well.

2. With just the central drawer, the desk becomes an elegant table.

3. Drawer units are mortised and tenoned directly into work top above and below the legs.

Because maple is so much in vogue, it is refreshing to see a design which sympathetically makes use of another timber—cherry. Perhaps it is this, combined with the shaped legs and thick top, that gives this dressing room table with three drawers a slightly oriental quality. It manages to convey a subtle blend of robustness and delicacy at one and the same time. The success of the design centres very much on the overall shape of the piece but shrewd use of the cross members dovetailed into the top highlights how constructional details can be made visible to provide a strong decorative element.

Anatomy of the table

The table top is made from 60 mm thick solid cherry boards planked together. The legs are cut from 70 mm square cherry and are reduced to 40 mm square at their thinnest, after they have been shaped. The drawer sides and backs can also be made from cherry, dovetailed at the corners. You could consider using a contrasting timber to show off these dovetails even further. The drawers will also give off a pleasant aroma when opened if cedar of Lebanon is used for the bases. All the panels are loose-fitted and again they are made from cherry. The front and back rails underneath the drawers are cut in towards their centres by 10 mm on their outside edges.

How to make the table

Plank up the top from cherry boards so that the finished surface is 1200 × 550 × 60 mm. The frame is made using mortise and tenon joints throughout while the panels are fitted without gluing into routed grooves.

The inside faces of the legs remain straight, and it is only the outside faces which are shaped. At their tops, the legs are 50 mm square in cross-section; a third of the way down they are reduced to 40 mm square, but they flare out to 70 mm square at the bottom. It is best to make a template to mark this curve all the way along the length. The dovetail crosspieces can be cut on a circular saw using the tilt arbor; plane them to fit just

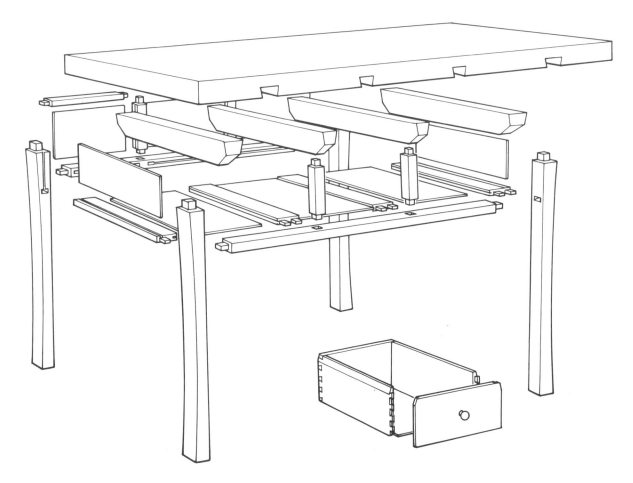

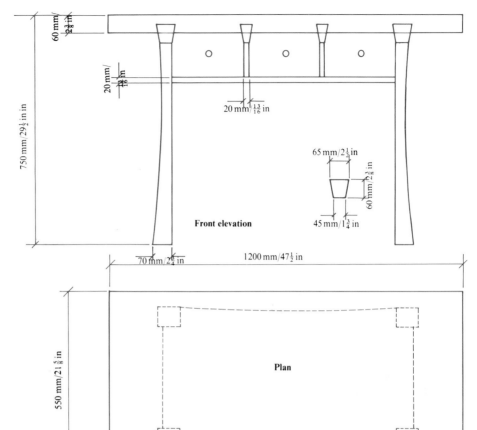

60 mm/2⅜ in

20 mm/¾ in

750 mm/29½ in

20 mm/1 3/16 in

65 mm/2½ in

60 mm/2⅜ in

45 mm/1¾ in

Front elevation

70 mm/2¾ in

1200 mm/47½ in

550 mm/21 5/8 in

Plan

before they are assembled. The curves in the bottom front and back rails are cut on the band saw, and finished with a compass plane, or spokeshave.

With the frame clamped up dry, mark where the dovetail slots fall on the underside of the top. Then rout these out using a dovetail cutter and a batten clamped to the underside of the top as a fence.

Next pre-finish all the inaccessible surfaces in the final assembly and then glue up the base. Start with the bottom frame, add the back frame to it followed by the side frames. Tap the dovetail crosspieces into position in their slots, gluing them just at the front edge, so allowing the top to move along them. Now glue the base to the dovetailed crosspieces, using clamping battens across the ends of the legs, under the frame, and across the top.

The drawers, dovetailed at the back corners and lap dovetailed at the front with the solid bottoms, are located in routed grooves, and fixed only at the front, so being free to move. The drawer fronts should be cut from one piece of timber so that the grain matches across the drawer fronts. When fitting the drawers, you will have to plane an angle on the top of the sides because of the dovetailed crosspieces which guide the drawers.

The small dowel handles can be turned on a lathe and then glued into pre-drilled holes.

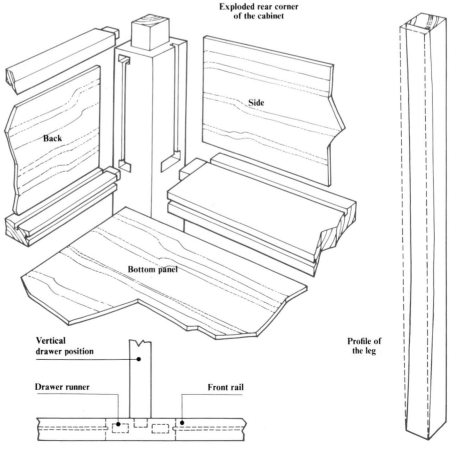

Exploded rear corner of the cabinet

Back

Side

Bottom panel

Vertical drawer position

Drawer runner

Front rail

Profile of the leg

LOW TABLES / David Field

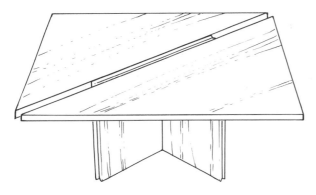

David Field's low table uses traditional methods in a contemporary design. The top is divided in two and joined to a cross-shaped base with V-moulded edges. Part of the base can be seen through the gap in the table top. There are both visual and structural reasons for

constructing the table this way. Visually, the strong diagonal accent created by the break and by the direction of the veneer can be used to complement the symmetry in a room; for example, to guide the eye through a corner between two sofas. Secondly, the fact that part of the base can be seen from the top helps to unify the parts of the table. The V-moulding on the base reflects light and emphasizes the break in the top while at the same time linking the two halves.

Structurally, the fact that the two halves of the top join the base on both horizontal and vertical axes makes the construction much stronger than it would be if they were joined on just one axis as is usual. The V-groove on the base provides a neat and secure fixing for the feet; it would be difficult to break these off if the table were dragged across the floor. The two-piece top means that there is less surface to be veneered, and the job can be handled without a press.

Anatomy of the table
The table is made from solid yew and yew-veneer over an 18 mm thick chipboard ground. It is 375 mm high and the top is 1 metre square overall. The three base pieces are arranged in a cross which measures 650 mm down its longest axis.

Blocks of ebony are used for the feet and these are glued into the V-groove cut in the edge of the solid yew lipping which runs all around the long base piece and the outside and bottom edges of the smaller crosspieces.

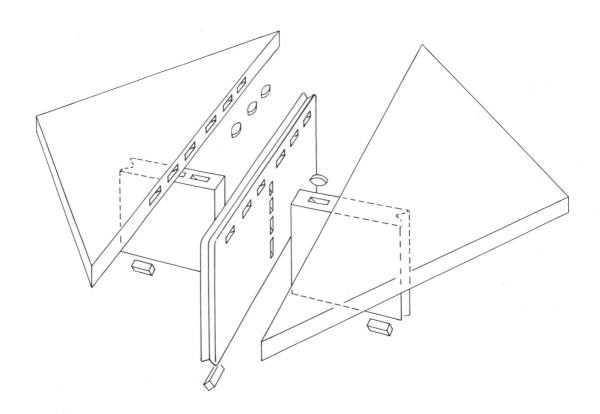

102

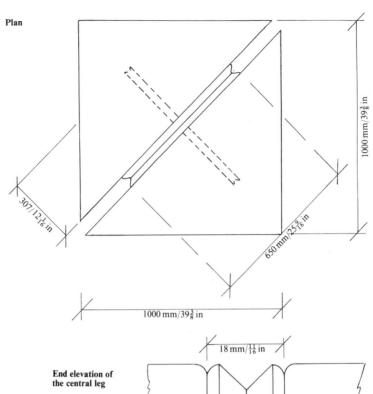

Plan

307/12$\frac{1}{16}$ in

650 mm/25$\frac{9}{16}$ in

1000 mm/39$\frac{3}{8}$ in

1000 mm/39$\frac{3}{8}$ in

How to make the table

Cut out the sections of chipboard and veneer and lip as necessary. Make up the base by biscuit jointing the two crosspieces to the centre of the long base section. The top edges of the crosspieces must be the depth of the table top below the top edge of the long section. Now centre the two table tops on the base, butting the diagonal edges against the sides of the long base section so that this now forms part of the top. Mark out where the biscuit joints are to go and cut the recesses with a biscuit jointer. Glue the biscuits into the two tops first, then locate these in the recesses cut along the side of the base section and lower the tops from the outside corners so that all the other biscuits are located.

Using bar clamps and bearers, gently clamp the tops and base together; check that everything is in place and then tighten slightly. Next use two sash clamps and two clamping blocks across opposite corners to ensure the diagonal edges are held firmly against the sides of the base section.

When dry glue up the feet and then finish the piece with two coats of lacquer to preserve the qualities of the yew.

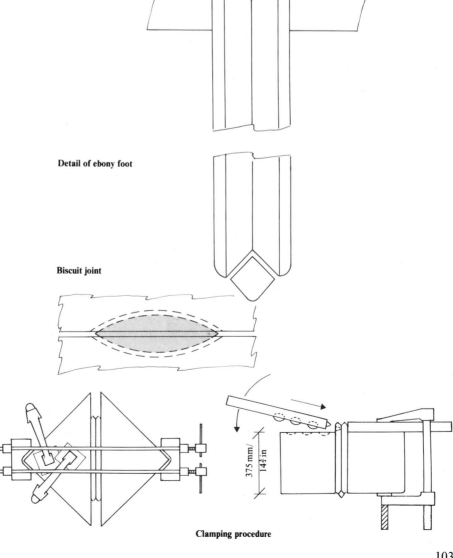

18 mm/$\frac{11}{16}$ in

End elevation of the central leg

Detail of ebony foot

Biscuit joint

375 mm/ 14$\frac{3}{4}$ in

Clamping procedure

103

LOW TABLES / David Field

The basic themes used to construct both the rosewood table on the facing page and the yew table on pages 102 and 103 can be modified to produce an imaginative range of related designs. The variations can be adapted to suit specific needs, but they have in common the dramatic split top and segmented base of the yew table.

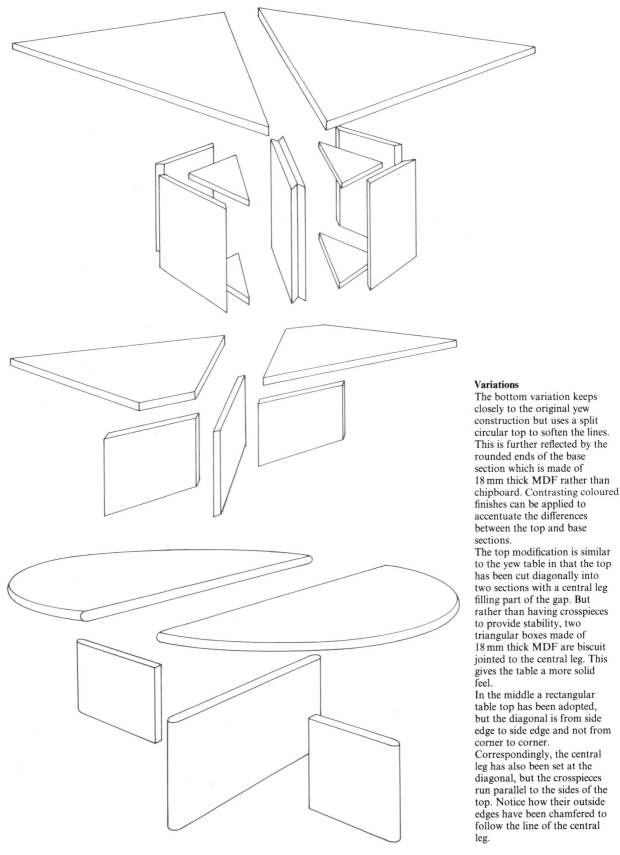

Variations

The bottom variation keeps closely to the original yew construction but uses a split circular top to soften the lines. This is further reflected by the rounded ends of the base section which is made of 18 mm thick MDF rather than chipboard. Contrasting coloured finishes can be applied to accentuate the differences between the top and base sections.

The top modification is similar to the yew table in that the top has been cut diagonally into two sections with a central leg filling part of the gap. But rather than having crosspieces to provide stability, two triangular boxes made of 18 mm thick MDF are biscuit jointed to the central leg. This gives the table a more solid feel.

In the middle a rectangular table top has been adopted, but the diagonal is from side edge to side edge and not from corner to corner.

Correspondingly, the central leg has also been set at the diagonal, but the crosspieces run parallel to the sides of the top. Notice how their outside edges have been chamfered to follow the line of the central leg.

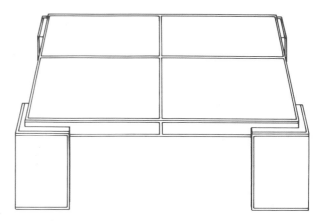

Apart from the clean and sturdy lines of this low table, it is noteworthy for the use it makes of veneering, stringing and inlay. The very nature of a rosewood veneer exudes a sumptuous feel. But here the alignment of the grain of each veneer panel has also been used to produce a beautiful decorative effect, with the grain running to the corners and then folding over the sides at 45°. This is further highlighted by the addition of inlaid boxwood banding across the top and along the prominent edges.

How to make the table

Sandwich up the top and glue on the hardwood lippings, tongued and mitred at the corners. Then veneer the top (with balancing veneer on the bottom) in four equal squares with the grain diamond matched. Rout 1.5 mm grooves across the top and sides where the veneers meet and glue in 1.5 mm square boxwood stringing. Veneer the edges, with the grain running at 45° away from the centre of the top edge.

Block up the leg pieces out of three pieces of 16 mm plywood. Lip the top, bottom and outside edges with solid rosewood, mitring the corners. Next veneer each piece, with the grain running vertically, so that each corner will be bookmatched when jointed. Now mitre the legs to form the L-section before gluing them up. Cut a rebate 25 mm square along the inside of the top edges to take the table top. Glue up and then let in 1.5 mm boxwood stringing round the outside edges. Finally apply two coats of lacquer, and attach the top using dowels or biscuits.

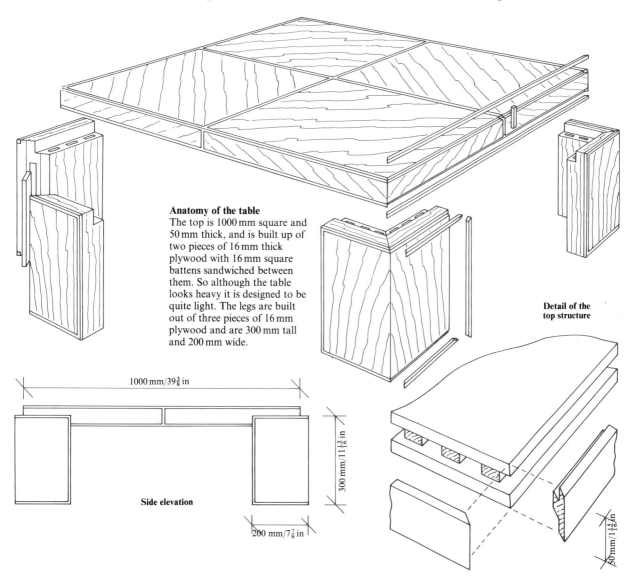

Anatomy of the table

The top is 1000 mm square and 50 mm thick, and is built up of two pieces of 16 mm thick plywood with 16 mm square battens sandwiched between them. So although the table looks heavy it is designed to be quite light. The legs are built out of three pieces of 16 mm plywood and are 300 mm tall and 200 mm wide.

Detail of the top structure

1000 mm/39$\frac{3}{8}$ in

Side elevation

300 mm/11$\frac{13}{16}$ in

200 mm/7$\frac{7}{8}$ in

50 mm/1$\frac{15}{16}$ in

LOW TABLES / Floris van den Broecke

Like **Floris van den Broecke**'s occasional table on pages 108 and 109, the attraction of this particular table rests on its simplicity and strong geometric form. It is based on the British "A" series of standard paper sizes (see Variations). The angular lines and square edges maintain a refreshingly clean look, while the overhanging top gives it a slightly oriental feel. An interesting little feature is made of the side rails which extend beyond the line of the legs. In turn, the legs are allowed to come through the top in the form of a wedged tenon to provide the only touch of decoration on the table.

Anatomy of the table

The table is made from solid maple or ash, which you can later stain. The top is made up from 16 mm thick planks to an overall size of 420 × 300 mm. The four legs are each 297 mm long and are cut from timber with a 42 × 30 mm cross-section. Use the same sectioned timber for the two top side rails which are 190 mm long and the two bottom side rails which are 260 mm long.

How to make the table

Start by planking up the top, planing the boards so that the tenons of the legs will not go through a joint. Next mortise the rails to the legs. Note how the top rails sit centrally on the uprights, but the side rails extend 16 mm beyond the outside edges. Having glued up the base frame, glue on the top, and increase the strength of the mortises by driving down wedges between the ends of the tenons and the edges of the mortises. Trim the wedges flush with the top of the table, before applying stains and lacquer.

Wedged tenons in table top

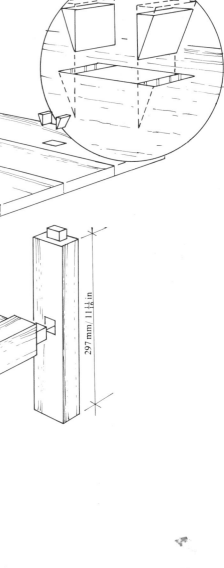

180 mm/7 1/16 in

150 mm/5 7/8 in

297 mm/11 11/16 in

216 mm/8 1/4 in

149 mm/5 7/8 in

16 mm/5/8 in

Overhanging shoulder

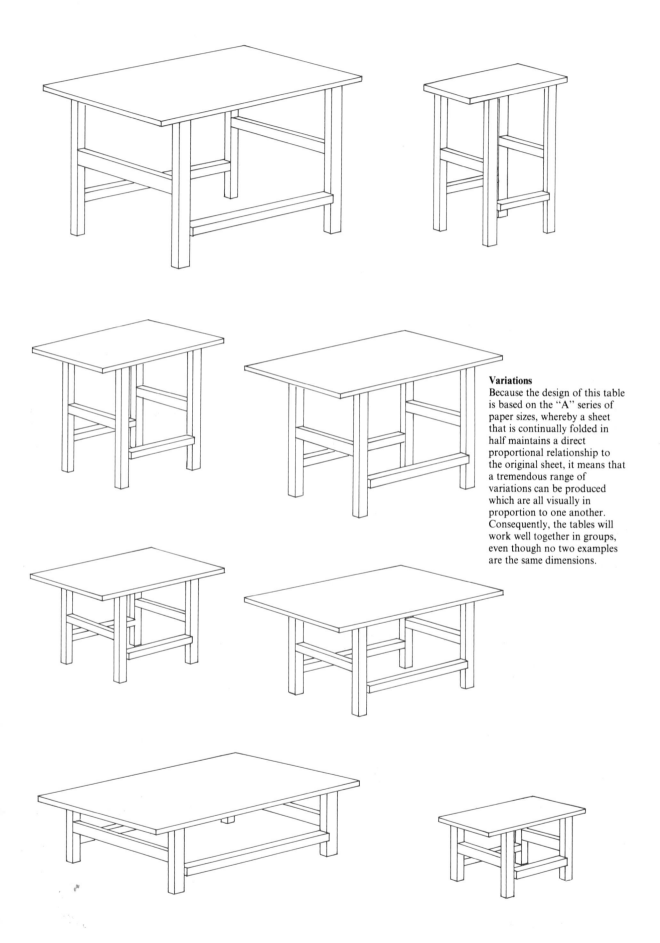

Variations
Because the design of this table is based on the "A" series of paper sizes, whereby a sheet that is continually folded in half maintains a direct proportional relationship to the original sheet, it means that a tremendous range of variations can be produced which are all visually in proportion to one another. Consequently, the tables will work well together in groups, even though no two examples are the same dimensions.

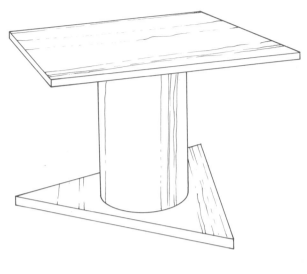

Floris van den Broecke's occasional table derives its appeal from his unusual, highly original and confident use of strong geometric forms. The result is a somewhat stark design which has the appearance more of an art object—almost a sculpture—than of a practical table. The seemingly simple arrangement of shapes belies the considerable design thinking that went into developing the correct proportions between each of the sections, allowing the strange alignment of square, triangle and cylinder to work as a piece of furniture. Here the use of timber is of secondary importance to the design, and wood has been used as a means to make the design rather than for its intrinsic qualities. Indeed, the design would work equally as well in plastic or metal. However, the use of different woods—mahogany for the top, stained brasswood or lime wood for the column and maple for the base—provides the subtle contrasting colours and textures, which are sometimes lacking in other materials and which cleverly accentuate the combination of shapes.

Anatomy of the table

This piece comprises a square top made of solid mahogany, 1160 × 1160 × 21 mm; a triangular base made from solid maple. The sides of the equilateral triangle measure 1132 × 41 mm; and a column made from eight pieces of basswood 681 × 175 × 50 mm that have been mitred together to form an octagon which is 425 mm from face to opposite face. Holding the top to the cylinder are two pieces of aluminium 800 × 25 × 25 mm held in place by two right-angle brackets 1015 mm wide, with 50 mm long arms. Four of these brackets fasten the base to the cylinder, screwed onto the octagonal faces inside the cylinder.

Making the top and base

Make from the top and base from solid timber butted together and held by loose tongues (see pages 162–163). After gluing and clamping (see pages 178–179) and allowing the assembly to dry, cut the resulting boards to size and shape.

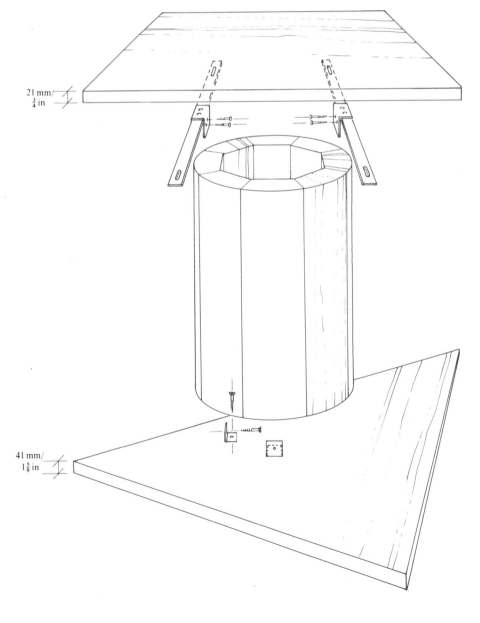

21 mm/ ¾ in

41 mm/ 1⅝ in

Making the column

Shoot the mitres of each piece of basswood to an angle of $67\frac{1}{2}°$. Then glue and clamp the cylinder together all at once, using band clamps to hold all the parts secure. At this stage the column should be slightly oversized so that if any pieces slip during the gluing and clamping operation the whole piece can be evened up afterwards.

When the glue is dry, trim the ends so that they are square and finish at 681 mm. Then mark a circle on each end of the octagon 420 mm in diameter. Lay the column on its side and plane the edges down to the line of the circle to form the cylinder.

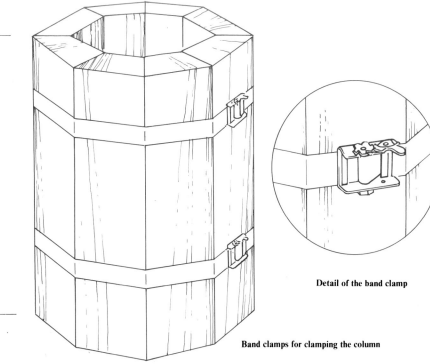

681 mm/$26\frac{13}{16}$ in

Detail of the band clamp

Band clamps for clamping the column

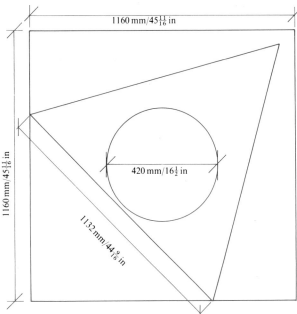

1160 mm/$45\frac{11}{16}$ in

1160 mm/$45\frac{11}{16}$ in

420 mm/$16\frac{1}{2}$ in

1132 mm/$44\frac{9}{16}$ in

Locating the top, column and base

Locating the base

On the base, find the centre of the line AB and draw a perpendicular to point C. Then centre the foot of the column on this line with the circumference 45 mm away from line AB.

To attach the base in place, screw four right-angle brackets to the inside foot of the column and then reach down inside the column to screw through the brackets into the base for a concealed join.

Once this has been completed, the top can be screwed on.

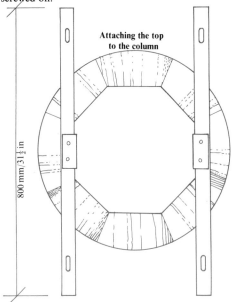

Attaching the top to the column

800 mm/$31\frac{1}{2}$ in

Locating the top of the column

The column is located centrally under the top and the two are held together by the aluminium sections and right-angle brackets which are first screwed to the inside face of the column. Before fastening, slotted screw holes should be drilled into the aluminium to accommodate any expansion and contraction of the top.

Turn the top upside down and place the column, with aluminium sections attached, in position on the underside. Use this as a guide to mark where the sections and brackets touch the top, then rout out this area so that the sections and brackets will lie flush with the underside when the top and column are brought together (see pages 172–173).

Before joining the pieces for the last time, it is necessary to attach the base to the column.

LOW TABLES / Floris van den Broecke

These three variations on **Floris van den Broecke**'s table all use the same basic geometric shapes arranged in different combinations, sizes and materials for the base, column and top.

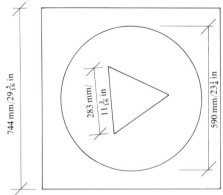

(1) All the sections of this arrangement can be made from medium-density fibreboard (MDF) or multi-ply plywood sprayed

with coloured lacquer. The aluminium sections can be screwed directly to the top.

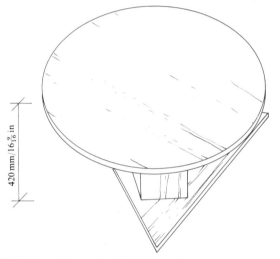

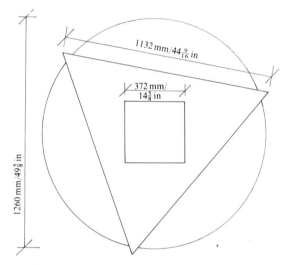

(2) This low table version with all the sections centred on the same point again uses MDF or plywood and the same attaching

methods as the original. The aluminium sections can be screwed directly to the top.

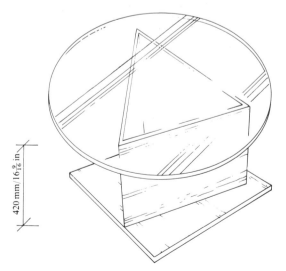

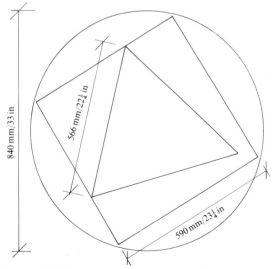

(3) Here MDF is used for the square base and triangular column, but the top is 6 mm thick glass resting on rubber pads. Because it is possible to see inside the column, the inner surface should also

be finished. The base/column join is concealed by screwing up through the base into the bottom edge of the column.

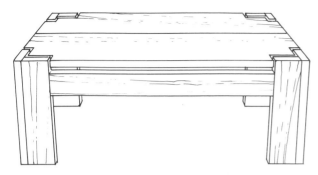

Tim Well's side table makes a positive feature of the fact that timber expands and contracts across the grain—hence the use of a split top to accommodate any movement. The 10 mm gap around the top of the legs is more for decorative purposes to give the table top an illusion of floating. Using the same cross-section of timber throughout (ash was used for the original), the table is simply made using butt joints and mortise and tenons. Two coats of lacquer provide a protective finish.

Anatomy of the table
The table is made with eight legs, 25 × 65 × 350 mm, paired at right angles, a pair at each corner. Two rails, 25 × 65 × 830 mm overall and 25 × 65 × 770 mm to the shoulders, run the length of the table and two rails 25 × 65 × 530 mm overall and 25 × 65 × 470 mm to the shoulders, run the width. In addition, there are two cross rails, 25 × 65 × 580 mm overall and 25 × 65 × 550 mm to the shoulders. The top is in two parts, each 25 × 295 × 900 mm. Eight steel screws fasten the top to the base. Finally the table is finished with lacquer.

Detail of the corner of the leg frame

Making the table
First cut all the timber to the finished sizes required, then cut all the mortise and tenon joints, using double mortise and tenons for the unseen cross rails. The side rails should be 35 mm below the top of the leg while the cross rails should protrude 10 mm above the side rails.

The tops are attached by screwing up through the cross rails, so drill pilot holes counter-bored for the screws to reach into the underside. The holes by the tenons are 25 mm in from the shoulders and the holes nearer the centre are 240 mm in from the same shoulder. The latter should be slotted to allow the top to expand and contract towards the outside edge.

Now glue up the legs with a simple butt joint, then glue up the frame in two stages—first joining the longer side rails to the legs, and then the other four rails all in one operation.

Top corner, cut out to accept the leg

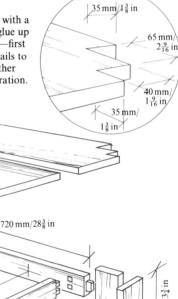

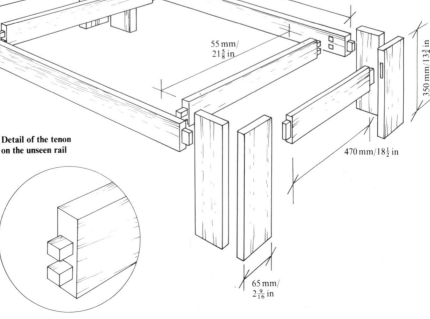

Detail of the tenon on the unseen rail

Attaching the top
The two tops are made up out of as many planks as it takes to get a finished width for each piece of 295 mm. Cut out the spaces for the legs allowing an additional 10 mm for the gap all around. Then fasten them down by screwing up through the pilot holes drilled in the cross rails.

LOW TABLES / Ron Carter

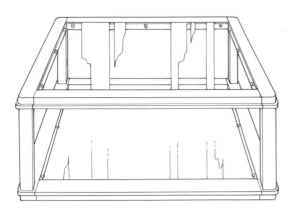

The paradox of **Ron Carter**'s occasional table, made in solid mahogany, is that a simple design with a small amount of decoration has resulted in a sophisticated piece of furniture which can double as a display cabinet. This designer's work is characterized by clean and elegant lines, and a sense of proportion that produces complete and satisfying shapes. In this example, glass has been used to give the structure lightness, yet it still retains an unobtrusive feeling of rigidity. Note how the sides have been left open to give easy access to the shelf below.

Anatomy of the table
The overall dimensions of the table are 920 × 920 × 340 mm. The inside measurements of the top and bottom frames are 802 mm square, and they are both cut from 58 × 30 mm solid mahogany. This should have a 6 mm wide × 19 mm deep rebate cut from a corner in the longer face. When marking out individual lengths remember to make allowances at each end for the relevant tenons. Two 800 mm square sheets of glass 6 mm thick complete the top and form the bottom shelf—make sure the edges of the glass have been polished. Twelve 13 mm diameter × 23 mm long metal or wood dowels are also needed to support the glass. The four legs are each 320 mm long and are cut from 48 mm square solid mahogany. A 12 mm radius should be cut in the outside edge.

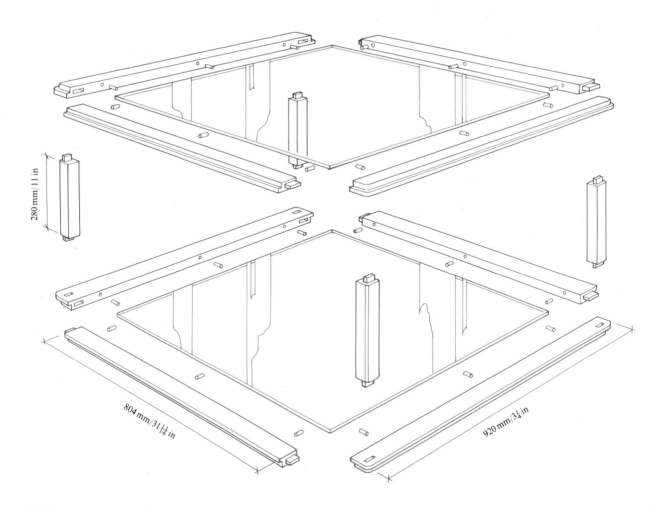

280 mm / 11 in

804 mm / 31 $\frac{11}{16}$ in

920 mm / 3 $\frac{1}{4}$ in

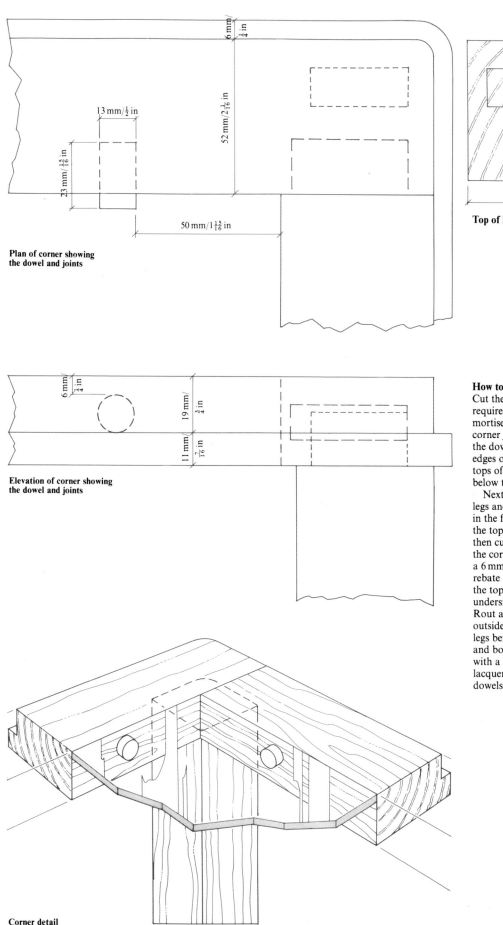

13 mm/½ in

23 mm/$\frac{15}{16}$ in

52 mm/2$\frac{1}{16}$ in

6 mm/¼ in

50 mm/1$\frac{15}{16}$ in

Plan of corner showing the dowel and joints

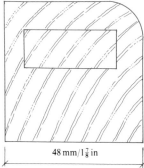

48 mm/1$\frac{7}{8}$ in

Top of leg showing tenon

6 mm/¼ in

19 mm/$\frac{3}{4}$ in

11 mm/$\frac{7}{16}$ in

Elevation of corner showing the dowel and joints

How to make the table
Cut the mahogany to the
required sizes, then cut the
mortise and tenons for the
corner joints. Mark and drill
the dowel holes in the inside
edges of the frames so that the
tops of the dowels are 6 mm
below the top surface.

Next cut the tenons in the
legs and the reciprocal mortises
in the frame corners. Glue up
the top and bottom frames and
then cut a 12 mm radius on all
the corners. Use a router to cut
a 6 mm wide × 19 mm deep
rebate around the outside of
the top surface and the
underside of the bottom frame.
Rout a 12 mm radius on the
outside edges of all the four
legs before gluing to the top
and bottom sections. Finish
with a stain and two coats of
lacquer before inserting the
dowels and putting in the glass.

Corner detail

LOW TABLES / Ron Carter

This low side table allows its contents to be displayed at close hand, while protecting them from prying fingers. Again, it bears the hallmark of **Ron Carter**'s work. It is a refined piece of furniture, simple yet elegantly proportioned and beautifully made in stained solid mahogany. Access to the display cabinet is by a lift-off top which sits over the glass panel. The base is made of plywood covered in fabric, and a suitable colour can be chosen to highlight the contents to best advantage. In fact it is a straightforward job to re-cover the base if a new coloured fabric is required.

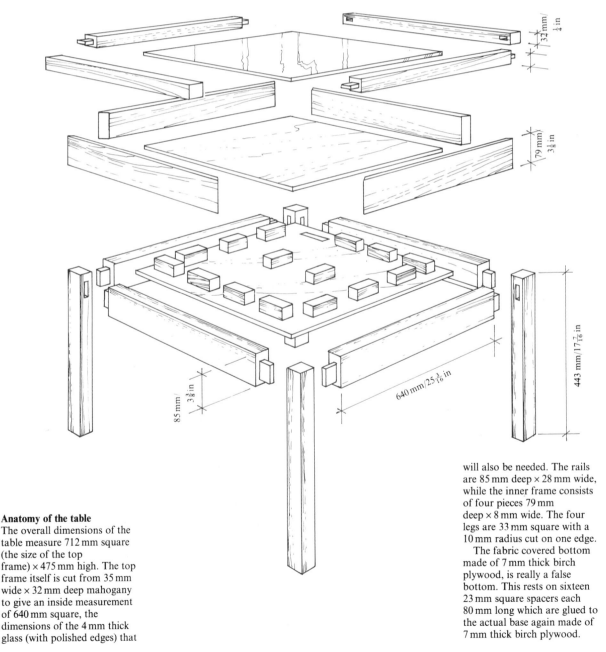

Anatomy of the table
The overall dimensions of the table measure 712 mm square (the size of the top frame) × 475 mm high. The top frame itself is cut from 35 mm wide × 32 mm deep mahogany to give an inside measurement of 640 mm square, the dimensions of the 4 mm thick glass (with polished edges) that

will also be needed. The rails are 85 mm deep × 28 mm wide, while the inner frame consists of four pieces 79 mm deep × 8 mm wide. The four legs are 33 mm square with a 10 mm radius cut on one edge.

The fabric covered bottom made of 7 mm thick birch plywood, is really a false bottom. This rests on sixteen 23 mm square spacers each 80 mm long which are glued to the actual base again made of 7 mm thick birch plywood.

Anatomy of the table

The overall dimensions of the table measure 712 mm square (the size of the top frame) and 475 mm high. The top frame itself is cut from 35 mm × 32 mm mahogany to give an inside measurement of 640 mm square, the dimensions of the 4 mm thick glass (with polished edges) that will also be needed. The rails are 85 mm × 28 mm, while the inner frame consists of four pieces 79 mm × 8 mm. The four legs are 33 mm square with a 10 mm radius cut on one edge.

The fabric-covered bottom made of 7 mm thick birch plywood is really a false bottom. This rests on sixteen 23 mm square spacers each 80 mm long which are glued to the actual base, again made of 7 mm thick birch plywood.

How to make the table

Having cut all the timber to size, cut the mortises and tenons in the rails and legs. Then use a router to cut a rebate in the bottom inside edges of the rails to take the base so that it is flush with the underside. You will have to cut squares out of the corners of the plywood panel to go around the legs. Drill a 25 mm hole in the base to enable the false, fabric-covered bottom to be pushed out when the table is assembled. Then rout a 10 mm radius on the outside edge of each leg.

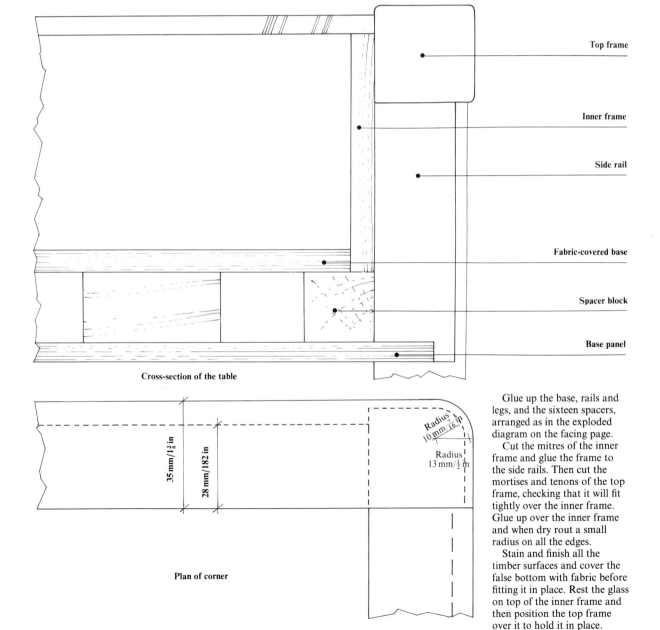

Cross-section of the table

Top frame

Inner frame

Side rail

Fabric-covered base

Spacer block

Base panel

35 mm/1⅜ in
28 mm/182 in
Radius 10 mm/⁷⁄₁₆ in
Radius 13 mm/½ in

Plan of corner

Glue up the base, rails and legs, and the sixteen spacers, arranged as in the exploded diagram on the facing page.

Cut the mitres of the inner frame and glue the frame to the side rails. Then cut the mortises and tenons of the top frame, checking that it will fit tightly over the inner frame. Glue up over the inner frame and when dry rout a small radius on all the edges.

Stain and finish all the timber surfaces and cover the false bottom with fabric before fitting it in place. Rest the glass on top of the inner frame and then position the top frame over it to hold it in place.

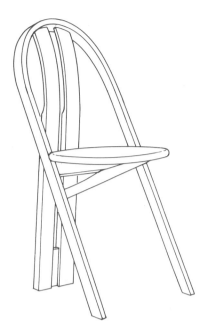

David Colwell's chair was designed to be produced in a small workshop, using steam-bent green ash. Look for unseasoned ash, freshly felled, preferably in the fall when the sap is low in the tree. The chair seat is made of maple or oak, and is slightly dished.

On the whole, this chair is a straightforward mortise and tenon affair holding the cantilever construction together. The key to its great strength is a steel pin at the fulcrum point (see pages 24–31 for more on cantilever chairs).

The steaming box necessary to make this chair is simple to construct, using supplies available at a hardware store; so is the former for shaping the steamed wood (see pages 180–181). The economy of this design is that only part of the section of wood need be steamed, considerably simplifying the operation. Note: any stains left from the metal in the former can be removed from the wood with oxalic acid (see pages 206–207).

Anatomy of the chair

The chair consists of two steam-bent components. One piece 50 × 25 mm and 3048 mm long, of which 910 mm have been bent to a radius of 215 mm to form the back and the front legs of the chair. A second section, 15 × 203 mm and 1512 mm long, has been bent to a radius of 508 mm to form the backrest and back legs of the chair. The piece has been sawn down its length to obtain its matching pieces.

A circular seat of maple has been turned on the faceplate of a lathe to make a disk 330 mm in diameter, with a dish of 25 mm deep. The grain on the seat runs from front to back to prevent the front edge from breaking.

Two cross rails support the seat. One runs from front to back made of timber 305 mm long, and 25 × 50 mm in cross-section. The rail running from side to side, also 25 × 50 mm, is 381 mm long, and tenoned at both ends to fit into mortises in the front legs. A small block 127 mm tall thick with a 75 mm tenon at either side fits into a mortise at the bottom of the back legs.

A 9 mm stainless steel pin 76 mm long passes through the front-to-back seat rail and into holes in the back legs, held with epoxy adhesive. A 76 mm long 5 mm bolt holds the cross rails together. Three 38 mm screws fasten the seat to the

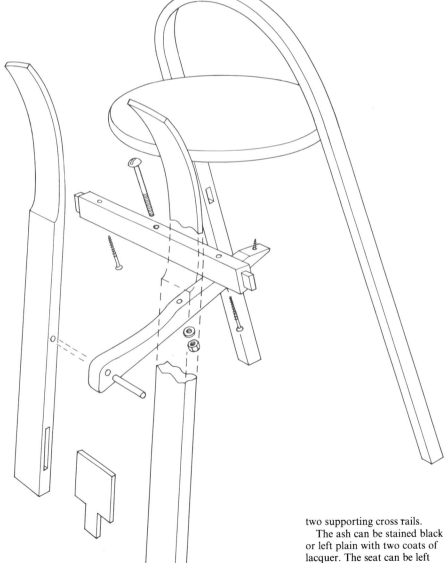

two supporting cross rails.

The ash can be stained black or left plain with two coats of lacquer. The seat can be left plain or it can be padded and covered with fabric.

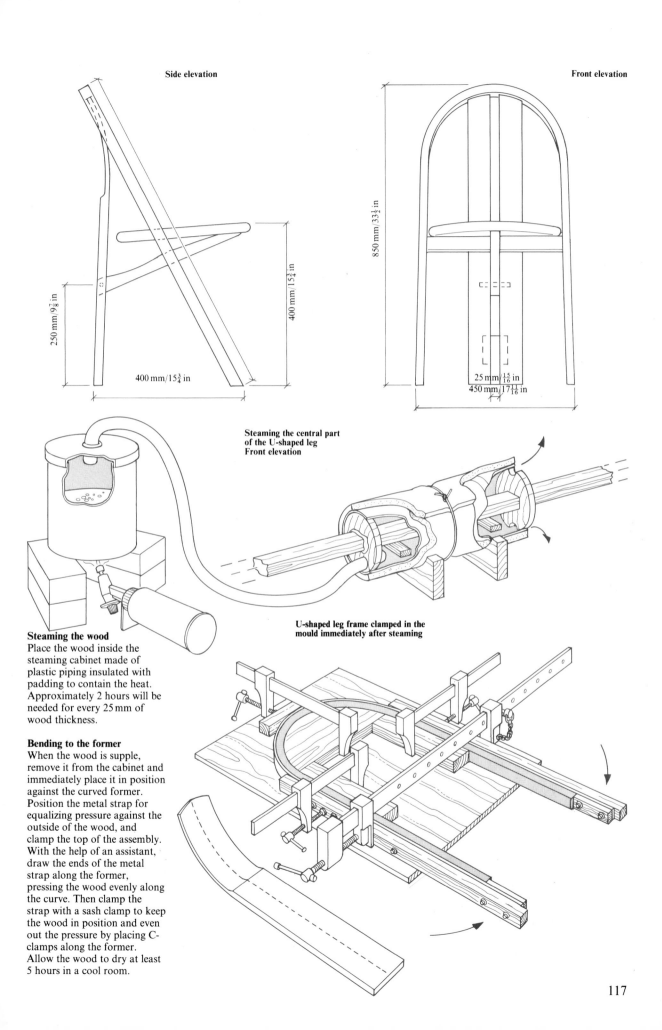

Side elevation

Front elevation

250 mm/9$\frac{7}{8}$ in

400 mm/15$\frac{3}{4}$ in

400 mm/15$\frac{3}{4}$ in

850 mm/33$\frac{1}{2}$ in

25 mm/$\frac{15}{16}$ in

450 mm/17$\frac{11}{16}$ in

**Steaming the central part
of the U-shaped leg
Front elevation**

Steaming the wood
Place the wood inside the
steaming cabinet made of
plastic piping insulated with
padding to contain the heat.
Approximately 2 hours will be
needed for every 25 mm of
wood thickness.

Bending to the former
When the wood is supple,
remove it from the cabinet and
immediately place it in position
against the curved former.
Position the metal strap for
equalizing pressure against the
outside of the wood, and
clamp the top of the assembly.
With the help of an assistant,
draw the ends of the metal
strap along the former,
pressing the wood evenly along
the curve. Then clamp the
strap with a sash clamp to keep
the wood in position and even
out the pressure by placing C-
clamps along the former.
Allow the wood to dry at least
5 hours in a cool room.

**U-shaped leg frame clamped in the
mould immediately after steaming**

117

As a result of **Toby Winteringham**'s interest in Shaker furniture, this carver chair has been consciously designed with utility foremost in mind; it is virtually devoid of decoration. The framework is made mainly of 25 mm square beech with the back rails steam bent to provide extra comfort. The seat is plywood with a 10 mm deep perforated circular dish.

The appeal of the chair therefore rests very much in its simplicity and proportion. While the framework may appear fragile it is nevertheless remarkably strong due to the number and positioning of the rails.

Interestingly, Winteringham is aware that some people may resist the design because it does not look as if it could safely support a person, although in practice it can do this more than adequately. His plan is now to use thicker cross-sectioned timber purely to give the impression of greater strength.

Anatomy of the chair
The legs and arms are cut from 23 mm square beech. The seat rails are cut from 23 × 40 mm timber while all the other rails are 23 × 10 mm. The three back pieces are steam bent in one piece and then cut to 23 × 10 mm. The seat is made from plywood with a 280 mm diameter dish, 10 mm deep in the centre.

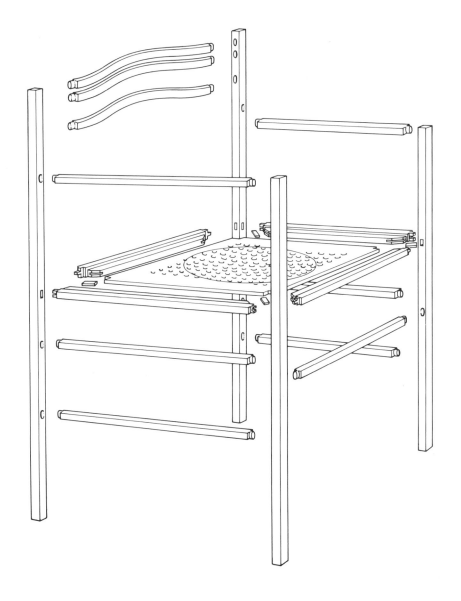

How to make the chair
The chair is assembled mainly using mortise and tenon joints, but note the complexity of the seat rails. The outside section is mortised into the chair leg while the inside rebated section is cut to avoid the leg and then mitred to join the rebate meeting it at right angles. Inset tongues in the mitre provide extra strength. The seat fits into the rebate and is cut out around the legs.

In order to form the dish of the seat, glue together three

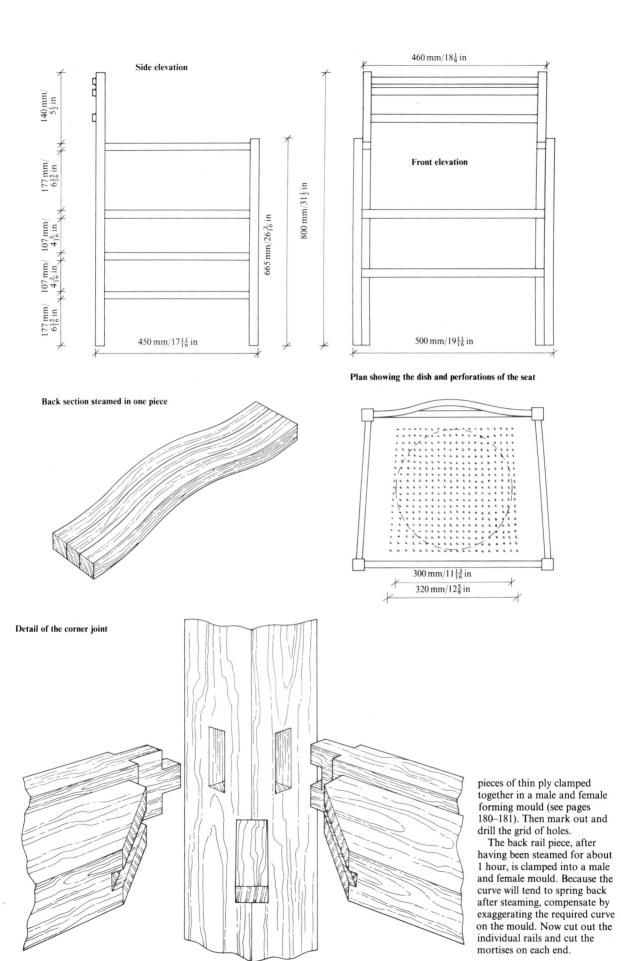

Side elevation

140 mm/ 5½ in

177 mm/ 6 15/16 in

107 mm/ 4 3/16 in

107 mm/ 4 3/16 in

177 mm/ 6 15/16 in

450 mm/17 11/16 in

665 mm/26 3/16 in

800 mm/31½ in

460 mm/18 1/8 in

Front elevation

500 mm/19 11/16 in

Plan showing the dish and perforations of the seat

300 mm/11 13/16 in

320 mm/12 5/8 in

Back section steamed in one piece

Detail of the corner joint

pieces of thin ply clamped together in a male and female forming mould (see pages 180–181). Then mark out and drill the grid of holes.

The back rail piece, after having been steamed for about 1 hour, is clamped into a male and female mould. Because the curve will tend to spring back after steaming, compensate by exaggerating the required curve on the mould. Now cut out the individual rails and cut the mortises on each end.

119

SEATING / Ron Carter

A complete and satisfying design to look at, with oriental undertones, and at the same time a very comfortable piece to sit on—these are the key elements at the heart of **Ron Carter**'s highly successful chair. It is also the only chair to be featured in this section which incorporates upholstery, with natural wool fabric stretched over foam and webbing to form the back and lift-out seat. This, combined with the generous proportions and arms to provide the user with added support, gives the chair an inviting and sumptuous quality that timber constructions sometimes lack.

Anatomy of the chair
Ideally, the chair should be made in either maple or cherry. The legs are made from 38 × 38 mm timber, the rails 63 × 25 mm and the back 49 × 32 mm. The arms are cut from 40 × 38 mm sections. Natural wool fabric, polyether foam and elastic webbing are used for the upholstery of the seat and back. Leather could also be used.

How to make the chair
First cut out all the components, ensuring that the back legs and top of the back make maximum use of grain strength,
Next cut the side faces of the legs to thickness, then roughly shape the faces that point forwards on the bandsaw before planing to a right angle. Cut the thickness of the legs on the circular saw, working up to the elbow and stopping and then repeating the cutting from the other end. Clean up with a chisel and plane.

Front elevation
631 mm/24 $\frac{7}{8}$ in

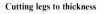

585 mm/23 in

420 mm/19 $\frac{9}{16}$ in

440 mm/17 $\frac{5}{16}$ in

440 mm/17 $\frac{5}{16}$ in

518 mm/20 $\frac{3}{8}$ in

505 mm/19 $\frac{13}{16}$ in

581 mm/22 $\frac{7}{8}$ in

610 mm/24 in

860 mm/33 $\frac{7}{8}$ in

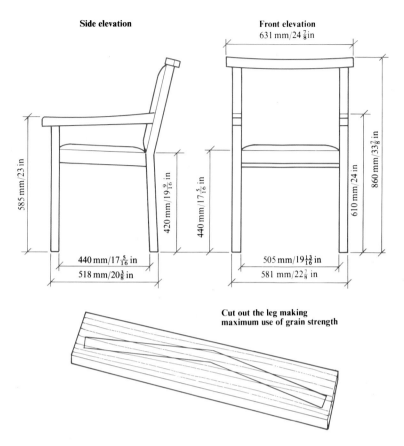

Cutting legs to thickness

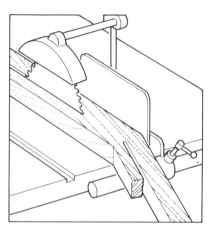

Cut out the leg making
maximum use of grain strength

Joint the legs and rails using mortise and tenon joints, then connect the back and arms to the legs and shape with a spokeshave. Drill three holes in the back rail for screwing up into the upholstered back panel later. Now glue up all the parts.

You will also need to make four triangular corner blocks and screw these to the inside corners of the seat frame 22 mm down from the top edge. Finish the piece with two coats of lacquer.

To fit the upholstery first make up two frames, tenoned at the corners, one for the back and one for the seat. These should be a loose fit so they can accommodate the padding and fabric cover. Interlock the elastic webbing across the frame and staple onto the top edge to hold it in position. Glue 32 mm thick foam onto this and stretch over heavy muslin and then the fabric to make a good shaped seat before stapling it to the underside of the frame. For the back frame, staple onto the outward facing side edges and cover the back itself with another piece of fabric, again stapled to the sides. The edges will be hidden when the panels are in place.

To locate the back panel match up the dowels previously fitted into the top edge with holes drilled in the top rail. Then screw up through the bottom rail to hold it fast. The seat unit drops into its recess and is screwed in through the corner blocks.

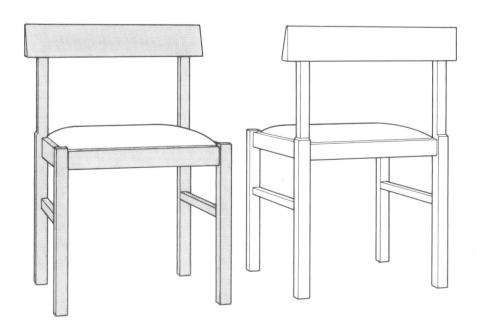

Variation
A simpler version of this seat can be made by omitting the arms and the upholstered back. But a deeper rail at the top of the back should be added to give adequate support to the person using the chair.

SEATING / Adrian Reed

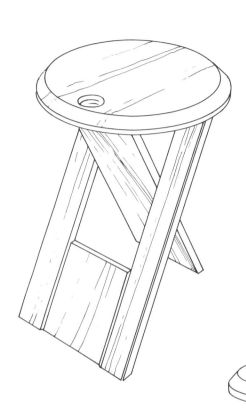

The clever simplicity of **Adrian Reed**'s stool belies the amount of design thinking and inventive engineering that have gone into its making. It is very much a complete design with all the parts working well together. It is easy to handle; it packs flat for storage; and it is clean and neat in appearance. A hole in the seat is carefully positioned so that the stool can be hung from a peg on the wall—a great space-saving consideration.

The angle of the seat can be adjusted for added comfort while sitting on the stool as the brass pivot dowel slides up and down in the groove routed in the central leg.

Anatomy of the stool
All the major components are made of solid white beech. The seat is 320 mm in diameter and 25 mm thick. The single inside leg measures 648 × 140 × 20 mm; the two thin legs are 648 × 50 × 20 mm; and the short crosspiece joining the two is 140 × 164 × 20 mm. Eight birch dowels 6 mm in diameter and 50 mm long are also needed as well as two stainless steel dowels 5 mm in diameter and 40 mm long. The legs pivot on four brass butt hinges 25 mm long.

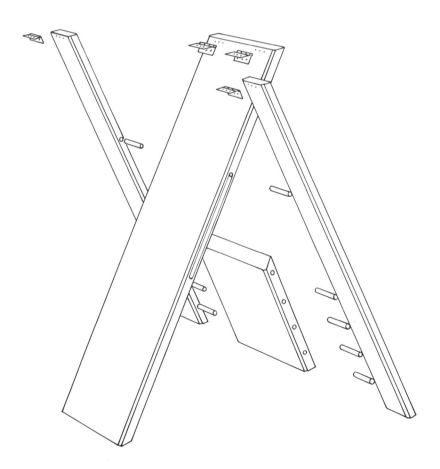

How to make the stool

Plank up the top and thickness it to 25 mm. Then cut the rough shape for the seat on a band-saw or jigsaw. Use a lathe or a router fixed to a pin and bar on the underside to bring the seat to the finished size. Then, if you are using the lathe, cut a 14 mm chamfer on the top edge and a 6 mm chamfer on the bottom edge. Alternatively, use a 45° router cutter with a pin to produce a 14 mm chamfer on top and a 5 mm chamfer underneath.

Next cut a 25° angle on the ends of all the leg pieces and on the spacer in the appropriate direction so that when the seat is opened they rest flat against the underside of the seat and flat on the floor. Then cut 5 mm chamfers down the length of all the edges, but not across the ends.

Drill holes for the dowels in the inside edges of the two outer legs and a 5 mm groove down both edges of the wider single leg, leaving the rounded end of the router cutter at the end of the cut. These grooves allow the metal dowels to slide up and down as the stool is opened and closed.

Before the final assembly, all the pieces should be lacquered and waxed. Then glue the metal dowels into the two thinner legs and glue these legs to the wooden spacer, with the single leg in position over the metal dowels. Drill the hanging hole in the top, and rout a 5 mm chamfer round the inside edge. Mark out and screw the hinges to the top and the single leg, and screw the hinges to the outside legs. Stand the stool up until it is perfectly level and then you will be able to mark and fit the hinges (already screwed to the outside legs) to the underside of the seat.

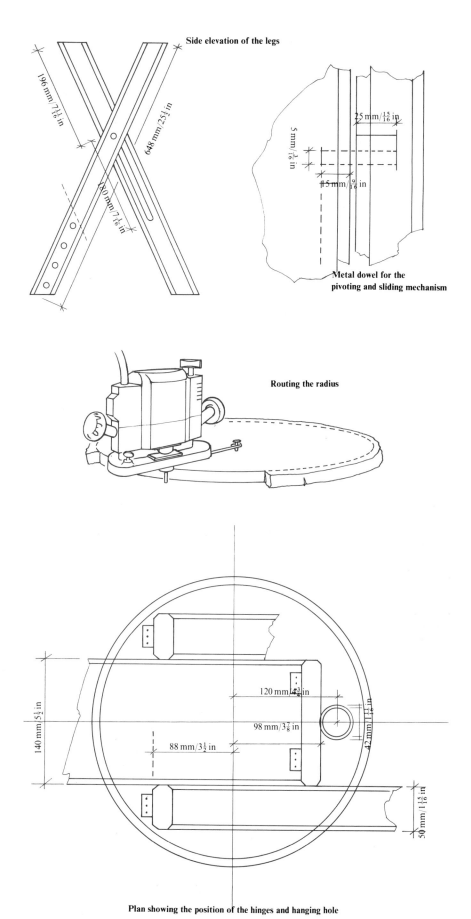

Side elevation of the legs

Metal dowel for the pivoting and sliding mechanism

Routing the radius

Plan showing the position of the hinges and hanging hole

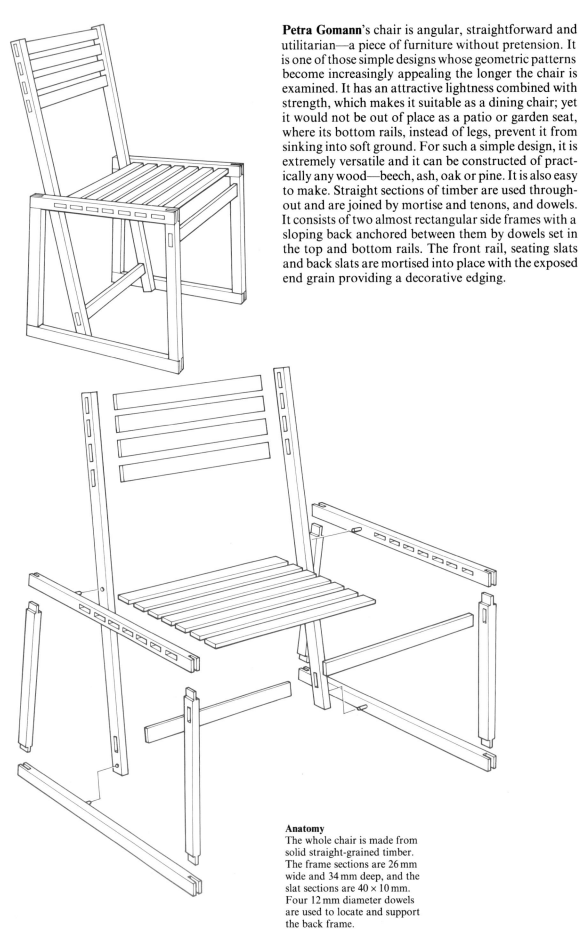

Petra Gomann's chair is angular, straightforward and utilitarian—a piece of furniture without pretension. It is one of those simple designs whose geometric patterns become increasingly appealing the longer the chair is examined. It has an attractive lightness combined with strength, which makes it suitable as a dining chair; yet it would not be out of place as a patio or garden seat, where its bottom rails, instead of legs, prevent it from sinking into soft ground. For such a simple design, it is extremely versatile and it can be constructed of practically any wood—beech, ash, oak or pine. It is also easy to make. Straight sections of timber are used throughout and are joined by mortise and tenons, and dowels. It consists of two almost rectangular side frames with a sloping back anchored between them by dowels set in the top and bottom rails. The front rail, seating slats and back slats are mortised into place with the exposed end grain providing a decorative edging.

Anatomy
The whole chair is made from solid straight-grained timber. The frame sections are 26 mm wide and 34 mm deep, and the slat sections are 40 × 10 mm. Four 12 mm diameter dowels are used to locate and support the back frame.

Side elevation

Front elevation

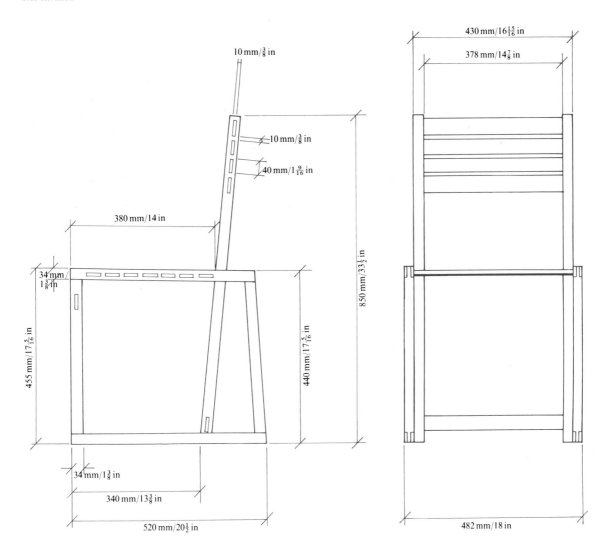

10 mm/$\frac{3}{8}$ in

10 mm/$\frac{3}{8}$ in

40 mm/1$\frac{9}{16}$ in

380 mm/14 in

34 mm/1$\frac{3}{8}$ in

455 mm/17$\frac{5}{16}$ in

440 mm/17$\frac{5}{16}$ in

850 mm/33$\frac{1}{2}$ in

34 mm/1$\frac{3}{8}$ in

340 mm/13$\frac{3}{8}$ in

520 mm/20$\frac{1}{2}$ in

430 mm/16$\frac{15}{16}$ in

378 mm/14$\frac{7}{8}$ in

482 mm/18 in

How to make the chair

First cut all the timber to the required sizes and lengths, then start by cutting the bridle joints for the corners of each of the side frames. Next mark out and cut the mortise and tenons to fix the front rail and seating slats into the side frames and the back slats into the two uprights. If you do not want the end grain of the tenons to be exposed, cut stopped joints instead.

Glue up the side frames and tighten a C-clamp over the joints to improve adhesion. Remember to use a suitable adhesive if the chair is intended for outside use. Next position the back uprights against the side frames and mark and drill where the dowel holes go. Use the measurements on the side elevation (above) to ensure that the uprights are set at the correct angle.

Glue up the back and side frames, then bring the two together by locating them over the dowels. The front rail and seat slats should also be set in place as this is done. Again tighten C-clamps over the tenons.

Finish the chair either with two coats of lacquer, if used inside, or brush on several coats of oil or leave natural, if it is to stand outside.

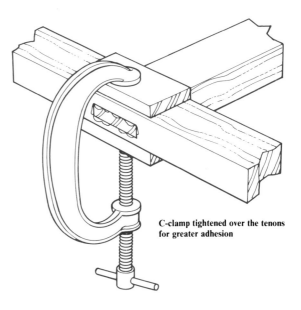

C-clamp tightened over the tenons for greater adhesion

STORAGE / David Field

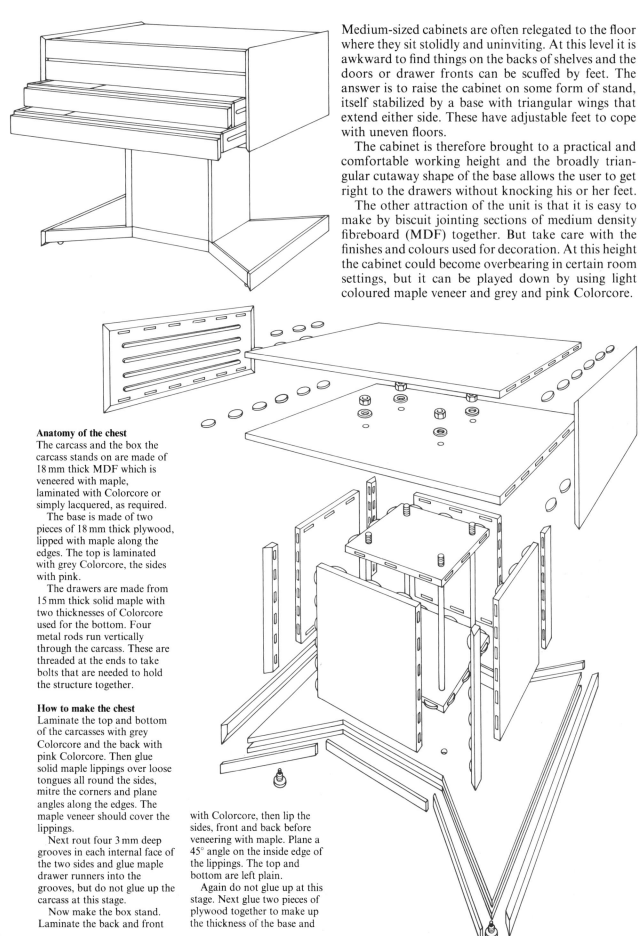

Medium-sized cabinets are often relegated to the floor where they sit stolidly and uninviting. At this level it is awkward to find things on the backs of shelves and the doors or drawer fronts can be scuffed by feet. The answer is to raise the cabinet on some form of stand, itself stabilized by a base with triangular wings that extend either side. These have adjustable feet to cope with uneven floors.

The cabinet is therefore brought to a practical and comfortable working height and the broadly triangular cutaway shape of the base allows the user to get right to the drawers without knocking his or her feet.

The other attraction of the unit is that it is easy to make by biscuit jointing sections of medium density fibreboard (MDF) together. But take care with the finishes and colours used for decoration. At this height the cabinet could become overbearing in certain room settings, but it can be played down by using light coloured maple veneer and grey and pink Colorcore.

Anatomy of the chest
The carcass and the box the carcass stands on are made of 18 mm thick MDF which is veneered with maple, laminated with Colorcore or simply lacquered, as required.

The base is made of two pieces of 18 mm thick plywood, lipped with maple along the edges. The top is laminated with grey Colorcore, the sides with pink.

The drawers are made from 15 mm thick solid maple with two thicknesses of Colorcore used for the bottom. Four metal rods run vertically through the carcass. These are threaded at the ends to take bolts that are needed to hold the structure together.

How to make the chest
Laminate the top and bottom of the carcasses with grey Colorcore and the back with pink Colorcore. Then glue solid maple lippings over loose tongues all round the sides, mitre the corners and plane angles along the edges. The maple veneer should cover the lippings.

Next rout four 3 mm deep grooves in each internal face of the two sides and glue maple drawer runners into the grooves, but do not glue up the carcass at this stage.

Now make the box stand. Laminate the back and front

with Colorcore, then lip the sides, front and back before veneering with maple. Plane a 45° angle on the inside edge of the lippings. The top and bottom are left plain.

Again do not glue up at this stage. Next glue two pieces of plywood together to make up the thickness of the base and

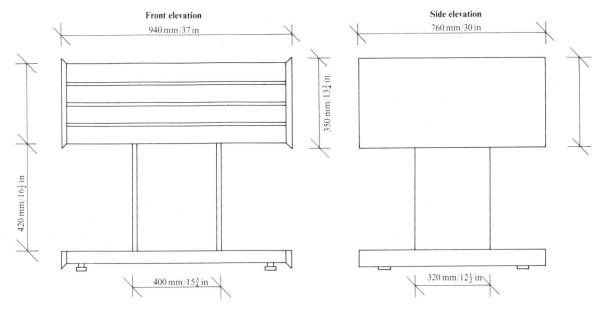

Front elevation

940 mm/37 in

420 mm/16½ in

400 mm/15¾ in

Side elevation

760 mm/30 in

350 mm/13¾ in

320 mm/12½ in

cut to the right shape.
Laminate the top surface with
grey Colorcore and the front
and back edges with pink, then
glue on oversize maple lippings
to the side edges.

Before gluing up the

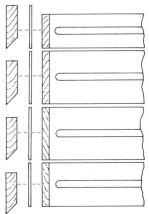

carcasses line up the three top
and bottom sections of the
cabinet, stand and base and
mark and drill the holes for the
fixing studs in one step.
Counterbore the nuts in the
bottom of the main carcass
and the underside of the base.
Now glue up the carcasses and
connect the sections.

The drawers are made up
from solid maple using biscuit
joints in the corners. Groove
down the outsides to
accommodate the runners on
the cabinet sides. Glue two
pieces of Colorcore together
for the bases. Laminate the
front and then screw on a false
front with an angle along the
bottom inside edge to act as a
handle. Depending on the size
and position of the false front
it is possible to create different
decorative effects.

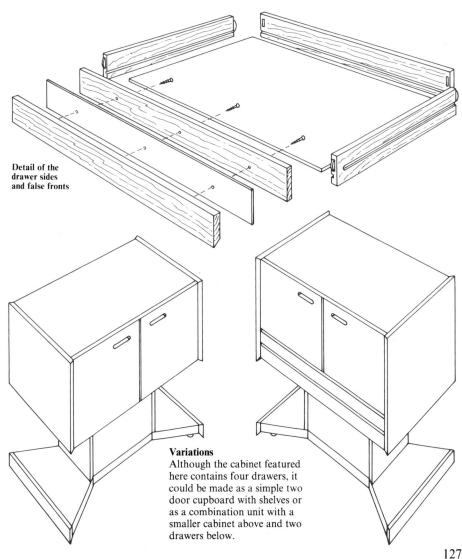

**Detail of the
drawer sides
and false fronts**

Variations
Although the cabinet featured
here contains four drawers, it
could be made as a simple two
door cupboard with shelves or
as a combination unit with a
smaller cabinet above and two
drawers below.

STORAGE / David Field

While most storage units tend to be conventional affairs that strive to satisfy the functional requirements demanded of them, **David Field**'s 5° dresser is eye-catching as an object—visually interesting whether its doors are opened or closed. Something potentially ordinary has been transformed into something dynamic by setting the angles 5° off the horizontal and vertical so that nothing looks quite square. The central row of shelves becomes wider at the top, for example, and the carcass flares slightly outwards from the bottom. It may sound complicated to make, but there is a simple, methodical approach to making the cuts.

Maple is ideal for a piece like this (the brightly coloured restraining wires on the inside shelves provide the only spots of colour). It gives a necessary lightness, and produces the hard, straight edges this design requires. But the design is not only about looks; it is still highly functional. The doors are hinged from the back, allowing additional shelves to be fitted to them so that the contents can be unobtrusively stored, close at hand, without detracting from the objects displayed on the centre shelves.

Anatomy of the dresser
All the solid planks which make up the doors, shelves, uprights and base are made of maple 22 mm thick. The backs are 15 mm thick plywood, veneered with maple. The posts to which the doors are hinged are 30 mm square maple, the feet are cut from 90 × 200 mm blocks. The restraining rails around the shelves are 6 mm diameter steel rod, epoxy coated or painted. Six brass hinges hold the doors open; two magnetic catches close them.

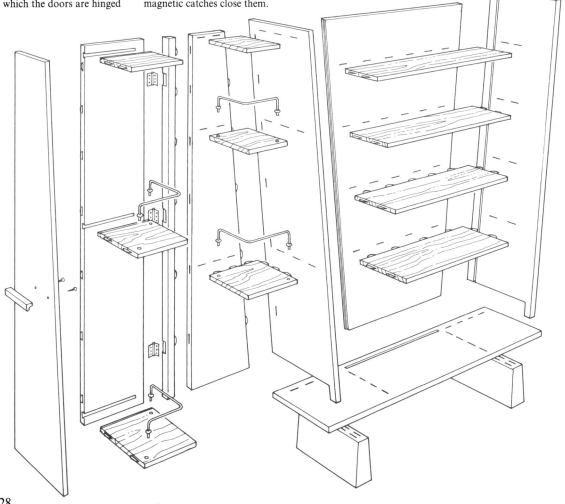

How to make the dresser

Having cut out all the pieces (the grain of the shelves should run the length, and not across the shelves), cut the backs to size and veneer in maple. The central back panel is grooved into the base and the 5° uprights, while the outer back panels are biscuit jointed to the 5° uprights and to the base. The two uprights are biscuit jointed into the outside edges of these two panels and are mortised into the base. The doors are hung from the two uprights.

All the shelves are biscuit jointed to the back and the 5° uprights, while the 5° uprights, which overhang the front of the base, are biscuit jointed to the bottom.

Now make the doors and join the shelves to them, using a dry dovetail slot where the grain of the shelf runs at right angles to the grain of the door, and use biscuit joints where both grains run in the same direction. Apply two coats of lacquer to the components.

Cut out the base blocks, stain them grey and lacquer them, and then biscuit joint them to the base.

Make up the steel retainers for the door shelves and drill and glue them into place. Then hang the doors on the 30 mm square uprights before fitting the catches and handles.

Variations

These nine variations can be made using largely the same construction techniques and materials as the 5° cabinet. All of them are based on creating a composition of horizontal and vertical lines of shelves, doors, drawers and uprights. The faces of these would be well suited to staining or painting in various colours, or to added inlay, to exaggerate their geometry and lines.

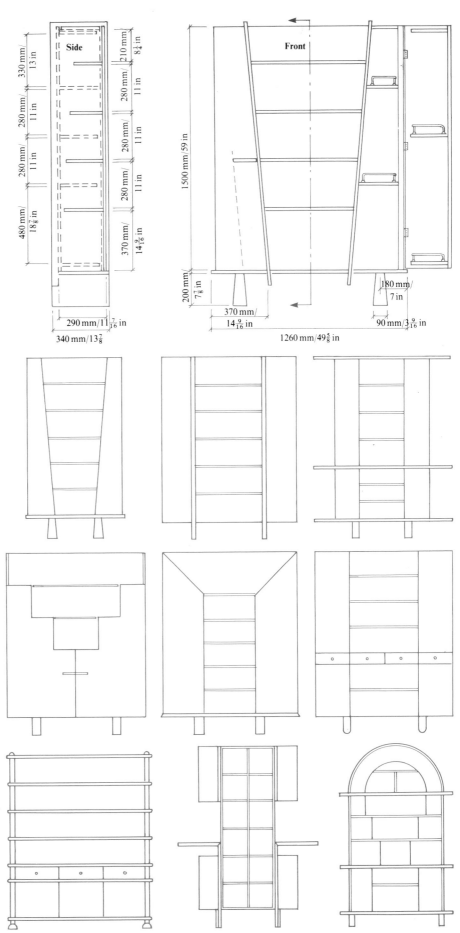

129

STORAGE / David Field

Strong geometric form and striking colours combine to produce an elegant, totem-like cabinet that looks more like a sculpture than a piece of furniture. It appears made up of separate blocks of colour, something like the brightly coloured children's plastic building blocks called Lego, which snap together to make angular shapes—hence its name, the Lego cabinet.

Because of its height relative to its width, the cabinet has a high centre of gravity, and it could become top-heavy and unstable if the top shelves were heavily loaded and the bottom shelves left empty. The problem is overcome with fin-like stabilizers at the base.

The piece is exceptionally beautifully lacquered in a matt red finish.

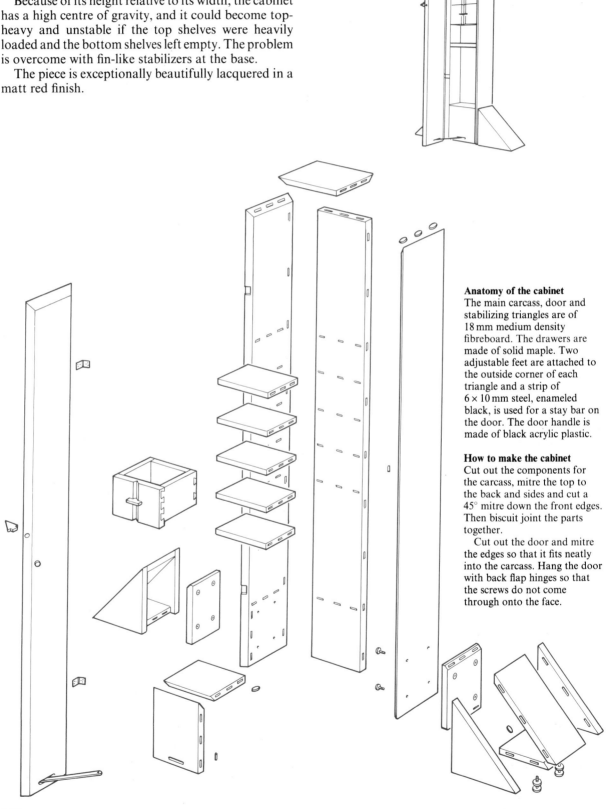

Anatomy of the cabinet
The main carcass, door and stabilizing triangles are of 18 mm medium density fibreboard. The drawers are made of solid maple. Two adjustable feet are attached to the outside corner of each triangle and a strip of 6 × 10 mm steel, enameled black, is used for a stay bar on the door. The door handle is made of black acrylic plastic.

How to make the cabinet
Cut out the components for the carcass, mitre the top to the back and sides and cut a 45° mitre down the front edges. Then biscuit joint the parts together.

Cut out the door and mitre the edges so that it fits neatly into the carcass. Hang the door with back flap hinges so that the screws do not come through onto the face.

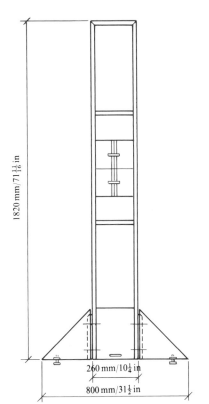

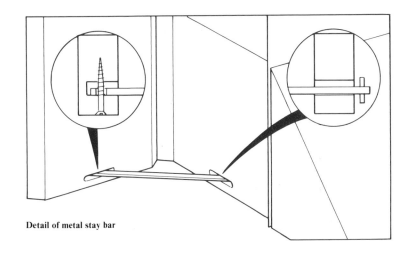

Detail of metal stay bar

Door hinge and handle

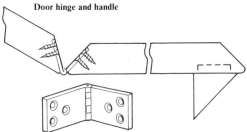

Cut a blind slot in the bottom of the door and attach one end of the stay bar in this by screwing up into it through the bottom edge of the door. The other end of the bar is passed through a slot cut at the same height in the bottom piece of the carcass. A pin is then glued into the end of the bar and thus prevents the door from being opened too far. Before the pin is finally fitted in, lacquer the cabinet red.

The door handle is made of 6 mm thick black acrylic and is tongued into the door and secured with epoxy adhesive after the door has been lacquered red.

Now biscuit joint the triangles together, letting the face that touches the carcass stick out by 3 mm. And into the same face fix four threads. Before actually gluing up the triangles, use the threads to mark the corresponding hole positions on each side of the cabinet and fit the adjustable feet. Also drill the fixing holes in the cabinet. Coat all the faces of the triangle with matt white acrylic paint, and use a 3 mm black acrylic plastic spacer between the carcass and triangle. Then attach the triangles to the cabinet.

Make the drawers out of solid maple, dovetailing the corners at the back and using lap dovetails at the front. For the handles, rout a 6 mm deep

Door front with acrylic handle

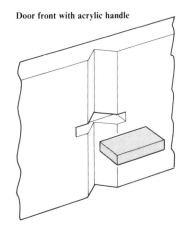

groove into the front and then rout a V-groove down the middle of the front, from top to bottom. Glue a piece of black acrylic into the horizontal groove to act as a handle.

Finally, attach a magnetic catch to the door to keep it closed.

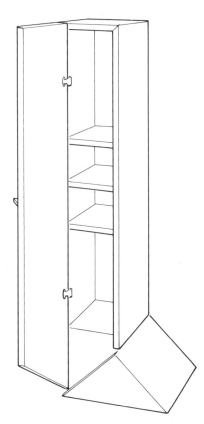

David Savage's cabinet is a fine example of a classical cabinet. Tall and slender and beautifully proportioned, it makes an excellent showcase without seeming to dominate its contents. The carcass and shelves are made of pearwood, the back is cedar of Lebanon, renowned for its pleasant smell. The method of hanging the door is worth noting because it enables the knuckles of the hinges to be concealed when looking at the cabinet from the front and forms a continuation of the moulding on the side. The detail necessary to achieve this is repeated on the opposite side of the cabinet to maintain symmetry. When the door is opened a small drawer is revealed on the bottom of the carcass. The contrasting strip of maple that runs vertically up the centre of the rosewood drawer front protrudes and acts as a handle. It is ingeniously recessed into the shelf above when the drawer is closed.

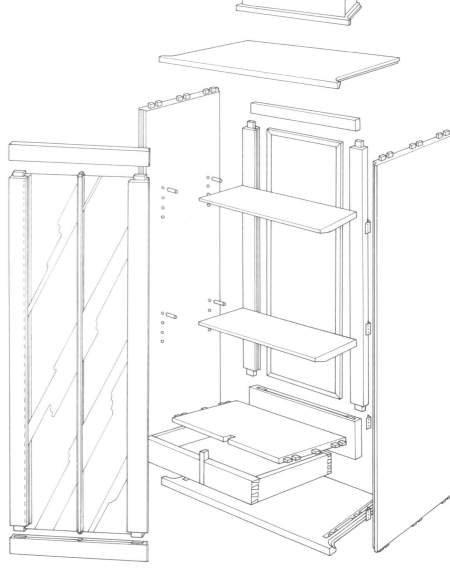

Anatomy of the cabinet

The cabinet is made predominantly of pearwood, the top and bottom having cross-sections of 185×18 mm; the back is cedar of Lebanon. The two 13 mm thick adjustable shelves rest on brass dowels while a third fixed shelf acts as a top for the drawer at the bottom of the cabinet. This again is made of pearwood, with a rosewood (or ebony) front. A strip of maple acts as a handle. The door frame is pearwood, with beading acting as a central divider. The panels are fitted with 3 mm thick glass and the door is hung on four brass hinges.

How the cabinet is made

The bottom shelf is mortised and tenoned, and housed into the sides of the cabinet. In turn, the sides are similarly jointed into the top and base. Before gluing up the outside carcass, shape the top and base using a router, with a ring fence running against a template clamped in place. Also drill the holes for the brass dowels to take the shelves, which should be chamfered on the lower front edges.

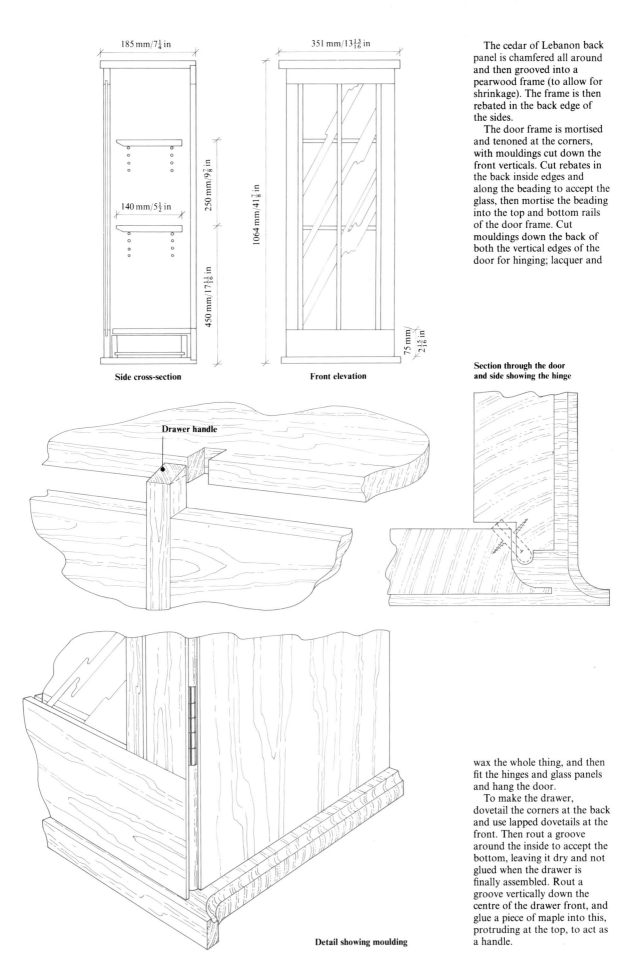

185 mm/7¼ in

351 mm/13¹³⁄₁₆ in

250 mm/9⅞ in

140 mm/5½ in

1064 mm/41⅞ in

450 mm/17¹¹⁄₁₆ in

75 mm/2¹⁵⁄₁₆ in

Side cross-section

Front elevation

**Section through the door
and side showing the hinge**

Drawer handle

Detail showing moulding

The cedar of Lebanon back panel is chamfered all around and then grooved into a pearwood frame (to allow for shrinkage). The frame is then rebated in the back edge of the sides.

The door frame is mortised and tenoned at the corners, with mouldings cut down the front verticals. Cut rebates in the back inside edges and along the beading to accept the glass, then mortise the beading into the top and bottom rails of the door frame. Cut mouldings down the back of both the vertical edges of the door for hinging; lacquer and

wax the whole thing, and then fit the hinges and glass panels and hang the door.

To make the drawer, dovetail the corners at the back and use lapped dovetails at the front. Then rout a groove around the inside to accept the bottom, leaving it dry and not glued when the drawer is finally assembled. Rout a groove vertically down the centre of the drawer front, and glue a piece of maple into this, protruding at the top, to act as a handle.

CLOTHES STORAGE / Alan Peters

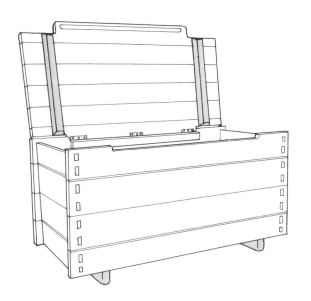

Here is a linen chest that displays all the skills of the designer in combining structural considerations with the intelligent use of decoration. Visually a simple piece, the clean lines have been enhanced by raising the chest on feet to give it lightness, and by slightly tapering the front and back panels and making a feature of the through-tenons, giving them bullnoses.

On closer inspection it is readily apparent just how much thought and ingenuity has gone into solving a number of design problems, notably of how to deal with shrinkage, how to support the hinging mechanism and how to incorporate an unobtrusive handle to lift the lid. Scots pine originally was chosen as a timber that would complement the design, but any straight-grained timber can be used.

Anatomy of the chest
The sides, front, back and lid (and the hinge support) are made from 21 mm thick Scots pine. The feet and dovetailed supports for the lid should be cut from a 50 × 32 mm section of dense hardwood. Plywood 15 mm thick can be used for the bottom.

How to make the chest
Plank up the front, back and side panels, using stopped plywood tongues in the grooves. Then square off all the panels and cut the final lengths required.

Mark out the mortises and tenons so that the mortises can be cut with a 12 mm router cutter. And when measuring allow extra length for the protruding tenons.

Now cut the mortises and a 3 mm housing between them using the router. The rebate on each side of the tenons can be

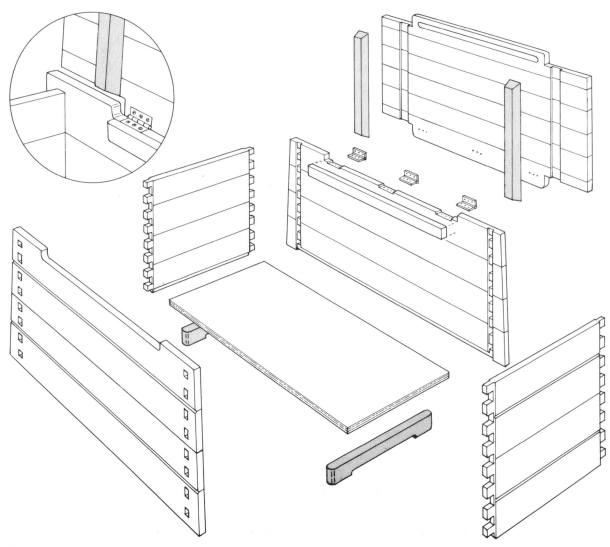

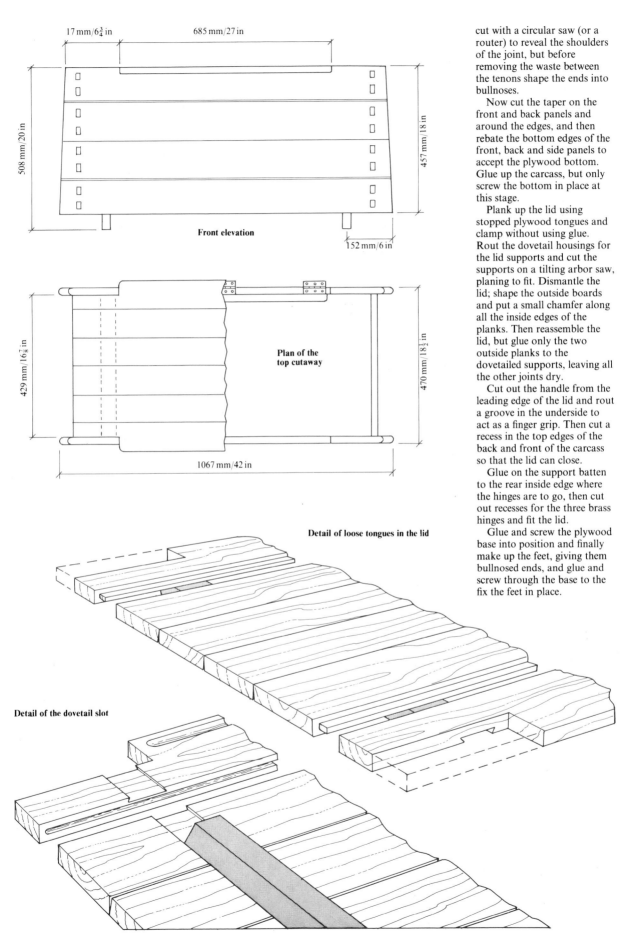

17 mm/6¾ in

685 mm/27 in

508 mm/20 in

457 mm/18 in

Front elevation

152 mm/6 in

429 mm/16⅞ in

470 mm/18½ in

**Plan of the
top cutaway**

1067 mm/42 in

Detail of loose tongues in the lid

Detail of the dovetail slot

cut with a circular saw (or a router) to reveal the shoulders of the joint, but before removing the waste between the tenons shape the ends into bullnoses.

Now cut the taper on the front and back panels and around the edges, and then rebate the bottom edges of the front, back and side panels to accept the plywood bottom. Glue up the carcass, but only screw the bottom in place at this stage.

Plank up the lid using stopped plywood tongues and clamp without using glue. Rout the dovetail housings for the lid supports and cut the supports on a tilting arbor saw, planing to fit. Dismantle the lid; shape the outside boards and put a small chamfer along all the inside edges of the planks. Then reassemble the lid, but glue only the two outside planks to the dovetailed supports, leaving all the other joints dry.

Cut out the handle from the leading edge of the lid and rout a groove in the underside to act as a finger grip. Then cut a recess in the top edges of the back and front of the carcass so that the lid can close.

Glue on the support batten to the rear inside edge where the hinges are to go, then cut out recesses for the three brass hinges and fit the lid.

Glue and screw the plywood base into position and finally make up the feet, giving them bullnosed ends, and glue and screw through the base to the fix the feet in place.

CLOTHES STORAGE / Jonathan Baulkwill

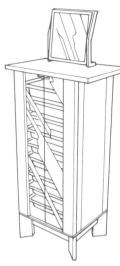

The design of **Jonathan Baulkwill**'s elegantly proportioned and very attractive storage unit originates from the old glass-fronted cabinets once found behind the counters of gentlemen's outfitters. The idea has been given a modern twist by replacing the shallow fixed shelving with preformed, clear Plexiglass trays, edged in mahogany, which can be pulled out like drawers to gain easy access to the contents. Combined with the glass doors, this feature also allows the user to see what is in the cabinet without having to open it up.

The freestanding pivoting mirror on top of the unit has also been designed as very much a part of the overall composition. It is the finishing touch which "lifts" the piece and turns it into a complete and highly functional cabinet.

Anatomy of the dresser
The dresser is made predominantly from 18 mm thick chipboard. A mahogany veneer, stained red, is used on the top while an ash veneer is applied to the sides and bottom. Solid ash is used for the doors, legs and corner uprights, and solid mahogany dowel for the edging to the trays. Two panels of 4 mm glass, with polished edges and predrilled fixing holes, will also be needed, as will 10 Plexiglass trays.

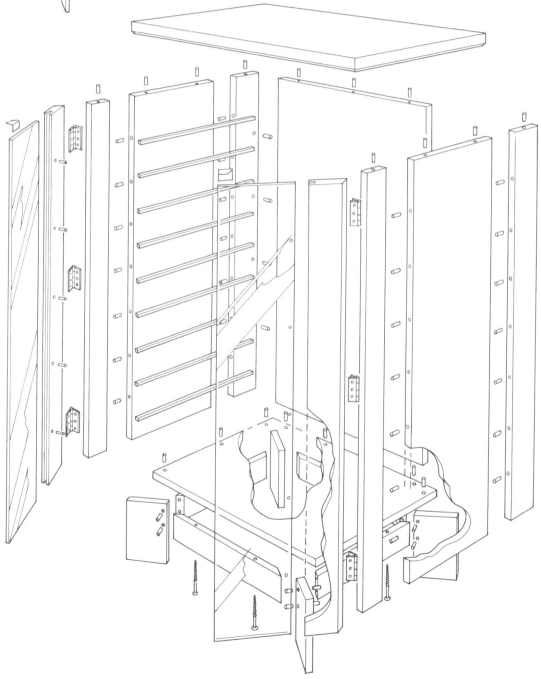

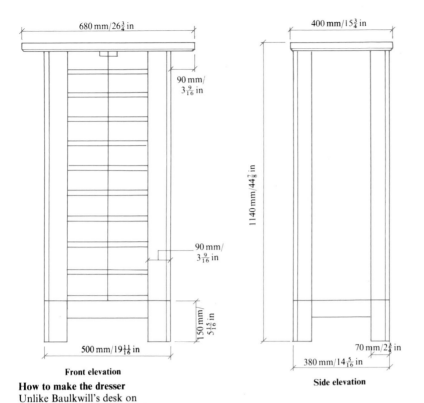

680 mm/26¾ in

90 mm/
3 9/16 in

90 mm/
3 9/16 in

1140 mm/44⅞ in

150 mm/
5 15/16 in

500 mm/19 11/16 in

Front elevation

400 mm/15¾ in

70 mm/2¾ in

380 mm/14 5/16 in

Side elevation

How to make the dresser

Unlike Baulkwill's desk on pages 90–91, which perhaps is over-elaborate in its use of complex joints, this cabinet is simply dowelled together. First make up the side panels and fit the runners for the trays. Then make up the base unit, mitring the corners so the legs can be set at a 45° angle. Now make up the slab areas by dowelling the side and back panels onto the base and to each other. Then fit the top.

Each of the two doors is made up of a solid ash rail which has a chamfer cut down its outside edge and is hinged to the carcass using ordinary butt hinges. A deep groove is cut into its other edge to accept the glass panel. This is held in place by dowels driven from the back of the rail through

predrilled holes in the glass into stopped housings, thus giving an invisible fixing from the front. The handles are simply glued to the top and rear edge of the glass.

To make up the trays rout two grooves down opposite sides of the mahogany dowel, one of which will slip over the runner fixed to the cabinet side and the other will accept the lip of the Plexiglass tray. Now cut and mitre the doweling and glue it to the tray. Alternatively, the containers can be made from cotton or canvas suspended from the doweling and stiffened with a hardboard bottom.

The mirror frame and holder are both made of solid ash. Mitre the corners for a neat finish and strengthen the joints with veneer tongues. Note how

Freestanding mirror

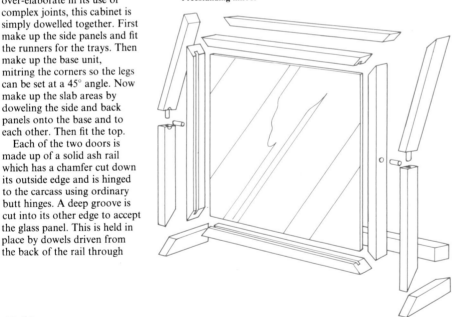

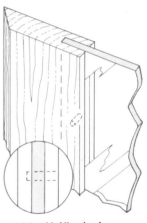

Metal dowel holding the glass

the top half of the holder is angled away from the bottom half. This is done by cutting a shallow angle across the two uprights and then refixing them with dowels. Dowels are also fitted into the elbow and mirror frame to allow the mirror to pivot.

The cabinet can be finished by spraying on a clear cellulose lacquer and then applying a light coat of wax polish.

Plexiglass tray

CLOTHES STORAGE / Ron Carter

It is the subtle decorative touches of **Ron Carter**'s design, combined with a well-proportioned cabinet, that has resulted in this simple, yet highly attractive chest of drawers. The overlapping top visually reduces the height of the piece and adds width. The triangular-shaped handles spaced apart at the top corners of the drawer fronts, and the triangular profile of the rails between the drawers promote the illusion of breadth.

The chest is simple to construct using housings and mortises and tenons. The fronts to the drawers are connected with through-dovetails, and then the false drawer fronts are screwed on from inside the drawer, which gives the impression of lap dovetails at the front corners of the drawers.

Anatomy of the chest
The top is made of 25 mm thick chipboard veneered in ash, with 60 mm wide solid ash lippings. The sides and back are also made of veneered chipboard 18 mm thick, with solid lippings.

The drawer fronts and sides are made of 12 mm thick solid ash, and have 18 mm thick false fronts screwed on which extend 16 mm beyond the width on each side. The drawers therefore appear wider than they actually are. The drawer bottoms are made from 6 mm thick plywood.

All the other components are made of solid ash.

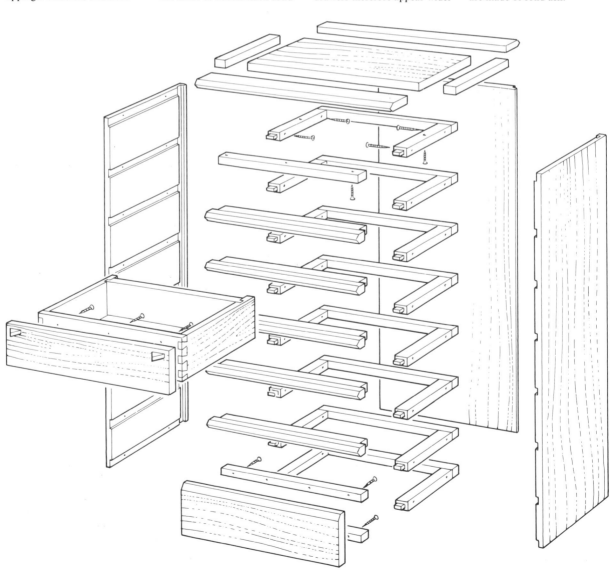

138

How to make the chest

Make up the top using butt joints, rather than mitres, for the lippings. The triangular profile of the front lipping can be cut with either a router or a circular saw. Cut out the sides and back, and lip all the edges of the sides—but just the top and bottom of the back— before veneering. Make up the eight internal frames, six of which act as drawer runners, using mortises and tenons, and drill holes in the frames where they screw into the plinth, and into the 3 mm housings grooved in the sides. Glue up and fit them in position. Next glue the triangular lippings to

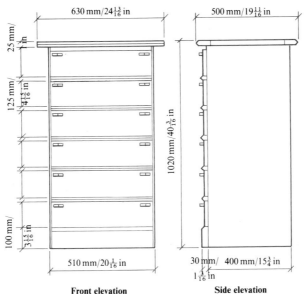

630 mm/24 $\frac{13}{16}$ in
25 mm/ 1 in
125 mm/ 4 $\frac{15}{16}$ in
100 mm/ 3 $\frac{15}{16}$ in
510 mm/20 $\frac{1}{16}$ in

Front elevation

500 mm/19 $\frac{11}{16}$ in
1020 mm/40 $\frac{3}{16}$ in
30 mm/ 1 $\frac{3}{16}$ in
400 mm/15 $\frac{3}{4}$ in

Side elevation

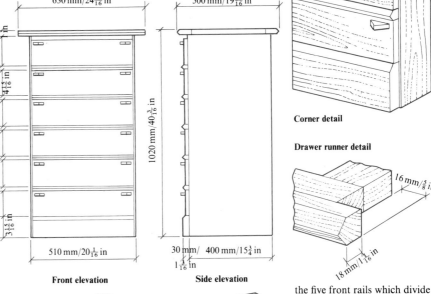

Corner detail

Drawer runner detail

16 mm/ $\frac{5}{8}$ in
18 mm/ $\frac{11}{16}$ in

the five front rails which divide the drawers.

To fit the back panel, cut a rebate down each edge of the back panel. Cut grooves 3 mm in from the back edge so the tongue of the rebate can be slotted into it. Pre-finish with two coats of lacquer.

Having cut out the plinth, the chest is now ready to be assembled.

Glue the back into the grooves, cut out of the side panels and screw in the internal frames. Screw up through the top frame to secure the top of the unit. The plinth then is screwed on from the inside.

Next make up the drawers using housing joints at the back and dovetails at the front; the bottom is grooved into the sides. The false fronts are screwed on from inside the drawer. The handles are made from 8 mm thick solid ash cut so that the grain runs away from the drawer front leaving end grain exposed in the sloping faces. The handles are tenoned into the fronts for a firm fixing.

Variations

These are a series of storage chests and cabinets suitable for most kinds of household storage. Their method of construction is similar to that of the chest opposite. On three of these modifications, the characteristic Ron Carter chamfer (see page 52, top) appears again.

BOOKCASE / Jonathan Baulkwill

Jonathan Baulkwill's book storage unit (see page 72) breaks away from the convention of storing books against a wall on some form of shelving system. Made from solid maple and maple-veneered plywood panels, the unit revolves on a turntable, thus allowing easy access to the shelves. This rotational movement is also reflected in the design by the spoked arrangement of the internal rails. It also means that the unit can sit happily anywhere in a room, next to a reading chair or even in a corner, where it can be turned around to reach the books facing the walls.

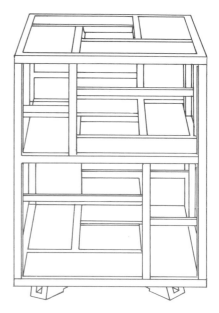

Anatomy of the bookcase

All the structural members are cut from 21 mm square solid maple except the built-up feet and the horizontal frames which separate the books—the latter are made of 15 × 11 mm maple. The panels in the top, central and bottom frames are 12 mm thick plywood veneered with maple. A similar panel is rebated into the middle of the bottom frame to provide a fixing for a 12.5 mm deep lazy-susan unit with sealed bearings. It is this which allows the entire unit to rotate.

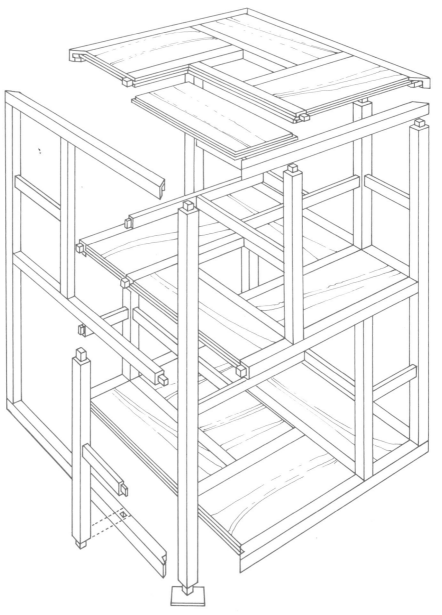

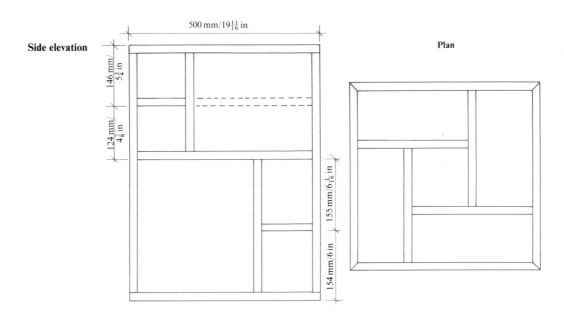

Side elevation

500 mm/$19\frac{11}{16}$ in

146 mm/$5\frac{3}{4}$ in

124 mm/$4\frac{7}{8}$ in

155 mm/$6\frac{1}{16}$ in

154 mm/6 in

Plan

How the bookcase is made

The carcass: The top and bottom sections are mitred at the corners with a supporting tongue inserted into each joint. Because the four uprights are tenoned into the mitres and into the tongues, it is important that the tongues are bigger than the cross section of the tenons, otherwise the mitres will be weakened. The top, middle and bottom sections have veneered panels grooved into the framework so that the veneered surface is flush with the top of the rails. The outside horizontals of the middle section are tenoned into the four corner uprights. The two frames supporting the books are tenoned into the horizontals which in turn are tenoned into the crossrails above and below. Where the two frames supporting the books meet in the centre, dowels are used to join them. Careful planning is needed for the stages of gluing up.

The base: Use a router to cut a rebate in the underside of the opening left in the bottom frame to accept a 12 mm thick panel of veneered plywood. When glued in place the panel should be flush with the underside of the frame. This is what the swivel mechanism is later fitted to. The feet are made up of black walnut sandwiched between two pieces of maple. The two sections are halved together and then the 12.5 mm thick turntable with sealed bearings is first screwed over the halving, and then screwed into the underside of the plywood base.

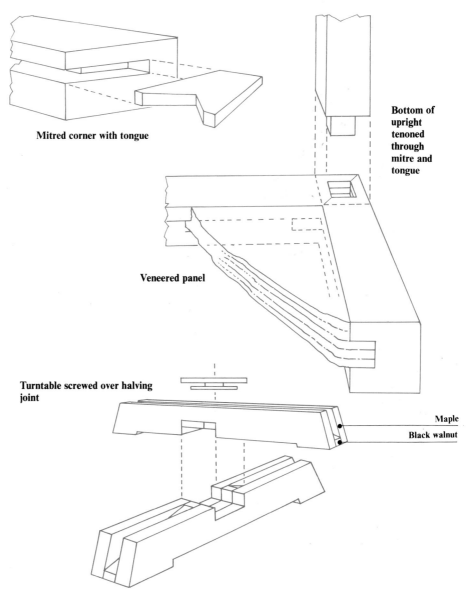

Mitred corner with tongue

Bottom of upright tenoned through mitre and tongue

Veneered panel

Turntable screwed over halving joint

Maple

Black walnut

MIRRORS / Paul Connell

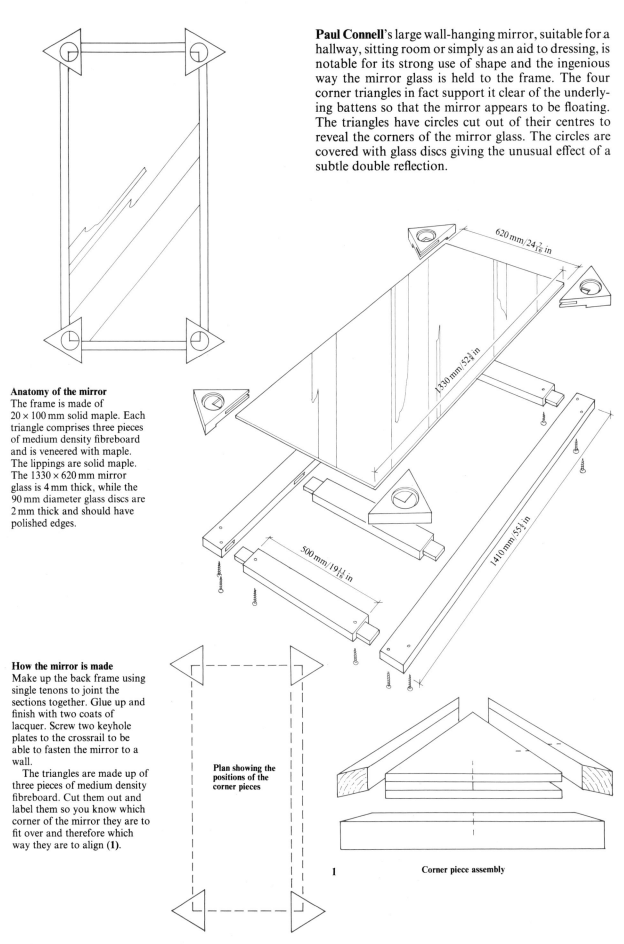

Paul Connell's large wall-hanging mirror, suitable for a hallway, sitting room or simply as an aid to dressing, is notable for its strong use of shape and the ingenious way the mirror glass is held to the frame. The four corner triangles in fact support it clear of the underlying battens so that the mirror appears to be floating. The triangles have circles cut out of their centres to reveal the corners of the mirror glass. The circles are covered with glass discs giving the unusual effect of a subtle double reflection.

Anatomy of the mirror
The frame is made of 20 × 100 mm solid maple. Each triangle comprises three pieces of medium density fibreboard and is veneered with maple. The lippings are solid maple. The 1330 × 620 mm mirror glass is 4 mm thick, while the 90 mm diameter glass discs are 2 mm thick and should have polished edges.

How the mirror is made
Make up the back frame using single tenons to joint the sections together. Glue up and finish with two coats of lacquer. Screw two keyhole plates to the crossrail to be able to fasten the mirror to a wall.

The triangles are made up of three pieces of medium density fibreboard. Cut them out and label them so you know which corner of the mirror they are to fit over and therefore which way they are to align (**1**).

620 mm/24 $\frac{7}{16}$ in

1330 mm/52 $\frac{3}{8}$ in

1410 mm/55 $\frac{1}{2}$ in

500 mm/19 $\frac{11}{16}$ in

Plan showing the positions of the corner pieces

1

Corner piece assembly

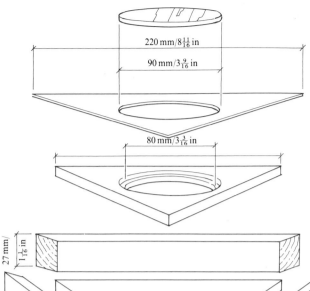

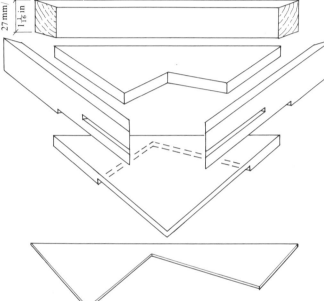

220 mm/8$\frac{11}{16}$ in

90 mm/3$\frac{9}{16}$ in

80 mm/3$\frac{3}{16}$ in

27 mm/1$\frac{1}{16}$ in

Exploded view of the corner piece

Take the middle sections of the triangles and cut away a right-angled section to allow the corner of the mirror glass to be recessed into it. Now glue up the three sections and add the mitred lippings, marking on their faces where the cut-out comes, before veneering.

Having glued veneer on both faces of each triangle, use a thin piece of plywood with a circle cut out of it as a template for the router. Using a large cutter and a ring fence, rout the hole in each triangle to take the glass disc. Then,

using a smaller cutter and the same template, cut down 13 mm into the edge of the hole, leaving a 5 mm rebate to support the glass disc.

Then rout a 4 mm wide groove through the centre of the lipping into the recess so that mirror can be slipped in.

Finally, cut a rebate in the underside of the triangles so they can sit over the corner of the frame and secure them in place by screwing up through the back of the frame. The glass discs are simply glued into the circles.

Corner piece in place

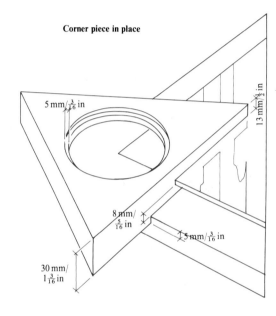

5 mm/$\frac{3}{16}$ in

13 mm/$\frac{1}{2}$ in

8 mm/$\frac{5}{16}$ in

5 mm/$\frac{3}{16}$ in

30 mm/1$\frac{3}{16}$ in

Variations
This mirror is made to exactly the same dimensions except that 130 mm squares are used on the corners instead of triangles. Contrasting colours can also be used inside the circles for greater decorative effect.

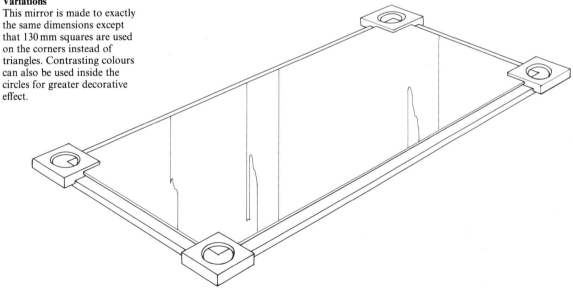

MIRRORS / Petra Gomann

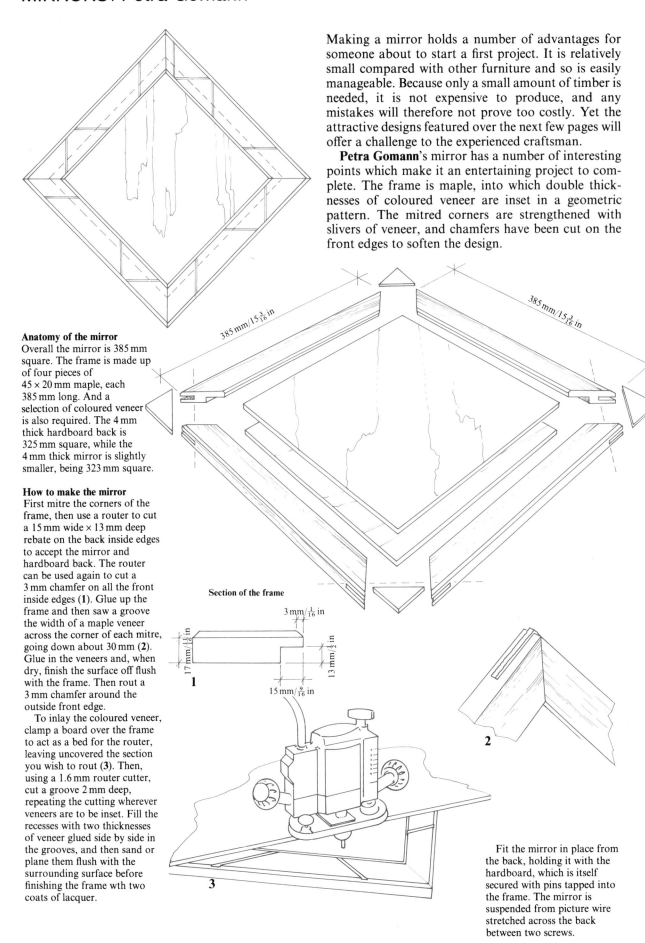

Making a mirror holds a number of advantages for someone about to start a first project. It is relatively small compared with other furniture and so is easily manageable. Because only a small amount of timber is needed, it is not expensive to produce, and any mistakes will therefore not prove too costly. Yet the attractive designs featured over the next few pages will offer a challenge to the experienced craftsman.

Petra Gomann's mirror has a number of interesting points which make it an entertaining project to complete. The frame is maple, into which double thicknesses of coloured veneer are inset in a geometric pattern. The mitred corners are strengthened with slivers of veneer, and chamfers have been cut on the front edges to soften the design.

385 mm/15 3/16 in

385 mm/15 3/16 in

385 mm/15 3/16 in

Anatomy of the mirror
Overall the mirror is 385 mm square. The frame is made up of four pieces of 45 × 20 mm maple, each 385 mm long. And a selection of coloured veneer is also required. The 4 mm thick hardboard back is 325 mm square, while the 4 mm thick mirror is slightly smaller, being 323 mm square.

How to make the mirror
First mitre the corners of the frame, then use a router to cut a 15 mm wide × 13 mm deep rebate on the back inside edges to accept the mirror and hardboard back. The router can be used again to cut a 3 mm chamfer on all the front inside edges (**1**). Glue up the frame and then saw a groove the width of a maple veneer across the corner of each mitre, going down about 30 mm (**2**). Glue in the veneers and, when dry, finish the surface off flush with the frame. Then rout a 3 mm chamfer around the outside front edge.

To inlay the coloured veneer, clamp a board over the frame to act as a bed for the router, leaving uncovered the section you wish to rout (**3**). Then, using a 1.6 mm router cutter, cut a groove 2 mm deep, repeating the cutting wherever veneers are to be inset. Fill the recesses with two thicknesses of veneer glued side by side in the grooves, and then sand or plane them flush with the surrounding surface before finishing the frame with two coats of lacquer.

Section of the frame

3 mm/1/16 in

17 mm/11/16 in

13 mm/1/2 in

15 mm/9/16 in

1

2

3

Fit the mirror in place from the back, holding it with the hardboard, which is itself secured with pins tapped into the frame. The mirror is suspended from picture wire stretched across the back between two screws.

In contrast to the Gomann mirror, **Anthony Thompson**'s design makes a feature of each constructional technique. Note how the mitres have been left open to expose the corners of the mirror. The gap here is exaggerated by a maplewood tongue which contrasts with the darker walnut of the rest of the frame. Again, chamfers along the edges soften the overall lines.

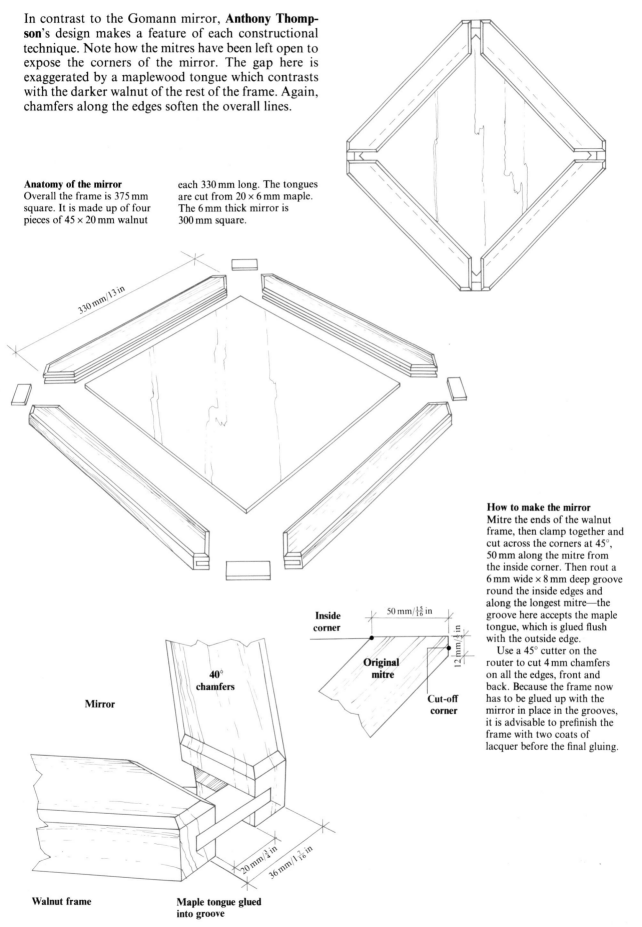

Anatomy of the mirror
Overall the frame is 375 mm square. It is made up of four pieces of 45 × 20 mm walnut each 330 mm long. The tongues are cut from 20 × 6 mm maple. The 6 mm thick mirror is 300 mm square.

330 mm/13 in

Mirror

40° chamfers

Walnut frame

Maple tongue glued into groove

20 mm/¾ in

36 mm/1 7/16 in

Inside corner

50 mm/1 15/16 in

12 mm/½ in

Original mitre

Cut-off corner

How to make the mirror
Mitre the ends of the walnut frame, then clamp together and cut across the corners at 45°, 50 mm along the mitre from the inside corner. Then rout a 6 mm wide × 8 mm deep groove round the inside edges and along the longest mitre—the groove here accepts the maple tongue, which is glued flush with the outside edge.

Use a 45° cutter on the router to cut 4 mm chamfers on all the edges, front and back. Because the frame now has to be glued up with the mirror in place in the grooves, it is advisable to prefinish the frame with two coats of lacquer before the final gluing.

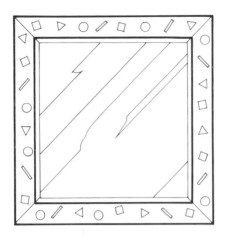

As with Petra Gomann's mirror, on page 72, **Toby Winteringham**'s mirror develops the idea of using coloured veneers to decorate the frame. Here, however, it is the colourful geometric shapes of the veneer set in a pale contrasting maple surround that provide the visual interest. The pattern is so flexible that only your imagination will limit the final design that can be created. Yet to be completely effective, a high degree of accuracy is needed when inlaying the veneer.

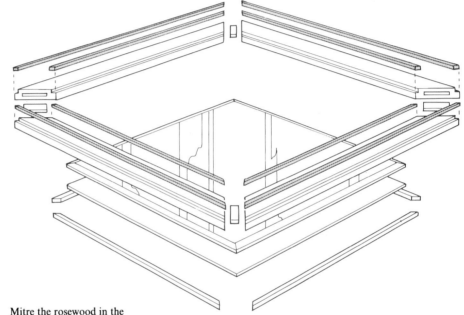

Anatomy of the mirror

The main frame of the mirror is made of solid maple 750 × 75 × 22 mm and this takes a 4 mm thick 600 mm square mirror glass with a 20 mm bevel on its edge. The four outside rosewood fillets are 6 × 5 × 750 mm and the four inside fillets are made of the same thickness timber. The four backing pieces are 9 mm square maple. You will also need one piece of 3.2 mm thick 600 mm square hardboard as a backing for the mirror, four plywood tongues 70 × 20 × 6 mm and some pieces of coloured veneers.

How to make the mirror

Cut the mitred corners of the frame. Using a dovetail router cutter, rebate a 6 mm wide × 5 mm deep recess on the outside front edges and glue in the 6 × 5 mm fillets of rosewood. Repeat the process on the inside edges, but make the rebate only 3 mm wide so that when the 6 × 5 mm rosewood fillet is added it overhangs the edge by 3 mm.

Mitre the rosewood in the corners, then rout grooves along the mitres to accept a 10 × 6 × 70 mm plywood tongue. When this is done, glue up the frame.

Next, cut the geometric shapes and colours needed for inlaying into the frame. Use the shapes as templates to trace out the area of wood to be removed. Use a chisel and router to remove the waste and glue in the veneers. Then clean up and finish the frame.

Finally, cut the hardboard back to fit. Insert the mirror and cover it with the back, holding them in with strips of maple mitred at the corners.

The mirror can be hung against the wall using a keyhole plate.

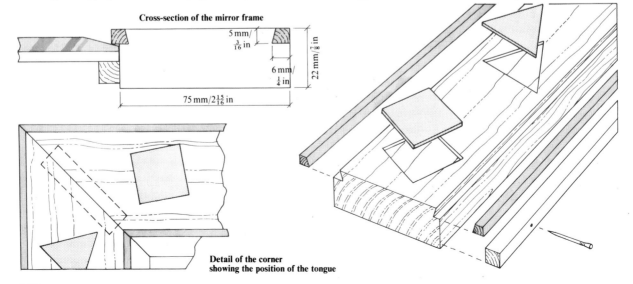

Cross-section of the mirror frame

5 mm/ $\frac{3}{16}$ in

6 mm/ $\frac{1}{4}$ in

22 mm/ $\frac{7}{8}$ in

75 mm/ $2\frac{15}{16}$ in

Detail of the corner showing the position of the tongue

The basic design of **Ron Carter**'s coatstand could not have been simpler—a solid central column supported by four feet provides a stable base that will not tip over when coats are hooked over the arms. Yet what could have been a rather ordinary piece has been transformed into an elegant and original stand by a few selective details. The triangular cross-section of the feet, repeated in the arms, lightens the chunkiness of the stand. This is aided by the angled grooves running the entire length of the upright on opposite faces. The triangular section of the arms also makes it far easier to hook coats on.

Anatomy of the stand
All the hangers are cut from 28 × 64 mm solid ash. The post is cut from 50 × 64 mm timber as are the legs and the feet underneath the ends are 10 × 38 × 50 mm in size.

How to make the stand
Cut the main post to size, and then cut two 8 mm wide grooves with a router, using a jig to hold the cutter at the correct angle (see pages 172–173). Before cutting the triangular sections of the arms and legs, cut the notches. This can be done either by routing a groove across the top of each rectangular block or by clamping two blocks together and drilling down where they meet to make a semi-circular recess in both faces. The triangular faces can be cut on a circular saw. The arms and legs are then joined to the upright and the stand is finished with two coats of lacquer.

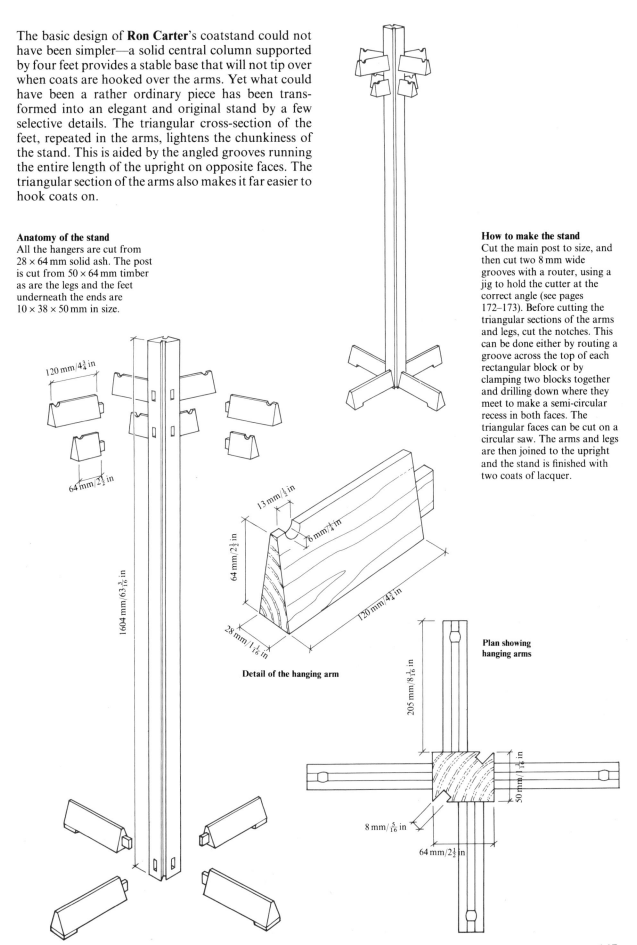

120 mm/4¾ in

64 mm/2½ in

1604 mm/63³⁄₁₆ in

13 mm/½ in

6 mm/¼ in

64 mm/2½ in

120 mm/4¾ in

28 mm/1¹⁄₁₆ in

Detail of the hanging arm

205 mm/8¹⁄₁₆ in

Plan showing hanging arms

50 mm/1¹⁵⁄₁₆ in

8 mm/⁵⁄₁₆ in

64 mm/2½ in

BEDS / David Field

There is often the problem, when designing a bed that is simply a mattress support, of finding a complementary headboard and side units to go with it. If a headboard is required, there is much to be said for designing it as a part of the bed itself. The **David Field** bed does this relatively simply by incorporating side shelves and drawers. The result is a thoroughly integrated piece, adaptable to a range of bedroom schemes.

The bed is straightforward to construct, primarily of medium density fibreboard (MDF). The surfaces are covered with strong-coloured lacquers and by plastic laminate, a finish that has been unnecessarily restricted to the kitchen. Here, the uniformly coloured surfaces, in grey, decorate the design.

The bed frame consists of two box units which function like rafts to support the platform base so that it floats above the floor.

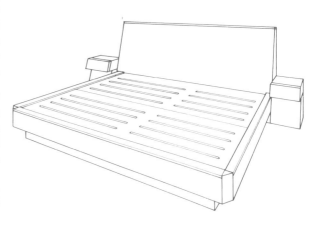

Anatomy of the bed
The bed is made of 18 mm thick medium density fibreboard covered with laminate. Similarly, the shelf is made of MDF, but this has been lacquered red. The side cabinets are made of 12 mm thick MDF and the drawers are 12 mm solid beech with 6 mm plywood bottoms. The drawer fronts are lacquered red. The boxes for the base are also made of 18 mm thick

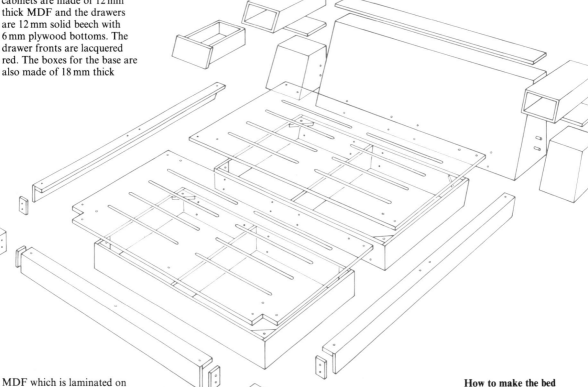

MDF which is laminated on the exposed faces and corner blocks are used to strengthen the corners. Each box is covered with a sheet of 18 mm thick plywood. A plywood L-shape protects the edges and the sections are joined by triangular beech wedges at the corners. The two boxes are bolted together, as are the side cabinets to the headboard.

How to make the bed
Cut out all the pieces and make up the headboard using biscuit joints. Cover the front and sides with laminate. Lacquer the shelf red and fasten it down from inside the carcass using wood screws.

Cut out the sections of MDF for the side drawer unit and make them up using biscuit joints. The platform base does not have a bottom, so that the

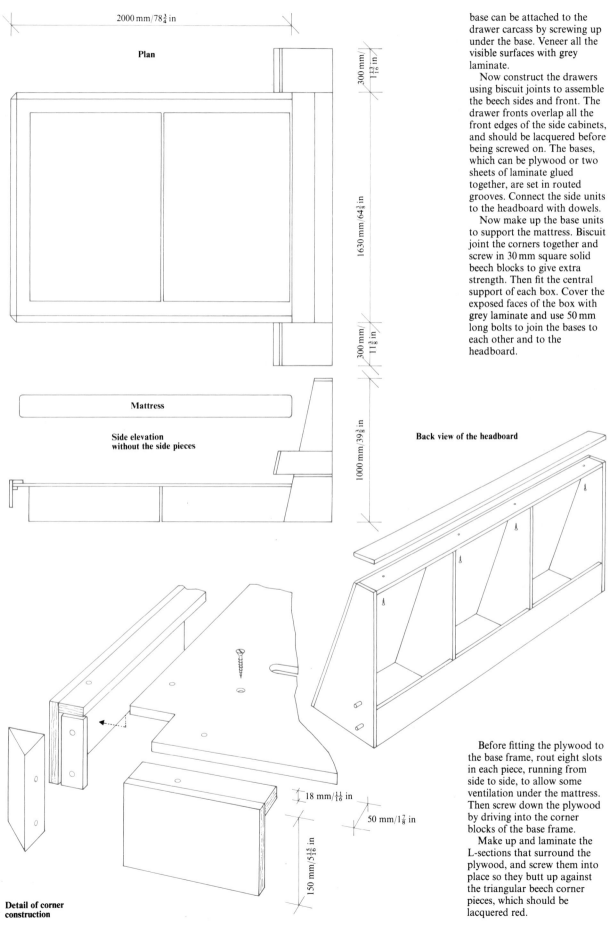

Plan

2000 mm/78¾ in

300 mm / 11¹³⁄₁₆ in

1630 mm/64¼ in

300 mm / 11⅞ in

1000 mm/39⅜ in

Mattress

Side elevation without the side pieces

Back view of the headboard

18 mm/¹¹⁄₁₆ in

50 mm/1⅞ in

150 mm/5¹⁵⁄₁₆ in

Detail of corner construction

base can be attached to the drawer carcass by screwing up under the base. Veneer all the visible surfaces with grey laminate.

Now construct the drawers using biscuit joints to assemble the beech sides and front. The drawer fronts overlap all the front edges of the side cabinets, and should be lacquered before being screwed on. The bases, which can be plywood or two sheets of laminate glued together, are set in routed grooves. Connect the side units to the headboard with dowels.

Now make up the base units to support the mattress. Biscuit joint the corners together and screw in 30 mm square solid beech blocks to give extra strength. Then fit the central support of each box. Cover the exposed faces of the box with grey laminate and use 50 mm long bolts to join the bases to each other and to the headboard.

Before fitting the plywood to the base frame, rout eight slots in each piece, running from side to side, to allow some ventilation under the mattress. Then screw down the plywood by driving into the corner blocks of the base frame.

Make up and laminate the L-sections that surround the plywood, and screw them into place so they butt up against the triangular beech corner pieces, which should be lacquered red.

David Field's simple and practical bed on the preceeding pages can take on a variety of shapes depending on your needs: with a headboard or a footboard or even an overhead canopy; and with a multitude of storage possibilities.

The simplest variation is to modify the side units, reducing them to little more than wing tables (left). To give them a floating look, they should be supported by unobtrusive braces or triangular brackets made of medium density fibreboard (MDF) which attach to the side of the headboard. Alternatively, the headboard can be extended to provide the required support.

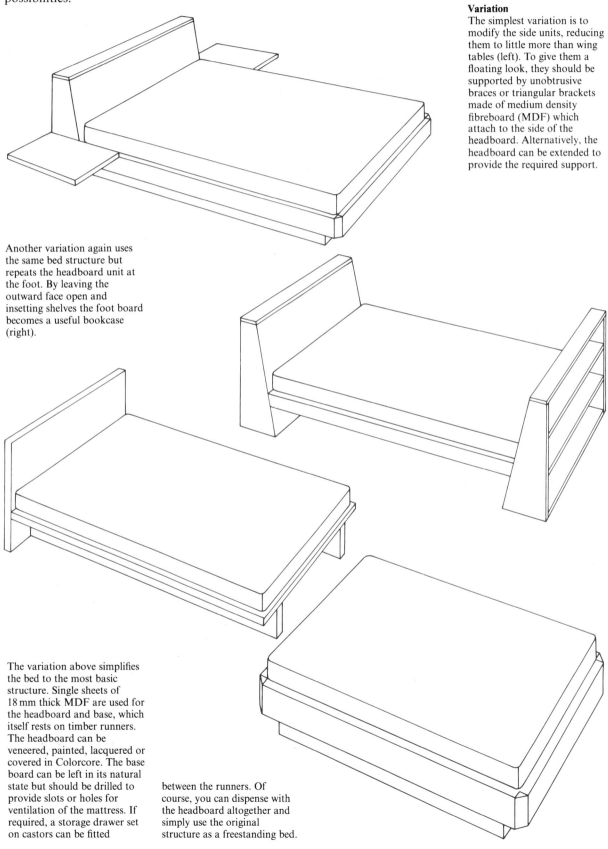

Another variation again uses the same bed structure but repeats the headboard unit at the foot. By leaving the outward face open and insetting shelves the foot board becomes a useful bookcase (right).

The variation above simplifies the bed to the most basic structure. Single sheets of 18 mm thick MDF are used for the headboard and base, which itself rests on timber runners. The headboard can be veneered, painted, lacquered or covered in Colorcore. The base board can be left in its natural state but should be drilled to provide slots or holes for ventilation of the mattress. If required, a storage drawer set on castors can be fitted between the runners. Of course, you can dispense with the headboard altogether and simply use the original structure as a freestanding bed.

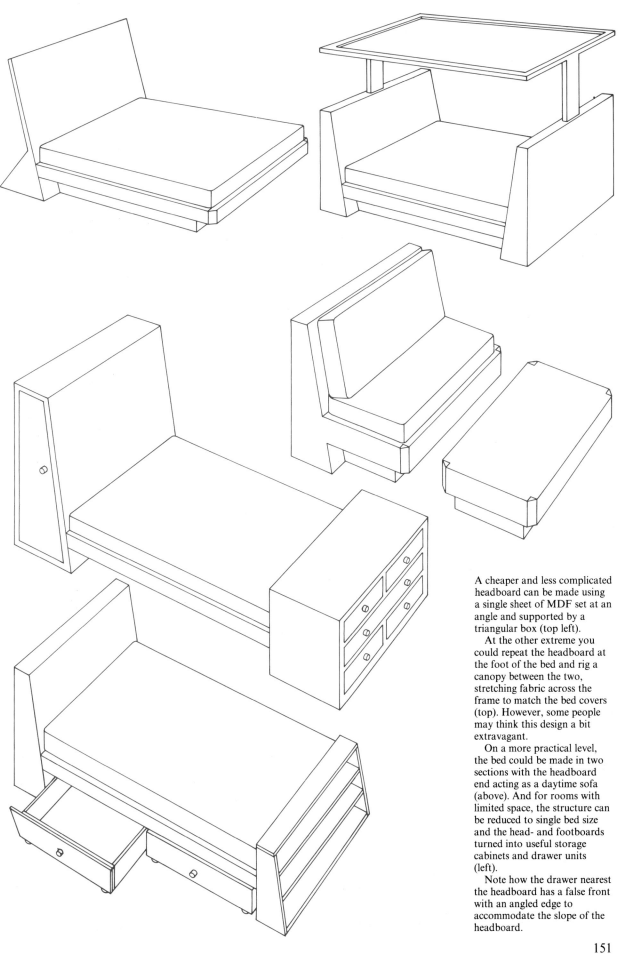

A cheaper and less complicated headboard can be made using a single sheet of MDF set at an angle and supported by a triangular box (top left).

At the other extreme you could repeat the headboard at the foot of the bed and rig a canopy between the two, stretching fabric across the frame to match the bed covers (top). However, some people may think this design a bit extravagant.

On a more practical level, the bed could be made in two sections with the headboard end acting as a daytime sofa (above). And for rooms with limited space, the structure can be reduced to single bed size and the head- and footboards turned into useful storage cabinets and drawer units (left).

Note how the drawer nearest the headboard has a false front with an angled edge to accommodate the slope of the headboard.

BEDS / David Colwell

Because the actual structure of a bed is obscured by the mattress and bed linen, a better criterion to judge it would be how it functions, rather than how it looks. The **David Colwell** bed rates high. It incorporates a unique system of double slats to provide uniform springiness along the full width of the bed and to prevent sagging toward the centre. The slats rest on two rails which in turn are supported by two end frames. The structure is held together by removable dowels, so that the bed can be taken apart and reduced to flat components, which is useful when the access to a bedroom is restricted. The slats are spaced apart by wooden blocks and are strung together with waxed cotton cord so that they can be rolled into a neat bundle to pack away.

Anatomy of the bed
The bed is made of solid ash which itself is naturally springy. The 48 slats are each 15×47 mm; their length depends on the width of the mattress. The two side rails are 60×35 mm, while the front end rails are 50 mm square, separated by four uprights 95×35 mm thick. Two lengths of 15 mm square ash brace the structure and prevent it from racking. Forty-eight spacer blocks $75 \times 43 \times 21$ mm will also be needed as well as a length of 12 mm diameter dowel and waxed cotton cord or washing line.

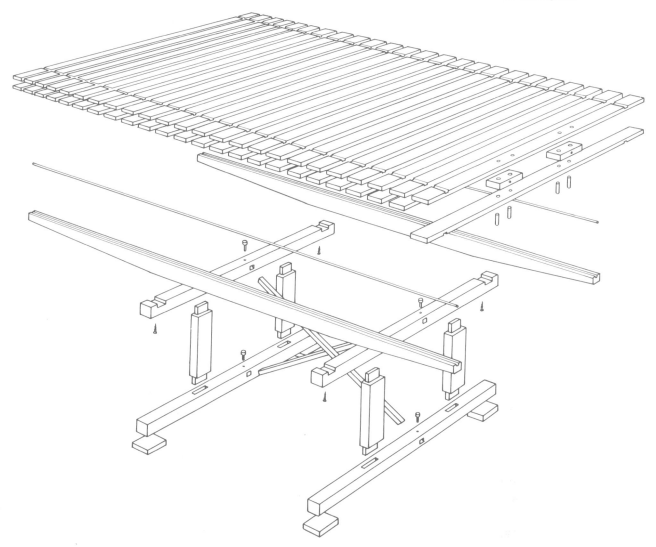

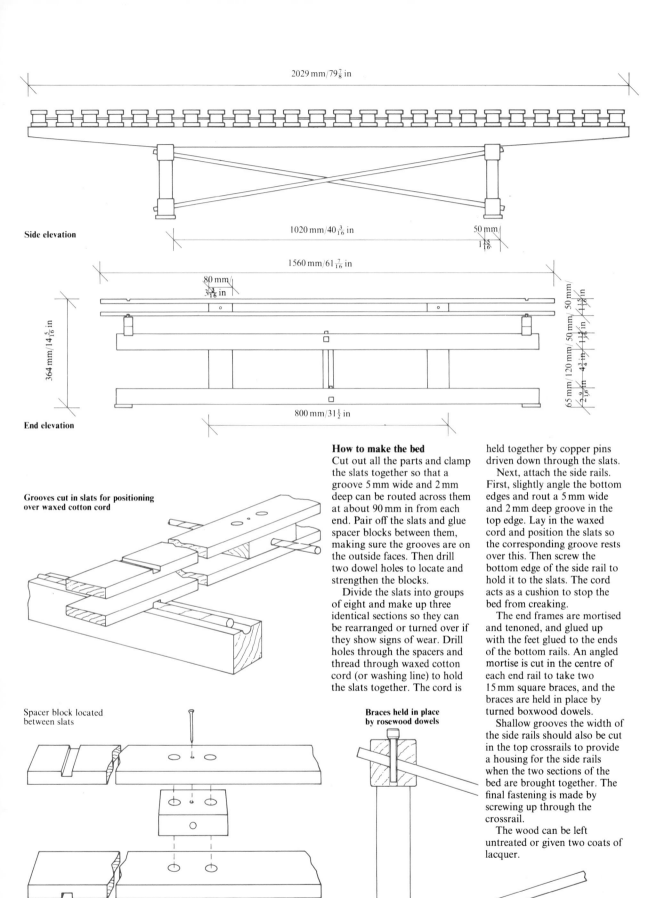

2029 mm/79$\frac{7}{8}$ in

Side elevation

1020 mm/40$\frac{3}{16}$ in

50 mm/1$\frac{15}{16}$ in

1560 mm/61$\frac{7}{16}$ in

80 mm/3$\frac{3}{16}$ in

50 mm/1$\frac{15}{16}$ in

364 mm/14$\frac{5}{16}$ in

65 mm/120 mm/50 mm/50 mm
2$\frac{9}{16}$ in/4$\frac{3}{4}$ in/1$\frac{15}{16}$ in/1$\frac{15}{16}$ in

End elevation

800 mm/31$\frac{1}{2}$ in

Grooves cut in slats for positioning
over waxed cotton cord

Spacer block located
between slats

Braces held in place
by rosewood dowels

How to make the bed

Cut out all the parts and clamp the slats together so that a groove 5 mm wide and 2 mm deep can be routed across them at about 90 mm in from each end. Pair off the slats and glue spacer blocks between them, making sure the grooves are on the outside faces. Then drill two dowel holes to locate and strengthen the blocks.

Divide the slats into groups of eight and make up three identical sections so they can be rearranged or turned over if they show signs of wear. Drill holes through the spacers and thread through waxed cotton cord (or washing line) to hold the slats together. The cord is held together by copper pins driven down through the slats.

Next, attach the side rails. First, slightly angle the bottom edges and rout a 5 mm wide and 2 mm deep groove in the top edge. Lay in the waxed cord and position the slats so the corresponding groove rests over this. Then screw the bottom edge of the side rail to hold it to the slats. The cord acts as a cushion to stop the bed from creaking.

The end frames are mortised and tenoned, and glued up with the feet glued to the ends of the bottom rails. An angled mortise is cut in the centre of each end rail to take two 15 mm square braces, and the braces are held in place by turned boxwood dowels.

Shallow grooves the width of the side rails should also be cut in the top crossrails to provide a housing for the side rails when the two sections of the bed are brought together. The final fastening is made by screwing up through the crossrail.

The wood can be left untreated or given two coats of lacquer.

GARDEN BENCH / Ron Carter

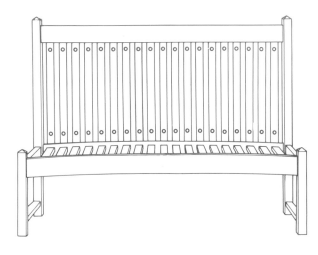

Essentially, **Ron Carter**'s Liverpool bench is little more than an elaboration of a typical park bench. Yet it has taken a clever and subtle designer's eye to transform a traditionally conventional and unobtrusive piece of furniture into an inviting seat which has a touch of grandeur about it.

The most important modification is to set the horizontal back and seat rails on a slight curve, with the seat slats running front to back. Instantly, the seat is given an unusual and unexpected appearance. And the curve is made more pronounced by raising the height of the back and setting the slats close together. Additional decorative touches also play their part, with holes drilled in the back slats and pyramids cut into the tops of the uprights. The large cross-sectioned legs give the structure stability and prevent it sinking into soft ground.

Despite the modifications, this design is no more difficult to make than an ordinary bench. Oak, beech, or teak are ideal timbers, which can be left natural, oiled or lacquered.

Anatomy of the bench
The three curved rails (two at the back and one at the front) are 100 × 33 mm; they can either be steam bent or cut out of solid wood. The legs are cut from 50 mm square timber, the slats from timber 19 × 44 mm. The holes in the back slats taper from a 30 mm diameter at the front to 25 mm at the back. The larger mid rails are 100 × 33 mm and the smaller ones 40 × 22 mm.

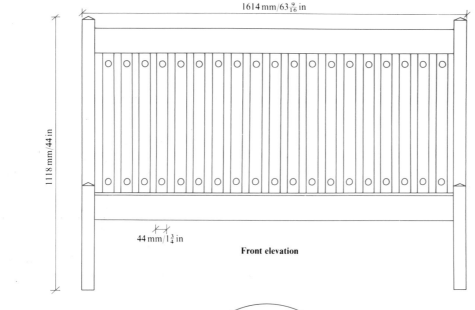

1614 mm/63 9/16 in

1118 mm/44 in

44 mm/1 3/4 in

Front elevation

How to make the bench

First, form or cut out the curved rails, then cut out the mortises for the slats; there are 38 of these spaced at 29 mm intervals. Use mortise and tenons to join the curved rails to the legs and to make up the side frames. Cut out all the slats, drilling the holes in the back slats with an angled router cutter and a circular template for the ring fence clamped to the slat.

Slightly chamfer all the edges of the bench and detail the tops of the legs using a disc grinder (see diagram).

Glue up the side frames and then glue them to the curved rails with the slats all in position.

The bench can be left as natural timber, lacquered or oiled depending on what the wood is, and where it is to go.

Detail of the top of the leg

75 mm/2 15/16 in

100 mm/3 15/16 in

Side elevation

580 mm/22 13/16 in

100 mm/3 15/16 in

290 mm/11 7/16 in

430 mm/16 15/16 in

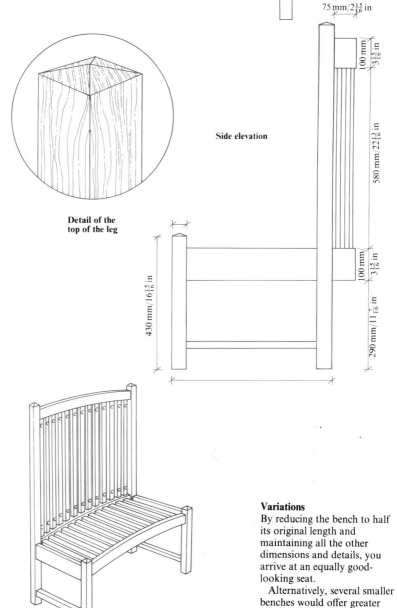

Variations

By reducing the bench to half its original length and maintaining all the other dimensions and details, you arrive at an equally good-looking seat.

Alternatively, several smaller benches would offer greater flexibility in arrangement than a larger bench and might better suit certain locations.

155

GARDEN BENCH / Ashley Cartwright

Most garden furniture is quite predictable, consisting of some form of chair and a table. For those who want something more unusual and enterprising, however, **Ashley Cartwright**'s bench is an alternative which provides a neat and flexible system of garden seating. Employed with care, it can blend with any type and size of garden, either by running it in an interesting zig-zag pattern or by bringing the ends together to create a hexagonal bench. The design breaks away from using only wood, and the stone and brick of the supporting piers provide additional textures and a sense of solidity to the structure.

The seating section is made of solid teak planks, an ideal timber for outside use, and these form an attractive interlocking detail where they join over the piers. The planks are held in place by screws driven through into a metal plate; and in turn the plate is screwed to the piers. This means the planks can easily be removed in winter when the seating is not in use.

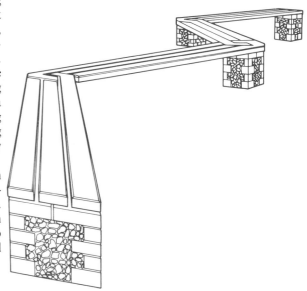

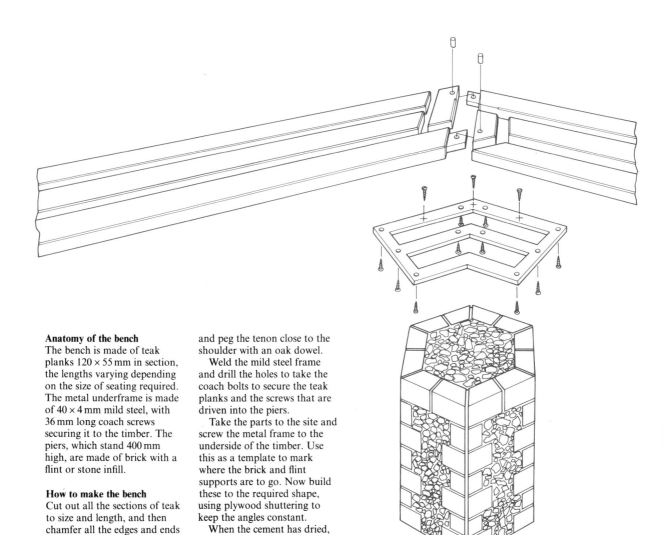

Anatomy of the bench
The bench is made of teak planks 120 × 55 mm in section, the lengths varying depending on the size of seating required. The metal underframe is made of 40 × 4 mm mild steel, with 36 mm long coach screws securing it to the timber. The piers, which stand 400 mm high, are made of brick with a flint or stone infill.

How to make the bench
Cut out all the sections of teak to size and length, and then chamfer all the edges and ends where there is no joint. Next cut the mortises and tenons where the planks are to be joined over the piers; glue up and peg the tenon close to the shoulder with an oak dowel.

Weld the mild steel frame and drill the holes to take the coach bolts to secure the teak planks and the screws that are driven into the piers.

Take the parts to the site and screw the metal frame to the underside of the timber. Use this as a template to mark where the brick and flint supports are to go. Now build these to the required shape, using plywood shuttering to keep the angles constant.

When the cement has dried, screw the seating unit in place after having finished the timber with teak oil.

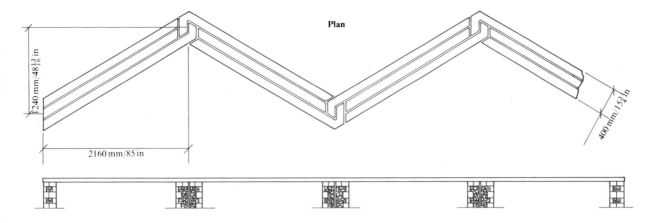

Plan

240 mm/48$\frac{13}{16}$ in

2160 mm/85 in

400 mm/15$\frac{3}{4}$ in

Front elevation

**Plan of the wooden seat, the metal frame
and the stone and brick pier**

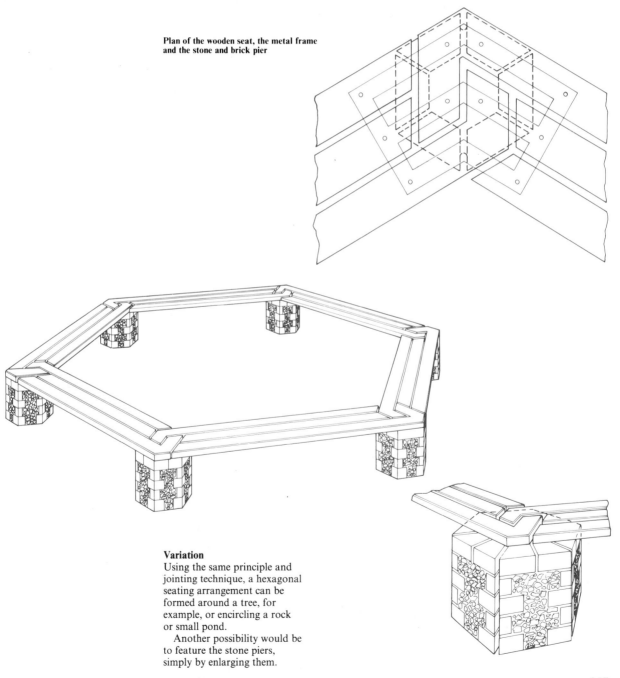

Variation
Using the same principle and
jointing technique, a hexagonal
seating arrangement can be
formed around a tree, for
example, or encircling a rock
or small pond.

   Another possibility would be
to feature the stone piers,
simply by enlarging them.

GARDEN TABLE / Ashley Cartwright

This is a fairly robust solid oak garden table which holds an interest from the design viewpoint in the way in which it has been constructed. The slats have been given a double bracketed profile which is repeated in the circumference, and they are spaced 10 mm apart to allow rainwater to drain off the top. A welded metal frame provides the base to which they are screwed. This frame, in turn, is connected to a solid oak split frame which also incorporates the legs. These are inclined towards the centre to improve the overall appearance of the table.

Anatomy of the table
The top is made up of 130 × 27 mm solid boards of oak and the metal frame is welded together from 40 × 4 mm sections of mild steel. The rails of the split frame are 32 × 50 mm, and although the legs are also 32 mm thick, they need to be cut from a board wide enough to give the shape illustrated top far right. You will need 40 mm spacers to keep the two sections of the frame apart.

How to make the table
First make up the metal frame by welding the sections of mild steel together in a shape that resembles an elongated octagon. If you wish, you can spray paint it. Cut out the top planks; cut out or stick on the details (bottom left) and then give all the edges a 2 mm chamfer.

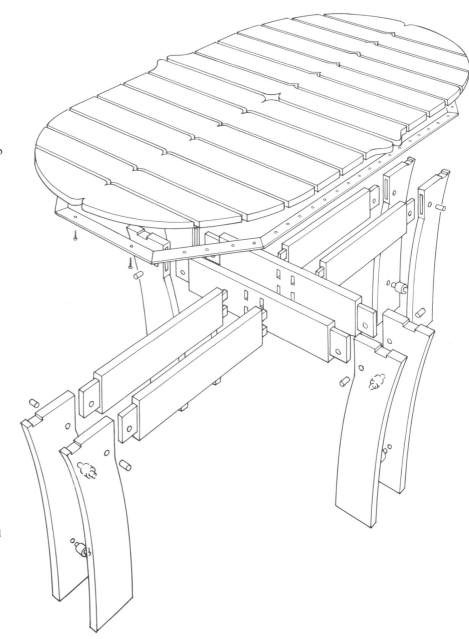

158

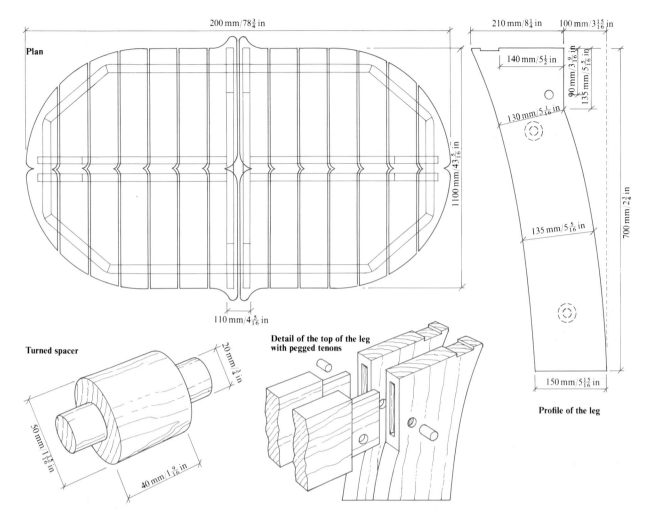

Plan

200 mm/78¾ in

1100 mm/43⁵⁄₁₆ in

110 mm/4⁵⁄₁₆ in

210 mm/8¼ in

100 mm/3¹⁵⁄₁₆ in

140 mm/5½ in

90 mm/3⁹⁄₁₆ in

135 mm/5⁵⁄₁₆ in

130 mm/5¹⁄₁₆ in

135 mm/5⁵⁄₁₆ in

700 mm/27¾ in

150 mm/5¹⁵⁄₁₆ in

Profile of the leg

Turned spacer

20 mm/⁴⁄₅ in

50 mm/1¹⁵⁄₁₆ in

40 mm/1⁹⁄₁₆ in

Detail of the top of the leg with pegged tenons

Next cut out the pieces for the legs and split frame. Cut the final profile of the legs using a spokeshave and drill holes for the spacers. Then cut the mortises and tenons to join all the sections together. Note how the shorter rails joined to the crossrails are double-tenoned.

Glue up the legs over the spacers and then connect them to the shorter support rails. These should have spacers temporarily inserted between them so they do not distort during clamping. Then insert the pegs near to the shoulders

of the joint to hold the assembly firmly in place. Glue up the other legs to the ends of the crossrail, and then glue and clamp the three sections together.

Cut a recess on the top of the legs with a router to take the metal frame and screw

down through the frame into the leg to secure the two together. Finally, screw the planks to the frame by driving up through the metal frame.

Depending on the timber you select, the table can either be left in its natural state or finished with oil.

Variation
While the overall effect of this variation is still similar to the table above, it is simpler and easier to construct. Here the round top, consisting of straight-sided planks, is screwed down onto an identical metal frame. The wooden base is made up from only a single section of timber rather than a split frame, but the legs and crossrails are cut from the same timber dimensions to compensate. Where the crossrails meet they are halved into each other, instead of being mortise-and-tenoned.

Once a piece of furniture has been designed, the plans must be turned into a physical object. To begin with, a well-lit workspace is of prime importance to the work because it can so easily affect the quality of the end product. Some people are satisfied with working in a garage or basement, but these spaces tend to be damp and drafty, and provide little natural light. Yet good light, and especially natural light, is a particularly wonderful aid that discloses unmercifully any defect in finishing. If possible the bench should be illuminated by indirect light because the changeability and inconsistency of direct sunlight creeping across a half-finished board can do irreparable damage. Machine areas can have artificial light, but neon tubes behind a lathe can give a strobe effect that makes spinning steel appear stationary.

Good access to a workshop is also important. One set in a loft may seem attractive, but having to carry unwieldy plywood sheets up narrow stairways is far from practical, as well as being time consuming. However, it is not necessary to go to the trouble of building a double-door loading bay, because most projects must be designed to go through domestic doorways anyway.

Pay particular attention to the way you look after your investment in materials, and avoid storing too much timber around the shop. Except for the materials you keep in the shop for the next project, to acclimatize to shop humidity, store the rest in a dehumidified space. Not too long ago it was perfectly acceptable to build fine furniture in damp, drafty barns because houses were also damp and drafty. But with the introduction of central heating and air conditioning, all this has changed. It is now necessary to consider lower humidity levels in households as well (see Storage, pages 192–193).

Along with humidity control systems, consider heating and ventilation, and their effect on your insurance policy. Electric heaters provide dry, safe heat—any other heating system will cause the insurance company to think twice. However, the ideal system from a practical point of view is a wood-burning stove. This changes the nuisance of waste scrap into a source of inexpensive heat. However, there is a price to pay. Your insurance company may demand that you build a concrete plinth and a fireproof back wall, and that you install fire extinguishers at every exit and water hose reels at every corner, apart from charging you the increased premiums.

Planning the workshop

In an ideal world the organization of a workshop would reflect the production process, with a storage area, machine shop, bench area and finishing room. But in reality this is seldom possible. So when planning either a major reorganization or an entirely new workshop, spend some time drawing up your ideas to scale on graph paper. And try to take into account how the workshop will evolve in the next year or two. Use scale cut-outs of benches and machines and move them around on the graph paper until you reach the most sensible arrangement.

If at all possible, separate the machine and bench areas, but keep a table saw reasonably close at hand because it will be used for most jobs, every day. The layout must also reflect whether the shop has a combination machine or individual function machines. There are very good combination machines available with three or four 2 HP motors that allow the functions of the machine to be changed over quickly. Unfortunately there is always some disadvantage, but if you are tight for space, the best combination machines can be an economical way of equipping a shop.

Position your machines with enough room to wheel a portable dust extractor between them. Plan to have an aisle wide enough for two people to pass down, shoulder to shoulder. It is easy to underestimate the amount of room required, particularly when carcasses are being manoeuvred into position. Consider grouping machinery in one corner, leaving the rest of the space wide and clear.

If pressed for space, try using the diagonal of the workshop. And, by tilting machine table tops or setting them at varying heights, most power machinery can be moved close together when not in use, their tops positioned out of each other's way. The test of a workshop plan is to be able to carry a 2 m/2 yd board through each machining process. This means the planer should have 4 m/4 yd of clear space fore and aft. Always try sorting out the layout on paper before juggling the machine around in real life. Once the workshop layout has been fixed, the plumbing and electrical services can be installed exactly where they are needed.

If you have the opportunity, install three-phase electrical wiring. The initial cost will be higher than single phase wiring, but it will make available to you the cheaper second-hand light industrial machines and tools. With the rapid advances in computer-operated woodworking machines, many companies are replacing table saws, shapers, padsanders and planers, which have many years life left in them. This is the ideal time for the handcraftsman to acquire precision tooling. The difference in capital outlay between the new, top of the range home-woodworking machines and second-hand industrial equipment is minimal, but the industrial machines will perform much better. Do not, however, underestimate the problems of locating and installing these heavy machines, although once in place they quickly pay their way.

The bench area
The layout of the bench area should be given special attention. Easy access to hand tools is essential, stored in a drawer or on a peg board mounted on a nearby wall. Decide also whether there will be two separate benches or one main bench with auxiliary assembly benches. A design table can be placed in the shop, but this is not recommended. Dust and noise do not mix with technical drawing.

A multi-function woodworking machine

A multi-function woodworking machine

1. A large heavy cast iron table with a 30.5 cm/12 in saw blade, which has a capacity to tilt to 45°. There is a sliding-table cross-cutting facility with an adjustable fence for mitres. The rip fence is located at one end only, and a separate motor drives the saw arbor.

2. Protruding from the saw table is a 3.2 cm/1¼ in shaper head. This is separately driven with three speeds. Fences and guards are provided, but to a lower specification than industrial shapers. The shaper is less convenient to use in this context because it is poorly positioned.

3. The planing facility is available in 25.4 cm/10 in and 43.2 cm/17 in widths, both with long bed, cast iron tables. The infeed table is adjustable, and the outfeed is fixed. With the planer powered by its own motor, this is a good facility.

4. Thicknessing is done by lifting the outfeed table and feeding timber on a cast iron table under the planer blades. Lifting the table involves removing the edging fence from the planer, but it is otherwise quick to do.

5. The mortising attachment is also powered from the planing/thicknessing motor. The mortiser is very efficient, but positioned between the infeed and outfeed tables it can make planing less comfortable.

Jigs and other devices allow the craftsman to use machines and workshop equipment to their full potential by extending their abilities beyond the merely obvious. But it is also possible to adapt some machines to perform tasks for which they were not originally designed. This can be extremely useful where, for the occasional operation, it would not be cost effective to buy a machine specifically to do the job. But at the same time, do not be tempted to modify a tool that is in everyday use. There is nothing more inconvenient and infuriating than having to take off some gadget just to bore a couple of holes. In a cabinet workshop, for example, a lathe would qualify as a machine to be modified, whereas a table saw would not. Ideally, any adaptation should be designed to interfere as little as possible with the original function of the machine.

A woodworking lathe also can be modified to work metal very successfully. Another useful addition would

The horizontal mortiser

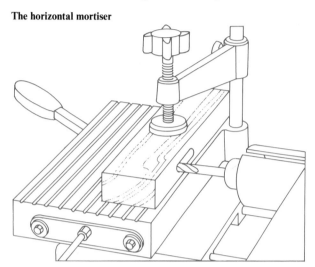

Mortiser used as disc sander

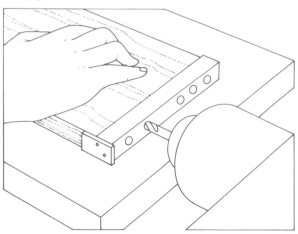

Doweling on the mortiser

The horizontal mortiser
Used for mortising, this drilling jig can produce very clean and accurate results. Stops are available for producing short-run batches, making this an attractive alternative to square chisel or router mortising. Using the machine is simple, even though the position of the mortiser at the side of the planer is somewhat inconvenient.

Mortiser used as disc sander
This machine should only be used for sanding as a last resort, where there is no other means of disc sanding. Although it may perform its task very well, beware of the set up and dismantling time should you wish to alternate between using the planer and mortiser.

Doweling on the mortiser
It is not necessary to have a complicated machine to dowel successfully. All that is required is a flat table set beneath a revolving chuck. A horizontal mortiser does this perfectly, but a workshop-built jig could function just as well.

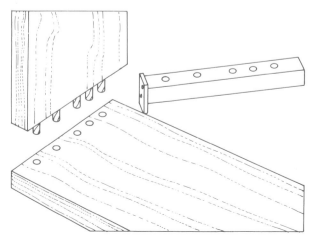

be a cross-slide large enough to turn the small odds and ends needed for furniture, such as drawer knobs and finials. Similarly, the outboard end of the lathe can be adapted into a convenient disc sander.

The drill press is also a good candidate for adaptations. It can be turned into a bobbin sander, a milling machine or a vertical mortiser. However, think carefully how much you use the press before adapting it to some other purpose. It might be worth buying a second smaller machine to do the odd jobs.

The planer has always been a favourite for modifying. The position of the central cutter block means that a horizontal power take-off mortising table can be fitted which will work on the same rise and fall mechanism as the thicknessing table. This could be used not only for mortising but also for doweling, disc sanding and for grinding planer knife blades, given the necessary fitments.

Converting a woodworking lathe to metalworking

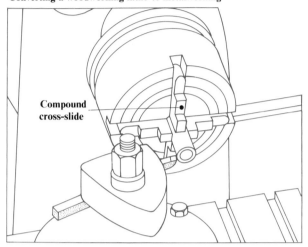

Compound cross-slide

Converting a woodworking lathe to metalworking
On some woodworking lathes it is possible to work metal by adding a compound cross-slide; many furniture designers and makers produce their own metal fittings such as door knobs, handles and hinges. The cross-slide has a limited capacity but it is perfectly suitable for small jobs.

The drill press as a mortising machine

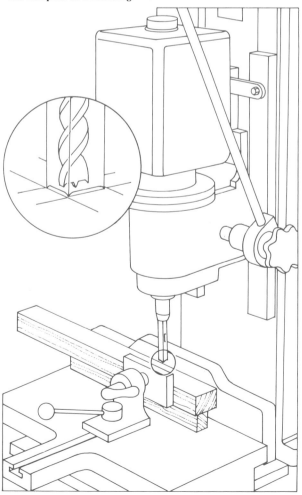

The drill press as a mortising machine
There are several available attachments to convert a drill press for hollow chisel mortising. This is not a temporary conversion that can be quickly fitted and taken down as needed, so a separate drill press machine would be needed. In this form it can function reasonably well. The results are not as clean as a router or a horizontal mortiser, but this is of little importance for making stopped mortises.

Grinding long knife blades

Grinding long knife blades
The horizontal mortiser has the capacity to grind planer knives, and many craftsmen depend on this jig to produce uniformly sharp long edges on these long blades quickly. Other machines, such as lathes, have similar grinding capabilities. However, it is generally not recommended to grind planer knives in place, or to use a grinding attachment such as this because it is bad practice to mix precision machinery with abrasive grinding material. The dust from the abrasive and the metal filings could destroy the machine bearings after a while. Fortunately, these bearings usually are sealed for life to protect them, but many craftsmen prefer not to take the risk, and instead sharpen long knife blades by hand, using a whetstone.

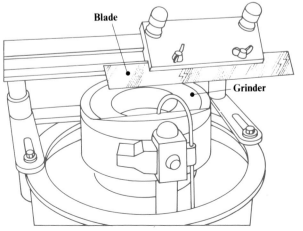

Blade

Grinder

The most widely used and most important machine in any furniture workshop certainly must be the table saw. It is inherently simple yet highly versatile, capable of accurate deep ripping and equally accurate crosscuts. Properly set up and then expanded by the use of jigs, this is the cabinetmaker's joint-cutting machine.

Table saws are so frequently used that it makes good sense to get the best affordable model. The table should be flat and heavy (many are made of cast iron), and the blade should run on a tilting arbor with a rise and fall mechanism that is simple to adjust. Do not be tempted by a machine that tilts the table instead; these are troublesome to adjust and not as satisfactory to operate. A blade of 25.4 cm/10 in or 30.5 cm/12 in diameter covers all the likely types of work, and this should be driven by a motor of 2 HP or more.

Some workshops have one heavy dimension saw and a second smaller machine for joint cutting and delicate work. This jointing saw usually has an 18.8 cm/8 in blade powered by a 1 HP motor. Being smaller it allows the worker to control the cut more effectively and, situated next to the bench area, can serve as a general-purpose saw.

On both saws, the table is traversed by a rip fence. This should slide easily back and forth and be capable of fine adjustment, and it should lock on both sides of the table. This last point is important, for any movement in the fence under pressure will create an inaccurate cut. The guide channel for the crosscutting or miter compass also crosses the table top.

The advantage of such a machine is that, by using jigs and templates, its usefulness and capacity to handle different types of work is greatly extended, thus reducing the need for several different machines. Instead, a surprising number of jobs can be carried out on only one or two good machines.

Setting up the saw
The machine as it comes from the manufacturer will be generally accurate, so the object of setting up is to fine tune it to absolute accuracy. First, check the rip fence. It should cross the table parallel to the blade, with less than 0.4 mm/$\frac{1}{64}$ in error, to prevent the timber from binding if it spreads during ripping. Next replace the removable steel plate around the blade with a matching hardwood piece. By winding the spinning blade up through this piece you make a cut in the new plate exactly the size of the blade. This custom-made plate will support your cut right up to the blade. Then set the blade tilt stops and measuring scales and remember to check them periodically for precision.

The blade should be of industrial quality, made of heavy steel plate with good tungsten carbide tips, especially for cutting manufactured boards. Lighter titanium-carbide tipped blades are available, but they sometimes resonate or vibrate and give a variable kerf.

Finally, set up the metal crosscut protractor so there is no play between the guide bar and guide channel. If necessary, hammer the guide bar oversize, then file it down to fit. Attach a hardwood auxiliary fence to the face of the protractor, extending the wood beyond the blade. Set the fence square and push the fence through, cutting off the excess wood. You will then have support for your job right up to the blade.

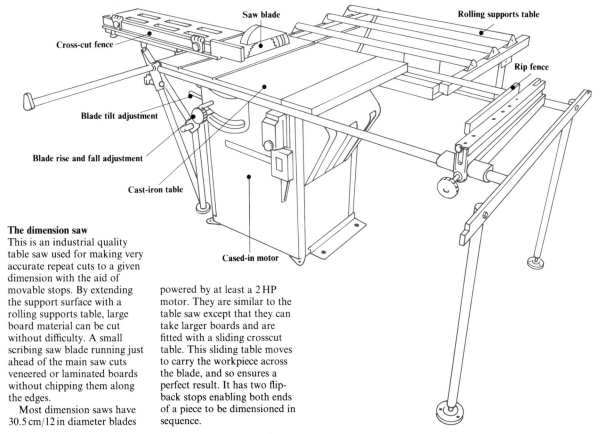

Cross-cut fence

Saw blade

Rolling supports table

Rip fence

Blade tilt adjustment

Blade rise and fall adjustment

Cast-iron table

Cased-in motor

The dimension saw
This is an industrial quality table saw used for making very accurate repeat cuts to a given dimension with the aid of movable stops. By extending the support surface with a rolling supports table, large board material can be cut without difficulty. A small scribing saw blade running just ahead of the main saw cuts veneered or laminated boards without chipping them along the edges.

Most dimension saws have 30.5 cm/12 in diameter blades

powered by at least a 2 HP motor. They are similar to the table saw except that they can take larger boards and are fitted with a sliding crosscut table. This sliding table moves to carry the workpiece across the blade, and so ensures a perfect result. It has two flip-back stops enabling both ends of a piece to be dimensioned in sequence.

Dado cutting on the table saw

Using two blades in a table saw cuts a variable-width kerf, either across the grain (dado cutting) or with it (grooving).

A tool steel dado set with two blades, the clippers and the spacers, will work infinitely variable kerfs between 6 mm/$\frac{1}{4}$ in and 3.2 cm/$1\frac{1}{4}$ in. This is adequate for most work in solid timber.

Moulding on the table saw

A table saw will, with the proper blades, produce mouldings. However, the speed, power and the design of the table saw do not always give good results.

Dado cutting on the table saw

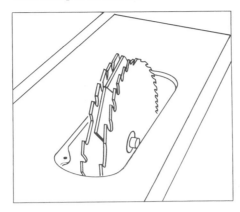

Moulding on the table saw

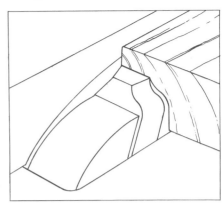

The radial arm saw

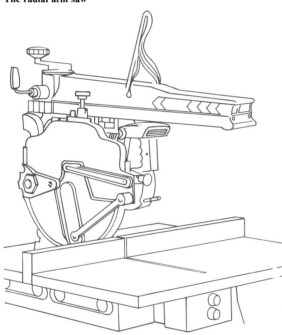

The contractor's saw

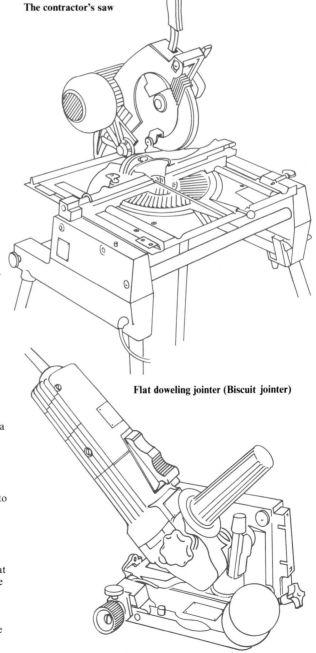

The radial arm saw

If used as originally intended, as a crosscutting saw, this machine does a very good job. By drawing the blade across the timber it will cut to length exceptionally cumbersome or heavy pieces. However, it takes up a lot of workshop space. A radial arm saw can also be used for other operations— none of them with reliable accuracy.

The contractor's saw

The contractor's saw or site saw has many uses within a workshop, notably for cutting large boards down to sizes more easily managed on a table saw. It can also be turned upside down to become a small table saw, but only if fitted with adequate guards and fences.

Flat doweling jointer (Biscuit jointer)

This portable tool is an excellent doweling jig. The small saw blade cuts a slot at a pre-determined position to accept a flat compressed ellipse, usually of beech and known as a biscuit. The grain of the biscuit on the diagonal swells when coated with glue to make an exceptionally strong joint.

In some instances one flat dowel can replace two conventional dowels holding, for example, a rail or stile. Flat dowels can replace the mortise and tenon joint, especially if used in pairs. The jointing machine has other applications, notably, to make stopped grooves.

Flat doweling jointer (Biscuit jointer)

Mitre jig

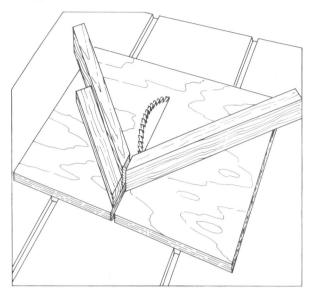

High fence jig

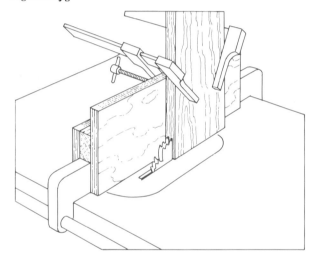

Ripping jig for waney-edged boards

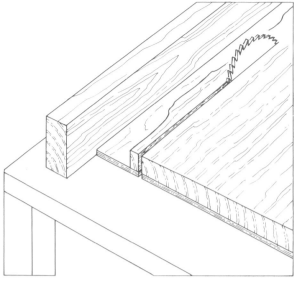

Pattern cutting jig

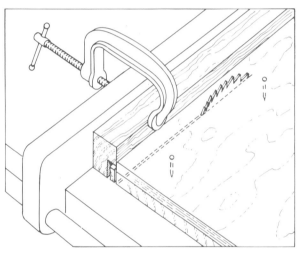

Taper and wedge cutting jig

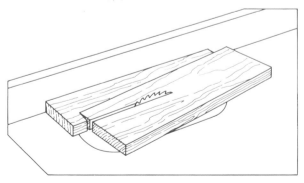

Mitre jig

To make a mitred joint, all sides to be joined must be of equal length and the joints cut at exactly 45°. This jig carries the parts to be mitred across the blade and allows cutting from both sides. The two arms of the jig must line up perfectly to a 90° square, and the two parts being mitred kept firmly together. To cut wide mouldings or rails, use several pins with the heads just protruding from the base of the jig to hold the workpiece securely against the fence. This prevents the slipping that can occur when cutting wide timber at 45°.

Ripping jig for waney-edged boards

When cutting a waney-edged board on the table saw, it is a problem to know where to begin. This jig creates a false straight edge. Select a piece of scrap plywood of similar length to your board with an existing straight edge. Tack this scrap to your board with the straight edge parallel to the cut you wish to make, and bear the jig against the rip fence as you push your cut through.

High fence jig

This device fits snugly over a rip fence and extends the full width of the table. It allows you safely to work long pieces of wood above the blade; for example, when tenoning the edge of a long board. The jig should be long enough to take a wide workpiece and sit squarely and securely on the table.

Pattern cutting jig

This is a simple way to produce any number of pieces to one pattern or template. The pattern is cut to size exactly in 12 mm/$\frac{1}{2}$ in plywood. An auxiliary fence is fitted to the rip fence with a wide rebate on the waste side. The pattern is pinned with small nails to the workpiece which has been pre-cut to rough size. When the pattern runs against the auxiliary fence, the blade will cut flush with the pattern edge.

Taper and wedge cutting jig

Tapers are best worked on the jointer to a finished dimension in one operation, but if a lot of stock has to be removed, a taper jig can be used on the table saw. Because the workpiece is not bearing against the fence directly, take care to keep it under control.

Splined mitre jig

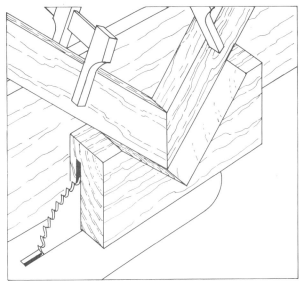

Combe joint jig

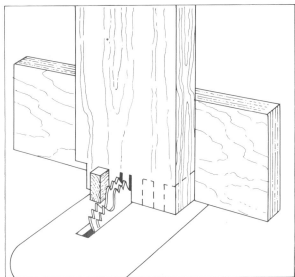

Crosscut jig

Dimension jig

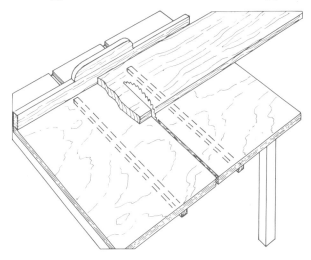

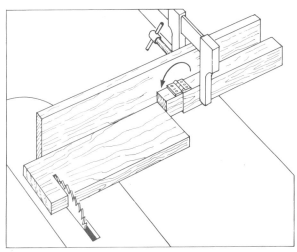

Radial arm dado jig

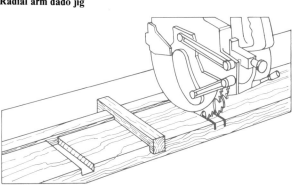

almost as strong, quite attractive and considerably easier to set up and produce than the dovetail. The technique involves setting a dado head to the width of the "finger" required and then regulating and repeating that cut at given distances down the carcass side. Build the jig only from dense, wear-resistant hardwood. The technique can be used to make mock combe joints cut across a mitre angled combe joints, mock dovetails cut with a router and many other machine joints.

Crosscut jig

The difficulty with using the crosscut device which accompanies most table saws is that it is adjustable and therefore sometimes inaccurate and that it *pushes* the workpiece across the blade. This jig, however, covers the

whole table top and *carries* the workpiece across the blade.

Dimension jig

This simple device is used with the crosscut jig or with the crosscut protractor to cut several pieces to a common length where both ends need trimming. Two stops are therefore required, one of which must be removable. The dimension saw has stops of this kind, but you can adapt any table saw using this simple jig to do the same work with the same accuracy.

Radial arm dado jig

Here the radial arm saw cuts dadoes at a regular distance down the length of a board. The fence is dadoed at the required distance and a removable locating piece is used to position the board for the next cut.

Splined mitre jig

With a mitred frame it is often necessary to strengthen the joint with a spline of plywood or decorative contrasting hardwood. This jig uses the high fence jig to assist with running the workpiece above the blade. Glue the frame parts before cutting the

groove to ensure that the joints align. Or dry clamp both parts to the high fence jig and proceed as if they were glued.

Combe joint jig

It is possible to make dovetail joints on the table saw, but it is a complicated procedure. The combe joint, however, is

The family of narrow blade machines includes the jig saw, the scroll saw and the bandsaw. The bandsaw, is a particularly versatile piece of equipment, and together with the planer and table saw, forms the modern workshop machine battery. However, the quality of work it produces does not match the work that comes off a precision table saw. It is at its best cutting to rough size, ripping, resawing and for cutting shallow curves.

A bandsaw consists of a continuous, narrow metal blade which is fed around either two or three rotating guide wheels. Only one of these wheels is driven, and because these saws need a lot of power to carry out their tasks, they should be powered by a motor of 2 HP or more. Rubber belts fitted around each wheel help to transmit this drive to the blade itself. The smallest bandsaws usually have three wheels to allow for a deeper throat, the horizontal distance between the blade of the machine and the vertical frame. Although this increased throat allows the machine to take wider pieces of timber, it loses in the depth of cut—the distance between the table and top guide, which is the maximum thickness of timber the saw will accommodate.

The frame of a bandsaw is put under great tension, especially when the blade is set for deep cutting, so a two-wheel machine is a more satisfactory design for general workshop use. The guides of a bandsaw are usually simple side blocks with a backing wheel. For straight cutting, common in furniture work, these are most useful. It should be possible to lower the top guide to just above the work piece so the cut can be controlled right to the point of entry.

Fine adjustments of the machine and well cared for blades are the requirements for getting good results with the bandsaw. Select the blade not only by its width, but also by the type and number of teeth and the hardness of steel. Narrow blades of $6\,\text{mm}/\frac{1}{4}$ in and $9\,\text{mm}/\frac{3}{8}$ in are less powerful than the wide blades normally used for deep cutting, but with 5 to 6 teeth per inch, they make clean cuts when cutting curves.

When deep cutting or resawing, ensure that dust is kept clear of the cut. If the blade gets trapped in the timber with no way for the dust from the cut to escape, the binding blade will veer into a curve. So it is best to fit as wide a blade as your machine will take—ideally $2.5\,\text{cm}/1$ in or $3.6\,\text{cm}/1\frac{1}{2}$ in, with widely spaced teeth at 3 teeth per inch in a skip-tooth blade configuration. Set the tension to somewhere near maximum and feed the work through at a gentle rate—never force the cut.

Ideally a workshop should stock two or three dozen blades so that they can be sent for sharpening at the machinist's in steady rotation. Two types of blade hardness are available: normal, which can readily be sharpened with a hand file; and blue or flexiback, which is a hardened tooth on a resilient backing. Contrary to some opinions this type can be sharpened by grinding, and specialized machinists will do the job. Normal blades can be shop-sharpened to a higher standard and blued blades can even be touched up on the bench grinder, but it is a laborious business.

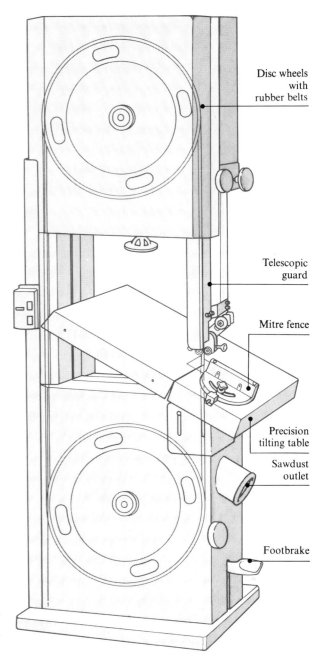

Disc wheels with rubber belts

Telescopic guard

Mitre fence

Precision tilting table

Sawdust outlet

Footbrake

Bandsaw
The most useful type of bandsaw for the small workshop is a two-wheel cast-iron machine with a 60 cm/24 in throat and a depth of cut of between 30 cm/12 in and 35 cm/14 in. For small scale work such as model making, musical instruments and some types of furniture, a small three-wheel bandsaw should suffice.

Resawing on the bandsaw

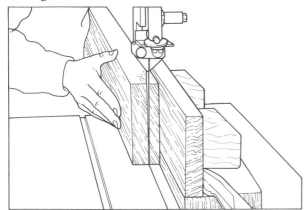

Veneer cutting on the bandsaw

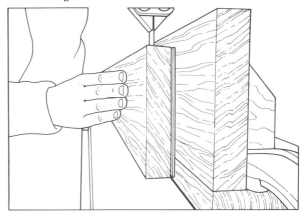

Cutting cabriole legs

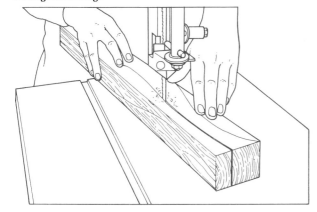

Jig saw

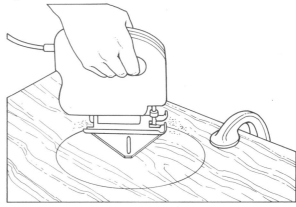

Resawing on the bandsaw
Set up the blade table and the additional high fence so the cut can be made parallel to the fence. Before adjusting the width of cut, check that the blade is straight; a re-sharpened blade could angle to the left or right. To check this, feed a test strip through the blade cutting to a gauge line. The attitude of the strip will show to which side the blade

Scroll saw or jig saw

tends and the high fence can be set accordingly.

Veneer cutting on the bandsaw
Essentially, this is the same technique as resawing. It will be necessary to use the planer to reface the veneer surface that bears against the bandsaw fence. Cutting leaves of $3\,mm/\frac{1}{8}$ in is the most economical way of using a figured board, and the veneers

will be of sufficient thickness to be planed or sanded. It is important to change the saw band frequently to prevent uneven cutting.

Cutting cabriole legs
A bandsaw is good for cutting compound curves making it ideal in the manufacture of cabriole legs. First mark out each curve or profile on the top and side. Saw one profile, then

re-attach the waste wood with tape. This sandwich retains the marking out and holds the job square to the blade.

Jig saw
The jig saw is a valuable tool when reducing large sheets and boards to manageable sizes and for cutting the inside of curves. It is extremely useful for on-site work, but in the workshop a bandsaw is a better choice.

Scroll saw
The scroll saw has a place in any workshop where precise, curved saw cuts are needed. This model has some advantages in that the blade is under less pressure because it is held under tension in a moving frame.

Blade sizes can vary from quite robust 0.7 mm/0.028 in thick for sign-making, for example, down to 0.02 mm/0.008 in for the hairline cuts required for marquetry. These blades, known as jeweller's saws, have rounded backs to help turn difficult corners. They are very delicate and are often made more resilient by tempering them in a bath of molten lead.

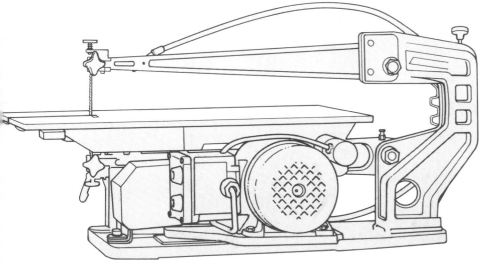

Planing machines are among the most welcome labour-saving pieces of equipment in the workshop. There is a wide range of machines to choose from including edge planers, planers, jointers, thicknessers, under/overs, planer thicknessers and planers with thicknessing capacity. As they all have different functions, it is essential to know what each can do and to select the ones that will be of most use for your workshop needs.

All planing machines work on the principle of a spinning block, which houses two or more long tool steel planer knives. These are precisely located in the block so that each knife cuts on the same arc both along its entire length and in relation to the other knives. The timber is fed across the knives from the infeed table (the register table) to the outfeed table which is set slightly higher, the difference in height determining the depth of cut.

For surface planing and edge planing machines, the critical dimension is not the width of the knives but the length of the tables themselves. These determine the machine's capacity to produce a flat, true surface even from a warped and twisted board. A surface planer should have a total table length of at least 1.3 m/4 ft so that it can deal with the sizes of timber commonly needed when making furniture. The planing width can be as narrow as a few centimetres or inches but 30 cm/12 in is regarded as a useful width.

Edge planers or jointers are similar to surface planers. In fact the addition of an adjustable vertical fence to a surface planer allows it to perform both functions. But if a fence is added it is essential that it can be fastened securely. On many models it moves under pressure resulting in inaccurate cutting. Consequently, many commercial workshops have a separate purpose-made jointer.

Having established a flat surface with an edge at right angles, the workpiece can be planed to thickness and to width. First turn the board over, then, using a register table below the blades, set it parallel to, and at the required distance from, the cutting arc. Generally the board is pulled under the blades by a power feed at a pre-determined speed. For a good finish on hardwood, 6 m/20 ft per minute is slow enough; for softwood, faster feed rates may be used.

A thicknesser compatible with a 30 cm/12 in planer has the capacity to handle most projects in a home workshop. One with a cast iron register table at least twice as long as the width of the knives and driven by a $1\frac{1}{2}$–2 HP motor is ideal. The larger machines which allow boards to be surfaced, edge jointed, glued and planed in one sequence are useful, but these are more suitable for the production shop. An alternative for the home workshop is a combined machine known as a planer thicknesser which performs both functions.

The addition of a thicknessing plate to a planing machine is a final option. Although laborious to use, because there is no power feed, this system offers total control and is able to reduce a board down to the thickness of sawn veneer. It may provide a solution where very small amounts of timber are worked, but does not compare well with a power feed thicknessing system for general use.

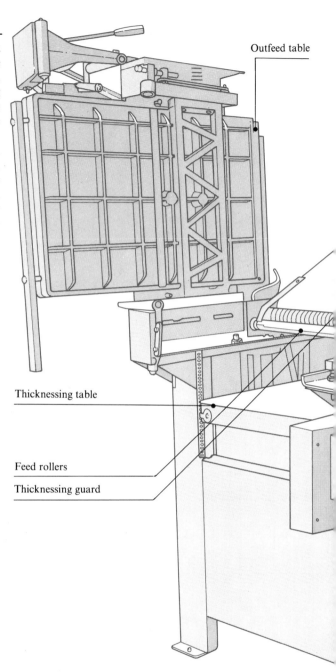

Outfeed table

Thicknessing table

Feed rollers

Thicknessing guard

Planer thicknessing machine
This machine has a 43 cm/17 in capacity for both planing and thicknessing. To plane timber, lower the rear table and feed each piece by hand from right to left across the cutter block. Complete a batch of timber, stacking each piece in the same grain direction before moving on to the next process. For thicknessing, lift the rear outfeed table, fit the dust extractor, and wind the thicknessing table to the appropriate height. Timber is fed with the planed side face down underneath the cutters; rollers pull the workpiece through at a pre-set speed.

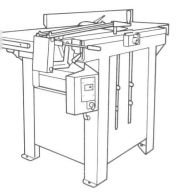

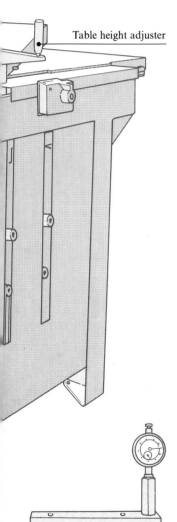

Table height adjuster

Knife setting jig
Each of the planer knives must cut in exactly the same arc. To check this, a dial gauge is fixed in a steel block and the readings are taken from the outfeed table to the top of the cutter arc. Readings should also be taken at intervals along each blade to ensure that it is square to the line of cut.

Jointer edge-planing jig
The vertical fence on most machines is adjustable and consequently so open to inaccuracy that a shop-built fence made precisely 90° to the table is often regarded as a more reliable piece of equipment.

Bevel planing
If the vertical face is made to tilt, it is possible to cut a bevel down the entire length of a piece of timber. In order to ensure a constant angle to the bevel the timber is kept in position by adjustable guides.

Stopped chamfers and stopped planing
A more useful reason for tilting the fence is to produce stopped chamfers. This involves attaching an auxiliary fence with two stops which determine the length of cut. Both infeed and outfeed tables are lowered by the same amount and the chamfer cut at one pass. To start the cut, hold the workpiece against the rear starting block with the front end raised. Gradually lower it on to the cutter, keeping a firm hold as the cutters enter. Then feed through until the forward stop is reached and carefully raise the back of the piece off the cutter. With the fence set vertically, a recess cut can be made. This technique is called stopped planing and can be used, for example, for the bottom of table legs, leaving the ends uncut to make block-like table feet.

Rebating
Planing machines can be set up to cut rebates. But because this means removing the guard it is a practice which is considered unsafe in a number of countries. Rebates can be cut just as well with a shaper or router.

Jointer edge-planing jig

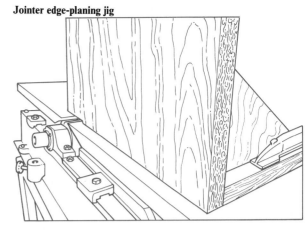

Bevel planing

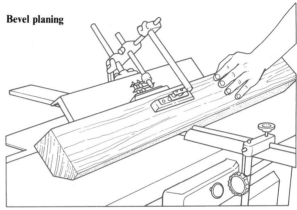

Stopped chamfers and stopped planing

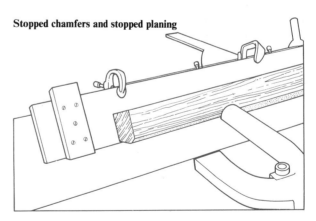

Rebating

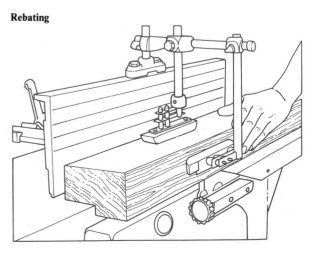

The router has been in use for many years, not only as a hand tool for finishing the bottom of dadoes, but also as a builder's power tool used widely in chopping out staircase stringers and for making decorative mouldings. With the development of the plunging router and the extension of the range of cutters to fit it, the woodworker now has a power tool which allows him to completely rethink his conventional workshop practice. In some shops the plunging router is almost a replacement for the chisel. Many busy workshops will have two or three routers with different bases or power ratings, plus one permanently turned upside down for light spindle moulding (see Shapers, pages 174–175).

Two types of routers are available. The first is large and powerful with a rating of 1600 watts or more; it is really a joiner's power tool used for heavy mortising and rebating. With a capacity to take $6\,\text{mm}/\frac{1}{4}\,\text{in}$, $9\,\text{mm}/\frac{3}{8}\,\text{in}$ and $12\,\text{mm}/\frac{1}{2}\,\text{in}$ shanked router cutters, this tool will do everything a router can do. The second is the smaller cabinetmaker's router; it has a motor of about 600 watts and is small and light, with precise well-balanced controls. The capacity is limited to $6\,\text{mm}/\frac{1}{4}\,\text{in}$ shanked cutters, but for most work this is not a restriction. Most craftsmen prefer this smaller, lighter machine, especially for light-duty cabinet work.

Carbide-tipped cutters are available in an ever-increasing range of types and sizes and they are essential for cutting manufactured board with a high glue content such as plywoods. High-speed steel cutters are considerably less expensive and will give a better finish on solid timber. Although they lose their edge fairly quickly, the face side of most cutters can, with a little care, be honed back.

A router gets its best results using speed, not power, so allowing the cutter to spin at the maximum revolutions per minute possible and make several light paring cuts. If the note of the router changes or if your arm muscles tense up, these are warnings that you are removing too much stock too quickly.

Many craftsmen adapt the guidance systems and machine bases to suit their needs. A simple and effective modification is to extend the length of the side fence to between 30 cm/12 in and 38 cm/15 in to give greater support at the beginning and end of a cut. For freehand work, replace the base with clear Plexiglass, plunge through with a very small cutter, then score target sight lines to this centre.

Always wear eye protection when using a router because it spews out dust and shavings.

The plunging router

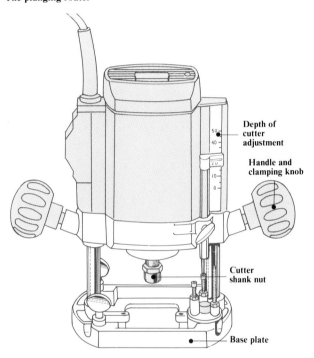

- Depth of cutter adjustment
- Handle and clamping knob
- Cutter shank nut
- Base plate

The cut-off jig
This is a simple and very useful guiding device. A straight batten is attached to a plywood sheet about 10 cm/4 in longer than the proposed cut. The router is run against the batten, cutting a parallel channel; this indicates the exact position the router will cut if the jig is clamped to a workpiece.

The halving jig
Another simple guidance jig, this can be used if a stopped rebate or dado is needed. It may be used, for example, to make the recesses for locks, hinges or handles on a batch production run. The U-shaped jig, usually made of plywood, is clamped to the workpiece. The router is then kept hard up against the inside face to cut the perimeter of the halving, and is then worked back and forth to remove the waste.

The cut-off jig

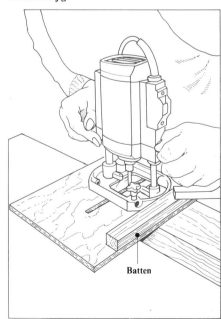

Batten

The halving jig

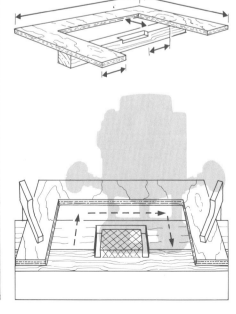

The mortise box
Use a powerful router for cutting mortises. Plunge down at each end to give a stop cut, then remove the waste with a series of shallow runs. For through-mortising, the router will cut clean, round-ended mortises to a standard only equalled by the horizontal mortising machine. But the set-up time is longer and repeats are a little slower to produce.

The template jig
This is based upon the same technique used by the shaper and overhead router. Templates are nailed to the workpiece temporarily by short pins. When using a profile guide inside a template avoid letting the waste jam the cutter as the cut is completed.

The dovetail jig
Machine dovetail jigs have been used for years but many craftsmen have shunned them because the regularity of the pins looks clumsy and lacks the elegance of hand-cut dovetails. But a machine jig is now available that offers the variety of spacing necessary to imitate hand-cut dovetails.

Inlay routing
The profile guide used for template routing is also the guide system for inlay routing. One template is used to cut the inlay and the recess. The difference between them is taken up by a collar made in thickness to the exact diameter of the router cutter, usually $3\,\text{mm}/\frac{1}{8}\,\text{in}$. The profile guide and collar should be made by an engineer, otherwise the simple precision of the technique will be lost.

The veneer edging jig
When fitting solid edge lipping to manufactured board, it is usual to plane the lipping flush with the board. A quicker alternative is to use a router jig while holding the cutter parallel to the board. Adjust the cutter to board level and then the excess lipping can be removed quickly and easily.

A bench jig
Working small objects is frequently a problem when using even a small router. One solution is to adapt a bench vice into a combined clamp and guidance jig. The clamp and guidance surfaces must be absolutely parallel to avoid inaccuracy.

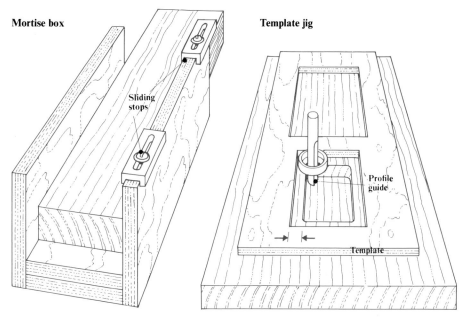

Mortise box

Sliding stops

Template jig

Profile guide

Template

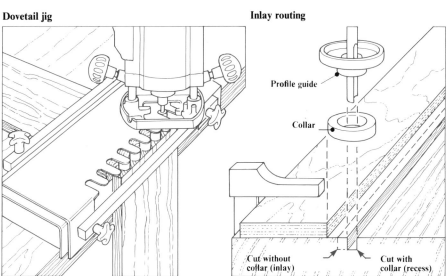

Dovetail jig

Inlay routing

Profile guide

Collar

Cut without collar (inlay)

Cut with collar (recess)

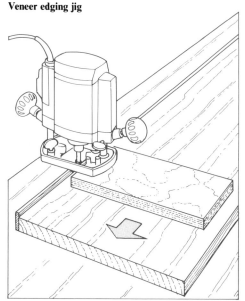

Veneer edging jig

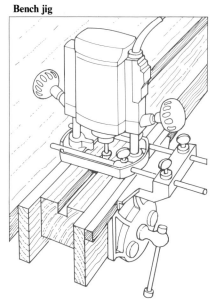

Bench jig

WORKSHOP / Shapers

The shaper is often the most under-used machine in the workshop, perhaps because of the misconception that it is just for making mouldings.

In principle, the shaper is similar to a router which has been turned upside down and hung beneath a work surface. In practice, however, they are quite different because a router functions well with low power and extremely high speed, while a shaper spins comparatively slowly at between 4,000 and 8,000 rpm. The shaper depends on torque, high power and heavy weight behind the cutter to make deep clean cuts.

For the best results, choose a model with a motor of at least 2 HP which drives a 3.2 cm/1¼ in diameter spindle through an aperture in a heavy cast iron table. Lightweight shapers are not recommended. The top piece of the spindle or the entire spindle should also be removable permitting speedy changes of tooling. It also allows the option of using either an English or a French head. Concentric rings in the table top around the spindle can be removed to give a different aperture for small or large cutter blocks.

A spindle brake may be provided for in the design, as well as a locking device, which is useful when changing tooling, but neither are essential features on this very simple machine. A sliding table may be a useful addition when producing machine tenons in batches, but otherwise jigs can be invented to perform this function.

Although it cannot be regarded as the most essential machine in a new workshop, anyone planning to extend either the quantity or the variety of their products should consider buying a shaper. Do not be put off by the idea that this is an industrial machine. Although it has been developed for industry, many single spindle machines are ideal for small workshop use.

One word of caution: all spindles have the capacity to throw out cutters at alarming speed at just around waist level. When learning to use the shaper, either seek the advice of an experienced machinist or take a course in machine operation.

The shaper

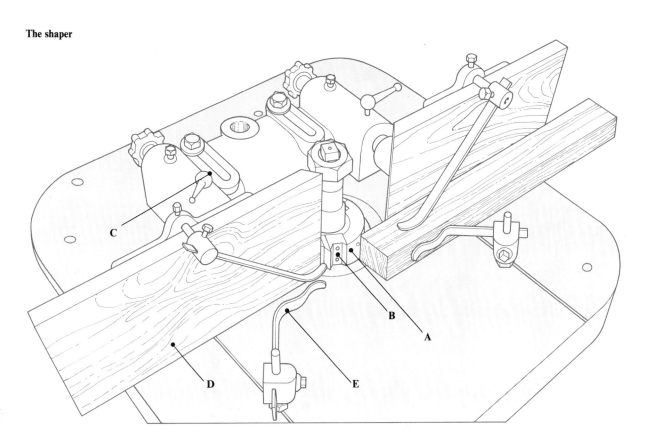

The shaper
A good quality shaper will have a solid fence with several adjustments. It will either be a two-part system or a one-piece horseshoe fence.

This is positioned in the most convenient place relative to the cutter block (A). Each individual fence will have some micro adjustment (B). This enables the fences to be stepped so that support can be given to a workpiece where the entire bearing face is planed off. These fences have a sideways adjustment (C) that can bring the fence as close as possible to the cutter block. Usually an auxiliary high fence is fitted permanently (D). This gives support to the job right up to the cutter block and allows other temporary fences to be attached with pins. These thin auxiliary fences straddle both sides of the horseshoe and are used with the French head to give additional support. When working against the straight fence it may be necessary to use either hold-down units of the sprung block type (E) or shop-built guides. A bonnet guard covering the cutter should always be used.

The rebating head

Most rebating can be done quickly and cleanly on the shaper using only this one item of tooling. Choose as large a block as your machine will accept; the inertia generated by spinning the weight of a large cutter block is an aid to a clean finish. An 11 cm/4$\frac{1}{2}$ in diameter, 4.5 cm/1$\frac{3}{4}$ in deep block is a good size. This can have tungsten-carbide-tipped cutters with two usable faces, and scoring knives top and bottom with four usable faces. Though not re-sharpenable, these blades last a very long time.

Rebating head

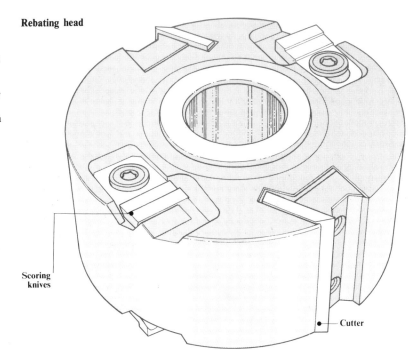

Scoring knives

Cutter

English and French heads

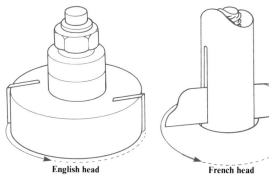

English head

French head

Whitehill block

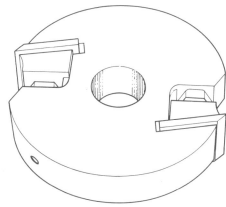

Safety head

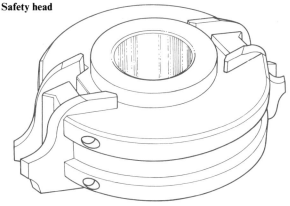

Standard profile cutters

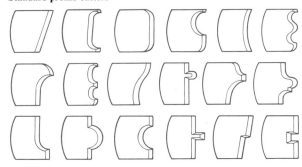

English and French heads

Most machines fit tooling of at least 3 cm/1$\frac{1}{4}$ in in diameter to the English head. The French head cutter scrapes at 90° to the job with a hook similar to a cabinet scraper; these cutters can be ground to exactly the moulding required. French head cutters are cheap, versatile, and produce a good finish on short runs.

Safety head

This is a basic tooling block. The cutters are factory ground to suit the most used profiles, though it is possible to grind your own cutters. Generally, one cutter does the work while another cutter of similar weight provides the balance. The design makes it unlikely for this type of block to throw a knife.

The Whitehill block

This is a more versatile version of the safety block because it allows one cutter to be angled and turned to produce several moulds. Because of the weight of the block, a balancing cutter is only occasionally needed. Tenoning can be done using rebate cutters and two Whitehill blocks mounted one above the other. This system is versatile, but it lacks the safety features of other tooling.

Similarly the slotted collar block uses two discs mounted one above the other. This traps two cutters in a cutter block sandwich. This type of block needs to be set up with great care in order to equalize the cutter projection and to seat the cutters (shown in the diagram above) properly.

Tenoning disc

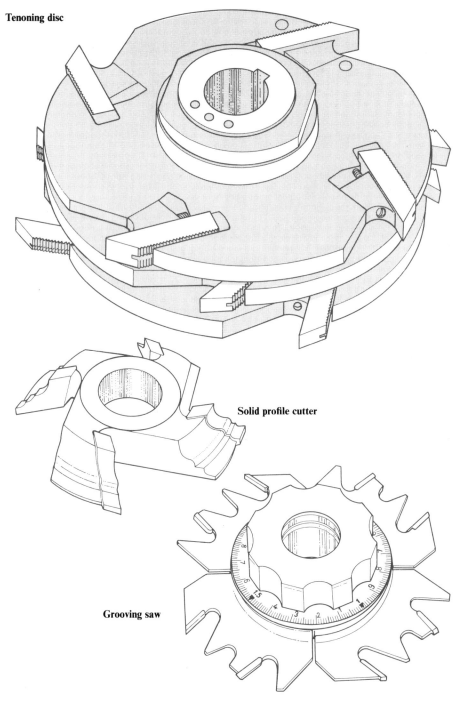

Solid profile cutter

Grooving saw

Tenoning disc

This is really an industrial form of tooling which is used on single- or double-headed tenoning machines. However, in some instances it can be used on a shaper to cut cheeks and shoulders at the same time. Spacers are available to vary the tenon width by placing the discs farther apart or closer together.

The workpiece is pushed through the tool, either on a sliding carriage, or held square with a shop-built jig.

Solid profile cutters and grooving saws

These are special-purpose shaper tools usually purchased with a particular job in mind. The familiar three-lip cutters are very solid and are less liable than other models to throw small scraps. They are available in a wide range of profiles and can be face-honed easily in the shop. Two-wing solid profile cutters are a more expensive version based on the same principle; because they are short, both can operate at much higher spindle speeds.

Grooving saws are available in many widths and are used with and across the grain. Tooling similar to a dado head is also available to give a better finish than dadoing on the table saw.

The ring fence

Do not confuse this with the ring guard which should sit above it. The ring fence introduces the workpiece gradually to a deep cut. The fence is placed off-centre to the cutter. The positions of minimum (A) and maximum (B) cutter projection are marked on the machine and the workpiece pivoted around between the two marks.

The ring guard

This item should be used whenever the straight fences and bonnet guard are removed. The concentric rings around the spindle are removed to the width of the cutter block and the last ring inverted. This gives a raised lip, which can be used as a fence below the tooling against which a template can run. Some operators may use it in the same way as a ring fence to introduce the cut gradually. Be aware that this is a dangerous practice because the cut is not guarded at its greatest projection.

The ring fence

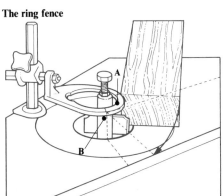

The ring guard

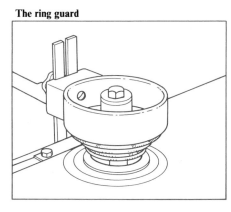

Template moulding

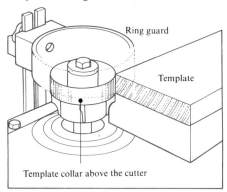

Ring guard

Template

Template collar above the cutter

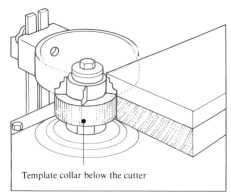

Template collar below the cutter

Shaping against collar

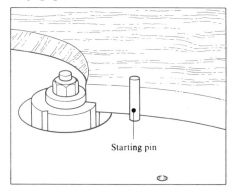

Starting pin

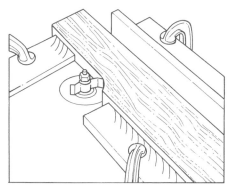

Circular moulding jig

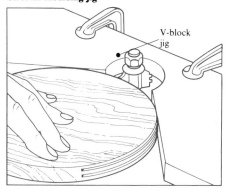

V-block jig

Mini-spindle with small grooving saw

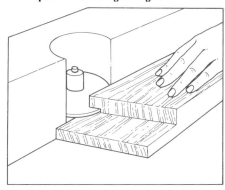

Mini-spindle

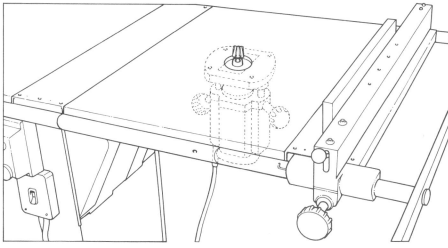

Template moulding

This time-saving production technique employs jigs and templates that are temporarily attached to the workpiece. The templates can be made of plywood faced with plastic laminate or of solid plastic, which slips easily on the machine table and give better control. The template runs against, and is guided by, a collar which is either above or below the cutter. The advantage of having a template guiding the cut is that the entire face of the workpiece can be worked. Collars are available with ball bearing centres and outer rings of differing diameter so that the depth of cut may be varied. Ring fences or a starting pin may be used to begin the cut.

Shaping against a collar

This is similar to template moulding, without the template. The technique can be used only when the workpiece has been cut and planed to shape. Collar shaping allows a mould to be worked along one part of the edge of the workpiece only. Small solid profile or three-wing cutters are ideal for this function. The collar is fitted to suit the depth of cut and the workpiece itself guides the cut. Because the spinning collar can burn when rubbing against timber, ball bearing collars are fitted. A starting pin may be used to introduce the job to the cutter.

Circular moulding jig

By replacing the fences with a simple V-block jig, decorative moulds can be worked or rebates cut to suit the job.

Mini-spindle

A router that has been inverted and hung beneath a workbench is known as a mini-spindle. It is most usefully placed between the extension rails of the table saw, so that the table saw fence system can be used for the mini-spindle as well. Make an enlarged plastic base for the router: by positioning it in a rebate flush with the work surface, it can then be lifted out for adjustment.   This is a useful way to extend the capacity of an already invaluable machine for working small items.

The mini-spindle can also be fitted with a small grooving saw (above) for cutting relatively deep yet narrow channels along the edges of the workpiece.

A well-designed workbench is important because it holds a workpiece in position to be glued, cut or bent. For this reason it is sometimes seen as the biggest clamping jig in the shop. Ideally, the bench should be as large as possible, heavy and stable, and should support the workpiece at a convenient height. This is the key to maximum accuracy.

The bench is therefore an essential workshop fixture, and perhaps the most important tool any woodworker will build. However, the types of bench vary according to the type of work done and the type of person doing it. A precise worker with an engineering approach will design an absolutely flat bench top which can be used in the same way that an engineer uses a drafting board. Timber is likely to be an unsuitable material for this kind of bench because its warps will cause inaccuracies, and because it can easily be damaged with an edge tool. A more practical approach is to build the bench from timber and to recognize that in the course of having to work quickly, it will almost certainly get damaged. However, when the damage reaches the point of adversely affecting the work, the bench can be planed flat or resurfaced with a thin sheet of plywood.

Whatever the type of bench, there will be common features. First, it should be as wide and as long as possible with a base built from heavy timber to add to its stability. The height of the work surface can be adjusted to personal requirements. If, for example, you have a history of back injuries, the bench should be built higher than normal.

A bench made from 7.5 cm/3 in thick solid beech which is, perhaps, 2 m/$6\frac{1}{2}$ ft long and 45 cm/18 cm wide would satisfy most requirements. Along this surface should be built a back rail and a tool well which provides a natural repository for general workshop clutter.

Secondly, the bench should be the work centre around which the most constantly used tools are stored. A cabinetmaker may well keep bench planes, a selection of chisels, marking gauges and squares stored on a rack beneath the bench. The less frequently-used workshop tools should be stored in a more central position.

Most benches should have at least two vices built-in. The main vice is best situated at the extreme left-hand end of a bench to allow the workpiece to be sawn clear of the bench end. A modern metal vice is the most useful because of its quick action, wide jaw capacity and considerable clamping strength. Giving the jaws an inner facing of some hardwood such as beech will

Main bench vice
This shows the way in which a conventional metal vice can be faced with timber to provide a jig or guide for routing small objects. The vice should be flush with the bench top and square with the end of the bench.

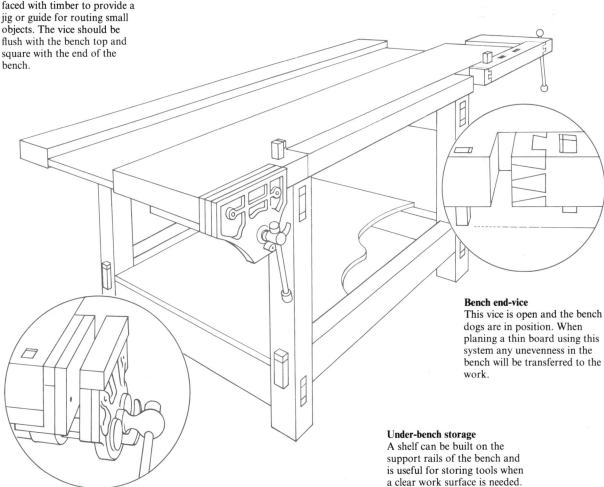

Bench end-vice
This vice is open and the bench dogs are in position. When planing a thin board using this system any unevenness in the bench will be transferred to the work.

Under-bench storage
A shelf can be built on the support rails of the bench and is useful for storing tools when a clear work surface is needed.

prevent timber from being damaged on the metal corners of the jaws and enables the vice to act as a router jig.

A second end-vice or tail-vice is a versatile clamping system which has the advantage of being able to accommodate work in the normal way, but without any of the obstruction below that is common with other types of vice. The end-vice can also be used in conjunction with a series of bench dogs or stops. These are fitted down the length of the bench, making it possible to clamp large flat workpieces to the bench top. It is this facility for holding anything from a shooting board to a completed carcass that gives the end-vice is versatility. Bench dogs can be placed in mortises every 15 cm/6 in or so down the length of the bench. When not in use, the bench dog lies flush with the bench top and when needed it can be quickly pushed up. Slippery lignum vitae makes a good bench dog. The facing could be boxwood or horn beam, and yew is suitable for the spring.

Finally, remember that while a bench should be as rigid, solid and heavy as possible, it should also somehow be movable to allow you to change your shop layout without having to destroy the bench. Additionally, the bench should be able to move with the shifting daylight—the best light to work by.

Sash clamp storage

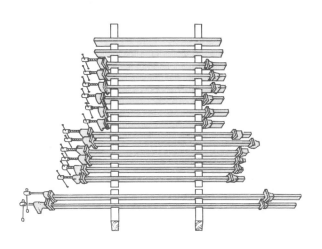

Sash clamp storage
Sash clamps are an important and expensive workshop tool. Keep them well waxed and free of glue. A horizontal storage rack will hold clamps of different lengths and also keep the end pins in position.

Speed clamp storage
General bench clamps should be close at hand and immediately accessible. This vertical rack prevents them from cluttering up the workshop.

Mitre clamping
It is frequently necessary to glue mitres together with just the end grain as a glue surface, if only as a temporary measure until a spline is inserted later. However, it still presents problems when clamps have to be positioned to hold the mitres together. A traditional solution is to glue small blocks, one on each side, to make a parallel clamping surface. The blocks are separated from the workpiece by a layer of brown paper. When clamped they hold well, but when tapped with a hammer the paper splits leaving only a little glue and half the thickness of paper to be cleaned away.

Speed clamp storage

Mitre clamping

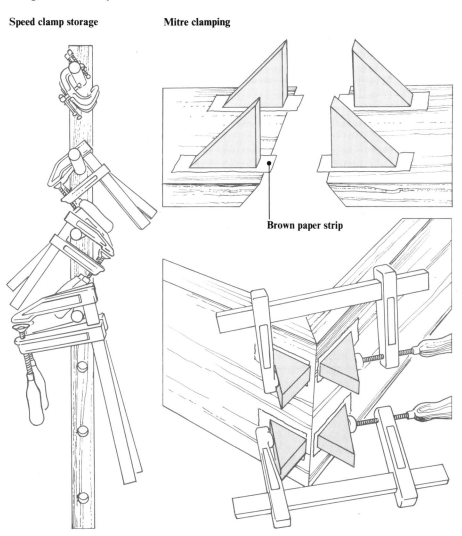

Brown paper strip

179

Bonding, veneering and laminating are all similar operations involving separate techniques that require their own types of jigs, formers or moulds. Holding the workpiece at a certain attitude with respect to the tool requires a holding jig; giving the workpiece some other shape, surface or configuration requires some different kinds of jigs.

Laying veneers

To lay veneers, many workshops get by with hot glue, veneer hammers and a lot of skill. Occasionally a composite veneering job will come up that demands the use of cauls and a veneer press. For the small job, a couple of heavy boards, a few battens and clamps will suffice, but for general use it really is best to build a small workshop press. The commercially available clamping systems made from steel beams weigh two hundred kilos or more, are fast to operate and cost a fortune. It is, however, possible to design a press for occasional use that is almost as efficient.

The problem is to clamp up an area of perhaps a square metre/yard or more, quickly and evenly. Modern resin glues have a delayed setting time of 10 to 15 minutes to allow the worker to get the job coated, the veneer positioned and the whole assembly put under pressure. At a moment like this, it is the worker and not the veneer which is under pressure. It takes great organization, calm and presence of mind to caul up a large surface single handed. Just as time is running out, the worker must resist the temptation to tighten all the clamps. Instead he should clamp up the work in a strict order, a little at a time, squeezing glue from the centre to the edges, trying only to press the surface evenly and no more.

A shop-built veneer press

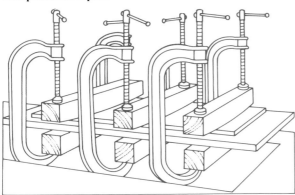

Wedge clamping

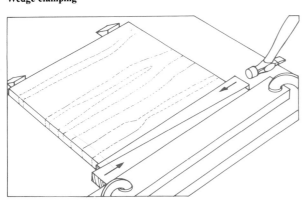

Bending to a former

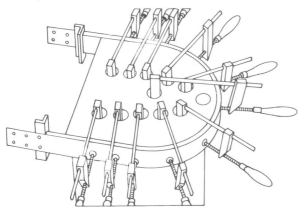

A shop-built veneer press
For occasional use, this system of clamps and shaped bearers will do a good job. Tighten up only until the bearers exert even pressure across the width of the press. On wide presses, the underside of the bearers should be concave so that adequate pressure is exerted on the centre of the workpiece. To do the job quickly before the glue sets two persons are needed to manipulate the parts of the press, although only one person should be adjusting the clamp tension to keep the pressure relatively even.

Wedge clamping
This is used in conjunction with a chairmaker's plate or a worktable with built-up stops to hold a workpiece under pressure. Two long wedges of the same size are forced against each other and remain in place, held by friction. It allows a flat workpiece to be held without obstructing its surface.

Bending to a former
A former is a shape around which the workpiece is pushed or pulled to bend it. With some assistance from a helper, it is possible to clamp up a job quickly with this kind of former. A steel strap pressed along the outside of the workpiece will distribute the pressure of the individual clamps evenly.

Note that any stains left by the steel strap on wood dampened by glue or moisture can easily be removed with oxalic acid (see pages 206–207).

A chairmaker's removable former
In this simplified jig, the pressure is exerted by wedges bending the workpiece around the former. The pegs are moved around the steel baseplate as the workpiece is pressed into shape.

A chairmaker's removable former

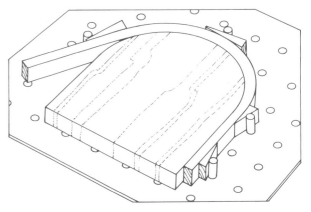

Bending jigs

Bending can be a steamy, sweaty business. Two similar types of jig are used especially for chairmaking. For occasional use, or for the one-of-a-kind job, it is sensible to bend to a former. It is very important to get both sides clamped up very quickly or the workpiece will chill unevenly and dry to a different curvature. A similar technique used in chairmaking is to bend the workpiece to a removable former. The stress is taken by a heavy steel plate drilled to accept steel pegs in various positions. Once the workpiece is bent to the former, a single sash clamp is placed across the bottom and the whole assembly is removed to dry out.

Laminating jigs

Laminating is an altogether more civilized technique performed in the dry comfort of the workshop.

Whereas commercial laminated boards are supplied flat in sheet form, the value of lamination to the craftsman is in its ability to hold a curved shape. Solid wood can be cut into thick veneer sections, stacked in the same order they came from the log and reassembled in a different curved or serpentine form.

The technique depends upon each lamination being held to a slightly different radius from its neighbour. Then the layers are glued together under mechanical pressure. Once set, the entire job retains the shape of the jig or mould in which it was produced. Simple laminating can be done with clamps to a jig or former. But sheet lamination or laminating more complex compound curves may require a mould that takes more time to build than to assemble the job itself, although once assembled it can be reused as often as necessary.

Laminating to a former

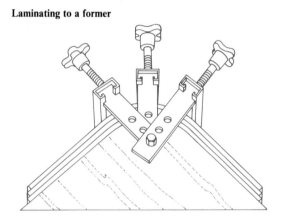

Laminating to a former
This simple example of bent lamination is curved around a fixed point. Specialized clamps such as these are useful, but it will still require two persons to set up the job.

Lamination using a mould
1. A mould is a two-part former that gives support on both sides of a bent shape. The framework of the mould bends the laminated parts of the workpiece and holds them under even pressure. The pressure is exerted by thick

beams held by bar clamps, which are slowly tightened to leave a thin, even glue line along the edges of the laminated boards.
2. A mould with a multiple curve should have sliding braces along the front to restrict sideward slippage.
3. The gap between the bottom and the top of the mould should be wider at the sides that in the middle so that it can exert enough pressure on the centre of the workpiece as the clamps are tightened to force the glue from the centre out.

Lamination using a mould

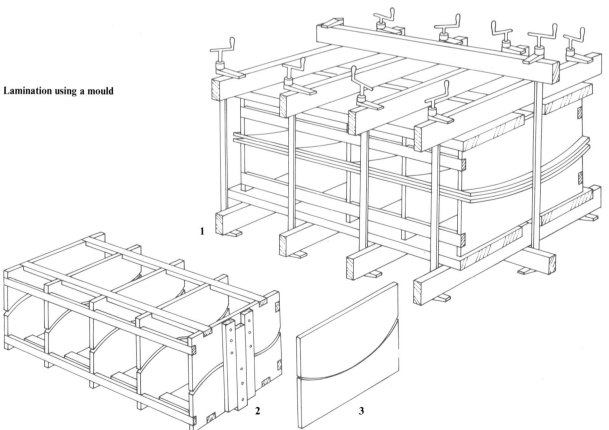

Traditionalists are wary of sanders, believing they give an inferior finish, cloud the grain or are generally too industrial. It is certainly less pleasant to use a noisy machine spewing clouds of dust than to hand-plane silky shavings from a cabinet side. But it takes great skill to plane correctly and in the end the planed surface will be neither superior to, nor smoother, than a machine-sanded surface.

The importance of the surface of an item should not be underestimated. Daylight will disclose all flaws without mercy and if they are not seen they will be felt. A fingertip will sense just how smooth a door edge is, or be pricked on the sharp point of a splinter.

For most tropical timbers with interlocking grain, good sanders and a dust extraction system are probably the only ways to get a smooth surface. Recent advances in finishing systems have been made with hard-wearing, cloth-backed abrasives used in conjunction with jointing systems for belt sanders. The market now offers sanding machines of many different types and capacities. The illustrations below display those which are most often used in the small workshop.

It is generally not worth purchasing abrasive belts heavier than an E weight paper. The cloth backing will generally outlast the abrasive. Depending upon the degree of finish required, grits of between 80 and 220 aluminium oxide are recommended, with 120 and 180 grits being the most commonly used.

Pad sander or stroke sander

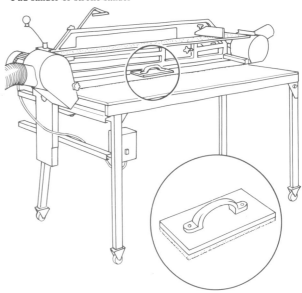

Pad sander or stroke sander
Perhaps the most useful big sander in a small workshop, the pad sander is capable of the finest of finishes, even on veneers. The mechanical system for placing the pad is usually discarded, thus adapting an obsolete industrial capacity machine to the sensitive touch of a hand operator. Capable of much greater control than other belt sanders, this machine is highly recommended.

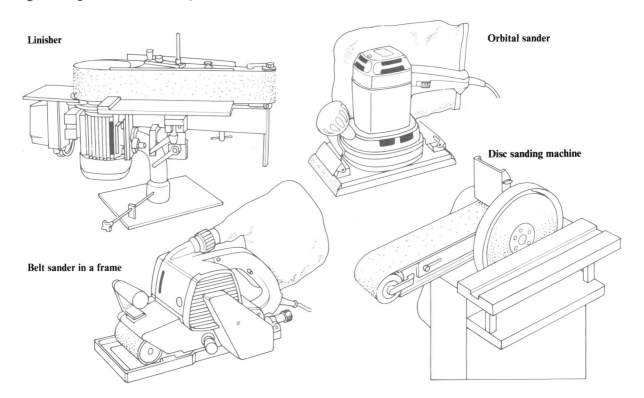

Linisher

Orbital sander

Disc sanding machine

Belt sander in a frame

Linisher
The static belt sander is a common sight in small workshops. It can also be used as a dimensioning tool to remove stock either across or with the grain at great speed and efficiency.

Belt sander in a frame
Like a mobile linisher, this belt sander has a removable frame which limits the depth of cut. To some extent this controls the force of the belt sander, but care is still needed to avoid removing too much material.

Orbital sander
This is strictly a finishing tool. When papers coarser than 100 grit are used to remove stock, problems arise because small rings are left in the finish which are impossible to remove with subsequent finer papers.

Disc sanding machine
For trimming square all end grain or for shaping small pieces, this sander is without equal. It is often used in conjunction with the linisher to finish and smooth out the rough shaping.

Working with power tools is not dangerous provided you follow carefully the manufacturers' operating instructions and use basic common sense. But home workshops are potential safety hazards because they are exempt from the strict regulations on machine practice that are enforced in small commercial workshops. And although it may be unrealistic to propose that home woodworkers should adopt industrial safety standards, it would be in their best interests to do so. Machine techniques such as cutting tenons above the blade of a table saw, when used by an inexperienced, tired or careless machinist, very often result in accidents.

The best defence against such accidents is a knowledge of what could go wrong when operating each machine. A table saw, for example, is always capable of throwing small pieces of timber back at you. This generally happens during ripping or cross cutting when timber binds between the blade and rip fence. The result is often a waist-level missile. However, a much greater danger occurs when the board pinches on either side of the blade itself. On these occasions a piece can lift off the table from the back, and fly towards the operator at eye level. So, when ripping always use a riving knife—a thin metal plate behind the blade that prevents the cut from closing—a guard and long push sticks. Loose ties, cuffs and clothing are constant hazards, particularly near planers. Thicknessers may pull a limb on to the cutter block.

Lathes and drill presses are comparatively safe machines but always check that there is nothing obstructing the movement of the spindle before switching on the power. Again, make sure that loose cuffs, neck ties and long hair are tucked in or removed.

Shapers can kill in the hands of a careless or over-confident machinist; the rattle of a loose cutter in a French head is a certain danger signal. Bandsaw blades can do more damage to the operator out of the machine than in it, but if they are folded properly the hazard is lessened. Remember that unfolding can be equally alarming, because the blade is likely to jump and spring around the shop.

The list of dangerous activities may seem almost endless, and a craftsman working alone in a workshop should take particular care. Every workshop should be equipped with a good first aid kit stocked not only with the usual small bandages for cuts and abrasions, but also with some large gauze pads and first aid tape to help stop bleeding. Remember that the victim is likely to be in shock and keep the telephone number of the emergency services written on the wall by the telephone. If someone has cut off a finger, take it with him to the hospital, preferably packed in ice.

Dust can do long term damage to your lungs, and some workers are allergic to certain exotic timbers. Mansonia, ebony, rosewood, iroko and black bean are only some of the species that can cause skin rashes and sore throats.

The vapours released from evaporating glue when cutting certain manufactured boards can also be toxic, so a good respirator mask is essential. Skin creams on hands and arms can help prevent rashes.

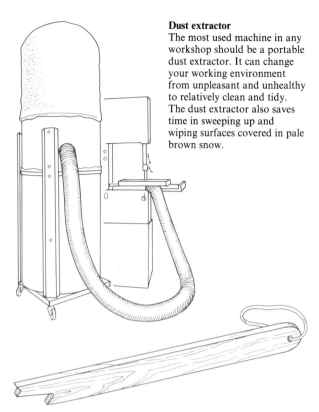

Dust extractor
The most used machine in any workshop should be a portable dust extractor. It can change your working environment from unpleasant and unhealthy to relatively clean and tidy. The dust extractor also saves time in sweeping up and wiping surfaces covered in pale brown snow.

Push sticks
It should be standard practice always to use long push sticks when feeding a cutting edge.

Make sure the handle end is rounded and smooth or a jerk from the blade will still injure you.

Ear defenders
Working with machines can easily damage your hearing, so buy good quality ear defenders with glycerine-filled seals. If you can press the defenders to your head and decrease the noise, they are not doing the job required.

Goggles and masks
Goggles tend to steam up and become unpleasant to wear after a time. Masks, which can be put on for short machining jobs and then taken off, are more practical. Always wear a mask for routing to protect you from the small chips that are thrown out.

Wood is a remarkable material. Its combined utility and strength are almost unmatched, and its flexibility and broad range of uses make it an ideal material around which to base a workshop and to experiment with furniture design ideas. If it is dried properly, protected from extreme heat and moisture and from the ravages of marauding insects, it will last indefinitely. And where solid woods cannot cope with the demands of a design, manufactured woods such as plywood and chipboard or specially laminated curved sections and beams will provide structural strength.

Appearance

It is a common mistake to think of trees as wholly alive. In fact, the central heartwood of the mature tree is dead and merely supports the living outer sheath of sapwood. Tree growth, which takes place in the sapwood during spring and summer, produces the distinctive ring marks in the timber. As the growing season ends the wood cells become smaller and thicker-walled. This belt of denser timber is called summer wood. The growth rings only become obvious when the tree is cut through, but it is these, along with other clearly visible groups of specialized cells, that give each species of timber its unique grain patterns. Grain varies not only by species, but also by the type of growth and the direction of the cut.

The colour of the grain varies also. Sapwood is usually white, tinged with red or brown. The colour of heartwood ranges widely, from the black of Ceylon ebony to the paper-white of fir. Other species tend towards green (American tulip) or red (Andaman padauk) heartwood. Infections may also change the true colour, for example, the rusty brown that English oak becomes when afflicted by "beefsteak fungus".

Smell

Many woods have distinctive scents, some pleasant such as sassafras and sandalwood, and some rank, such as virola and wet ramin. These scents may be sealed in by coats of finish, but strong-smelling woods should be avoided for food preparation surfaces such as cutting boards. This is why maple is a good choice for kitchen worktops.

Moisture content

When a tree is cut down it contains a considerable amount of water. This amount is measured as a percentage of the timber's weight if it were completely dry. Before the wood can be used for furniture making it needs to be dried so that its moisture content is around 9 percent. At this level the application of water repellents, preservatives, preservative stains, paints and varnishes is far more effective, and the timber itself is quite stable.

If the wood is well below the 9 percent level, when it comes into contact with moist air it will swell, particularly across the grain, resulting in distortion. A panel door will stick in its frame, for example. If the wood is too wet when it is placed in a dry, central-heated environment, it will shrink as it dries, causing previously tight-fitting joints to loosen up.

Swelling

Shrinkage

Dry wood

Moist air

A door swells across the grain and so could jam in the frame.

Loose fitting tongue and groove joints are caused by shrinkage across the grain.

Moist wood

Dry air

Testing for strength

A tensile-testing machine, such as the one illustrated far right, is used primarily in industry to assess the inherent strength of woods and adhesives.

Average shrinkage (mm) of a 100 mm wide board when dried from green to oven dry.

Softwoods	
Western Red Cedar	3.7
Douglas Fir	6.4
Pine White	4.1
,, Red	5.9
Yew	4.6

Hard woods	
Ash	6.3
Beech	8.1
Cherry	5.4
Elm	6.8
Mahogany	4.5
Maple	6.5
Oak	7.0
Sycamore	6.5
Walnut	5.5

Shrinkage in length 0.1 to 0.2%

Testing for strength

Density

Density, the apparent weight of wood, varies extensively among the species. It has only a loose connection with strength. Some heavy woods—rosewood, for example—are brittle, whereas light woods such as spruce are strong enough to use in the construction of light aircraft. Because wood contains water, its weight depends on its moisture content. Wood saturated with water can weigh up to three times more than an oven-dry sample of the same species.

Insulation

Wood is an insulator, and therefore a very poor conductor of heat, making it a peculiarly good choice as a casing material for fire-proof safes. Dry wood expands very little as temperatures rise—around a quarter as much as steel or glass—and loses little of its strength. Because fire consumes large wooden beams very slowly and their interiors remain cool and strong, research is showing that fires in buildings with wooden frameworks may be less destructive than previously thought.

Stability

Stability—the tendency of a material to retain its shape and size—is one of the chief assets of timber. At most, wood will change dimensions slightly, or move, in reaction to seasonal variations in atmospheric moisture, as the wood fibres shrink and swell with absorbed humidity. The greatest movement will be across the grain, rather than along it.

Strength

Assessing the strength of wood is difficult, involving a series of tests to check its suitability for particular purposes. A bending test evaluates timber for beams and support members by measuring its ability to withstand heavy loads. Because timber will fail suddenly when a maximum load is exceeded, it is important to know that limit to be able to design in a margin of safety. Similarly, a compression test checks the strength of supporting columns, such as chair legs.

Wood is also tested for hardness, its resistance to wear and knocks, and for shear strength. A further discussion of stress can be found on pages 28–31.

Laminating for strength

Characteristics affecting strength

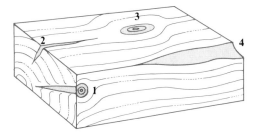

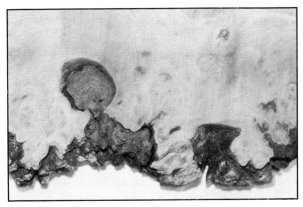

Laminating for strength
One way to increase the strength of timber is to laminate sheets together to produce plywood. This process can be extended to sizeable laminated beams such as these, which have the strength to support large buildings.

Characteristics affecting strength
Some of the inherent features of wood such as growth rings (1), fissures (2), knots (3) and waney or bark-covered edges (4) all tend to reduce strength.

Diseased burl wood
Diseases (5) also cause weakening, but the effects they produce, such as burl with its curly grain, can still be used for decorative veneered finishes.

185

Milling and design

The most important factor in the appearance of a piece of wood is its surface markings, loosely called "grain", or more correctly "figure". Figure is mainly determined by the species of timber, the way the grain naturally runs through it and the method used to convert the log to boards—that is, the milling. If the growth rings are at right angles to the wide face of the board, which occurs in quarter sawn logs, the surface will usually have a boldly striped appearance; growth rings near parallel to the surface usually result in a more irregular "water figure".

Cutting wood at an angle across the grain lines also gives an unusual figure, looking like flame or crown. But this is a wasteful method of milling timber for structural use and it is generally reserved for making saw-cut veneers.

In some species, such as English oak, distinctive markings called medullary rays add further variation to the surface appearance. The knots and occasional patches of pale sapwood can, with a little skill and ingenuity, be incorporated into a design and enhance the overall look of a piece.

Sawmill

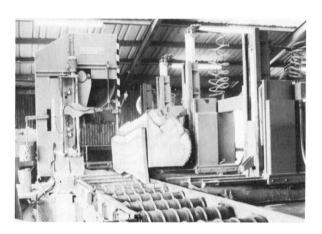

Saw-cut veneers

Until the 19th century, veneers for furniture were generally saw-cut. This produced a thicker veneer than the modern knife-cut veneers and resulted in a very durable surface when it was properly applied. Saw-cut veneers can be made in the small workshop using a bandsaw and surface planing machine, with a thicknesser or by hand saw. This way, small quantities of exotic, attractive woods can be "stretched" to cover larger areas. In addition, weak or unreliable timber can be stabilized by backing it with a strong, stable groundwork.

The efficiency of the bandsaw method depends on the ability to cut straight lines on the bandsaw. Having decided upon the angle and direction of the cut, use a wide blade in the saw to slice about 4 mm/$\frac{3}{16}$ in off the workpiece. Then set the surface planer to take off a small shaving and pass the workpiece over it, removing just enough to get rid of the sawmarks. Take off another 4 mm/$\frac{3}{16}$ in slice from the freshly planed surface, and then replane the cut side. Carry on until you have enough area of veneer to cover your project, allowing 10 to 20 percent for waste. The width of the

Methods of converting boards
Timber is converted into boards at a sawmill (left) using one of two methods. The simplest and most efficient way is known as plain sawing through-and-through, or slash sawing (**A**), which uses a band saw or circular saw to take slices down the length of the log. Because the growth rings run almost parallel through the boards, those on the outside of the log have a highly figured surface (near right), referred to as water figure. The boards cut from the centre of the log have a more even, striped grain figure.

The second method, quarter-sawing (**B**), is a more complex process. The log is first quartered along its axis, and then each segment is cut into boards. Most of the cutting is at right angles to growth rings, so most of the boards will have a plain, attractive figure (far right).

Veneers from quarter-sawn stock
Different patterns result, depending on the orientation of the saw blade to the grain: a cut parallel to the grain creates a "water" pattern; angled, it becomes a "crown" pattern; at 90°, the figure becomes a straight quarter-cut pattern.

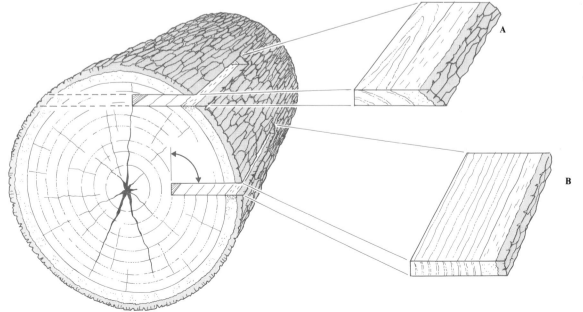

A

B

veneers is limited by the depth of the cut possible on the bandsaw, but narrow strips of veneer can look attractive. Careful adjustment of the saw guide, and a sharp, well-set blade will produce the best results. For safety reasons, attach a small workpiece or a larger scrap of timber before cutting. Sheets of cut veneer can be thicknessed to as little as 3 mm/$\frac{1}{8}$ in before laying. If a thicknesser is not available, the sheets are planed smooth after being laminated.

Using hand tools to make veneers takes work and practice. A panel saw, or a chair-maker's bow saw, is ideal for veneer cutting. Saw marks can be removed with a jack-plane. The production sequence is the same for both types of saws. Use PVA adhesive to laminate the veneer, planed-side down, to the groundwork. After 24 hours, the surface can be cleaned up with a plane and scraper in the usual way.

Grain figure and design

Figure can subtly affect the overall design in the way the grain directions alter the apparent size and shape of furniture. Two pieces of furniture, identical in size, can appear to have different proportions as a result.

Varying grain patterns can also influence the eye's perception of all parts of a design; asymmetric patterns may make furniture appear to lean awkwardly to one side or to bend in the middle. The best time to make these decisions is at the milling stage of the project.

On the other hand, by matching up the sections of the design by its figure, separate components of a piece can be unified. For example, if the figure on the front of a series of a drawers flow from one to the other, as they do on the John Makepeace sidetable on page 56, the drawers are seen as a visual whole.

Complete freedom of choice about grain direction is only possible with veneered furniture. The structural requirements can thus be satisfied, and then the piece layed with a decorative skin to achieve the visual effect required.

In general, however, figure effects should be avoided unless you are absolutely certain of the result. A strong horizontal figure, for example, will make low furniture look even lower and wider than a vertical figure. And doors tend to look odd if the veneer figure occurs from side to side. Sketch a project with the grain running in various ways before making a final design decision.

Veneers from quarter-sawn stock

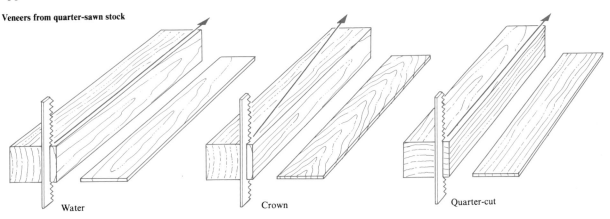

Water   Crown   Quarter-cut

The effect of figure on design
The same piece of furniture can seem to take on widley varying proportions, depending on the orientation of the grain figure. Certain optical illusions can be useful for the designer:
1. To create a sense of breadth and accentuate the horizontal lines of the drawers, run the figure horizontally. If the pattern is strong, the piece may look squat.
2. Crown veneers radiating toward the centre line of the piece create the illusion of narrowness.
3. The piece will seem elongated if the figure runs vertically. On a tall, narrow piece, the effect will be towering and monolithic.
4. Crown veneers radiating from the centre line will add breadth to the piece.

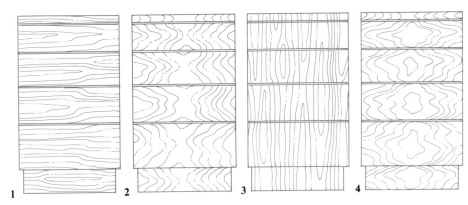

1   2   3   4

The illusion of sagging
Although the veneers on this sideboard have been expertly matched, from a distance the down-curving figure distorts the appearance of the piece, so that it seems to sag in the middle. It is best to run the grain vertically on doors unless the grain is straight and can be prefectly aligned.

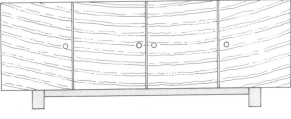

187

Timber is available from timber yards cut down to standard sizes. In this country these are based on metric lengths and thicknesses. The standard lengths of most thicknesses of hardwood and softwood start at 1.8 m and can get as long as 7.2 m, although this varies considerably from merchant to merchant according to the kind of wood sought. This is especially true of hardwoods, which are becoming increasingly rare. Short lengths of less than 1.8 m usually are cheaper than standard lengths.

The thickness and width of a board is measured in *nominal* millimetres, which means that the board was of those dimensions when it was cut from the log. However, at that point, the wood was still wet; in the process of drying, it will have shrunk down to its *actual* width and depth usually by as much as 6 mm to 12 mm. The chart on the next page shows the actual sawn softwood sizes that are available in Britain.

Most yards will offer a choice of rough-sawn or planed timber. The planed board will be about $\frac{1}{8}$ in thinner and narrower than the rough sawn board, but it saves planing and edging the wood at home.

The British timber industry being in the middle of converting from Imperial measurements to metric, wood is still ordered by the cubic foot, which is 12 ft by 12 in by 1 in. Large man-made boards are usually sized as 8 ft by 4 ft, or 5 ft by 5 ft, but smaller boards are sized in metric. If you prefer to work in Imperial measure-

ments, the timber retailer will convert for you.

The simplest route to quality is to ask for the best grade for furniture making. Plywoods are made in various coded grades, but vary with the manufacturer.

When buying timber, every piece of wood should be inspected. The boards should be straight, flat, free of checks or shakes or any unsound knots. On clean wood, freshly planed, the faults are easy to spot, but the final appearance of grubby, dusty or muddy timber is more difficult to determine. If timber has been improperly air-dried, or stored negligently, dampness will have seeped into the wood, staining it and causing it to warp. The stains can sometimes be bleached out (see pages 206–207) but unless the wood is quarter sawn, the warpage is probably irreversible. It is advisable to bring a knife or small block plane when visiting a yard to clean off a surface patch.

The moisture content of the wood is also a vital factor. For outdoor furniture, air-dried wood is adequate, but indoor furniture must be built of wood that has been kiln-dried with not more than 9 percent moisture content, or in the drier atmosphere of the house the joints will loosen and cracks appear.

The only reliable way to measure moisture content is with a meter. Inexpensive electronic moisture meters can help avoid costly mistakes. They work by measuring the wood's electrical conductivity; the higher the moisture content, the higher the conductivity. Read-

Overall appearance

End shakes

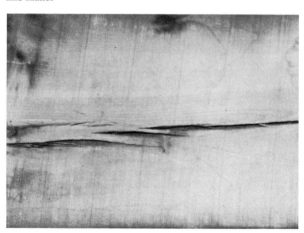

Knots and sap channels

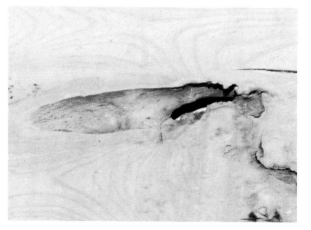

Inspecting timber
The more you buy timber the more you will become experienced in knowing what to accept and what to reject. Some common features to look out for include:

Overall appearance
Exposure to light and air may change the surface colour of timber considerably which may mean planing or cutting off a small section to reveal the true colour underneath.

End shakes
This is common at the ends of boards, and if the timber yard is not prepared to trim this part off allow for additional wastage when you buy your wood.

Knots and sap channels
Because these are both difficult to conceal, they are best avoided.

ings should be taken from several spots on the wood, and an average taken. This meter does not measure the moisture deep inside the wood, however, because its needle probe only goes into the timber surface. The merchant may therefore allow you to cut off a short piece of board to expose the core of the wood. Alternatively, use a meter with hammer electrodes which can be driven deep into the board.

Finding rare woods

Of the many thousand species of timber that exist, only a small number are readily available: mahogany, walnut, oak, maple, cherry, rosewood and teak among the hardwoods, and pine, hemlock, fir, redwood, spruce and cedar among the softwoods. Unusual or exotic woods may take some effort to find. One source is the small timber yards in rural areas, where the main business is to clear fields and orchards and to provide fence timber and firewood. From time to time they may have the odd log or two of unusual timbers to sell—nutwoods such as hickory or chestnut or fruit-woods such as cherry or pearwood. This wood will need to be seasoned at home, though you may be able to arrange for kiln drying at the yard.

Exotic timbers can also be found through suppliers advertising in crafts and woodworking magazines, and from veneer manufacturers who sometimes dispose of the scraps of exotic timbers they cannot process.

A glossary of timber terms

Air-dried or naturally seasoned timber. Unkilned timber usually of uncertain moisture content.

Bast. The layer beneath the bark.

Batten. A thin, narrow strip of timber.

Balk. A large square-sectioned timber, usually used for beams or rafters.

Blue stain. Discoloration of wood caused by moulds which attack sapwood. The stain can be brushed or scraped off in some cases, and is harmless to the wood structure.

Board. Wide timber usually 1 in thick or less.

Butt. A short length of heavy timber.

Casings. Low-grade softwood.

Case-hardened timber. Poorly seasoned timber that is given to twisting and warping. It is not suitable for cabinet-making purposes.

Checks. Splits and cracks in a board running across the grain.

Clean. Timber that is free from knots.

Clear timber. Timber that is free of knots and other defects.

Cross-grained timber. See **Wild grain.**

Dead or unsound knot. A loose knot, liable to fall out.

End grain. The grain visible in a cross-section of a board or at the ends of a board.

Figure. Attractive and decorative grain patterns.

Grain. The stratification of the wood fibres in alternating soft and hard wood.

Joinery-grade timber. Timber that is of average quality, adequate for cabinet-making purposes.

Kiln-dried or oven-dried timber. Timber that has been force-dried and has a known moisture content.

Knee. Short lengths of naturally curved wood. Also known as crook timber.

Movement. Shrinking or swelling of wood due to changing moisture levels in the atmosphere.

Natural seasoning. See **Air-dried** timber.

par. Planed all around.

Plain-sawn, through-and-through or flat-sawn wood. A method of milling a log into boards in which the log is sawn straight through, with each cut parallel to the next.

Quarter-sawn timber. A board with the end grain running at 90° to the board face. These boards are the least susceptible to warping.

Rough-sawn timber. Boards that have simply been cut from the log and allowed to dry or season.

Sawn size. The size of the board before machining (planing).

Shake. A split at the end of a board running along the grain that occurs because the ends dry faster than the middle. The end must be cut off.

Sound knots. Small solid knots that will not work loose.

t & g. Tongue and grooved boards.

tg & b. Tongued, grooved and beaded.

tg & v. Tongued, grooved and v-jointed.

Waney edge. A sawed board with untrimmed edges, produced by plain sawn-milling.

Wild grain. Timber with interlocked grain that makes decorative veneer.

	Softwood—available sawn sizes (mm)									
	Widths									
Thicknesses	50	75	100	125	150	175	200	225	250	300
16	*	*	*	*	*					
19	*	*	*	*	*					
22	*	*	*	*	*					
25	*	*	*	*	*	*	*	*	*	*
32		*	*	*	*	*	*	*	*	*
28		*	*	*	*	*	*	*		
44		*	*	*	*	*	*	*	*	*
50		*	*	*	*	*	*	*	*	*
63			*	*	*	*	*	*		
75			*	*	*	*	*	*	*	*
100			*		*		*		*	*
150					*		*			
200							*			
250									*	
300										*

Sizes may vary between areas within UK, these in accord with BS4471(1978).

Hardwood—available sawn sizes (mm)
Widths
Ranging from 50 mm to roughly 300 mm in 10 mm steps, the width varies widely because of the natural variations among the species, and the size and age of tree.

Thicknesses
19, 25, 32, 38, 50, 63, 75, 100, 125, 150 mm. Thicker than this now is rarely available.

Lengths
Shorts, or add-length pieces at reduced prices, are available from 900 mm to 1700 mm. Lengths usually from 1800 mm up to roughly 3 m. But this also is variable, depending on the species and the availability of the wood.

Manufactured boards such as plywood or fibreboards are especially useful for making many items of the same design and for getting shapes and thicknesses that would be impossible with solid timber. Because of their composition, manufactured boards are more stable and their dimensions are more predictable than solid timber. The drawbacks are that their joints have to be hidden and their exposed edges faced with either veneer or solid wood lippings, and that they are difficult to repair.

Plywood

The best known manufactured board is plywood, made of sheets of wood laminated with their grain running perpendicular to each other, accounting for its greater stability. It can be bought treated for outdoor use or faced with decorative veneer. Cheaper plywood contains knots and other imperfections in its inner plies, which weaken it and can mar the face veneer.

The thinnest plywood is aeroply, originally developed for aircraft manufacturers and now used for building laminated structures. It takes stain unevenly. And because aeroply is very thin, it should not be nailed; instead, the sheets should be glued.

At one time, birch multi-ply was the main material used to make furniture carcasses. Today it has been replaced by chipboard as the industry's all-purpose material. But for small work multi-ply is still preferable to chipboard, being stiffer, stronger and easier to cut and join, particularly if worked by hand.

Marine ply is an outdoor plywood sometimes finished with an attractive surface veneer. It can be expensive. It is used much the same way as birch multi-ply, where water resistance is important.

Blockboard and battenboard are good heavy-duty plywoods used for making sturdy flush doors because they are easy to veneer and they take screws well. The thick wooden core strips may shrink and cause the surface veneers to ripple slightly. If this is a problem, use laminboard which has thinner core strips.

Particleboard or chipboard and fibreboard

Weaker, and generally cheaper, than plywood are the recently developed board materials such as particle board and fibreboard. These are made of wood fibres that have been broken up and then pressed and glued back together, making them even more stable than plywood. They were originally intended for the furniture industry, but now they are sold by retail suppliers. They are especially good as groundworks for veneered or painted carcasses.

Particleboard or chipboard has been used for the past 40 years by manufacturers making furniture carcasses. Furniture grade particleboard is layered, using finer particles for the faces than for the core to save on materials and produce a lighter board. The best quality are high-density boards, made up of smaller particles that leave a smoother surface.

Particleboards can be bought plain, or veneered with wood or plastic. Wood-veneered board should be made of high density board covered with good quality stock. The face veneers are always balanced by a backing veneer—usually a lesser-graded wood.

Plastic-coated chipboard is popular for building furniture for kitchens, bathrooms and work areas because its tough surface wipes clean easily. However, the coating cannot be re-laminated easily, and therefore must be removed at the joint faces. A wide assortment of plastic knock-down fittings are available as an alternative to gluing the joints. Raw edges must be covered with a lipping; iron-on veneer is available for this in colour-matching rolls (see pp 202–203).

Fibreboard, sometimes known as medium density fibreboard (MDF), is a recent development of particleboard. It is composed of fibres so evenly distributed that it can be moulded and joined almost as well as solid wood. It makes an excellent ground for veneer and because its cut edges resemble the edge of a solid board, they do not need lipping. It is relatively inexpensive.

Trade or usual name	Description	Sheet sizes (ft)	Price range
Aeroply	Spruce 3-ply	3 × 1 8 × 4	High
Birch multi-ply	3–19 layers of birch veneer	8 × 4 10 × 4	Medium
Marine plywood	High quality multi-ply from tropical hardwoods	8 × 4 10 × 4 10 × 6	High
Solid core plywood (MR)	Low cost plywood with thick central plies	8 × 4	Low–Med.
Blockboard	Board made from 1″ strips glued together, faced with ply	8 × 4 10 × 4	Med–High
× **Battenboard**	As above, but core made from wider strips (2–3″ wide)	8 × 4 10 × 4	Medium
Laminboard	As above, core made from narrow strips	8 × 4 10 × 4	High
Hardboard or Masonite	High-compressed wood fibres	8 × 4 6 × 3	Low
MDF (Medium density fibreboard)	Compressed wood fibres	8 × 4	Medium
Chipboard or Particleboard	Compressed wood chips with resin binding agent	8 × 4 10 × 6	Low–Med.
Contiboard™ or veneered chipboard	Chipboard pre-veneered both sides	6 × $\frac{1}{2}$ up to 8 × 4	Medium
Contiplas™ Melamine-paper veneered chipboard	As above	6 × $\frac{1}{2}$ up to 8 × 4	Medium
Formica™ Wariete™	Hard laminate of paper and resin	8 × 4 10 × 4	Med.–High
Colorcore™	Hard resin plastic, engravable and machineable	10 × 4	High

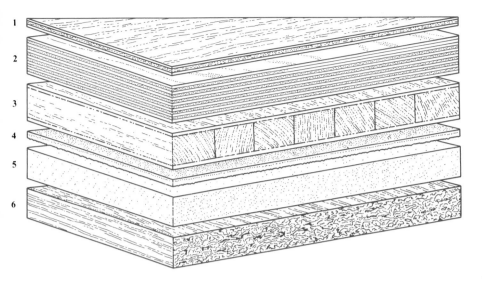

Common manufactured boards
1. Plywood is made in various thicknesses. The thinnest is a 3-ply about 4 mm/$\frac{3}{16}$ in thick.
2. Multi-ply has 13 veneers and is 18 mm/$\frac{3}{4}$ in thick. It produces a strong board which can be used for cabinet work.
3. Blockboard also comes in a range of thicknesses and can have outer decorative veneers.
4. Hardboard has little structural strength and so is limited to cabinet backs and bases of drawers.
5. Medium density fibreboard, a relative newcomer, is stronger than chipboard and can be worked like wood.
6. Chipboard is available with a veneer or a plastic coating.

Appearance	Characteristics	Machine workable	Hand workable	Use most traditional joints	Use special joint techniques	Inside/ outside	Relevant uses
Little figuring, pale creamy white	Light, flexible, strong, easy to glue	Yes	Yes	N/A too thin	Yes	Outside, limited	Lightweight or laminated structures
Slight water figure, creamy white colour	Stable, strong, easy to machine	Yes	Yes	Yes	N/A	Inside only	General furniture work of all kinds
May have plain mahogany type or decorative veneer face	As birch multi-ply but completely waterproof	Yes	Yes	Yes	N/A	Any outside use	Boats, buildings, signboards, garden furniture
Coarse fibres, pinky red hardwood face veneer	Hard to polish and splinters easily	Yes	Yes	With care	Yes	Limited outside use. Moisture resistant	General furniture carcassing, veneer groundwork
Pale creamy white or may be covered with hardwood veneers	Stiff, heavy, durable and load-bearing	Yes	Yes	Yes	N/A	Inside only	General furniture/ worktops, veneer groundwork
As above	As above, may show surface "rippling"	Yes	Yes	With care	Yes	Inside only	As above, but unreliable as a ground for veneers
As above	As above, smooth surface	Yes	Yes	Yes	N/A	Inside only	As above, but very good groundwork
Golden brown, one shiny side, one rough side	Cardboard-like, weak and may be brittle	Yes	Yes	N/A	Yes	Oil-tempered types only have some moisture resistance	Low cost furniture parts such as cabinet backs
Plain mid-brown, no visible structure, smooth	Easily machined, moulded and painted	Yes, needs T.C.T. tools	Yes, hard on tools	With care	Yes	Inside only	General carcass/ painted work, veneer ground
Light brown to creamy white, smooth and hard	Quality varies with density. Best is stiff and strong	As above	As above	N/A	Yes	Special types only outside	General furniture carcassing, good veneer ground
Varies according to surface veneers	As above	As above	As above	N/A	Yes	Inside only	General furniture carcassing
Smooth surface in white or pastel shades or in wood texture	As above	As above	As above	N/A	Yes	Inside only	As above, especially kitchen units
Available in 100's of plain colours and patterns. Smooth or textured	Hard, difficult to cut and work by hand. Brittle — handle carefully	As above	As above	Use as surface veneer only	Use as surface veneer only	Outside use when bonded to suitable ground	All hard duty surfaces
Available in 20 colours including black and white	Hard, brittle: colour goes right through	As above	As above	As above	As above	Outside apply to groundwork with waterproof glue	As above, including public areas

This section contains the information needed for storing, seasoning, and conditioning solid and manufactured boards so that they can be used dependably for cabinet-making. The space for storing timber correctly often is in short supply, particularly in modern houses. But with careful planning, even a loft or a garage can become an effective timber storage space, protecting the craftsman's investment in his timber stock.

Seasoning boards

The first step in storing boards, seasoning is sometimes necessary to reduce the amount of water, or plant juices, contained in freshly felled "green wood" to a very low level. The moisture content of timber is expressed as a percentage, based on the dry weight of the timber compared with its wet weight. An electronic moisture meter provides a quick reading.

The conventional method of seasoning solid timber is to stack boards flat, separated by "sticks" or small battens, that evenly space apart the boards and allow air to circulate, gradually reducing the moisture content. This decrease does not go on indefinitely, but ceases at a certain level, depending on the humidity of the surrounding air. In temperate climates air-dried timber is at about 13 percent moisture, which is still too high for timber to be used indoors. To remove more moisture, the timber is force-dried in a commercial kiln. The energy and space requirements of a commercial drying kiln are very high, making it an impractical investment for a small workshop. More useful is a compact and economical type of refrigeration unit—a dehumidifier—which removes water vapours from the air inside a storage cabinet. For a workshop with a small turnover, it may be even more economical to buy the more expensive kilned stock from a merchant. Some merchant will kiln-dry a batch of unseasoned wood for a fee.

A crude device for force-drying amounts of low-cost softwood is to convert an old steel office cupboard into a drying cabinet. Two large holes are cut at the top and the bottom of one side of the cabinet, and a 1 kw fan-heater, placed on the floor, directs a stream of warm air into the cabinet. This method can reduce moisture levels in 24 to 36 hours to a satisfactory level for softwoods. A few pieces of timber may twist and crack with this technique, but any that survives is certain to be reliable. Moving the heater closer or further away

Storing solid boards outdoors

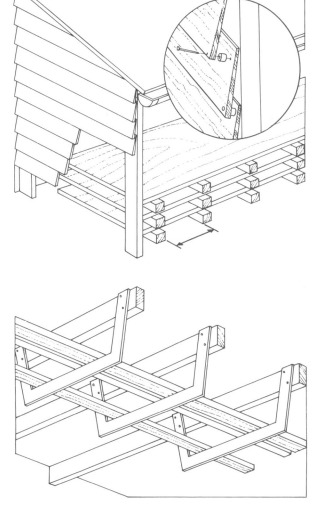

A force-drying cabinet

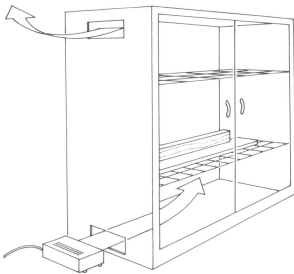

Storing solid boards outside
Solid boards can be stored outside for seasoning in a special lean-to set against a wall. The clapboard sides are made of 6 or 9 mm/$\frac{1}{4}$ or $\frac{3}{8}$ in exterior grade plywood with PVC spacers leaving a gap between the overlapping boards. This way the wood is kept dry, with a good circulation of air around it.

The boards should rest on 25 mm sq/1 in sq battens (sticks) of the same species of wood, spaced 30 to 45 cm/12 to 18 in apart. (Dissimilar woods in contact with each other can sometimes leave stains).

A force-drying cabinet
An old steel cabinet can be modified to form a force-drying cabinet. The timber is stacked on mesh shelves using the same methods as for outside storage. With the doors closed, warm air from a fan heater flows through the cabinet.

Roof storage
Good, out-of-the-way storage can be made under the roof rafters. Suspend the timber in brackets cut from 18 to 25 mm/$\frac{3}{4}$ to 1 in exterior-grade plywood. Make sure the brackets are well secured.

from the entry point controls the heat.

The ideal moisture level for indoor furniture timber is around 6 to 8 percent. To remain at this level, kilned timber must be stored indoors, because timber kept in an unheated shed will reabsorb moisture from the air and soon become unsuitable for furniture projects. In winter, the storage room should therefore be heated to a comfortable temperature. If this poses problems, a solution is to build storage racks of heavy plywood, which can be bolted to the roof beams of the work-shop. Storage of this kind retains the maximum floor space while making use of a good flow of rising warm air around the timber. Utility rooms and dry base-ments are good storage places, especially if they contain a central heating boiler. If the storage con-ditions are still too limited, it is best to delay purchas-ing the kilned timber until the project is about to begin.

Conditioning wood

Once seasoned the timber should, if possible, be conditioned to an environment similar to the one in which it will finally be used. When working at home, it is a good idea to store timber in the house for a couple of weeks before it is finally cut. The difference in humidity between the shop and the house often is considerable. It is heartbreaking to watch a much-labored piece of furniture crack and warp under the effects of forced-air central heating in winter, not to mention the added cost to the craftsman in time and materials repairing the work. And no amount of surface varnishing will prevent the loss of moisture when the timber is moved to a dry environment: tiny water molecules pass without difficulty through the varnish film.

Storing manufactured boards

Manufactured boards have already been seasoned, so all that remains is to store them in a dry environment, away from damp floors and walls and, preferably, with good air circulation. The boards can be laid flat, stacked atop each other, leaned against a wall or placed in a vertical storage rack. Stored vertically, they should not be allowed to sag in the middle or they will become misshapen. A safety chain should be strapped across the front of the stack to prevent the heavy boards from toppling over suddenly. And door stops should be placed at the foot of the stack to keep it from slipping out.

Vertical methods

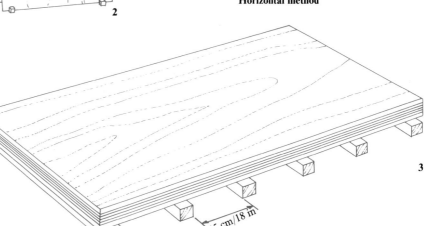

Storing wood indoors
1. The ideal method for storing manufactured boards is to lay the sheets horizontally. The stack should rest on 75 mm sq/3 in sq sticks so that they are raised off damp surfaces, and air can circulate.

The battens should be evenly spaced no more than 45 cm/18 in apart. Uneven support will cause the boards to warp or creep under their own weight. The battens should form a level plane so that the boards are kept perfectly flat.

Prevent thinner sheets from curling at the edges by sandwiching them between thicker, heavier boards.
2. Where space is tight, the sheets can be rested against a wall, with the bottom edges no more than 15 cm/6 in from the base. A safety chain across the top of the boards prevents them from falling forward, and door stops at the foot prevent them from sliding out.
3. However, the best vertical storage for plywood sheets is a special framework which allows individual boards to be taken out without the others having to be moved.

Horizontal method

45 cm/18 in

There is still a belief that veneer is an inferior alternative to solid wood. This is a misconception which must be corrected. In fact, veneers open up a range of design opportunities that would not be possible with solid timber constructions. Not only can they provide a range of decorative surfaces from the subtle shimmer of grain running in a straight pattern, to the wildly swirling lines found in burl. But also, the thin layer of veneer bonded to the structure beneath it stabilizes solid wood against natural expansion and contraction, especially in the long planks used for table tops or doors. And the veneering processes can be taken beyond just laying sheets over boards. String inlaying, crossbanding, parquetry and marquetry provide decorative treatments that are limited only by the designer's imagination.

Types of veneer

There are three main ways of cutting veneer, all of which use a knife and slicing action. Flat slicing is the most common and produces face veneers, used primarily for furniture making. Next comes slicing or half rotary cutting—less popular because in some woods it often results in a bland grain figure. And finally, rotary cutting, where the log is spun against a blade to give a continuous length of veneer. This method is least favourite because of the unnatural-looking grain pattern it produces. And the action of the blade against the log sometimes creates small parallel surface cracks in the veneer, making it unsuitable for fine furniture, and so it is reserved for backing veneers and for making plywood. Occasionally, saw-cut veneers come to light at the bottom of a veneer merchant's stack. These were produced by cutting the log with a large circular saw blade. But the method is no longer used because nearly half the log ends up as sawdust.

Buying veneers

Veneer merchants will probably be the most reliable source of good quality veneers, and it is worth getting on good terms with them so they will set aside the interesting veneers for you. Basically, there is a choice of four different types. Flat sliced is probably the most common, mainly because flat slicing is the favourite method of cutting. Yet it is also worth considering the many wild-grained veneers that are cut from particular sections of a tree, which offer a wider scope of decorative options. However, it is important to keep in mind the nature of the object to be veneered and the intended type of veneer covering. An all-burl table top, for example, can be difficult to lay and its busy pattern could overwhelm the design. Consequently, try to visualize how a veneer will look on a piece of furniture before it is laid.

Ways of cutting veneers
1. Flat slicing
2. Three methods of half rotary cutting
3. Rotary cutting

Some types of veneer
4. Flat sliced
5. Burl—cut from a wart-like outgrowth on the trunk which is normally caused by injury
6. Butt—from the swollen base trees such as walnut
7. Crotch—cut from the point where a branch or root grows from the main trunk

Pattern matching veneers
8. Book matched—the first leaf opens out along the second leaf's edge as in a book. The third leaf opens along the fourth's edge and so on.
9. Butt matched—as for book matched, but the ends, rather than the sides, are matched.
10. Running matched—created by laying the leaves side by side as they come off the bundle.
11. Diamond matched—four consecutive leaves are cut diagonally and side- and butt-matched
12. Reverse diamond—each of the four leaves of a diamond matched pattern are turned through 180° and then butted together.
13. Diagonal quartered—four consecutive leaves are side-and butt-matched.

Ways of cutting veneers

Types of veneer

Pattern-matching veneers

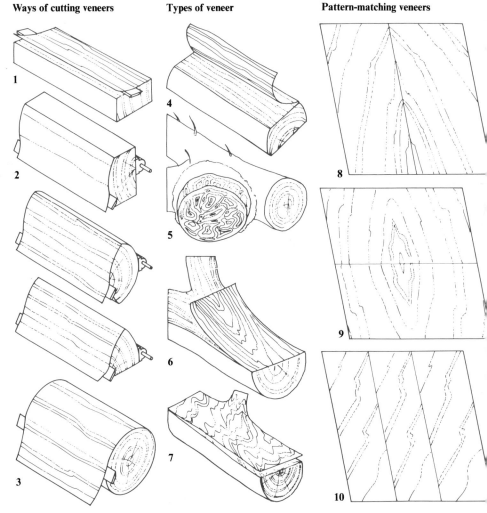

Veneers are sold either as single leaves or in bundles known as flitches. Some merchants may also sell a mixture of small off-cuts that can be used for parquetry or marquetry. It is essential to buy enough veneer to complete the job. If extra is needed later it may be difficult to match the colour or figure with the stock that is left.

When buying veneers look through the bundle to see if there are any obvious splits or large knot holes. If there are a fair number, reject the batch or negotiate a lower price, particularly if it is possible to use the veneers in such a way that the faulty sections can be discarded. Do not forget to check the width of the veneers as well. Narrower leaves may mean using three strips rather than the two planned for in the design, and some quick on-the-spot decisions may be needed.

Coloured veneers, different string inlays and assorted band inlay patterns can also be bought at veneer merchants. It is well worth stocking up on something interesting, which may yield ideas for future designs.

Storing veneers

Veneers are very fragile and should be stored with care, out of direct sunlight and stacked in the same position and orientation as they came off the log. This will help in later pattern matching. Ideally if there is space in the workshop, lay the veneers on a sheet of flat board and then place another board on top to keep them flat. Tape the ends of veneers with wild grain, such as burl, butt or curl, which have a tendency to split.

Laying veneers

The first step in veneering is to decide how the leaves of veneer will be matched when laid. It is something that takes care and experience to produce satisfactory results. Apart from selecting one of the six basic patterns (see the illustrations below), take into account the other forms of decoration such as inlay or coloured veneer.

Nearly all veneering is now done on manufactured boards, although solid timber is sometimes used as a base for shaped pieces like bow fronts. When a number of veneered panels are required, a press becomes essential. A hand operated screw press is probably the most suitable, being relatively cheap and quite easy to find second hand. If there is a compressor in the workshop, consider installing a pneumatic press.

A vacuum bag press is ideal for shaped work that is curved in one direction. The veneer is laid on the ground work and enclosed in a plastic bag. The air is then pumped out to create a vacuum, forcing the bag tightly against the veneer. A veneer hammer is then rubbed over the surface to ensure that there is total contact and that no air bubbles remain.

A veneer punch
Punch out the old veneer and clean up the area with a chisel. Coat the ground with glue and fit a patch over it. Cover with a damp cloth and press with a hot iron to swell the patch for a tight fit.

Cutting a veener Cut veneer by running a scalpel along a roofing square.

A glue spreader
A glue spreader has a hopper that contains adhesive, and a roller to apply an even coating on the ground.

A veneer punch

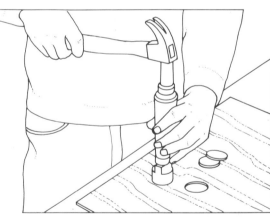

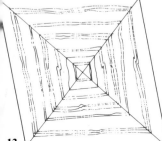

11

12

13

Cutting a veneer

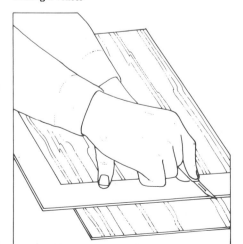

A glue spreader

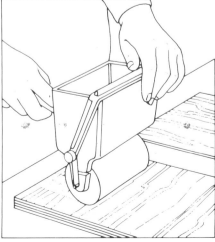

A caul makes an effective substitute for a press, particularly on small panels. Glue film is another alternative. This adhesive comes as a thin coat laid on a paper backing. It is applied by laying the glue side down on the base wood, or ground, and pressing a warm iron over the paper backing, which is then peeled away. Then the veneer is positioned over the glue film and fixed in place by pressing down firmly on it with a warm iron. In nearly all cases, panels should be veneered on both sides to prevent the board from warping. But a cheaper backing veneer can be used if it is not going to be seen.

If the veneers have buckled, they will have to be flattened, otherwise it is impossible to get a straight joining edge, and they are liable to split when put in the press. Flattening is done the day before veneering. First the veneers are dampened on both surfaces with a moist cloth and placed between two flat boards. They can be left in the press overnight, or, more simply, a heavy weight can be placed on top of them. By the next day the veneers should be flat and ready to use.

When cutting veneers to length allow an extra $12\,\text{mm}/\frac{1}{2}$ in at both ends. The best tool for cutting is a sharp knife or a scalpel. A builder's roofing square can be used for marking out and squaring up the ends, and for cutting against.

By using clear cellulose tape to tape the veneers together it is possible to see whether the seam is even. If it is not, the fault can be rectified. Some craftsmen argue that this kind of tape is difficult to get off the surface of the veneer, but it can be sanded away easily.

One of the most common mistakes when first veneering is to apply too much adhesive. This can cause the glue to bleed through the surface of the veneer, creating marks that are difficult to remove. Glue will also ooze out at the edges making it difficult to trim the edges without chipping the delicate veneer. Only a thin layer of adhesive on the ground is needed, but it must be absolutely even. In a small workshop, the most effective tool for spreading veneer glue smoothly is a hopper-fed glue spreader.

The adhesives used for veneering are normally either resin or PVA. The resin types are water and heat resistant. One kind comes in two-pack form consisting of resin and a powder hardener. The two-pack glues are less commonly found and they have a very limited shelf life, although they are excellent for veneering. The other type of resin glue comes in a powder form to be mixed with water, and it has a much longer shelf life. One of the advantages of using PVA adhesives is if bubbles occur under the veneer surface, they can often be flattened by covering the bubble with a damp cloth and pressing down hard with a hot iron. This softens the glue and re-adheres the bubble to the ground. However, PVA adhesives tend to creep, so that in time matched veneers may develop a small ridge of glue along the seam.

Veneers are pressed for varying lengths of time depending on the adhesives used. Some need only an hour, others almost 12 hours. Follow the instructions on the side of the glue container carefully. When the veneered board is taken out of the press, first check for bubbles by running your fingernails over the surface. If there is a bubble you will hear a whisper-like sound. If you have used PVA adhesive use the heat method to flatten the veneer. Alternatively, make a slit along the length of the bubble in the direction of the grain. Lift one side of the cut with the knife and squeeze glue underneath both sides of the slit. Then press the two sides down by hand and wipe off the excess glue. Finally, place paper over the repair, and cover with a block of timber clamped in position. Or, better yet, put the panel back in the press. If the repair is on a light coloured veneer, rub white chalk along the slit to help disguise the seam.

Laying wild grained veneers requires a good deal of patience. The veneers must first be dampened and flattened, and then patched. After pressing, more patching will probably be needed, and this is where a veneer punch becomes particularly useful to cut out neatly the faulty sections of veneer and replace them with exactly matching patches.

Stripping off a veneered board should be done with a belt sander. But this machine should be used with caution. It is a matter of working by feel, which can only be developed with practice. Ideally, you should be able to sand off a layer of plywood so that the second veneer is evenly exposed. Portable sanders will also strip off a veneered board, but the sander must have an underframe and fine adjuster to avoid gouging and rounding the edges. A portable orbital sander used with the finer grades of abrasive paper is an excellent machine for final finishing.

Lippings

When veneering manufactured boards there is often the problem of what to do with the edges. If medium density fibreboard or chipboard was used, lippings must be applied to prevent the edges from chipping. They also provide a base for hinges. However, the edges of plywood can be left bare, giving a laminated appearance. The surface veneer can cover the top of the lipping or the lipping can form a border for the veneer. These days, with resin and PVA adhesives, there is such a strong bond between the veneer and the board that there is little problem of the veneer lifting at the edges. Lippings can be attached with loose or fixed tongues, biscuit joints, or simply by butt joints. The choice really depends on which machine is available. Mitre joints are always a neat solution for corners. Alternatively, one set of parallel lippings can run through to expose their end grain.

Always cut lippings about $1\,\text{mm}/\frac{1}{16}$ in deeper than the board to ensure that the top edge does not dip below the surface of the veneer if the lipping slips while being glued in position. Once the lippings are fixed, use a plane or belt sander to take them down to size. Border lippings must again be cut slightly oversized, and must be worked with care to avoid digging into the veneer. Smooth the lipping with a try plane or a block plane, working it diagonally along the lipping, and letting the back of the sole rest on the veneered panel. It will cut the lipping at an angle until flush with the veneer. An orbital sander can be used for finishing.

Caul veneering

Veneer is applied to both sides of the ground and the surfaces are covered with sheets of newspaper. The board is then sandwiched between two cauls (two boards of 18 mm/¾ in blockboard). Pairs of braces are clamped in position down the length of the cauls. The top brace is slightly concave to apply even pressure outwards from the centre of the veneered board.

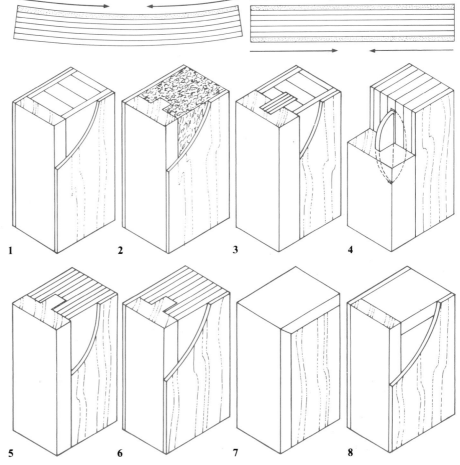

Bearer
Caul
Paper
Veneer
Ground
Veneer
Paper
Caul
Bearer

Counter veneering

1. A board veneered on one side only will bow with the pull of the veneer.
2. Counter veneering with a backing veneer overcomes this pull.

Ways of applying lippings

A lipping is little more than a strip of timber fixed to the edge of a board. It serves either as a simple form of decoration to frame the top surface, or to hide the central core of manufactured board and to provide a base for hinges. Lippings can be fitted in a variety of ways:
1. Butted lipping
2. Fixed tongue lipping on chipboard
3. Loose tongue lipping
4. Biscuit-jointed lipping
5. Border lipping
6. Lipping applied before veneering
7. Mitred lipping
8. Lipping carried through to expose the end grain top and bottom

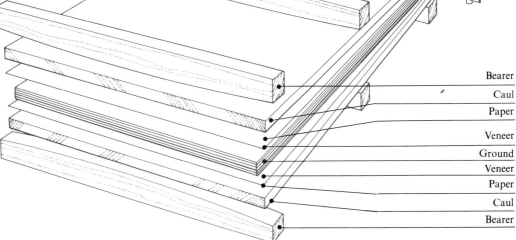

1   2

197

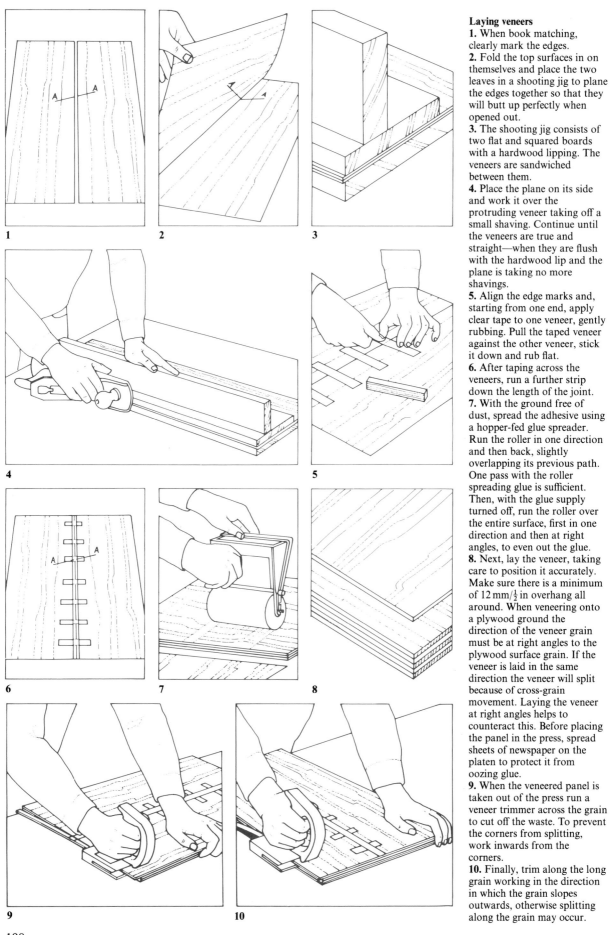

1

2

3

4

5

6

7

8

9

10

Laying veneers

1. When book matching, clearly mark the edges.

2. Fold the top surfaces in on themselves and place the two leaves in a shooting jig to plane the edges together so that they will butt up perfectly when opened out.

3. The shooting jig consists of two flat and squared boards with a hardwood lipping. The veneers are sandwiched between them.

4. Place the plane on its side and work it over the protruding veneer taking off a small shaving. Continue until the veneers are true and straight—when they are flush with the hardwood lip and the plane is taking no more shavings.

5. Align the edge marks and, starting from one end, apply clear tape to one veneer, gently rubbing. Pull the taped veneer against the other veneer, stick it down and rub flat.

6. After taping across the veneers, run a further strip down the length of the joint.

7. With the ground free of dust, spread the adhesive using a hopper-fed glue spreader. Run the roller in one direction and then back, slightly overlapping its previous path. One pass with the roller spreading glue is sufficient. Then, with the glue supply turned off, run the roller over the entire surface, first in one direction and then at right angles, to even out the glue.

8. Next, lay the veneer, taking care to position it accurately. Make sure there is a minimum of $12\,\text{mm}/\frac{1}{2}$ in overhang all around. When veneering onto a plywood ground the direction of the veneer grain must be at right angles to the plywood surface grain. If the veneer is laid in the same direction the veneer will split because of cross-grain movement. Laying the veneer at right angles helps to counteract this. Before placing the panel in the press, spread sheets of newspaper on the platen to protect it from oozing glue.

9. When the veneered panel is taken out of the press run a veneer trimmer across the grain to cut off the waste. To prevent the corners from splitting, work inwards from the corners.

10. Finally, trim along the long grain working in the direction in which the grain slopes outwards, otherwise splitting along the grain may occur.

One striking way to decorate a plain veneered or solid timber top is to inlay the surface with contrasting timbers, coloured veneers or other materials. Brass, Plexiglass, aluminium and plastic laminate all can be worked using woodworking tools and techniques. The chart on page 219 will indicate the best choice of adhesives to use. Inlaying can enliven a dull surface and it can help channel the eye to feature a particular detail.

Stringing, which is the process of edging the surface with fine lines, or banding, which is a wider inlay, can also be effective. Crossbanding around the edges of panels and in conjunction with stringing was particularly popular when animal glues were the main adhesive. It protects the edges and prevents the veneer from delaminating.

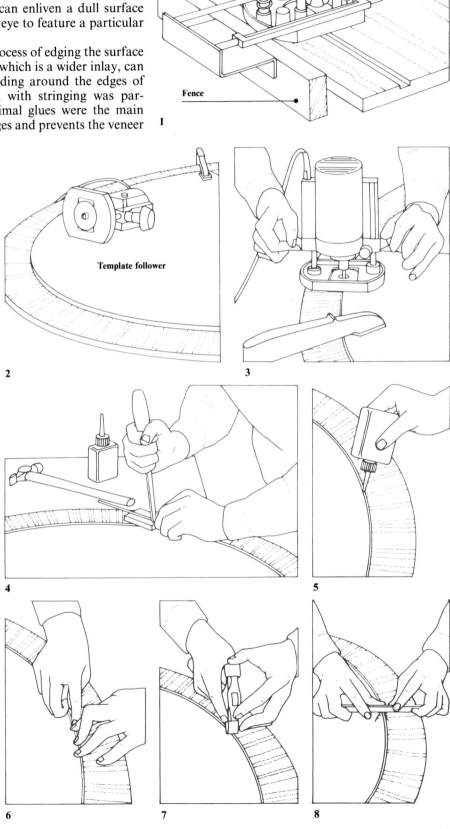

Fence

1

Template follower

2

3

How to inlay
To inlay stringing or banding, cut the groove with a router and fence (1) or use a template follower (2). Select the right cutter size to take the inlay. Experiment on a test piece first to check that the inlay fits. The groove should be slightly less deep than the inlay's height, so the inlay protrudes slightly from the surface.
3. Clamp the template to the surface, then cut the groove with the router, following the template.
4. Trim the stringing with a chisel. Mitre the corners for a rectangular pattern.
5. Squeeze resin or PVA adhesive into the groove.
6. Starting at one end of the groove, push the stringing firmly into place.
7. Then rub over it with the cross-pein of a hammer to bed it down, wiping off any glue that has squeezed out.

Now lay the next stretch of stringing. When the job is complete leave the work overnight to dry out to prevent the stringing below the panel surface from shrinking.
8. Clean up with a scraper, but be careful not to dig into the surface. Take extra care at corners using the scraper diagonally to prevent the wood from splitting. The final finish can be done with an orbital sander or by hand.
A note of caution: be wary of using dark or coloured inlays on light veneers. The dust from sanding the inlay may get worked into the light veneer and is then difficult to remove. Instead, finish the surface partially before the groove is cut. The pores of the veneer will then be filled with polish and will not take up any of the dark dust during sanding.

4

5

6

7

8

GLASS / Cutting and finishing

Glass has a long history as a design material. It is remarkably strong, yet it can fail suddenly and dangerously if the limits of its strength are exceeded. For obvious safety reasons it should therefore be used very cautiously as a load bearing material, and never used to bear the full weight of a person. Ordinary glass breaks into large jagged pieces and it is best suited for moderate-sized cabinet doors, small tops for occasional tables and protective overlays on solid polished surfaces. Stronger laminated glass, however, with its sandwich construction and flexible plastic core, can be used safely for certain load-bearing structures; glass columns, pyramids or cubes can form the bases of tables, and glass plinths can make carcass furniture look as though it is floating on air. However, it is important that the glass is not twisted or bent because it is particularly vulnerable to these forces.

Cutting and drilling

Ordinary flat glass can be cut simply by using a wheel or diamond-type cutter. A smear of paraffin on the glass surface will help the cutter to score evenly. The size of the glass is measured out carefully, positioning the cuts so there are no narrow margins. Glass is a potentially dangerous material, so it is essential to wear gloves and heavy stout shoes when handling it. The glass is placed on the bench atop a piece of old carpet or a blanket. A layer of newspaper can be used as a cutting surface. Then, using a straightedge to align the cut, and holding the cutter like a pencil with the wheel pressed gently down on to the surface, the glass is scored once all the way along the cut line. The straightedge is slipped underneath the glass to act as a fulcrum on one side of the score, causing the glass to snap by pressing down firmly with your hands on either side of the line.

Glass can be drilled with a special spear-point bit. The usual method is to make a well of putty around the spot to be drilled which is filled with paraffin. A low speed power drill, or hand drill, does the job using only light pressure. Laminated glass, or any plate more than $4\,\mathrm{mm}/\frac{5}{32}$ in thick, should be cut by a glass merchant. Toughened glass cannot be cut after the toughening process but it is not likely to be useful in domestic applications anyway.

Finishing glass

As well as cutting and drilling, glass can be ground smooth on the edges, or ground and polished. It is however, a slow process, using wet-or-dry paper lubricated with soapy water. The grinding begins with 240 grit, and finishes with 400 grit. The edges can be waxed to improve their appearance. Fine polishing can be done with 600 grit wet-or-dry and a liquid abrasive such as the compound used for restoring car paintwork. Most large specialized glass companies can do this work if required but it can be expensive.

Glass can be joined mechanically, with metal plates, or glued together in a variety of ways. Strong joints which are almost invisible can be made with modern, daylight-hardened adhesives, but close fitting surfaces are essential for this. The best adhesives for general use are probably the epoxy resins. These are fairly visible when used on clear plates, but are not a problem when used with the many types of bronze or grey smoked glass. Neat looking strong and flexible joints may be made with silicone rubber mastics.

Several specialized finishes can be applied to the surface of glass. Tinted aerosols, in shades of blue and green give a fine translucent colour to clear plate, and various metallized or coloured plastic films that permanently adhere to wetted glass are available. Glass may also be sandblasted, as a low-cost alternative to buying frosted material, or etched with patterns of any kind. All these require the sympathetic help of glazing professionals. Look for a supplier who is used to specialized jobs, and he will probably enjoy doing your work as a change from his usual routine.

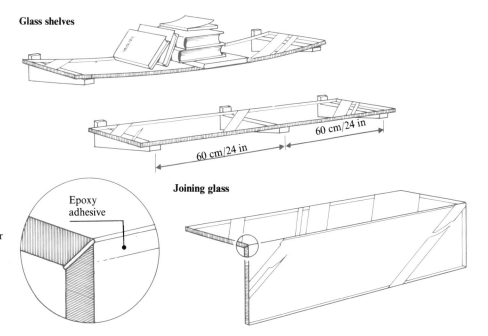

Glass shelves
A glass shelf can suddenly break if overloaded. A well designed shelf should use glass of the correct thickness (see table) which is adequately supported. All the edges should be ground smooth to prevent cuts and accidents.

Glass shelves

60 cm/24 in

60 cm/24 in

Joining glass
Glass panels can be butted together and held by metal brackets. Alternatively, epoxy resin adhesive can be used. For a neater finish, mitre the corners by grinding down the edges before bringing them together and attaching them.

Epoxy adhesive

Joining glass

Shelf fitting

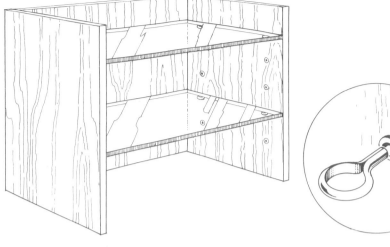

Glass table support

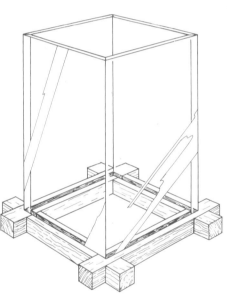

Glass door

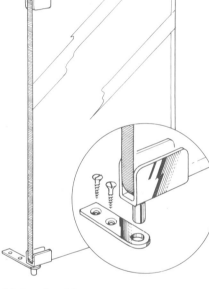

Traditional glazed door

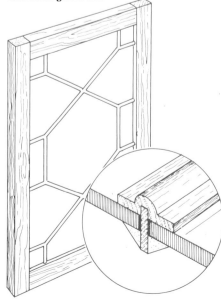

Modern glazed door

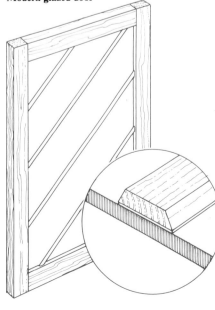

Shelf fittings

Glass shelves can be supported unobtrusively on brass split rings which slot into eyelets set at intervals in the sides of the carcass.

Glass table support

This simple design illustrates how a glass column can be made using half-lapped wooden battens with routed grooves to take the four panels. An identical frame fits on top of the column and a table top rests on this.

Glass doors

Glass doors can be fitted using special pivot hinges, which avoids having to drill the glass. The door fits into two metal slots which rotate on brackets attached to the top and bottom of the cabinet. Handles can be glued on or fitted into pre-drilled holes; or finger plates can be ground out of the glass if the doors are meant to slide instead of swing.

Glazed doors

The traditional way of making up a glazed door was to fit small panes of glass into a pattern of glass bars known as astragals. One favourite design was the 13-panel door popularized by Chippendale. The same effect can be produced now simply by sticking mock-astragals to a large pane of glass.

Selecting glass	
Thickness	Use
3 mm	Panel doors with small panes
4 mm	Glazed doors with single panes up to 70 × 35 cm/ 28 × 14 in
6 mm	Shelves up to 80 cm/32 in long (width 30% of length) bearing light loads only; small framed table tops; protective covers
9 mm	Long and heavily loaded shelves (at least 3 points of support are needed); frame-less table tops up to 210 × 90 cm/7 × 3 ft

Working with metal

The decorative use of metal mounts and inlays is as old as cabinetmaking itself. Base and precious metals have been used, as well as enamelled and plated finishes.

A good design incorporating timber and metal must take into account the different properties of the two materials. Avoid fastening a long length of metal inlay, for instance, across the grain of a wide solid board. The metal will expand as the room temperature rises, whereas the tendency of wood to lose moisture in a warm environment causes it to shrink across the grain. Neither of these opposite motions can be prevented easily, and can cause the inlay to lift or buckle.

The problems of delamination can be overcome using flexible contact adhesives rather than hard setting epoxy resin glues. Small gaps left between joints in metal inlays also allow for movement. Alternatively, use stable manufactured board such as chipboard instead of solid wood for the base material.

Rather than using plain finishes, it is possible to break down metals with various chemicals to produce special effects. Frosted aluminium is made by briefly dipping polished aluminium into a weak caustic soda solution. The mixture is corrosive, so wear protective clothing, and rinse off with plenty of water. Gun-blue used on steel inlay produces an unusual blue-black effect. Patterns can also be etched onto metal.

Working with plastic

Of the many types of plastic material, only two are of much interest to the woodworker: methyl methacrylate, sold under the brand name Plexiglass, and several varieties of reinforced formaldehyde resin, commonly described as the plastic laminate Formica, or as plastic-coated chipboard.

Acrylic plastics, or Plexiglass, are supplied in sheet form, as rods, tubes and blocks. The sheets come in sizes up to $1.22\,\mathrm{m} \times 1.83\,\mathrm{m}/1\frac{1}{3}\,\mathrm{yd} \times 2\,\mathrm{yd}$, and thicknesses up to $9\,\mathrm{mm}/\frac{3}{8}\,\mathrm{in}$. A wide variety of colours is available, transparent or opaque, from suppliers or from signmakers.

Always treat acrylics with care, because they are soft and easily scratched. Keep the protective paper wrapper in place until the job is complete. All the marking out of the job can be done on this paper, which often will have a helpful grid pattern printed on it. Cutting acrylics is difficult; they should be sawn slowly, using a coping saw for shaped work and a hacksaw for straight cuts. Power saws tend to melt the material, but a sharp tungsten-tipped wood blade will give a reasonable

Shrinkage plates

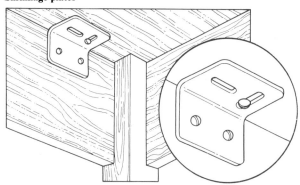

Shrinkage plates
Because of the amount of movement of timber across the grain, special metal shrinkage plates are needed to attach a solid wood top to a plastic-laminated carcass. Note the slots in the plate to allow the timber to move.

Similarly, when attaching metal legs to the underside of a table, special tube fittings are required with slotted screws to allow the two materials to expand and contract independently.

Setting in inlays
In most old furniture, metal inlays were inset flush with the surrounding surface. Nowadays, except for table tops and similar surfaces, they are recessed only slightly. Brass and aluminium inlays are the easiest to work with. They should be cut, filed to fit and polished before they are glued into place.

Setting in inlays

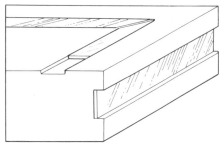

Applying edging strip

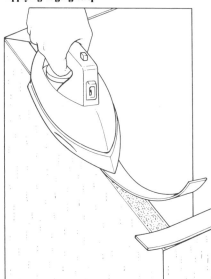

Shaping acrylic sheet
Acrylic sheet can be bent over a heavy metal bar. First heat the bar in a very hot oven around 350°C/662°F. Clamp it into a metal vice and cover it with a thin piece of cotton sheeting. Press the sheet of acrylic against the bar until it becomes hot enough to bend; any holes in the acrylic should be drilled while it is flat. Thick acrylic sheet may be easier to work if it is pre-heated in boiling water. Finally, saw all the edges smooth.

Applying edging strip
Chipboard-backed laminates can be finished with a special edging strip that is ironed on using an ordinary household iron set to medium heat (no steam). Alternatively, the raw edges can be filled with car-body filler which is then sanded smooth and painted.

Shaping acrylic sheet

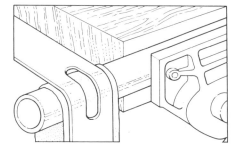

result. Goggles should always be worn because the fine acrylic chips are needle-sharp. It is best to allow a generous margin when sawing, and then to finish down to the line with a file and a sanding block.

Holes can be made with a hand-drill and twist-bit, larger holes with a slow-speed power drill and a hole cutter. Drilling must be slow, allowing the bit to cool for a moment between short bursts of work. The hole can be cleaned inside with abrasive paper. All edges should be finished with 400 grade wet-or-dry, and then polished with acrylic polish. This will remove the scratches and restore the transparency.

Acrylic sheets can be bent easily when hot and sections can be glued with epoxy resins. But a neat and strong joint is best achieved with a solvent adhesive.

Using plastic laminates
The cheapest plastic laminates are made from a layer of resin-impregnated paper, pressed during manufacture onto a chipboard core. This produces large sheets, up to $1.2 \text{ m} \times 2.4 \text{ m}/1\frac{1}{3} \text{ yd} \times 2\frac{1}{2} \text{ yd}$ of rigid, smooth-surfaced material in solid colours, or printed to imitate wood grain. This kind of material is a good veneer for kitchen cabinets and wardrobes. Quality varies and is determined by the thickness of the coating and the density of the chipboard core.

The other type of plastic laminate, often referred to by its brand name Formica, is very hard and quite brittle. It is made from layers of special paper soaked in resin and hardened under heat and pressure. This gives a thin (1 to $2 \text{ mm}/\frac{1}{16}-\frac{1}{8}$ in) springy sheet, which can be glued onto any smooth surface. It is an easy-to-clean surface with a great resistance to abrasion, making it very popular for kitchen worktops and door facings. Plastic laminates are available in literally hundreds of plain colours, wood grains and patterns, and textured to simulate wood or stone, with smooth or rough surfaces. Formica has recently developed a new material it calls Colorcore in which the colour penetrates through the sheet so there is no black edge to disguise.

Despite their toughness when glued onto a suitable base, sheets of laminate must be handled carefully, as they are liable to split and crack if bent or struck. Buy one of the several types of special cutting tools designed for this material. Laminates can be glued onto simple curved surfaces, but not around sharp or compound curves. Rubber-based contact adhesives are used to laminate the plastic sheets, but on small pieces that can be clamped, one of the waterproof resin glues such as Cascamite is better.

Finishing plastic laminate edges

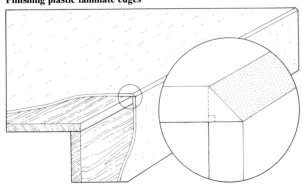

Finishing plastic laminate edges. Where Formica-type laminates butt together at a corner, the exposed black edge should not be butt-jointed or it will chip at the edges when it is knocked by a hard object. Instead it should be bevelled to an angle of 45° using a block plane once the sheets have been laminated into place.

Etching copper

1

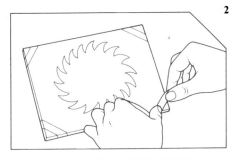

2

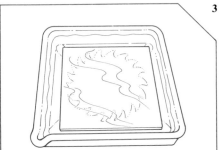

3

4

Etching copper
Copper-plate, with a ground metal of a contrasting colour to the copper, can be decoratively etched using a simple and safe process.
1. Spray copper-coated plastic sheet with a "photo-resist" aerosol.
2. Cut out the pattern you wish to create in a paper stencil and tape this to the plate using masking tape. Expose the plate to sunlight for half an hour.
3. Immerse the plate in a solution of ferric chloride and water for approximatey 20 minutes.
4. Then wash off the solution to leave the copper on the plate where it has been exposed to the light. Polish the surface and spray on a fixer. Alternatively, the plate can be protected by a sheet of glass, rather than fixer, if it is to be set into a table top.

Leather

Natural leather has special qualities that make it a splendid complement to wood. Its porous structure lets the underlying wood breathe and helps to prevent any warping or buckling of the ground. Its suppleness is also an asset, allowing it to move in degrees with the wood rather than splitting or lifting away from the surface. Leather, however, can be expensive. A good source is leather clothing manufacturers who may stock large pieces of hide, for some reason unsuitable for clothing, but which might meet the needs of a design. It is best to shop carefully, and to buy a whole bundle of skins at once, because each skin has an individual shade and texture that is difficult to match.

Leather can be stretched over wood or metal frames to make handsome and simple chairs. Thin hides of shaved leather make excellent coverings for desks and tables. The pieces are glued in position using starch wallpaper paste, brushed generously onto the ground-work and partially allowed to dry. The thin hide, known in the trade as skiver, is pressed onto the damp paste and cut to fit into its recess with a sharp craft knife. Cloth-backed vinyl and polyurethane sheets can be substituted for leather.

A more unusual use for leather is as a backing for a tambour door. This is a sliding shutter made from many narrow strips of wood, running in a groove. The strips are usually glued to a backing of linen or canvas.

An effective and unusual type of tambour can be made by using leather as a decorative facing material. The wooden strips are in this case glued to the back with PVA adhesive.

Felt

Felt is often used as a low-cost substitute for hide, and is the preferred surface for games tables of all kinds. Warm to the touch, it has excellent acoustic properties that make it an ideal sound-absorber. It comes in many varieties and weights. The thinner kind, usually green or blue, sometimes is erroneously called baize. The thickest and most expensive type is known as piano or hammer felt. The quality may vary widely, but reserve the best for surfaces on display. Good-quality felt feels firm to the touch, does not stretch easily when tugged, and looks smooth and uniformly thick. Felt may be laid in the same way as hide, and makes an interesting alternative to wood veneers on low-cost chipboard carcasses.

Cork

Natural cork is a product of the cork oak, where it is found as a spongy protective layer beneath the bark. Attractive and versatile, it is processed into many forms to use as wall and floor covering, and to make seals, insulation and soundproofing. Cork shares some characteristics of felt and it can be used for many of the

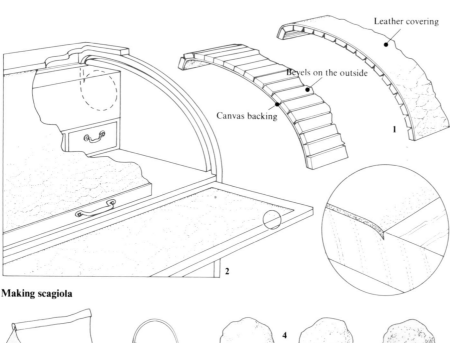

Leather covering

Bevels on the outside

Canvas backing

Using leather
1. Leather can replace the traditional linen when making tambour shutters for a desk. Here the leather is stuck to the outside of the slats which should have their bevels facing inwards, enabling the tambour to be rolled up.

2. Leather makes an ideal writing surface. It can be set into a worktop so that it is flush with the surrounding surface, or be laid directly on the desk flap. The edges are protected by being pushed into a shallow recess cut around the perimeter. Use a steel rule to rub the leather firmly into the corners and a sharp knife to cut away any excess material.

Making scagiola

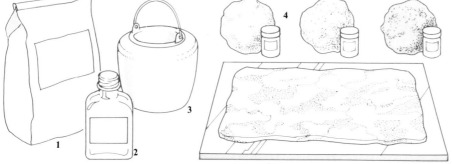

Making scagiola
To produce scagiola, first mix whiting (**1**) a calcium carbonate powder, to a stiff dough with linseed oil (**2**) and hot animal glue (**3**). The actual amounts will take practice. Divide the dough into three and tint each with a poster color (**4**). Next knead the three parts together to form a marble effect. Roll out onto a sheet of glass and leave to harden. Scagiola can be sawed and carved, and then sealed after two weeks with varnish.

same applications. Paper-backed cork wall coverings have recently become available, and these can be veneered onto chipboard or solid timber. One of the most interesting types of cork for furnishing is the variety known as Hallite. This is used as a gasket material for automobile engines, and is made from fine cork crumbs blended with rubber. It has an attractive feel and a pleasant colour, and it is practically indestructible. Hallite laminate provides a heavy-duty cover material that can be scrubbed, jumped on and scratched—all without visible damage. This type of cork can be obtained from large manufacturers. The price is high, but it is a special material.

Marble

Like timber, marble comes in many types and colours. One of the finest types of traditional marble is a white or cream Carrera marble from Italy. The smooth perfection and clean lines of good marble demand a very high quality fit and finish in the rest of the project.

Marble is fragile and also very heavy. Like a sheet of glass, it is a plane that is vulnerable to twisting and bending. At the same time, a typical slab can weigh as much as 100 kg/220 lbs—making it extremely awkward and unwieldy to manoeuvre in the workshop. It may be interesting to experiment with an old form of marble substitute called scagiola which is very easy and cheap to make.

Bone and mother-of-pearl

These materials were often used for small inlays on writing boxes, the escutcheon plates for locks, and to decorate musical instruments. Both materials can be obtained ready to use from musical instrument makers, or from specialists in decorative arts. But bone inlay can also be made in the workshop, using the shoulder blades of a cow as a source of workable bone. The bone should first be boiled in at least four changes of water, and then left outside to bleach in the sun for several months. The bleaching can be improved by dipping in 20 percent hydrogen peroxide. Bone and mother-of-pearl can be shaped with a fine piercing saw, and with files. The best glues to use are epoxy resins or old-style hot animal glue. Bone also can be turned on a wood lathe, using a scraping tool, to make knobs and other small furniture fittings.

Gilding

Gilding is a craft with five thousand years of history behind it. The techniques, tools and materials are surprisingly simple and inexpensive. The real gold leaf used to cover surfaces is very thin and flexible, and these qualities enable it to cover complex shapes with ease. A common belief is that gilding is only suited to very old-fashioned, ornate work. This is not true. Striking and imaginative results can be achieved using modern designs.

The gilder's tools

The gilder's tools
1. A gilder's palette or "cushion" is used to hold the gold leaf for gilding. The paper screen prevents the fragile leaf from being blown away in a light draft. Covered with chamois, the palette can also be used as a cutting surface.
2. A gilder's tip is used to transfer the leaf from the palette to the workpiece.
3. A quill or mop (**4**) is used for pressing the gold leaf into the surface of the workpiece.
5. A knife used for cutting gold leaf. No special type of knife is required. An old fruit knife with a sharp blade is ideal.

Patterns of gilding
6. Broken gold is a gilder's technique of laying torn scraps of gold leaf on a coloured ground of enamel paint.
7. and **8.** A decorative pattern—geometric edging for a door panel or curvelinear markings for a moulding—is produced by laying gold leaf on gesso and incising with a "V" gauge. Gesso is a mixture of glue, water and whiting. The grooves are then filled with enamel paint or coloured wax, and the surplus removed.
9. Thickly laid-on gesso produces a raised tear-drop effect to make a pattern on a frame.

On a well-designed piece of furniture, the final steps of finishing are as important as the first saw cut. Not only does the finish impart longevity by protecting the wood surface from the abuses of everyday use, but a carefully considered finish brings a design together and gives it meaning.

Despite the structural strength of wood, its surface is vulnerable and must be protected. Dirt dulls it, and grease and spilled food leave unsightly stains. Water raises the grain fibres and roughens the surface. At the same time, wood must be protected from too much dehydration, which causes shrinking and splitting.

A finish seals the surface by saturating the fibres and filling the pores, or by bonding to the surface in a tough, flexible film. It even helps to start the evaporation of moisture from the wood fibres. If the film is clear, light refracted through it enhances the colour and grain pattern. Unattractive wood, or a design incorporating unmatching pieces of wood, can be disguised by adding a coloured stain, or by bleaching the colour out. And a thick opaque layer of pigment, in the form of paint, obscures the wood completely.

To some extent, the design dictates the choice of finish. But there must also be the practical consideration of the eventual use of the piece. The finish must be able to withstand the wear and tear of use, and be easy to spot-repair.

Because finishing is a process of adding layer upon layer of material, thought must be given to the chemical compatibility of the materials, or the layers will not bond properly. To help plot a finishing sequence, consult the chart on page 208 and see pages 209 to 211.

Bleaching

There are three types of bleach, ranging from weakest to strongest. The weakest, sodium hypochloride, removes stains without altering the natural colour of the wood. Its bleaching action is stopped by neutralizing it with a water wash. Oxalic acid, mixed with water or methylated spirits and neutralized by acetic acid, is especially effective for removing metal stains. But the strongest bleach comes in two parts and is known as A and B bleach or superbleach. It will turn light woods white and considerably lighten darker woods.

Bleaches are sponged on with a rag or scrubbed on with a brush. Always wear rubber gloves to protect your hands. Repeat the application if the wood has not been lightened sufficiently.

Any trace of bleach and neutralizer must be washed away completely with water or it will break down the finish on top of it. But because of the water wash, the bleached wood must be lightly sanded with fine grade paper (240 to 320 grit) to remove the raised fibre ends.

Staining

Staining acts by either dying the wood fibres or by laying a very thin film of pigment over the surface. Dyes are best sprayed on, but can be brushed on or

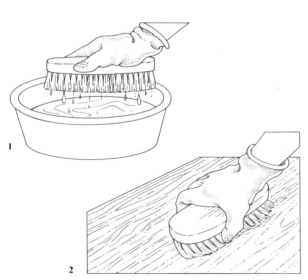

Bleaching the wood
The strongest bleach, the two-pack A and B type, must be used with great care. Wear gloves and avoid splashing it. The first solution is an alkaline. Dip a soft scrubbing brush into a pan of the liquid and apply it liberally. The wood may become temporarily darker. The bleaching action takes place when the second solution, a concentrated hydrogen peroxide, is brushed over the alkaline solution. Allow the wood to dry completely—wet wood appears darker. Then repeat the whole process if the resulting colour is still too dark. When the wood has dried completely for the final time, sand down the lifted grain with fine grade sandpaper.

Applying a stain
Be sure the wood is clean and completely smooth, because flaws will be accentuated by the stain. Wood that is to be given a bright colour should be bleached before staining. Then, wearing gloves to keep from discolouring your hands, dip a clean wadded rag into the stain and rub it thoroughly both with and against the grain, pushing the pigment into the pores. The pigment may at first obscure the grain; allow it to be absorbed 10 to 15 minutes, and then wipe off the excess. Do not allow the stain to dry completely before it is wiped off or it will cake on the surface and mar the finish. Caked-on stain can be wiped away with a rag soaked in turpentine.

wiped. They are absorbed at varying rates by the hard and soft grain, and so emphasize the figure of the wood. These dyes are either water or alcohol based, and are thinned by adding more solvent. The problem of raised grain with water-solvent dyes can be corrected by wetting the wood before staining, letting it dry and then sanding lightly with fine grade paper. Alcohol-based dyes will not raise the grain, and some varieties are light-fast.

The second type of stain consists of pigment suspended in oil; as the oil is absorbed, the pigment is left in a very thin film that should not obscure the grain. Pigment stains are thinned with turpentine or benzine, and if the stained wood is too dark, it can be lightened by wiping with a solvent-soaked rag.

Wood will also change colour in reaction to certain chemicals. Exposed to ammonia fumes, wood containing tannic acid will take on a golden brown colour. Commercial stains are available to simulate the colour but the effect is better achieved by exposing the bare wood to ammonia fumes trapped inside a specially made fuming cabinet for 24 hours.

Finally, the quality of the grain itself can be altered by plugging the pores with filler, brushed on and the excess rubbed off. Traditional filling is only moderately popular among modern woodworkers, who prefer the natural look and feel of wood. But the technique is used for a bleached effect known as liming which leaves a pale, silky finish on all types of wood.

Finishing options		
Preparing the wood: to smooth away flaws that will be magnified by the finish, by sanding through the grades of paper, wetting and resanding if a water-based stain, bleach or water-based latex paint will be used.		
Penetrating finishes	**Surface finishes —painted**	**Surface finishes —clear**
		Bleach: to lighten the wood if it is stained or is too dark, or if a pastel or bright stain is to be applied.
		Stain: to enhance the grain pattern, to match portions of the piece, to add colour to the grain.
		Filler: to close the pores of open-grained wood if a mirror-smooth finish is desired; to add very slight colour.
Penetrating oils: to protect and beautify wood that will not be exposed to hard use. Inexpensive and easy to apply.	**Sealer:** to assure even absorption of the primer by the underlying wood. **Primer:** to help the paint bond to the wood surface.	**Sealer:** to act as a buffer between the underlying layers and the final finish coats, by sealing off the chemicals in the wood and undercoats.
	Light sanding: to mechanically "key" the underlying layers so that the finish will adhere; to remove any raised grain fibres and bits of grit and dust embedded in the film.	
Waxing: to improve the protective properties of oil and add a slight sheen, if necessary.	**Paint:** to obscure the grain completely to unify the design, or to highlight a feature.	**Clear finish:** to cover the wood with a highly protective film that enhances the grain without obscuring it.
Buffing: to harden the wax and bring up a lustrous shine.	**Sanding and buffing:** to repair faults in the applied finish, dulling a high gloss, or burnishing up a matt surface.	

Anatomy of a fuming cabinet
A wooden frame is constructed allowing at least 8 cm/3 in of air circulation space around the piece to be stained—in this case, a table—so that the volatile ammonia fumes can come into contact with the whole surface evenly. The frame is then sheathed with black plastic sheeting, fastened with ducting tape to ensure a tight seal. Shallow pans of 26 percent ammonia are placed throughout the cabinet; several small pans distribute the fumes more evenly than one large one. A test scrap of wood is inserted through the sheeting and pulled out at intervals to check the degree of colour change. **Warning:** Work in a well ventilated space and try not to breathe the fumes.

Liming
1. Apply white filler—a mixture of chalk-like solids and pigment in oil—using a sturdy brush to push the material into the open pores. Work quickly to cover the entire surface before the filler dries.
2. When the filler turns dull, wipe across the grain with a rough cloth, such as toweling or burlap, to reveal the grain without pulling the filler from the pores. Allow it to dry overnight.
3. The next day, brush on white paint slightly thinned with solvent.
4. Wipe across the grain with a rough cloth before the paint has a chance to dry. Finally, finish with a coat of clear matt finish.

Wood finish can be anything from olive oil to Metal Flake car paint, but the ideal finish is any that forms a hard film to seal and protect the wood, and yet remains soft and flexible enough to allow the wood to expand and contract. The finish either is absorbed into the wood, penetrating and forming a film inside the fibres, or it bonds to the surface in a coherent film. Some finishes do a bit of both.

Penetrating finishes, such as linseed oil or tung oil which are absorbed into the wood, have the advantage of being flexible and also easy to apply; saturate the wood with finish until it can absorb no more, and then rub away the surplus. But being oils, they remain soft and may take months to dry, even with metal "driers" added to speed the process. And because the grain is still partially exposed, dirt and grime are trapped in the surface and the wood is difficult to clean. Additionally, to change the finish at a later date, the saturated wood must be sanded away.

Non-penetrating finishes, such as lacquers and varnishes, act as hard superficial films and are easy to clean. With added solids like silica to thicken and cloud the film, a wide degree of sheen is possible, from matt to satin, on to high gloss. The shine can be further modified by polishing. But hard film finishes develop by a complex chemical reaction and require careful application and sometimes expensive equipment, usually in the form of spraying equipment.

Chemically, finishes fall into two categories: the solvent-release type that forms a film by the evaporation of its solvent, and the reactive type that polymerizes in reaction with oxygen in the air or is triggered by a catalyst in the formula. These categories determine to some extent the properties of the finish, and the two types should not be mixed because they are chemically incompatible.

A solvent-release finish—shellac or nitrocellulose lacquer—dries to a hard film chemically similar to its liquid formula. It only lacks its solvent, alcohol or mineral spirits, which has evaporated. Because the film can be redissolved by its solvent, spilled alcohol from a cocktail or perfume will damage it. Even water, combined with heat, can cloud it. But the damage can easily be repaired by dissolving away the disfigured film with a solvent-soaked rag. A new layer of finish will then bond to the old by partially redissolving it.

The list of chemically-reactive finishes is longer and more varied. The range includes: "drying" oils such as linseed oil and tung oil; varnishes formulated with synthetic resins or from plastics such as polyurethane and polyester; and a mixture of oil and varnish known variously as Danish oil, antiquing finish or rubbing oil. Generally, reactive finishes form a film that is chemically changed from its liquid form, and so is highly resistant to solvents. The oils, and the varnishes that contain oil, are softer and less brittle than the solvent-release finishes, but scratch more easily and take longer to dry. And their insolubility makes them harder to spot-repair.

Plastic varnishes come ready-mixed or in two parts that must be combined to use. Once triggered into hardening, the plastic film will only bond properly to another layer within a particular "sensitive" period specified by the manufacturer, and requires a long curing time to finish hardening. But properly applied, the film is as durable as a plastic laminate. Some types are dissolved only by acetone.

Store reactive finishes in containers filled to the top to prevent air inside the can from reacting with the liquid and solidifying it in the can. And dispose of finish-soaked rags safely; stuffed into a closed container, they can ignite spontaneously.

Paints for wood basically are clear finishes with pigment, and the same rules apply. The most common are nitrocellulose, or plastic varnish based. They are usually sold as oil-based enamels in a range of glosses; water-based latex paints are impractical because water in the paint will raise the wood grain.

Two-part plastic car paints are available, some with unusual effects such as Metal Flake, pearl or crystal. These paints are brittle and are best used on stable woods such as manufactured board.

For toys and eating utensils, avoid toxic finishes—especially lead-based paints. Linseed oil, tung oil and most varnishes also contain poisonous lead or mercury to speed drying. Vegetable oils such as olive oil are adequate, but they can become gummy or rancid. There are several "wood bowl" finishes available from wood suppliers. Melted paraffin wax, poured on and scraped off, makes a good finish for cutting boards.

Solvent-release finishes			
Characteristics		**Shellac**	**Lacquer**
Properties	**Durability**	Brittle, but excellent resistance to wear	Good resistance to wear
	Water resistance	Good	Poor
	Alcohol resistance	Very poor	Poor
Application	**Rubbing**	No	
	Brushing	Yes, but better if sprayed	
	Spraying	Yes	Yes
Curing time		Dust free in 30 min; hard in 1 hour	
		Curing time is shortened if air can circulate and carry away evaporating solvent	
Shelf life		6 months: solvent evaporates and the finish loses the ability to dry	
Repairing		Easily done: solvent dissolves away damaged areas and new coats are easy to apply	
Polishing and Buffing		Excellent: can be polished and buffed to a mirror-like finish.	
Comments		Gives a thin coat which must be reapplied to build up any thickness. But rapid drying time means that many coats can be applied in a period of time, and that they will dry before dust has a chance to settle	

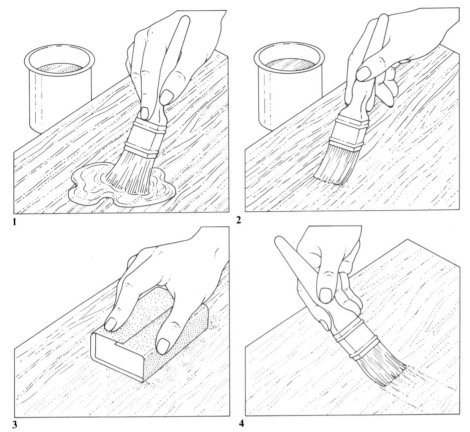

Brushing on a finish

1. Using a good quality varnish brush, make a pool of finish on the wood surface.

2. Spread the pool with the brush, using short strokes back and forth along the grain to "pull" the film smoothly onto the surface. Overlap the strokes to remove surplus finish and even out the film. After the surface is covered, leave the finish to dry, at least one hour for lacquer or shellac, and 24 hours for varnish, or the time recommended by the manufacturer.

3. When the film is dry, sand it gently with 320 grit wet-and-dry paper, being careful at the edges not to sand through the film. Clean the surface of grit and dust with a tack rag—a square of cheesecloth dampened with water, squeezed out, then dampened with turpentine and squeezed out.

4. Brush on another layer of finish going across the grain. Repeat the process as often as necessary, ending with a coat brushed along the grain, and gently sanded when dry with 400 grit paper.

			Chemically-reactive finishes			
Boiled linseed oil	**Tung oil**	**Danish or rubbing oil**	**Varnish**			**Plastic coatings**
			Spar	**Alkyd resin**	**Polyurethane**	
Poor: leaves a very soft film	Poor, but harder film than linseed oil	Good: the hardest penetrating finish	Poor resistance to wear	Good resistance to wear	Brittle, but good resistance to wear	Excellent
Very poor	Good	Good; better if it contains tung oil	Excellent	Good	Excellent	Excellent
Poor	Good	Good	Good	Good	Excellent	Excellent
Yes	Yes	Yes	No	No	No	No
No	No	No	Yes	Yes	Yes	Yes
No	No	No	Yes, but usually brushed			Yes
Never fully hardens	12 hours	1 to 2 hours	Dust free in 2 hours, hard in 24 hours, continues curing for 1 month		Varies with the manufacturer	
Curing time is shortened when the temperature is raised: raising the temperature 10°C/50°F halves the curing time						
6 months	2 months	1 month: exposure to air catalyses a reaction and congeals the liquid				8 hours, maximum
Easily done by sanding lightly and recoating	Poor to good: damaged areas must be sanded away and recoated				Poor: must be sanded down to bare wood and recoated	
None	Matt finish only; cannot be polished but can be buffed to a slight shine		Good: can be buffed and polished		Good	
An inexpensive finish, laborious to apply: must be rubbed on and allowed to dry 24 hours, repeatedly for several weeks	Some workers object to the smell of tung oil. Many coats are needed	A thin-bodied finish, time consuming to apply but it gives a beautiful natural looking finish	Formulated for exterior use to resist sun, salt air and water; may yellow in sunlight	Not as hard as polyurethane	Difficult to spot repair	The most expensive and complicated finish, it normally comes in a two-pack form. Emits toxic fumes: always wear a respirator mask
			A good all-purpose finish, heavier bodied than lacquer and shellac and so requires fewer coats. The film resists cracking.			

FINISHING / Application

Though any finish can be brushed on, many workers prefer to spray on certain fast-drying finishes such as dye stains, high gloss paints and solvent-release shellacs and lacquers. They find that spraying is quick and clean and leaves a high quality film without brush marks or streaks.

But perfect spraying takes practice, and the necessary equipment is expensive to rent or buy. Additionally, the process wastes the finish that is vapourized into the air and carried away. To do the job safely and efficiently it is necessary to set up an isolated spraying area—ideally a spray booth. And whatever the finish, you must always protect your lungs from poisonous fumes with a special carbon air filtration mask.

In fact, any finish can be sprayed. For small jobs all you may need is an aerosol can of finish. For larger jobs, which require a high degree of control, the best system is a compressed air gun. An air compressor takes air from the room, filters out the dust and moisture and regulates the pressurized air, which passes through a hose into the gun. The gun is connected to a paint supply, contained in a small can attached either over or under the gun's nozzle. An even better system has a separate pressurized paint container, which more precisely regulates the flow of paint

and avoids the problems of splattering and clogging. To spray, first the finish must be thinned with solvent, using a viscosity cup to determine the right consistency. Then the gun must be adjusted to control the volume of finish that flows from the nozzle, the air pressure used to atomize the finish, and the shape of the spray pattern.

Spray equipment must be carefully cleaned to prevent it from clogging up. Pump some thinner through the system until only clean thinner comes through. Then disassemble the gun and clean the interior; never immerse the whole gun in solvent, or the lubricants in the joints will dissolve away. To clean the hard-to-reach parts, use a toothpick or pipe cleaner and be careful not to damage the precision-machined openings.

Under ideal conditions, once the finish has been applied, nothing more needs to be done. But in reality the job is often far from perfect. Small flaws such as grit and dirt embedded in the film are easily sanded away with 400 grit paper or 0000 steel wool saturated with mineral oil. Then use a rubbing compound and silicon wax with a sheepskin buffing pad to enliven the dulled finish. Or apply paste wax with 0000 steel wool and buff it to a shine with a pad.

Anatomy of a spray booth

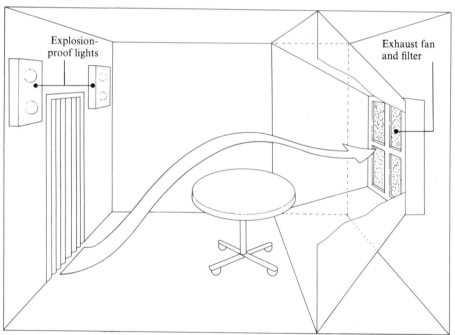

Explosion-proof lights

Exhaust fan and filter

Anatomy of a spray booth
At the heart of the spray booth is an exhaust fan with an explosion-proof motor. The fan keeps a steady flow of air passing throught the booth, expelling the fumes outside. It is preceeded by a paint arrestor filter. To funnel the exhaust air out of the booth, the filter wall is angled inward. At the other end of the booth are explosion-proof lights located behind the worker using the revolving table. The light is reflected off the surface of the work. The opening into the booth is large enough to accommodate a bulky object and is fitted with plastic strips to keep dust out of the booth, while still letting air in.

The equipment can be bought from car body shop suppliers.

Using a viscosity cup
Thin the finish to 1 part solvent to 4 parts finish. Then clock the time it takes for a filled viscosity cup to empty, following the manufacturer's advice.

Adjusting the fluid pressure
With the air pressure at 0, turn the fluid pressure to 50 lb psi and aim a flow of liquid into a measuring cup for 10 seconds. Multiply the amount of fluid in the cup by 6 to obtain the desired flow per minute—12 to 14 oz per min—and adjust the pressure to compensate.

Viscosity cup

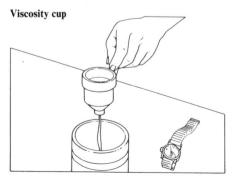

Adjusting the fluid pressure

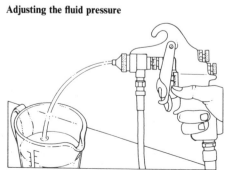

Adjusting the spray pattern

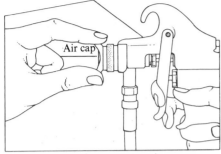

Finding the distance

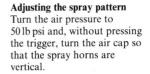

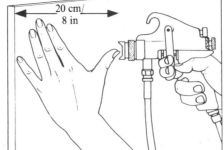

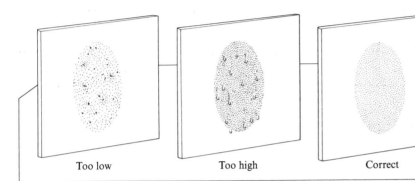

Too low   Too high   Correct

Checking the air cap

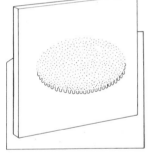

Making a stroke

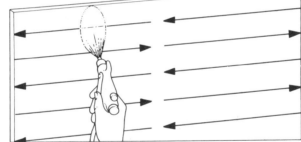

Spraying edges and corners

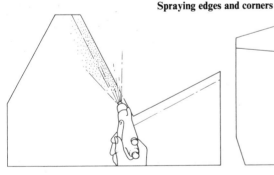

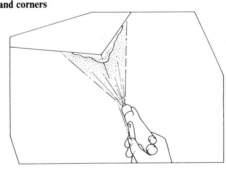

Adjusting the air pressure

Adjusting the spray pattern
Turn the air pressure to
50 lb psi and, without pressing
the trigger, turn the air cap so
that the spray horns are
vertical.

Finding the distance
Hold the gun perpendicular to
the test surface and a hand's
width (15 to 20 cm/6 to 8 in)
from it. Make sure that it will
remain perpendicular when
you move it from side to side
and up and down.

Adjusting the air pressure
Press the trigger in a short
burst to check the spray
pattern. If the pressure is too
low, the spray pattern will be
blotchy: the air pressure does
not evenly atomize the paint.
Raise the pressure by
increments of 5 lb psi and test
again.
   If the air pressure is too
high, a short burst will produce
a sagging film of finish.
   Proper pressure produces a
well-defined oval of finish.

Checking the air cap
Turn the air cap horns
horizontal. Then give a long
blast until the film begins to
drip. The drip lines should all
be the same length.

Making a stroke
Holding the gun 90° to the
work surface, trigger the gun
before the area to be coated,
sweeping beyond the spray
area. Keep the gun at 90° and
avoid letting the finish build up
and drip.

Spraying edges and corners
For complex objects with
irregular edges and corners,
spray the irregular surfaces
first, and then fill in the rest.
   To spray an edge, hold the
gun perpendicular to the edge
and flex your wrist to follow
the contours.
   To spray a corner, aim the
gun straight into the corner
and sweep the spray along the
corner edge, maintaining the
perpendicular angle.

Rubbing the finish
Rub gently and evenly to
remove grit and raised fibres
using 400 grit wet-and-dry
paper dampened with water or
white spirits. Wipe with a clean
towel wetted with spirits and
then repeat with 500 grit paper,
then with 600 grit paper. The
matt finish can be polished
using a sheepskin buff loaded
with rubbing compound, and
then with silicon wax.

211

At one time cabinetmakers would make their own hinges when hanging a door. Now with the tremendous range of high quality hinges available there is little need to do this. However, it is essential to select the correct hinge for a particular job, although in some situations more than one type will be suitable.

Apart from decorative hinges which are meant to be displayed and are mounted on the outside of a door and carcass, most hinges are designed to be as inconspicuous as possible when fitted. Butt hinges, for example, have to be recessed into the cabinet side and door edge so that the door fits tightly when closed, with no unsightly gap down the closing edge, and only the knuckle visible. Depending on how the door is set in relation to the carcass, and how wide it is to open, the flaps of the hinge can be recessed equally into the door edge and carcass or one flap may have to be fully recessed into the door while the second flap is tapered into the carcass. However, there is a flush hinge which does not need to be recessed. Instead the two flaps

interlock when closed and, because the hinge is made of thin metal, the door fits tightly.

On inset doors, hinges are usually positioned 150 mm/6 in from the top and 175 mm/7 in to 225 mm/9 in from the bottom, although on panelled doors they should line up with the rails. Pivot hinges tend to be fitted to the top and bottom edges of doors and as such they are relatively inconspicuous. A version for glass doors can be fitted without having to drill bolt holes in the glass. Concealed hinges can be hidden by the door when it is closed or neatly inset into the edges of the door and carcass.

Hinges are now made in a variety of materials. The best for cabinet work are either solid or extruded brass, which are superior to those of pressed or folded brass. The more decorative types are given a highly polished surface protected by a lacquer. It is important not to clean such hinges with abrasive polishes otherwise the lacquer will be removed and the hinge will discolour. Hinges are also made from steel and plastic.

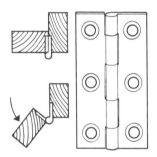

Butt hinge
This hinge is suitable for all doors. Although it can be surface mounted, it is more common to recess the two flaps so that the door fits tightly against or within the carcass. The basic type is made of steel, possibly with an electroplated brass finish, but solid brass hinges are best for fine cabinet work.

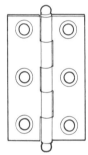

Loose-pin hinge
This is similar to the butt hinge. When fitted, all of the knuckle is exposed, which allows the door to swing clear of the carcass. One of the main advantages of this hinge is that it permits the door to be taken off without the flaps being unscrewed. Simply remove the balls of the finials at each end and gently punch out the pin.

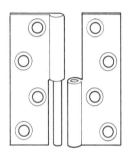

Lift-off hinge
This is suitable for room and cabinet doors. It is made in two parts, with the flap bearing the pin countersunk and side-facing on the carcass or frame, and the flap with the eye fixed to the door. This enables the door to be lifted off without the hinge having to be unscrewed. It also means that the hinge is "handed."

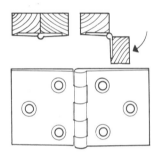

Back-flap hinge
This is a standard hinge for table leaves and fall-flaps on desks, cabinets and bureaus. It can either be surface fitted or recessed into the surface of the carcass and the flap, and it is fastened to the underside of the wood. The hinge flaps are especially wide to provide strong support for the weight on the hanging fall flap.

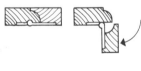
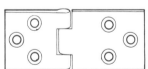

Rule-joint hinge
A hinge designed for the rule joint between the main surface of a table and a drop leaf. The longer flap is screwed to the leaf, it clears the concave section of the rule joint as it is dropped down. The knuckle, inset into the table, and the countersinks, are opposite to an ordinary butt hinge so the leaf can hang at 90°.

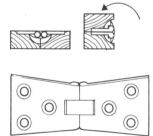

Counterflap hinge
For counters and tables or benches with lift-up flaps. The hinge pivots on a linked double pin mechanism which is inset into the edges of both the table and the flap. This allows a completely clear work surface when the flap is lowered. The most common has a double pin connected by a smooth link flush with the hinge surface.

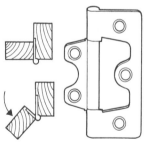

Flush hinge
A lightweight hinge that is best used on small cabinet doors. The hinge is made of thin coated metal and has one flap which rests inside the other when the hinge is fully closed. This means that the hinge does not have to be recessed and can be screwed directly to the edge of the door and carcass. Some have decorative finials.

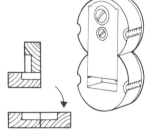

Flush fitting flap hinge
A hinge specially designed for fall-flaps, and which is often used instead of back-flap and counterflap hinges. The pivot action of the hinge allows the flap to rest flush with the inner surface of the cabinet. The two sections can be mounted separately and are connected by an adjusting screw when the flap is fitted.

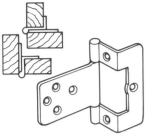

Single-cranked hinge

For lay-on or flush fitting cupboard and cabinet doors. Usually, the flap is screwed directly to the carcass without being recessed and the crank goes around the end of the door. This means the door is given additional support. Hinges are available with a zinc, bronze and electroplated brass finish.

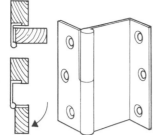

Cranked hinge

For lay-on cabinet doors. This is more a decorative hinge and is not really suitable for heavy-duty use. One of its advantages is that it allows the door to open through 270° and it can be used for right- and left-hand openings. A double-cranked version gives additional support to the door edge.

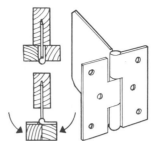

Oni semi-mortise hinge

Allows two doors to be hung from the same central division in a storage unit.   The long flap is mortised into a slot cut in the carcass or frame and held in place by screws driven through from the side. The narrow flaps are recessed into the rear edges of the doors. The knuckle is visible when the doors are closed.

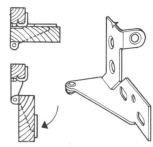

Pivot hinge

This is another hinge which is ideal for lay-on or inset doors. Its main advantage is that it allows the door to swing through 270°, thus providing unhindered access to the cupboard. However, fitting it can be difficult because a small angled cut is needed at the top and bottom of the door to give it a flush finish.

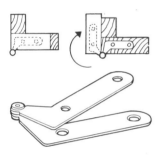

Necked pivot hinge

Although slightly less substantial than the pivot hinge, this hinge can be used in the same situations and is easier to fit. The hinges are recessed into the top and bottom of the door and into the body of the cabinet. The action allows the door to swing through 270°, well clear of the carcass.

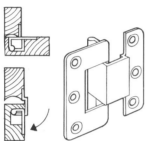

Oni semi-visible hinge

A substantial hinge made from extruded brass, suitable for all types of doors, and particularly those made from manufactured boards. It can be difficult to fit because the body of the hinge has to be recessed into the face of the door and the edge of the cabinet has to be hollowed slightly so that the door edge clears it.

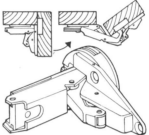

Standard 170° opening hinge

A concealed hinge suitable for lay-on doors. The opening action and the degree of swing means that it can be opened without disturbing the doors on either side of it. The arm connected to the carcass is surface mounted, but part of the section linked to the door has to be recessed. Some hinges are spring-loaded.

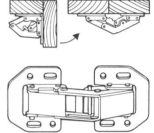

Lay-on concealed hinge

A highly useful hinge for cupboard and cabinet doors, because the 90° opening arc prevents adjacent doors from colliding with each other. Spring-loaded versions are available so the door can be held closed without the need for catches. The spring will also keep the door open and support a lift-up flap.

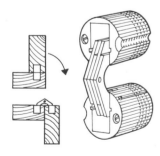

Cylinder hinge

An ingenious hinge suitable for inset and lay-on doors, fall flaps, flush tops and cabinet folding doors made of manufactured board. It is set into holes drilled in the edges of the door and cabinet and is completely concealed when the door is closed. Small adjusting screws allow for a tight fit. The angle of opening is 180°.

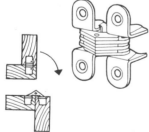

Soss hinge

More for use with lightweight doors, this is the original invisible hinge and the forerunner of the cylinder hinge. It consists of a number of interconnecting scissor joints which help to distribute the load of the door on the hinge and therefore make for a smoother opening action. The angle of opening is 180°.

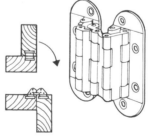

Sepa hinge

For inset and lay-on doors, fall flaps and flush tops. The hinge is screwed into round-end mortises cut in both the door and carcass, and when closed it is completely invisible. Its unique seven-pivot action allows an inset door to open through 90° and a lay-on door to 270°. Hinges of this type are usually made of solid brass.

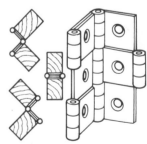

Parvent screen hinge

For multi-panel folding doors and screens. The hinge consists of three pivoting sections with the ends of the panels screwed to the outside sections. This arrangement allows the panels to move in both directions relative to each other. The hinge can cope with panels up to a maximum thickness of 25 mm/1 in.

213

DETAILS / Knock-down fittings

Strong trends in the furniture industry have led to a heavy dependence on metal and plastic hardware for assembly, instead of structural joints—and in particular to a reliance on knock-down (KD) fittings, which allow for dismantling. Some are designed for furniture which is made from flat panels of manufactured board; others for solid timber frames.

They reduce costs in two principal ways. They avoid the need to cut joints, often calling only for the boring of one or two holes instead of more complex machining; and, in the case of "flat-pack" furniture, they do away with factory assembly altogether. In addition, they eliminate gluing-up—a procedure which can often be tricky and time-consuming.

It is well worth getting to know the types available, because one or another may offer the best solution to a particular design problem. In general, they are unsuitable for traditional pieces of furniture, but their convenience makes them otherwise useful. They all require accurately drilled holes.

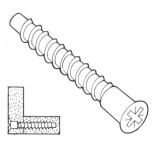

Chipboard screw
A blunt-ended steel fastener with a wide, shallow thread which gives it a holding power superior to that of even the most sophisticated conventional screw. It requires a drilled pilot hole the same diameter as the core (excluding the thread). Its head can be covered with a plastic cap for neatness.

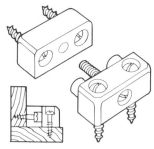

Block joint
A plastic fitting which secures right-angled butt joints between panels. Block joints come in pairs, and are screwed to the faces of adjacent boards before being linked with the machine screw supplied. A simpler type consists of a single block only. The double version is easier to fit because it allows individually accurate fixing.

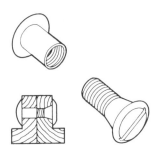

Cabinet connecting screw
Used more or less exclusively in built-in work for linking prefabricated units together against a wall—particularly in the kitchen. Made of plastic, it is designed for use with standard board thicknesses of 16 mm and 18 mm: no thicker. In most cases the carcass panels are of melamine-faced chipboard.

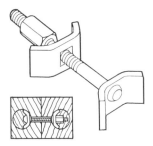

Panel-butting connector
A special-purpose metal fitting primarily for connecting lengths of plastic-laminated chipboard worktop, again usually in the kitchen. The twin metal plates are sunk into a pair of holes in the undersides of the adjacent pieces, connected by a channel to accommodate the threaded rod which links them.

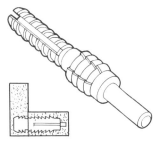

Chipboard dowel rivet
One of several specialized connectors for chipboard, this is not strictly a KD fitting since the joint cannot be taken apart once it has been assembled. Both parts fit into drilled holes, the barbs resisting withdrawal, and the pieces are then brought together. Accurate drilling is a necessity for the effective use of fittings such as this.

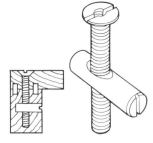

Bolt and cross-dowel
A strong and attractive fitting for solid timber frames, requiring two holes (drilled at right-angles to each other) for the bolt and the dowel. Made from steel with a brass finish, it comes with two knobs which screw (before assembly) into one of the joint's hidden faces to prevent it from twisting. Tighten with an Allen key.

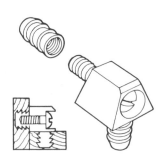

KD dowel fitting
A two-part plastic block joint which, rather than being screwed to the adjacent panels, is tapped into pre-drilled holes—one for the main body and one for its mating bush. Both parts are barbed. After assembly the screw is tightened to complete a rigid butt joint. As with most block joints, at least two are usually required.

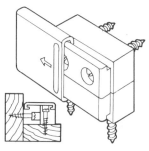

Metal-covered block joint
A two-piece plastic block connector, again for butt-joining panels at right-angles by fitting into the internal corner formed by adjacent boards. Its main distinguishing feature is the metal plate which is slid over the completed assembly for concealment—an asset where the internal appearance is important.

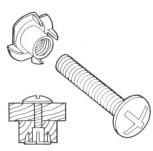

T-nut and bolt
A strong, simple fitting which works in either solid timber or manufactured boards. It operates exactly like an ordinary hexagonal nut except that no wrench is needed—its prongs enable it to grip firmly and immovably as a matching machine screw is tightened. The screw passes through a pre-drilled clearance hole.

Hanger bolt and table plate
Specially designed for attaching table legs to their linking rails, this "bolt" has a woodscrew thread on the pointed end that enters the leg, and a machine thread for a wing-nut on the other end. The point is driven into a 45° pilot hole in the leg's corner, and the metal plate positioned before the wing-nut is tightened.

Shelves and drawers are essential to a great deal of storage furniture, and for both there is a clear distinction between traditional and modern methods of fitting. Shelf hardware replaces the joints (usually housing joints—wide grooves cut into the uprights to receive the full thickness of the shelf) by which shelves are conventionally fixed to their supporting uprights. It may mean designing a carcass which incorporates the extra rigidity that the hardware alone cannot provide. With shelving, adjustability is a common requirement, and many of today's fittings are designed with this in mind. Inevitably, there is almost always some trade-off in terms of neatness—the most convenient or strongest fittings are not necessarily the least obtrusive or most attractive.

Drawer fittings replace the wooden bearers, runners, guides and kickers which support and align the box-within-a-box that is really all a drawer amounts to. In contrast to shelf fittings, drawer fittings present less of a problem in terms of appearance since the items are almost always concealed—although the appropriateness of metal and plastic hardware will always be a consideration, especially when using solid timber and veneers. The quality of the fitting must be as high as the quality of your work. The paramount needs are for strength, smooth running and resistance to wear. Modern runners in general are very well endowed in these respects, providing a quality of operation which—though it differs from that achieved by conventional cabinetmaking methods—can hardly be bettered except by the most meticulous craftsmanship and the best materials.

As with all fittings, it is always worthwhile taking the time to investigate products in some detail, so that you can discover which will best solve the particular design brief to which you are working. The changing demands of the industry have called forth an enormous variety of items from specialized manufacturers, and these (unlike most traditional fittings) are under continual development.

Adjustable shelving

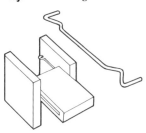

Stud shelf supports

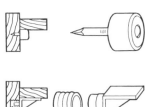
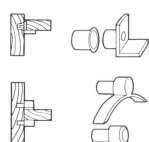

Magic wire
A completely invisible shelf fixing. The ends of the heavy-gauge wire fit into holes drilled in the upright faces, while a stopped groove—as wide as the wire is thick—is cut in each end of the shelf to slide over the fitting. The system provides considerable support, but the holes can of course be seen if the shelf is repositioned.

Bookcase strip
Favoured because it allows a very high degree of adjustability, this metal strip is sunk and screwed into shallow recesses which are routed the entire length of the supporting uprights. The shelves simply rest on the studs which clip into the slots closely spaced along the strip. Unfortunately, the strip remains visible.

Stud shelf supports
One of the simplest forms of shelf support. Usually two studs at each end of each shelf will be all that is needed. All types of stud allow removal of the shelves. They may be straightforward studs of rubber or plastic, simply nailed in (**1**), or small brackets inserted in bushes which are themselves tapped into holes first (**2** and

3). Another two-part fitting (**4**) incorporates a peg for support, plus a springy plastic upper part (also fitting into a drilled hole) which is used to steady the shelf. As with most shelf fittings, regular rows of drilled holes (as opposed to occasional ones at the desired shelf heights) will ensure that the studs are adjustable. All you have to do is move them.

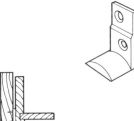

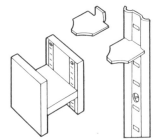
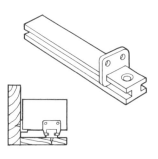

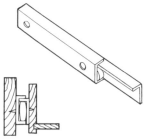

Drawer side saddle
A simple device which takes the place of more traditional guides to give smooth alignment in opening and closing the drawer. Its purpose is to prevent the drawer from angling sideways, and consequently from jamming. Its screw-holes are sized to allow precise adjustment of the drawer in the cabinet.

Drawer glide
A simple plastic runner which is attached to the interior of the cabinet with four wood screws through the push-in plastic pegs. A matching groove must be routed in the drawer side to complete the arrangement. This fitting is simply an alternative to the traditional timber runner performing the same function.

Central drawer-guide
This replaces traditional kickers in preventing a drawer from tipping up as it is pulled out, while also keeping it aligned. The plastic plate is simply screwed to the drawer-back at either its top or its bottom. This is a light-duty fitting and should not be relied upon where heavy loads or rough usage are likely.

Drawer-runner
These drawer-runners, with steel or nylon wheels, come in two or more parts; many are telescopic, extending forwards to considerable lengths, and some are extremely heavy-duty. They work equally well on solid or manufactured board. Runners are available for pull-out trays and very deep filing cabinet drawers.

DETAILS / Locks, catches and stays

Though it is sometimes useful to have the means of locking a flap, door or drawer of a storage unit, just how much security these locks provide depends on the materials of which the mechanism is made—brass is superior to steel—and the thickness and strength of the timber being used. Furniture locks will deter children and the casual browser, but they can be relatively easily forced open.

Locks may be left-handed or right-handed and, depending on the lock, can be surface-mounted on the back of a door, flap or drawer, recessed into the back edge or mortised into the timber thickness.

Catches are more convenient in frequently-used doors and flaps, where access does not need to be restricted, because the door can simply be pulled open. Devices made of plastic, or coated steel and plastic rollers, are the quietest and smoothest to operate. The most commonly used type is concealed when the door is closed.

Locks

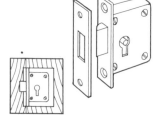

Drawer lock
Suitable for flush-fitted drawers, this lock is recessed into the back edge of the front panel. When the key is turned, the bolt is lowered into the top of the unit or cross rail. Some locks have keyholes at 90° to each other so that they can also be used upright. Locks like these are "handed," and have a limited security value.

Spring lock
A more substantial lock, it has a recessed fitting and is available left- and right-handed. The curved leading edge of the bolt and the spring-loaded mechanism allow the door or drawer to be shut without a key. A striking plate recessed into the timber face of the frame makes it more difficult to force the lock.

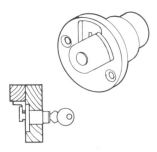

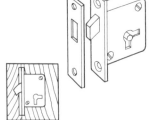

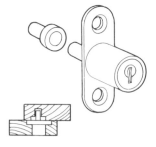

Fall-flap lock
Specially designed for the fall-flap of a bureau because it butts up to the carcass when closed, this lock can also be used on small cabinet doors. These locks can either be recessed or be mortised into position. When the key is turned, the bolt rotates and slides behind an L-shaped fitting under the bureau top.

Hook lock
This lock is suitable for inset sliding room doors. The body of the lock is recessed or mortised into the door itself, while the striking plate is fitted to a second door. When the key is turned, the bolt arcs into the plate, locking the door. A lock with a back-hood should be used on lay-on doors. It comes right- or left-handed.

Piano lock
Similar to the lock used to secure piano lids, it can fit any long lid. The lock is mortised into the framework and the striking plate fitted to the lid. As the key is turned, the bolt passes through the plate and then moves sideways to lock the lid. The mortise must be longer than the striking plate to receive the bolt.

Sliding door lock
The lock is used to secure overlapping sliding doors. The locking mechanism is recessed into the back of the facing door. When the key is turned, a bolt is driven into a corresponding socket in the rear door. The lock is normally supplied with an ecutcheon. It is usually finished in nickel plate.

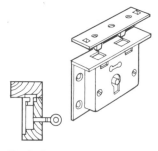

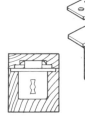

Box lock
Similar to the full-flap lock, this lock secures lift-up lids on storage units and blanket chests. It is recessed into the rear edge of the carcass and sits flush with the top. The striking plate fitted to the lid has two pins which locate into the lock when the lid is closed. When the key is turned, the bolt holds them in position.

Espagnolette lock
A lock which secures the top and bottom of a door against the carcass, and thus prevents warping. The lock is set on the inside of the door with the two long rod bolts supported in guides. When the lock is turned, a cam pins the bolts either behind small metal plates or into pre-drilled holes in the carcass.

Bird's-beak lock
Originally designed for roll-top (tambour) desks, the lock is mortised into the body of the desk while a striking plate is set on the leading edge of the top. When the top is closed and the lock turned, the bolt moves upwards through a sprung trap door on the striking plate, and two arms move sideways to lock the top.

Escutcheon
A ring, disc or plate that protects the key hole from damage by the key. The simplest types are just pressed into the key hole and held by a tight fit. Some disc types have a serrated edge and are tapped into position over the hole. The facing plate is secured over the key hole with small escutcheon pins.

Catches

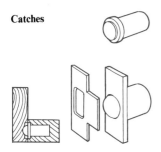

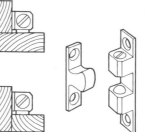

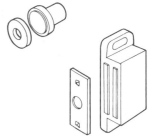

Single ball catch
An unobtrusive lock for cabinet doors consists of a small plastic or metal ball mounted over a spring set in a cylindrical housing let in the door edge. As the door is closed the ball is depressed by a striking plate. But it springs back into a recess in the plate when the door is fully closed, and so holds it fast.

Automatic latch
A device which opens a door simply by pressing lightly on the leading edge. The body of the latch is fitted to the door and incorporates a spring-loaded roller which locates over a catch attached to the underside of the carcass. When the door is pushed the mechanism is released and frees the roller.

Double ball catch
A superior and harder wearing version of the single ball catch, which usually is fitted into better quality furniture. The catch can be fitted on flush or lay-on doors. Unlike the single ball catch, both the spring-loaded steel balls can be adjusted by turning two integral screws. The catch is therefore always held tightly.

Magnetic catch
For all types of cupboards and doors. They can be either surface mounted or recessed, the latter being suitable for lay-on doors as they can be set into the edge of the frame. A metal striking plate has to be fitted to the door so that it makes contact with the magnet when the door is closed. Often, more than one catch is needed.

Stays

Stays reduce the forces acting on the hinges of a side-hung door or fall flap. By restricting the opening to 90° or less they also prevent doors and drawers from colliding with each other. Stays can also be used to keep a lift-up flap in the open position. Some are made for specific locations, but most can be used in more than one position. The more sophisticated have a braking mechanism for smooth opening and closing and to prevent slamming.

Stays

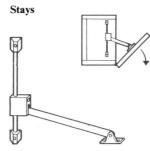

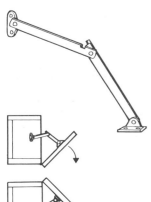

Cranked stay
This stay is for fall flaps and doors. The two arms, which are pivoted at a central elbow, are fixed at either end to the carcass and flap. The elbow, when lifted up, allows the stay to fold into the cabinet as the door is closed. When snapped straight, the stay holds the flap firmly in the open position.

Friction stay
These are suitable for all fall flaps. A metal rail is fixed vertically to the inside of the cabinet and the stay slides against this via a braking mechanism which controls the speed at which the flap falls open once released. It can be adjusted by turning a screw on the body. Stays are available right- and left-handed.

Quadrant stay
This simple stay can be used on fall flaps on bureau and cabinets. It does not incorporate a locking mechanism. The curved arm is screwed to the flap and the free end runs through a slot fixed to the carcass side. When the flap is shut the arm rests in a recess cut in the carcass bottom.

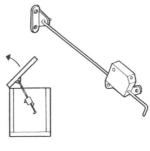

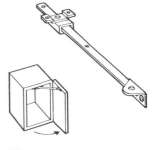

Lift-up flap stay
This is a useful mechanism for lift-up flaps on small units, particularly at the top of a wardrobe which is difficult to reach. The sturdy arm locks in the open position and the flap is closed by first lifting it slightly to release the locking mechanism. A friction mechanism prevents the door from slamming shut.

Up-and-over door mechanism
This is particularly suitable for wall units where wide access to a cupboard is needed, perhaps in a limited space. Two fixed stays attached to the cupboard top and two telescopic stays fixed to the door enable the door to be swung up and out of the way over the top of the carcass. No hinges are needed for the door.

Lid stay
This is a suitable device for storage units such as a hi-fi cabinet, where the lid must be held open. The stay slides through a braking mechanism concealed in a plastic housing fitted to the side of the cabinet. The mechanism can be adjusted so that the lid closes quietly and smoothly without slamming the door.

Silent stay
This is commonly used on cupboard and wardrobe doors where a quiet action is required. It can also be used on fall-flaps. The steel stay is pivoted to a bracket attached to the door and passes through a plastic guide screwed to the underside of the cabinet top. It can be adjusted to restrict the door swing to less than 90°.

Screws

At one time cabinetmakers made their own screws when required, hence no two screws were ever identical. But now all screws are made by machine to uniform standards from brass, steel, stainless steel or aluminium. From the wide range available, it is essential to select the right type for a particular job. Working with chipboard, for example, requires special screws where the thread extends to the underside of the head. In damp atmospheres steel screws may rust and stain certain woods such as sycamore, afromosia and oak.

Specifying the type of screw needed can be an extensive process. First, quote the length and gauge size (thickness). The narrowest gauge has a diameter of 0; the largest is 32, but the gauges most commonly used range up to 12. Also indicate what the screw is to be used for as this will have a bearing on the material it should be made of and its finish: untreated, zinc or chrome plated, black japanned, or cadmium or bronze coated. The other main feature to consider is the type of head. Screws are available with a flat countersunk head for flush finishing, a domed countersunk head or a round head. These usually have a slot to take a conventional screwdriver. Cross-head screws, now sold under the label of Phillips, although there are similar types known as Posidriv and Supadriv screws, require a special screwdriver. The table below shows the various screw types that are commonly available.

Abrasives

Abrasives are used to shape and smooth the workpiece before applying the final finish. They consist of a paper, cloth or metal backing sheet which is covered on one side with a layer of grit—crushed glass, garnet or some synthetic material.

Unfortunately, there is no common grading system for all abrasives. Flint sandpaper, with a grit of powdered quartz, is inexpensive and good for sanding waxy and resinous surfaces in both hard- and softwoods. More expensive and longer lasting garnet paper is the favourite of the furniture industry. It is used for sanding in between coats of finish and comes in grits from 12 to 320. Aluminium oxide paper with its bauxite abrasive is even harder wearing and is appropriate for sanding bare hardwoods. It is also used for the sanding belts of drum sanders. Finally, there is the extremely hard silicon carbide paper, otherwise called "wet-and-dry" or carborundum paper. It can be used wet for flattening brush marks and runs in paintwork but should be used dry on bare hardwood surfaces and particleboard. The coarsest grades are from 60 to 120, medium grades range from 150 to 240 and fine grades from 280 to 600.

Adhesives

Despite all the developments in modern adhesives, there are craftsmen who still prefer using animal glue. They argue that its slow setting period gives them time before hardening in which to make final adjustments. In addition, they maintain that the workpieces need less clamping and that the gluing process is reversible and so allows joints to be dismantled if necessary. But for most craftsmen these benefits are far outweighed by the greater convenience of using a modern adhesive.

Screw lengths and gauges

Legend: Countersunk ⵛ · Round head ⌄ · Raised head ⌄ · Straight head ⊘ · Cross head ⊕ · Straight and cross head ●

Length	0	1	2	3	4	5	6	7	8	9	10	12	14	16	18	20
6 mm/¼ in	⊘⊘	⊘	⊘⊘		⊘⊕											
10 mm/⅜ in		⊘	⊘⊘	●●	●●⊘	⊕	●●		⊘⊕							
13 mm/½ in			⊘	●●	●●●	●●	●●●	⊘	●●		⊘					
16 mm/⅝ in				⊘	●●⊘	●●●	●●●	●⊘	●●		⊘●					
19 mm/¾ in				⊘	●●●	●●⊘	●●●	●⊘	●●●	⊘	●●	⊘⊘				
22 mm/⅞ in				⊘			●⊕	●	●⊕							
25 mm/1 in				⊘	●●⊘	●⊘	●●●	●⊘	●●●		●●●⊘	●●	⊘			
28 mm/1⅛ in							●									
31 mm/1¼ in					⊘	⊘	●●●	●⊘	●●●		●⊘⊘	●⊘⊘				
38 mm/1½ in					⊘		●●●	●	●●●		●●●	⊘⊘	⊘			
44 mm/1¾ in							●	⊘	●●⊕●		●●●⊘	⊘	⊘			
50 mm/2 in							●⊘	⊘	●⊘●●		●●●●	⊘⊘	⊘⊘	⊘	⊘	⊘
56 mm/2¼ in							⊘		●		●	●	●			
63 mm/2½ in							⊘		●●⊘	⊘	●●⊘	●●●	⊘			
69 mm/2¾ in									⊘		⊘	⊘	⊘			
75 mm/3 in							⊘		●		●⊘	●●●	⊘⊘	⊘		
81 mm/3¼ in											⊘	⊘				
88 mm/3½ in									⊘		⊘	⊘	⊘			
100 mm/4 in									⊘		⊘	⊘	⊘	⊘	⊘	
113 mm/4½ in											⊘	⊘	⊘			⊘
125 mm/5 in											⊘	⊘	⊘			
150 mm/6 in												⊘	⊘	⊘		

Polyvinyl acetate (PVA) adhesive is now one of the most popular. A white liquid ready for use straight from the container, it dries clear in about an hour and forms a strong bond in 24 hours. However, it is not effective at bridging gaps and is best avoided if the joint being glued is eventually to be put under any stress. It is also weakened by damp conditions. The alternative is to use a casein adhesive available in powder form which has to be mixed with water.

Even stronger are the urea formaldehyde adhesives which have a wide range of woodworking applications. They come in two parts with a resin that has to be mixed with a hardener. Although they are not particularly good gap filling glues, once set they are extremely resistant to water and are excellent for outdoor woodwork. Resorcinol formaldehyde has similar applications. A word of caution: all these adhesives are prone to staining hardwoods so do a test run before using them.

Hot-melt glue guns for resin glues are extremely useful when quickly making a wooden mock up to test a design, as the adhesive sets within 30 seconds of being dispensed. But because they set so fast, these glues are of limited use in general furniture construction.

As the chart below indicates, there are a number of other glues available for sticking various materials to each other. It is essential to follow the manufacturer's instructions carefully to get the desired results. And be sure to work in a well-ventilated space, so that the fresh air carries away the noxious glue fumes.

Adhesives, trouble-shooting the failures

Joint failures	Causes	Remedy
1. Parts of joint separated, little or no glue visible.	Glue too thin. Clamps squeezing glue out. Wood too dry—glue soaking in. Joint too tight—glue forced out.	Change glue. Reduce clamp pressure. Brush joint faces with water before assembly. Increase play in joint.
2. Glue visible but not spread over surfaces.	Glue too thick. Not enough glue.	Dilute glue. Apply more glue.
3. Glue visible on one surface only.	Assembly too slow, thus allowing glue to dry.	Change glue type. Work in a colder environment. Speed up assembly.
5. Joint fails in use, but surfaces appear normal.	Adhesive creep or slipping.	Use a two-part resin adhesive.
6. Discoloration around glued parts.	Reaction between glue and wood. Bad cleaning up or dirty equipment.	Change glue type. Clean mixing equipment.

Adhesives for various materials

	Metal to:											Manufactured board to:											Wood to:										
	Leather	Fabrics	Metal	Plastics (soft)	Plastics (hard)	Pexiglass	Manufactured board	Wood	China and glass	Cork tiles	Ceramic tiles	Leather	Fabrics	Metal	Plastics (soft)	Plastics (hard)	Pexiglass	Manufactured board	Wood	China and glass	Cork tiles	Ceramic tiles	Leather	Fabrics	Metal	Plastics (soft)	Plastics (hard)	Pexiglass	Manufactured board	Wood	China and glass	Cork tiles	Ceramic tiles
PVA adhesives							○											○	○										○	○			
Resorcinol formaldehyde							○											○	○										○	○			
Urea formaldehyde							○											○	○										○	○			
Contact	○	○				○			○	○	○	○		○	○																		○
Latex						○								○																			
Cyano-acrylate		○		○			○	○	○						○						○					○	○	○			○		○
Epoxy		○		○		○	○	○	○						○			○			○					○	○	○	○		○		○
Acrylic		○		○			○	○	○						○			○			○					○	○	○			○		○
Specialized adhesives																		○	○													○	○

INDEX

CREDITS

The author and publishers wish to acknowledge the contributions to the book made by these specialized writers:

Tim Imrie, a photographer and writer specializing in the crafts, who wrote several of the designers' profiles and contributed some photographs of them. He worked in conjunction with **Maggie Ellis**, a furniture consultant, who conducted the interviews and contributed photographs.

David Savage who wrote the chapter on the Workshop. He has been running his own workshop since 1971 and has written about woodcrafts for several publications.

Peter St. Hill, who wrote about veneers in the chapter on materials. He has had extensive experience as a wood-craftsman and as a journalist in Britain and Australia.

Alan Smith, who wrote about wood and other materials in the chapter on materials. He is a lecturer at the Royal College of Furniture and a consultant in the British furniture industry. He has also written a number of books on the crafts.

Particular thanks are due to these manufacturers and distributors of woodworking materials: All Screws Limited, Hammersmith, London; Black and Decker, Slough, Berkshire; the DeVilbiss Company, London; Elu, Slough, Berkshire; GKN, London; Luna Tools and Machinery Limited, Bletchley, Milton Keynes; F. T. Morrell and Company Limited, Dartford, Kent; Rustins Limited, London; Startrite Machine Tool Company Limited, Dartford, Kent; Watkins Limited, Castle Donnington, Derby; Woodfit, Chorley, Lancashire.

Additional thanks are due from the author to these individuals and organizations for permission to use their furniture in this book: Birmingham City Art Gallery (Twin Towers, page 65); Amanda Carpenter (Folding table, page 49); Bob Maclaren (Lego cabinets, page 64, and the red and grey bed, page 76); D. Misell Esq. (rosewood table on the cover); Shipley Art Gallery (plan chest, page 64) Simon Toner (yew occasional table, page 57).

Photographs: Martin Dohrn (76); Maggie Ellis (51, 56, 71, 75, 78); Tim Imrie (48, 54, 58, 70, 74); Dr. Ivor Johnson (55); Mike Murless, Farquharson-Murless (56); Steve Tanner (1, 3, 6, 49, 52 bottom, 57 bottom, 61, 64–65, 69, 72); Alan Wakeford (62, 63, 66); Mary-Sherman Willis (67).

Quilt (76) by Andrea Coggins, from Rainbow Quilts, London.
Artwork: Trevor Lawrence; Coral Mula; Stan North; Paul Williams.
Additional artwork: Kuo Kang Chen; Paul Emra; Guy Smith; Valerie Hill.

Converting decimals to fractions:	
0.93	$\frac{15}{16}$
0.87	$\frac{7}{8}$
0.81	$\frac{13}{16}$
0.75	$\frac{3}{4}$
0.68	$\frac{11}{16}$
0.62	$\frac{5}{8}$
0.56	$\frac{9}{16}$
0.5	$\frac{1}{2}$
0.43	$\frac{7}{16}$
0.37	$\frac{3}{8}$
0.31	$\frac{5}{16}$
0.25	$\frac{3}{4}$
0.18	$\frac{3}{16}$
0.125	$\frac{1}{8}$
0.06	$\frac{1}{16}$

Conversion factors

Multiply by 2.54 to convert inches to centimetres
25.4 to convert inches to millimetres
0.3937 to convert centimetres to inches
0.03937 to convert millimetres to inches

A table of conversion from mm to in

6 mm	$= \frac{1}{4}$ in	140 mm	$= 5\frac{1}{2}$ in
11 mm	$= \frac{7}{16}$ in	150 mm	$= 5\frac{15}{16}$ in
13 mm	$= \frac{1}{2}$ in	200 mm	$= 7\frac{7}{8}$ in
18 mm	$= \frac{11}{16}$ in	250 mm	$= 9\frac{7}{8}$ in
40 mm	$= 1\frac{9}{16}$ in	300 mm	$= 11\frac{13}{16}$ in
48 mm	$= 1\frac{7}{8}$ in	400 mm	$= 15\frac{3}{4}$ in
50 mm	$= 1\frac{15}{16}$ in	450 mm	$= 17\frac{3}{4}$ in
70 mm	$= 2\frac{3}{4}$ in	500 mm	$= 19\frac{11}{16}$ in
75 mm	$= 2\frac{15}{16}$ in	700 mm	$= 27\frac{1}{2}$ in
80 mm	$= 3\frac{3}{16}$ in	800 mm	$= 31\frac{1}{2}$ in
90 mm	$= 3\frac{9}{16}$ in	850 mm	$= 33\frac{1}{2}$ in
100 mm	$= 3\frac{15}{16}$ in	1000 mm	$= 39\frac{3}{8}$ in
120 mm	$= 4\frac{3}{4}$ in	2000 mm	$= 78\frac{3}{4}$ in